SHAPING THE STORY

A Step-by-Step Guide to Writing Short Fiction

MARK BAECHTEL

Grinnell College

PEARSON
Longman

New York   San Francisco   Boston
London   Toronto   Sydney   Tokyo   Singapore   Madrid
Mexico City   Munich   Paris   Cape Town   Hong Kong   Montreal

Vice President and Editor-in-Chief: Joseph Terry
Managing Editor: Erika Berg
Associate Editor: Barbara Santoro
Senior Marketing Manager: Melanie Craig
Production Manager: Ellen MacElree
Production Coordination, Text Design, and Electronic Page Makeup: Stratford Publishing
    Services, Inc.
Cover Designer/Manager: John Callahan
Cover image by Gary Hunter, courtesy of Getty Images.
Manufacturing Buyer: Roy Pickering
Printer and Binder: Courier Corp.
Cover Printer: The Lehigh Press

Library of Congress Cataloging-in-Publication Data

CIP is on file with the Library of Congress.

Please visit us at http://www.ablongman.com

ISBN 0-205-33719-8

2 3 4 5 6 7 8 9 10—CRS—06 05 04

CONTENTS

3 Point of View   35

4   Tone of Voice   56

PART TWO: *Building the Scene*   71

8   Dramatization   123

PART THREE: *Moving from Scene to Story*   133

9   Plot   137

Short Stories

A PREFACE FOR INSTRUCTORS

Most students sign up for a beginning fiction writing course thinking they would love to spend a semester writing stories. Odds are, they've spent some time reading short fiction and—especially if they're English majors—pulling stories apart, analyzing them, discussing them in class, writing papers about them. They've learned what makes stories tick. How hard, they reason, could it be actually to write one?

Ay, and there's the rub. Their instructors know that the answer to that rhetorical question is most often "Very hard indeed." Theory is vastly different from practice, and the flame of the students' enthusiasm may begin to flicker as it begins to dawn on them how hard it is to create believable characters, real-seeming action and dialogue, plots that work, vivid settings, well-modulated tone, proper pacing, and—of course— how many revisions it will most likely take to get all the story's parts and pieces to mesh. So how are instructors to keep the flame of the students' beginning intention burning bright while helping students to acquire all these necessary skills? And how, on top of that, can they ensure that the students still have time during a semester to accomplish what they came to the course most wanting to accomplish—that is, the writing of a story?

A Step-by-Step Approach

Shaping the Story began as a meditation on these questions and as a search for an alternative to the two most common forms of beginning fiction-writing courses—the exercise-based class and the workshop-based class—and the student frustration they all-too-commonly engender.

The exercise-based class, while it helps students build the skills they need to write characters, dialogue, scenes, and conflict, or to manage point of view, too often leaves them feeling lost. What they have to show for a semester's effort is a disarticulated stack of sketches and little notion of how to employ their newfound skills in writing a complete story. *Shaping the Story* incorporates the virtues of the exercise form, but its twelve exercises interlock to lead students from their story's first rough conceptualization through its completion and revision. This unique structure teaches them the skills they need while teaching them how to use them in concert to write a satisfying story.

In the workshop-based class, instructors invite their students to submit their best attempts at short stories for consideration in class. Careful instruction, careful management of in-class discussion, and skillful editing can show the students how these first attempts can blossom into satisfying stories, but too often workshop-based classes seem to teach story writing in much the way an autopsy teaches the investigator the cause of death: the procedure may be instructive, but the subject lies dismembered on the table, never to be resurrected. *Shaping the Story* shows students how to move their story through a natural evolution that preserves their story's integrity and their sense of discovery while helping them to avoid common narrative problems. It's worth stressing here that *Shaping the Story* doesn't offer a magical formula for the well-made story. Indeed this is something that's emphasized in the book's Introduction, and for that reason students should be urged to read the Introduction before they begin working. Instead, this book is meant to introduce the student simply and straightforwardly to the challenges and rewards of writing the short story.

Key Features of the Book

- A linked, twelve-chapter structure, including lessons on beginnings, point of view, tone of voice, setting, characterization, dialogue, dramatization, plot, time, endings, and revision
- Two student responses which follow each linked exercise, along with instructor commentary, to enable students using the book to see how their peers have used the book's plan to build a story
- In addition to the linked exercise, each chapter also includes four non-linked exercises. This will accommodate the student who wants more exercises on a given subject of story writing craft, as well as the instructor who may want to spend additional time on a given topic or to bypass the linked exercises altogether
- In appropriate chapters, students will also find a half-dozen "Questions for Revision" that will guide them as they reconsider their unfolding story in light of what they learn from each new lesson

A Mini-Anthology

The final important feature of *Shaping the Story* is a group of award-winning stories from contemporary and classic writers. Clearly, a carefully chosen anthology can be an invaluable tool as you try to teach students what makes for a successful short story. One story—plus a brief commentary and a half-dozen reading questions—has been selected to buttress the lesson offered in each of the first eleven chapters. Featured authors include Jorge Luis Borges, Kevin Brockmeier, Sandra Cisneros, Louise Erdrich, Kazuo Ishiguro, James Alan McPherson, Judith Claire Mitchell, Flannery O'Connor, Tillie Olsen, Wallace Stegner, and Tobias Wolff. As a bonus, the anthology includes "final drafts" of the stories written by Jeremy Blodgett and Sarah Cornwell, the students whose exercise responses were featured as part of each chapter.

Acknowledgments

Thanks are due first of all to the University of Iowa, which originally commissioned the writing of six of these chapters for its Correspondence School's introductory course in fiction writing. Patrick Irelan, who was in charge of the project there, was the best kind of editor, both hands-off and hands-on, in each case where it counted. I'm grateful for his help and respectful attention.

I also owe a debt of gratitude to a number of people who helped me with the book, either by reading it closely in manuscript form or by allowing me to incorporate into it stories, ideas, and materials they had gleaned from their own teaching and writing experience. These benefactors include Frank Conroy, Director of the Iowa Writers' Workshop; Connie Brothers, the Workshop's Administrator (a human dynamo and cherished friend); James A. McPherson; Marilynne Robinson; Christine Kinneally; Thisbe Nissen; Sara Ominsky; Judith Claire Mitchell; Kevin Brockmeier; and (at Grinnell College) Elizabeth Dobbs and Paula V. Smith.

Helyn Wohlwend, also at Grinnell, lent cheerful support on many fronts. She was indispensable in the early going when the manuscript was not yet as orderly as it would ultimately become, and she read it closely as it came close to being in its final form. The process of pulling the book together would have been much more difficult without her help, as well as administrative help from Sara Barr, Vicki Bunnell, Nova McGiffert, Lisa Mulholland, Eric Otoo, Kathy Schwartz, and Robyn Wingerter.

I reserve special thanks for the students in my Undergraduate Fiction Writing workshops at the University of Iowa and in my Craft of Fiction class and Fiction Seminar at Grinnell College, most especially for Jeremy Blodgett and Sarah Cornwell, whose responses to each exercise are included in this book. My students were my guinea pigs as I tested these chapters and the ideas behind them, and if this final product in any way speaks usefully to the needs of apprentice writers, it is largely owing to my students' hard work and feedback.

I'm very grateful to my agent Beth Vesel and her assistant Emilie Stewart for their able representation and their patience with a client who moves as slowly and deliberately as I do. I also want to thank Joe Opiela, Kristen Desmond, Erika Berg, and Barbara Santoro at Longman for shepherding the manuscript through its various incarnations as it moved from prospectus through finished book.

My thanks also go out to the following reviewers without whom *Shaping the Story* would not be the book it is: Marcia Aldrich, Michigan State University; Jane Bernstein, Carnegie Mellon University; Richard Duggin, University of Nebraska at Omaha; Lucy Ferriss, Hamilton College; Stephen Gibson, Utah Valley State College; Jack Harrell, BYI–Idaho; Steve Heller, Kansas State University; Fern Kupfer, Iowa State University; Michael Latza, College of Lake Country; Keith Long, Southwestern Oklahoma State University; Sharon Oard Warner, University of New Mexico; Alyssa O'Brien, Stanford University; Thomas Palakeel, Bradley University; Stephen Pett, Iowa State University; Michael Raymond, Stetson University; Mark Sanders, College of the Mainland; and Brent Spencer, Creighton University.

Finally, I'd like to thank my wife Bridget and my daughter Sophia. Their support and encouragement stand behind every line, and this book is dedicated to them.

Mark Baechtel

A Note from the Publisher

The following supplements can accompany *Shaping the Story*.

A Student's Guide to Getting Published (0-321-11779-4)
This "how-to" guide steps students through the process of publishing their work. It discusses considerations of submission and contracts, how to research markets, how to self-edit and be edited, and how to produce a "well-wrought manuscript." Available FREE when packaged with *Shaping the Story*

Journal for Creative Writing (0-321-09540-5)
This journal provides students with their own personal space for writing. Helpful writing prompts and strategies are included as well as guidelines for participating in a workshop. Available FREE when packaged with *Shaping the Story*

A Workshop Guide for Creative Writing (0-321-09539-1)
This laminated reference guide offers suggestions/tips for students to keep in mind in a workshop situation—both as a participant and as a presenter. Blank space is provided for students to record additional guidelines provided by their instructor. Available FREE when packaged with *Shaping the Story*

INTRODUCTION

One of the oldest and sweetest requests in human experience is *Tell me a story*. We ask this almost as soon as we can form the words, and really, we never do stop asking. We enter every exchange in our lives ready to tell stories or to listen to them—to chat about the day's events, spin yarns, pass along parables, tell amusing anecdotes, relate cautionary tales. Stories lull us to sleep and wake us up; they teach us what we need to know, they frighten and console us. Stories are a species of magic: unreal worlds that inform the real world in which we live, an endless laboratory for human meaning in which we test our hypotheses about existence.

Because storytelling is so central in our lives, to a greater or lesser extent we all end up hanging out our shingles as story-tellers. Some of us take this activity so se-riously that we decide we'll try to practice it formally, and we start to write.

Odds are, though, when the would-be writer sits down to produce her first short story, it's a disaster. The writing sounds flat or else too flowery. The story's set-tings are over-described and chaotic, im-possible to visualize, or else the writer makes so little use of the physical world that it's as if the action were taking place in a vast, empty room. When characters talk to each other they sound like bad actors and when the writer prods them into motion they seem like even worse actors, striking poses, sawing their arms around or bashing through the story's scenes with all the grace of runaway dump trucks. What they do seems unreal, and it never seems to add up to much. The spark of interest with which the writer began gets quickly smothered; she crumples her story up and pitches it, muttering: *I guess I'm just no good at this . . .*

If this has happened to you, take heart: it's happened to most if not all writers. Even fiction writers who publish their work regularly must still struggle to create real-seeming characters, vivid and appropriately detailed evocations of setting, compelling action, believable outcomes, and struggle, too, to get it all to work together so that it's not just a collection of events, but a *story*. Every newly begun story is a challenge. It requires its writer to return again to that territory where the story hangs like a protostar in space: not quite there, but not quite *not* there—a ball of swirling potential. Making this murk

> "*There's no such thing as a born writer. It's a skill you've got to learn. You've got to write X number of words before you can write anything that can be published, but nobody is able to tell you how many words that is. You will know when you get there, but you don't know how long it will take.*"
>
> —LARRY BROWN

coalesce and getting it to ignite and to shed light takes some work, a willingness to explore, to experiment, or even to fail.

Guiding you through this work is what *Shaping the Story* is all about. There are many books that offer the beginning fiction writer exercises that will help her to master such issues of story writing as beginnings, point of view, narrative tone, setting, characterization, dialogue, dramatization, plot, pacing, endings and making good use of the revision process. Many of these books are very useful. There are none currently on the market, though, that, in addition to addressing these pieces of the process, also aim to teach the student how to knit those pieces into a whole—that is, to make them into a fully integrated, fully functioning short story. *Shaping the Story* fills that gap.

What This Book Is . . . and What It's Not

Memorable short stories aren't written by the numbers. That might seem a strange thing to say in the introduction to a book that lays out a step-by-step plan for the writing of a short story. But it's important to say at the outset that the interlocking series of exercises *Shaping the Story* contains isn't meant to provide a guaranteed formula for use in writing short fiction. That would be a foolish, as well as an impossible thing to try: stories are endlessly various in the ways they emerge, develop structurally and find their way to an ending. That's part of the joy of writing them, and of reading them.

> "*Y*ou've got to be smart enough to write, and stupid enough not to think about all the things that might go wrong."   —SARAH GILBERT

Instead, these interlocking chapters are meant to provide you with an experimental framework in which you can examine the short story's elements—elements which in reality, at all times, function as parts of a whole. It's important to keep this wholeness in mind as you work. In his essay, "The Art of Fiction," Henry James says:

> I cannot imagine composition existing in a series of blocks, nor conceive in any novel worth discussing at all, of a passage of description that is not in its intention narrative, a passage of dialogue that is not in its intention descriptive, a touch of truth of any sort that does not partake of the nature of incident, or an incident that derives its interest from any other source than the general and only source of the success of a work of art—that of being illustrative. A novel is a living thing, all one and continuous, like any other organism, and in proportion as it lives will it be found, I think, that in each of the parts there is something of each of the other parts.

James may have been speaking of the novel, but what he said holds true also for the short story. All parts of a story partake in the work done by all other parts of the story. Therefore, even though this book carves the process of story writing up into twelve assignments (which, it must be admitted, could be interpreted as "a series of [compositional] blocks"), and even though each assignment is meant to help you to deeply explore the effects you can achieve by operating a different piece of the narrative's machinery, you should never forget how interdependent the elements of a good story are.

Each story has its own lessons to teach us as we struggle to write it, and as you complete each of the book's twelve assignments, you'll benefit from the particular and focused attention you'll be paying to each component of your story and each stage of your story writing process. This will help you to gain confidence and learn about the many ways there may be for you to enter that strange territory where stories are produced. Try to throw yourself fully into each exercise, even if you've already written quite a few stories and the idea of writing a story this way—in stages—seems strange to you.

Letting Your Story Surprise You

Many beginning writers labor in the shadow of a very large and erroneous assumption: that good short stories emerge from their creator's fevered imaginations in a single draft, like Athena sprung fully armed from Zeus's brow. It's an understandable assumption—in a well-written story (to mix metaphors for a moment), the threads of character, physical setting and action that make up each scene are deftly interwoven with the threads making up all the other scenes, and the published story seems to the reader like a bolt of woven cloth—all of a piece. The reader has no conception of the struggle that went on during the story's composition—how much frustration and sometimes outright despair the writer felt before she finally struck on the right combination of narrative elements that allowed the story to emerge as it wanted to.

Note where the agency is placed: the story emerging as *it* wants to. Every story follows its own unique evolutionary track, and experienced writers know this track may wander far away from the track they might have predicted the story would take, when first they sat down and wrote what they thought were the piece's opening sentences. It can feel almost as if the story had a will and a life of its own, like a dream that dreams itself.

You may be beginning your story with very definite ideas about how it's going to unfold, what it's going to be about. Set aside those intentions for now, and try to throw yourself fully into the process of writing your story as a series of responses to this book's linked exercises. These exercises may take you down paths you've never considered traveling before. You may begin your story thinking one character is at its center, but after you've finished the characterization exercise, you may find yourself more interested in another who had, until that point, seemed peripheral. When you complete the setting exercise, you may find yourself wanting to use the main character's living room or car or kitchen as the frame for a scene you hadn't expected to write at all, but which is crucial to expressing the mystery at the story's heart. You may start out writing a story in first-person and end up writing your story in third-person, or vice versa. You may decide you prefer a more formal and objective voice for your narration over the more casual and intimate voice you began with. Experienced short story writers are quite familiar with these sorts of changes-in-intention. As was implied above, the writing of a story is very seldom a sure and steady movement from the idea that provides its beginning spark through the closing mark of punctuation. Instead, it is an unfolding that proceeds in fits and starts, with every new scene—with its descriptions of setting, speech and action, its evocations of character—adding to and modifying what the writer has learned about what came before, and necessitating changes to keep the flow of events plausible and evocative. If you think of short story writing as a continual process of *revision*—that is, of re-*seeing*—in addition to its being a process of *creation*, you come closer to capturing what the experience is like, and how it works. Treating your story as a piece of experimentation can be a healthy thing. Let yourself stretch a bit; it will do your fiction good.

The Order of the Lessons

Naturally, the lessons that make up this book had to be put in some kind of order. The order in *Shaping the Story* reflects its author's beliefs and experience, and his attempt to use these beliefs and experience to put the stages of story writing in approximately the order in which he believed a beginning writer would most usefully encounter them.

This order is not ironclad. Different writers think different issues are of primary importance (indeed, if you're using this book as part of a course, your instructor may have you pursue an alternate order in moving through the book's chapters). You may find, as you move on in your writing career, that your stories emerge most often out of character sketches, or else you may find yourself more interested in plot and the intricate web of causality a plot constitutes than the personalities who end up caught in it. You may begin by working hard to capture a particular atmosphere as the setting for your story and *then* imagine the characters and action that atmosphere will contain. You may hear a clear and particular narrative voice speaking to you, and then set yourself to take down what that voice tells you as though you were taking dictation.

> "*I like pushing the form, over-reaching, going a little too far, just on the edge, sometimes getting your fingers burned. It's good to do that.*"
>
> —GAY TALESE

The point is this: there are as many ways to embark on the writing of a story as there are writers, and as you serve your own writing apprenticeship you will find your way to the approach that feels most natural, most comfortable, for you. This is one method—and an experimental method, at that. Take it as that, and not as any sort of Gospel.

How It Will Work

We often learn best by doing, and this book is founded on the notion that you'll best learn the ways of the short story by writing one—beginning at its beginning, working your way through its middle, pushing on to its finish and then revising your first draft. To this end, you'll start by working on your story's opening, and each chapter you work through after that will move you forward to a further stage in your story's evolution. The book's chapters are grouped into four sections: Section I, "Getting the Idea;" Section II, "Building the Scene;" Section III, "Moving from *Scene* to *Story*" and Section IV, "Ending and Revising."

GETTING THE IDEA

The four chapters in this section—"Beginnings: Part I," "Beginnings: Part II," "Point of View" and "Voice"—will help you to explore and begin to bring order to your early ideas for your story. You'll learn how to set your initial ideas for your story down on the page, and then how to rework them into an opening scene that draws your reader in and involves him. You'll learn how to manage the reader's relationship with your story's characters and events by choosing the right point of view, and you'll learn why your storytelling voice is an important tool you can use to establish a tone which keeps your reader anchored in the world you're creating and keeps him interested in what you make happen there.

BUILDING THE SCENE

The second section's four chapters—"Setting," "Character," "Dialogue" and "Dramatization"—will help you learn to integrate setting, character, dialogue and physical action in one of the basic building blocks used to create almost every short story, the dramatized scene. The exercises in this section will help you to evoke the physical world of your story. You'll learn how to populate this world with characters who seem to live and breathe on the page. You'll learn how dialogue can function to make your characters realer and more vivid. Finally, you'll learn how to set your characters in motion, bringing setting, character and dialogue in scenes that pump energy into the story and add narrative momentum.

MOVING FROM *SCENE* TO *STORY*

By working your way through the third section's chapters on "Plot" and "Time," you'll learn how to bring your scenes together so they function as a narrative. You'll learn to pace this assemblage-of-scenes so that, in its unfolding, it carries the reader ever more deeply into your story's themes, and builds toward—and past—a climax.

ENDING AND REVISING

In the fourth section you'll explore what makes a good ending, and in writing the exercise that concludes the eleventh chapter, on Endings, you'll work to bring your story to a natural and satisfying conclusion. By the time you've finished this exercise, the work you will have produced will form a rough mosaic that, with some further cutting and polishing, will constitute a first draft of your short story. The twelfth chapter, on Revision, will lead you through this cutting and polishing process, demonstrating why some of the most important work you'll do on your story—work that deepens and completes it—will often take place after you've finished your first draft, and will continue for multiple drafts after that.

Though *Shaping the Story* was written under the assumption that you would be using this book as a part of a course taught by a working writer, it would also be possible for any sufficiently motivated writer to make her way through the book's course of study on her own.

REVISION AS A PART OF YOUR PROCESS

As was suggested above, writing a story is a process made up partly of writing, but largely of rewriting—framing what you've written in new ways, literally *re-seeing* character, event, action and object in light of the new information you gain through the creation of each new scene. To help you to make revision an ongoing part of your story writing process, after the linked exercises for the chapters on beginnings, point of view, voice, setting, characterization, dialogue, dramatization, plot, time and endings, there will be a half-dozen revision questions meant to set you rethinking your responses to the previous exercises in light of what the just-finished exercise has shown you about your story.

EXAMPLES FROM STUDENT STORIES

Theory is one thing and practice is another. It may be helpful, as you ponder how you're going to use each of the writing assignments to help you write your story, if you can see how other writing students have responded to each exercise. Each assignment will be followed by an example from the work of two students—Jeremy Blodgett and Sarah Cornwell—who used this plan during an introductory fiction writing course at Grinnell College. Their finished stories—"Not Even Angels Are Immortal" in Jeremy's case, and "Pretty Little Things" in Sarah's—are also printed at the end of the book.

> *"I read not only for pleasure, but as a journeyman, and where I see a good effect I study it, and try to reproduce it."* —LAWRENCE DURRELL

READING EXERCISES

In addition to the exercises, eleven of the course's twelve chapters also include a reading assignment. The assigned stories, printed in the back of this book, are by both "classic" writers who will probably be familiar to you, and by contemporary writers whose work you may be reading here for the first time. Each of these stories was chosen for the illustration it offers of the issues of craft under discussion in a particular chapter. Each story is accompanied by a half-dozen questions that will focus your attention on the example the story provides of the issue of craft addressed by the chapter and the way the particular story addresses them.

ALTERNATIVE EXERCISES

Some people using this book may not want to use the interlocking plan, or there may be some who will want to spend more than one exercise working, for instance, on characterization or dialogue or setting. To accommodate these writers, each chapter is accompanied by four alternative exercises. If you like (and, if you're using this book as a part of a class, if your instructor approves) you could use these exercises instead of following the more formal structure, or treat them as an opportunity to sharpen your skills.

> *"Real literature, like travel, is always a surprise."* —ALISON LURIE

That's enough about ways and means and pedagogical philosophy; now let's move on to what you came to this book to do. Let's make a start on your story.

PART ONE

GETTING THE IDEA

Human life is driven forward by its dim apprehension
of notions too general for its existing language.

—Alfred North Whitehead
Adventures in Ideas

At some point you've probably read a story that left you feeling moved and changed, impressed by the writer's ability to conjure a world that seemed real in all its particulars and strange as life itself can be strange. You may have come away from reading this story wishing the writer were at your elbow as you read the last words, so you could ask her, *How* did you come up with that?

It may surprise you to hear that her answer might be, I don't know.

Where Do Stories Come From?

Readers don't have access to the mysterious and messy origins a story had in the writer's imagination. Stories rarely arrive fully formed, with a completely articulated plot, living, breathing characters, entertaining and real-sounding dialogue, vivid scenes and settings, an elegant and balanced mix of thought and action. Instead, they most often begin obscurely, and arrive in bits and pieces with maddening and tantalizing slowness, and with the coherent narrative the finished story presents to us most likely emerging only after the writer struggled through many revisions.

Sometimes a story will have its beginning in a few overheard words—like the torn-off corner of a photograph, suggesting something larger. A story might begin

"When I have a chance to write about a period of my life, and experience, and I can rework it into the life of my hero, then everything changes and I can no longer remember what happened in reality. That is why when I am not writing, I am suffering, because I remember too much of concrete life. I have to destroy my past in order to win my own freedom."

—ANDREI BITOV

to form the way a painful memory surfaces over and over—not the memory itself, but a hint of it that comes to you in the shower, or while you're cooking a certain dish. Sometimes a story will emerge from the reading of a poem, a newspaper article, or a prayer, or from that desire familiar to most of us, which grows increasingly familiar as more time passes: to go back and live a piece of life over again, to find out how things might have gone if you had done things another way, or if events had fallen out differently.

One of the most maddening and essential questions any writer ever confronts is: *What do you write about?* It's a question you'll often hear when someone finds out you're serious about writing. How will you reply?

If you don't have a ready answer, don't worry. It's a question any writer dreads hearing—indeed, it is a question only nonwriters ask, because, as the quote at the start of this section suggests, there *is* no easy way to answer it. If you were Sandra Cisneros, how would you explain what you were after when you detailed a dull afternoon a little girl spends at a church in Mexico with her brothers and her grandmother in "Mericans" (p. 291)? If you were Flannery O'Connor, fresh from finishing a first draft of "Revelation" (p. 217), how would you even begin to express the story's action or its themes? Could Tillie Olsen have done "I Stand Here Ironing" (p. 312) justice with a summary sentence? What kind of reaction might Jorge Luis Borges have received if he tried to synopsize his story "The Aleph" (p. 248) by saying "It's about the inadequacy of art, expressed through the confounding metaphor of a three-centimeter sphere located beneath a set of cellar steps in a house in Buenos Aires, in which it is possible to view all space and all time simultaneously?" Borges's hypothetical questioner might have heard his reply and looked at him as if he were crazy.

Stories *are* a species of insanity, if sanity is defined as the orderly and sober forward marching of a logic-bound mind, intent only on *making sense* in a world in which nothing surprising ever happens. Stories are worlds and people the writer conjures amid the vapor hanging above the soup of the unconscious—visions set on the page in the form of character and situation as though they actually *were* real and the writer weren't making them up, but only recording their actions like a journalist. Described this way, story writing seems a pretty dodgy enterprise. Despite what was said above about the impossibility of giving a straight answer to the What do you write about? question, you should consider your answer here at the beginning, as a preface to this section dedicated to beginnings. What do you write about? is a question that rises before each of us as we sit down and face the blank first page of the draft that we hope and pray will become that grail of every writer, *The Best Thing I've Ever Written.*

> "*I usually write about things that frighten me. Otherwise, what's the point? Kafka once said we need books not to be entertained by them but for them to be like an ax on the frozen sea of our souls.*"
>
> —DAVID GROSSMAN

What do you write about? What does *any* writer write about? Doctors, lawyers, car thieves. Housewives. High school principals. Convenience store clerks and exotic dancers whose best friends are priests. Long-haul truckers. Prisoners trapped in cells of concrete and steel, or in the bottomless jails their minds have become. The strange and moving loyalty of animals. Families. Friendship. Love gone wrong, or persisted in beyond good sense or reason so that at last it goes right. Any face that can be imagined, any image that ever appeared within the endless and eternal labyrinth of the human heart. Relativity and loneliness and fear and trembling unto death. Truth, in all the faceted and multiple forms it assumes; lies, which are equal in their variety. Christmas, Hanukkah, Ramadan. Ghosts, God, the midnight realization that the world is empty of holiness. Chess. The damage a couple inflicts upon each other in choosing kitchen appliances. Death or birth or both at once. Leaving home or finding a home. The light that falls into the breakfast room and shatters your heart.

Does this begin to convey it? Anyone who tells you "You can't write about that" is wrong. You can write about anything, if only you work diligently and with integrity sufficient to the framing your subject requires and deserves. For most of us, this freedom can be frightening. Reality is so big, and even a single day in the most mundane lifetime is so packed with meaning that it can render material enough for entire volumes of fiction (witness James Joyce's *Ulysses*, which takes place in a single day in Dublin). And this is only one day; it doesn't even touch memory, that inexhaustible treasure trove of days and nights and years that every brain, including yours, contains.

> "*I* write about the things that trouble me. I write about the things that disturb me, the things that won't let me alone, the things that are eating slowly into my brain at three in the morning, the things that unbalance my world. Sometimes these are things I've said or done; sometimes they're things I've heard about or seen. Sometimes they're only sentences, sometimes scenes, sometimes complete narratives. I carry these things around inside my head until I'm compelled to write them down to get rid of them. I sit down and begin."
>
> —ROXANA ROBINSON,
> "IF YOU INVENT THE STORY,
> YOU'RE THE FIRST ONE
> TO SEE HOW IT ENDS"

So, taking it as a given that you have whole libraries' worth of material packed between your ears, how do you start to write that elusive thing, a short story?

You may be lucky. You may be the kind of writer to whom the entire story occurs seamlessly, with a beguiling beginning; a vivid setting replete with metaphor; fully fleshed characters; a complete, well-rounded, and pleasing plot; graceful transitions from scene to scene; and a lovely ending that ties up all loose threads without tying them too tightly, leaving the reader grateful and satisfied. For such a writer, story writing is just dictation.

If you're like the vast majority of writers, though, what you start with is a vague intuition, like a hard-to-scratch itch, the uneasy feeling that accompanies something—an errand, an anniversary, a date—you've forgotten, but that lurks in the mind's corner, a nagging specter. This is how stories most often begin: small apprehensions, a twinge of spiritual discomfort, a certain stillness in the house, a turn of phrase your father uses, a snatch of conversation you overhear while pumping gas. Wherever you feel meaning struggling within the surrounding silence, trying to find the air, is the place to start. Begin there and have patience: it is spring and you are planting a seed, hoping it will grow.

Because conceptualizing and writing an opening scene for your story are such crucial stages in its evolution, you'll be working on your story's beginning for the next two chapters. After this, you'll work on point of view (who's telling your story and to whom they're telling it) and tone of voice (the *sound* or *style* of the writing, which imbues the narrative with a certain personality and attitude). It should be said, too, that every beginning is provisional, and may change many times as your story begins to come into focus—something that will be addressed directly in the revision questions that follow the second chapter.

1

BEGINNINGS (PART I)

Work, work your thoughts . . .

> —William Shakespeare
> Chorus, in *Henry V*,
> Prologue to Act III

When you set out to write a short story, you're presuming a lot. You're presuming your reader will take time out of a busy life to pay the closest kind of attention to the world you've imagined and that is not the greatest of your presumptions. You're also asking for access to your reader's mind and heart. Your story may challenge his most closely held beliefs. You may want to disturb, educate, or inform him. Even to try to make someone laugh is to ask for his trust and belief. At the very least, you're asking your reader to relax and be entertained, and your reader, as stand-up comedians say, may be a very tough "room."

Obviously this means a lot of pressure comes to bear on the very beginning of your story, when the reader is consciously or unconsciously asking a very simple but very important question: *Why is this story being told?*

What Makes a Story a Story?

Before you can begin to answer the Why is this story being told? question as regards your own story, though, it may be useful to define what we mean when we say *story*. The American Heritage Dictionary defines a story as ". . . an account or a recital of an event or a series of events. . . ." This is accurate, as far as it goes, but it doesn't really address what's most important about stories—that is, the reasons writers tell them, and what readers come to them hoping for.

> "*The ark was built by amateurs, and the* Titanic *by the experts. Don't wait for the experts.*"
>
> —MURRAY COHEN

Ultimately, a story has to add up to something more than just "a recital of an event or a series of events" if it's going to command your reader's interest and hold him until it's finished.

What *is* this something more? That's hard to define. It's more than the story's *plot*—the order the writer uses in his retelling of the story's events. It's more than *theme* or *subject*; these are words that seem too reductive. It's not a *moral*—a sermon the story's preaching or a lesson it's meant to teach. Modern readers resist such didacticism. The French term *donnée* comes close to capturing it, describing as it does an assumption—not necessarily explicit—out of which a work develops.

For our purposes, though, another, older source may make it possible for us to frame a good working definition of what makes a story a story. In his *Poetics*, Aristotle said:

> Objects which in themselves we view with pain, we delight to contemplate when reproduced [in a work of art] with minute fidelity: such as the forms of the most ignoble animals and of dead bodies. The cause of this . . . is that to learn gives the liveliest pleasure, not only to philosophers but to men in general. . . . Thus the reason why men enjoy seeing a likeness [in a work of art] is that in contemplating it they find themselves learning or inferring, and saying perhaps: "Ah, that is he."
> (Aristotle's *Poetics*, translated by S. H. Butcher, New York: Hill and Wang, 1961.)

It is at this moment—when, as Aristotle puts it, the reader says "Ah, that is he"—that the story truly becomes a story. Aristotle called the reader's experience in this moment *recognition*—literally a moment of "rethinking," when the story acts on the reader to produce an insight or realization. As readers, our recognition of the emotional, spiritual, or experiential truth a story contains is a deep, even a visceral experience. It is when the story's heart declares itself to us.

Every story has a heart. Unlike the heart in the body, though, it doesn't exist in an identifiable place—when, for instance, the story reaches a climax. Although a climax can present us with a story's heart (as in Shirley Jackson's often anthologized story, "The Lottery"), more often it exists as a sum—a quantity the story presents when all the action it contains, all the characters it enables us to know, all the descriptions of place and circumstance it presents to us, combine to make it possible for us to have an understanding, an appreciation of some essential truth that it would have been impossible to reach in any other way.

> *"A*rt is a shutting in in order to shut out. Art is a ritualistic binding of the perpetual motion machine that is nature. . . . Art is spellbinding. Art fixes the audience in its seat, stops the feet before a painting, fixes a book in the hand. Contemplation is a magic act."* —CAMILLE PAGLIA

For an example, let's turn to Louise Erdrich's story, "The Red Convertible," which is included on page 293. Here is the story's first paragraph:

> I was the first one to drive a convertible on my reservation. And of course it was red, a red Olds. I owned that car along with my brother, Henry Junior. We owned it together until his boots filled with water on a windy night and he bought out my share. Now Henry owns the whole car, and his younger brother Lyman (that's myself), Lyman walks everywhere he goes.

This opening paragraph tells us the narrator, Lyman, is a Native American living on a reservation, who owned the car of the story's title with his brother Henry, until

Henry "bought out [Lyman's] share" on the night Henry's "boots filled with water." But for the bit about Henry's boots, this would seem to be a fairly straightforward statement of facts, and it is the bit about the boots—the first faint statement of the story's heart—that drives us forward into the story, where we learn that what happens to Henry and Lyman and their car is anything but straightforward.

In the first 1,400 words of the story, Lyman tells us that after buying the convertible on impulse, he and Henry spent an entire summer road tripping, an idyll that ended only with the coming of winter, when they returned to the real world and Henry had to leave for Marine boot camp and, after his training, transshipment to Vietnam.

It is after this opening that the story truly begins: Henry returns from the war utterly changed by his three years in combat. He is barely able to move or speak and Lyman—at a loss for what else to do to help his brother—secretly sabotages

> *"In the sense that there was nothing before it, all writing is writing against the void."*
>
> —MARK STRAND

the car to give Henry something useful to do. Henry eventually discovers the damage and sets about repairing it, and in her characteristic simple, clear prose, Erdrich details the loving attention Henry pays to the car and the uneasy but hopeful way Lyman looks on, hoping for Henry's transformation and the resurrection of their close relationship.

Finally, the repairs are complete and Henry proposes a drive to a nearby river. The brothers' young sister takes a picture before the drive, and the way Erdrich describes how Henry puts his arm across Lyman's shoulder for the snapshot—"very carefully, as though it was heavy for him to lift and he didn't want to bring the weight down all at once"—lets the reader know that working on the car has made some healing possible for Henry, but that deeper wounds remain untouched. It's an impression deepened by Lyman's description of Henry's face as it would appear later in the photograph: ". . . the shadows on his face are deep as holes. There are two shadows curved like little hooks around the ends of his smile, as if to frame it and try to keep it there—that one, first smile that looked like it might have hurt his face. He has his field jacket on and the worn-in clothes he'd come back in and kept wearing ever since." With this description firmly in mind, we know the drive they take can't but be a sad echo of the idyllic drive they took together during the summer before Henry left for the war, and we are prepared for it to lead to some sort of crisis. Erdrich takes us to a moment when it becomes clear—as Lyman and Henry sit together by a fire they've made on the banks of the river which is "full of winter trash . . . just at its limit, hard swollen, glossy like an old gray scar"—that Henry will never be able to come back to himself again. The brothers drink and fight, then Henry begins a strange dance, "something between a grass dance and a bunny hop, no kind of dance [Lyman] ever saw before, but neither [had] anyone else on all this green growing earth" and then jumps into the river, where (recalling the cryptic statement in the story's beginning), he tells Lyman his boots are filling with water and drowns. As a final gesture, Lyman sends the car in after him.

Without the influence of the odd phrase in the opening paragraph, and without Erdrich's careful efforts to take us inside the brothers, their world, and their relationship, Henry's death and Lyman's sinking of the car might have seemed perverse. Instead, presenting us as they do with a summation of all the story's elements, Henry's death and the car's end have a sad and transcendent beauty. Henry's death, as the reader is able to understand in a moment of Aristotelian recognition, was inevitable.

As this example may make clear, the process of unfolding a story's heart in a way that excites the reader's sense of recognition may be neither direct nor easy. Nor should it be. The thing we call consciousness is a vastly mysterious quantity. Sometimes we apprehend the truths of our experiences only obliquely, and sometimes the truth we apprehend can be difficult if not impossible to express easily or quickly. Because this is true, stories often take indirect paths to make contact with the reader's sense of recognition. In the best stories, despite the satisfaction they provide us with, it's often very, very tough to say what they're about, or to summarize all the ambitions the author seems to have had for them. As Flannery O'Connor said in her essay, "Writing Short Stories," "When you can state the theme of a story, when you can separate it from the story itself, then you can be sure the story is not a very good one." This is not an argument for obscurity in short story writing; rather, it is a recognition of a good story's *subtlety.*

> *"The material's out there, a calm lake waiting for us to dive in."*   —BEVERLY LOWRY

The Reader's Questions

Whatever the heart of a story may be, from its first sentence we, as readers, are trying to make contact with it. We are continually asking questions as we move deeper, take in more, learn more about the characters the story contains, the actions they perform, the situations and settings through which they move. As writers, it can help us to keep some of these readers' potential questions in mind as we ponder our story's beginning. In addition to the question posed above—Why is this story being told?—you might add a few others:

> Who's telling this story, and why?
> Who does this story "belong" to?
> Who am I with as the story opens?
> Why does the story begin at this moment in the character's/characters' life/lives?
> Where am I as the story opens?
> What are the physical features of this place? What do I see?
> What action is taking place?
> When—at what time of day, what time of year, in what part of life—is this story unfolding?
> What's at stake for the main character(s)?
> What does/do the character(s) want? What stands between (him/her/them) and that which (he/she/they) want(s)?
> What does/do (he/she/they) fear? What is pushing (him/her/them) into contact with that feared object?

Putting yourself in your reader's place and thinking your way through these questions can help you to establish the frame and basic outline of your narrative.

The Arc of the Story

A story can also reach out to the reader's sense of recognition through its structure. Stories most often travel through a course of increasing tension and rising complication as they move toward a crisis point—a point (to quote the *Poetics* again) of *peripety* or *turning*—after which they pass through a period of decreasing tension and complication. This process of rising and then falling complication might usefully be compared to the flight of an arrow. A skilled archer knows she must aim the arrow *above* the target in order to strike it, and so the arrow travels in an arc—first rising, then, after reaching the top of its arc, falling toward and finding the target.

It's important to add that this is only a rough and imperfect analogy. You can damage a story by aiming too deliberately at a particular target, draining the story of surprise. Very few stories actually follow a perfect arc, and the narrative energy that moves a story along can rise and fall irregularly. Not every story offers only one discernable turning.

> "*The* form chooses you, not the other way around. An idea comes and is already embodied in a form."
> —MICHAEL FRAYN

Nevertheless, it's useful to consider the idea of the story's arc and its turning as you think about the story's beginning and the function of each of the scenes and transitions that follow it. As you're pushing your story through its various stages in the exercises that follow, you should at some level be considering how a scene or passage of explanation or summarized action contributes to the rising or the falling arc of the story.

To provide an illustration of how this works, let's analyze "Goldilocks and the Three Bears." As the story opens, Goldilocks heads into the forest in search of adventure. She comes on the three bears' house, and the familiar sequence of events follows: she tries the three bowls of porridge, the three beds, and then she falls asleep. The bears return and (depending on which version you've read) either eat Goldilocks or frighten her, so that she runs all the way home, having learned her lesson. Represented as points along an arc, the story's events look like this:

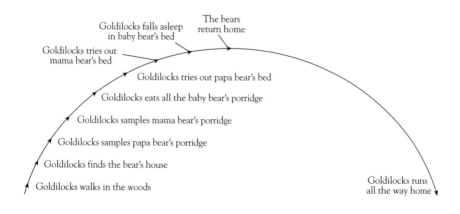

Goldilocks falls asleep
in baby bear's bed

The bears
return home

Goldilocks tries out
mama bear's bed

Goldilocks tries out papa bear's bed

Goldilocks eats all the baby bear's porridge

Goldilocks samples mama bear's porridge

Goldilocks samples papa bear's porridge

Goldilocks finds the bear's house

Goldilocks walks in the woods

Goldilocks runs
all the way home

At each point along the arc of the story, the tension the reader feels (knowing the bears *must* return at some point) rises. The longer Goldilocks is in the bears' house, the greater the chance they'll return and catch her. Finally, she falls asleep, and it is at this moment, when the unfolding of the narrative has created the greatest tension in the reader, that the bears return. This is why the return is at the top of the story's arc: it's the story's turning point, after which it falls toward its ending.

Progressive Writing Exercise #1:
The Story Cloud Diagram

You may already have an idea in mind for the story you'd like to try to write. You'll be using this exercise to explore your idea, working your way toward some notion of where the story might begin and how it might unfold. If you don't yet have an idea for a story, this exercise will help you to develop one. It's a variation on the notion of *clustering*, a technique for conceiving and arranging ideas for themes and papers which may be familiar to some students from composition classes they've taken in the past. This variation—which here is called the *story cloud diagram*—will help you to map your story's possibilities, and will help you begin to speculate about where—in what combination of scenes, in what emotional alchemy, in what interaction of characters—the heart of your story might reside.

Proceed this way: take out a blank, unlined sheet of paper and try to form a picture of your main character. Give this character a name, and put that name somewhere near the center of the sheet of paper. Now, as if in a cloud around it, write some of the emotional states you think the story will contain. Try not to settle on overly simple expressions of these emotional states, avoiding—for example—"fear" in favor of "terror of heights" or "sexual panic,"or using "nostalgic melancholy" or "suicidal bleakness" in the place of "sadness." Try to come up with at least a dozen of these emotional states.

Once you've done this, make a second cloud that surrounds and contains the first, this one composed of a dozen or so possible situations which might provoke or contain these emotional states—a bar fight, for instance; a church service, a first date, or the discovery of a lover's murder.

Now make a third cloud that contains the other two, this one composed of a dozen or so possible secondary characters. Try to go beyond the obvious with these characters, giving them more than two-dimensional presence in the diagram. You might list your main character's boss as one of the secondary characters, but she's a human being before she's a boss. What kind of human being is she? Can you—in a word or two—render her as more than just a job title? Is she a kindly boss? An incompetent boss? A wise boss? A boss with a savage temper, who has it in for your main character?

Once you've got your three clouds sketched in, ask yourself if you sense relationships, both within and among the levels of your diagram—character to emotional state, emotional state to situation, situation to secondary character, etc. If you do, you might draw lines between these elements.

Remember: at this point you're just speculating, making some guesses about what your story might ultimately contain. Don't worry that you'll need to represent all the emotional states you've proposed in the first cloud, or that as you write your story you'll have to include all the situations and characters you posit in the second and third cloud. You should also feel free to add new emotional states, situations and characters as they come to seem necessary.

What you'll learn: Creating your cloud diagram provides you with a form in which you can explore, and see the urging of your unconscious at work. You're not creating a plot here; you're trying to get a rough sense of what your story *might* be about.

STUDENT EXAMPLES

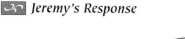 *Jeremy's Response*

Commentary One measure of a story cloud's strength is the breadth of narrative possibility it presents—the number of possible answers it may provide to the reader's opening questions (p. 14). These answers are suggested both by tensions existing within the individual clouds and by tensions suggested by possible relationships between the clouds' elements. For instance, if we look at the second cloud—the cloud of possible situations—and consider that Jeremy's main character, David, might break up with his girlfriend *and* have surgery, one possible story begins to suggest it-self. Why might a young man facing surgery break up with his girlfriend? Would the two events be somehow connected, or purely coincidental? What might it mean if he breaks up with her *after* he finds out he has to have surgery, or vice versa?

Another story possibility: Among the emotional states in the first cloud, Jeremy lists David's sense of "wonder at the natural world." If we were to connect this ele-ment to "moves to the city" in the cloud of situations, we can see that a story might emerge from the seeming contradiction. If David feels intimately connected to the natural world, what effect would it have on him if he were to move to the city, where the sort of intimate contact with nature to which he may have been accustomed is made more difficult? What conditions would move him to act in this way against his tendency? Would he be forced to? Would it be his choice? How would he cope with the internal conflict this move would create for him?

Jeremy's diagram offers many such possibilities. In resolving the tensions, frictions, and contradictions here—whether these are present within a character, produced by the interaction of characters, or implied by the interaction of character and environment—energy is produced that propels the story, moving it (like the arrow of the analogy above) through its scenes and through the arc of its narrative. The character is faced with a problem, and the story becomes the working out of the answer.

Concerns We've read many, many stories that feature some of the situations Jeremy has put in the second level of his diagram. That doesn't represent an insurmountable problem; one of the things the reader hopes to find in a story is a fresh perspective on life events—like road trips, breakups, and major philosophical questions—that are so familiar they have come to seem like refrains in our lives, repeated into meaningless-ness. If Jeremy chooses one or several of these situations to incorporate into his story, though, he will need to be sure he so freshly observes the details of David's ex-perience that the story rises above the general and generic, becoming specific and particular.

Also, Jeremy's listing of secondary characters seems a little flat-footed. "Friends" tells us very little about the people David cares about enough to call them that; likewise "landlord," "girlfriend," "doctor," and "neighbor" don't give us much to hang our hat on, in terms of speculation about the role these characters might play in the unfolding of David's story. It's instructive to notice that the one character who's given a tiny bit of nuance—"small town gas station attendant"—draws a disproportionate amount of no-tice, precisely because he or she is mentioned, however briefly, with just enough detail to begin to raise him or her from two-dimensional to three-dimensional.

Sarah's Response

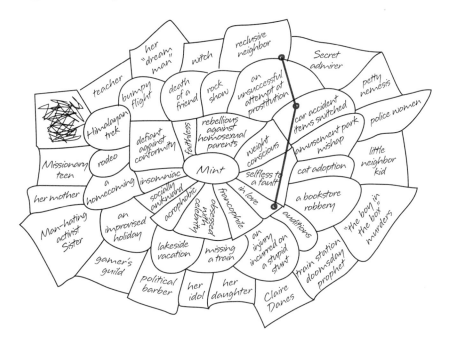

Commentary Human beings are bundles of contradictions, and stories are often kindled from the sparks struck when these contradictions are brought forcefully together. An examination of the emotional states in Sarah's cloud diagram turns up a number of promisingly contradictory states. For instance, Sarah tells us her main character, Mint, is both "obsessed with celebrity" and "defiant against conformity," which seems (at least on the surface) to be contradictory, because the cult of celebrity is the soul of conformity. How would Sarah have Mint wrestle with this contradiction? A story could arise from this struggle, and Sarah's situation cloud provides a number of promising possibilities for scenes of action in which this working-out could take place.

Another possibility: in one part of the diagram Sarah tells us Mint is in love, while in another part she tells us Mint is rebellious against her homosexual parents. What, precisely, might Mint be rebelling against? Is the fact that her parents are gay central or tangential to her rebellion? Does she resist the picture of love and identity her parents have presented her with? How does this struggle affect Mint's feelings about love?

The connections Sarah herself suggests—between Mint's feelings of love, a car accident in which some unnamed items are somehow switched, and a reclusive neighbor—is interesting. Accidents are by definition departures from routine, and can serve as the fulcrum that levers a character out of her accustomed patterns and into new realizations, new relationships, new approaches to her life. It would be interesting to see how this might play out for Mint, and to discover what connection there might be between her feelings of love and the reclusive neighbor.

Concerns Contradictions are, ultimately, only interesting and useful in the telling of a story if the story, in its unfolding, shows that the contradictions are more apparent than real. The writer must help the reader to understand how these seeming contradictions can actually be understood as facets of a single character. This is a challenge Sarah will need to meet as she ponders the variety of emotional states, situations, and secondary characters she wants to bring onto the stage of her story.

Alternative Writing Exercises

1. **What's the news?** Pick up a daily newspaper and read a) the local news section, b) the personal notices in the classified section and c) the obituaries. If you look carefully, you should be able to find the basic elements of narrative suggested amid some of the items that run in these three different sections. For this assignment, select a likely item or story from each section, and make a four-part list of story components suggested by each of these items. Your list should include 1) a *primary character*, 2) the *emotional states* your story might contain, 3) possible *situations* which might involve these emotional states, and 4) a list of potential *secondary characters*. *What you'll learn*: The world provides an endless stream of story ideas to the writer who's open to them, the newspaper being only one place you can turn to search for them. Much of life and many events, pondered with sufficient depth, will yield the germ of a narrative.

2. **She wants what she wants when she wants it.** This exercise assumes that you have a main character in mind. Try to form a picture of that character, and ask yourself the question: *What does she want?* Once you have an answer, try to imagine an obstacle—something that stands in the way of the satisfaction of her desire. Speculate on what that character might do to overcome that obstacle, what would happen to that character if she could overcome that obstacle, and what would happen if she *couldn't* overcome it. *What you'll learn*: Stories often rise out of our meditations upon the mechanics of desire, its frustration or its satisfaction after a character has struggled through difficulty, and the ways this struggle can create, change or destroy. By going directly to the notion of this struggle in considering your characters, you may tap into the energy that produces a narrative.

> "*I collect lines and snippets of things somebody might say—things I overhear, things I see in the newspaper, things I think up, dream up, wake up with in the middle of the night. I write a line down in my notebook. If I can get enough of these things, then characters begin to emerge.*"
>
> —RICHARD FORD

3. **What is there to be afraid of?** Begin the same way as you did with the preceding exercise, only substitute the question: *What person, place, thing or event does my main character fear?* As in the cloud diagram, go for *complex* and *specific* fears rather than *simple* and *abstract* fears—"fear of drowning"

rather than "fear of injury," or "fear of growing old" rather than "fear of being alone." Ask yourself where that fear comes from. Now try to imagine what would happen with your character if he were to come in contact with the feared person, place, thing or event. What would he do to prevent this contact, and what would the success or failure of that action mean to him? *What you'll learn:* Desire and fear can be seen as two faces of a single human coin, a coin that gets spun pretty often in our stories. One name we give this spinning coin is *conflict*. As with desire, an exploration of the nature of a character's fear may set a story in motion.

4. **Toto, I don't think we're in Kansas anymore . . .** This exercise assumes you already have a character and a situation in mind for your story. Now ask yourself a few questions from among those basic reader's questions about this character and situation—for instance: *Who's telling this story? Why here and why now? What is it about this particular place and this particular time that seems critical to my character or characters?* This is another way of considering the question—asking: *What makes me think there's a story here? What you'll learn:* Whether we're conscious of it or not, we often begin to write our stories by making a few assumptions about narrator and setting, and with some notions of why we want to locate our characters in a particular time, place and situation. You're going to be making that process of assumption-making conscious here, to see whether it doesn't suggest a course for your narrative.

Reading Exercise:
Recognition in Flannery O'Connor's "Revelation"

To use the poet Richard Wilbur's phrase, one of the things writers often try to capture with their work is "the buried strangeness which nourishes the known." Few writers of fiction offer so many occasions to recall the phrase as has Flannery O'Connor, and few of her stories so essentialize this strangeness as well as does "Revelation."

QUESTIONS

1. As was said at the beginning of the chapter, among the questions a reader will ask as he starts to read any story are: Whose story is this? and Why does this story begin at this moment and no other? What tells you this is Mrs. Turpin's story, and what does O'Connor do for the story by beginning it with Mrs. Turpin in a doctor's office?

2. What does Mrs. Turpin's conversation with the other patients in the doctor's office help us to understand about her, aside from the very obvious fact of her racism and snobbery?

3. What do you think O'Connor intends by having Mrs. Turpin notice when, after Mary Grace has attacked her, she looks into the girl's eyes and concludes that

"[t]here was no doubt in her mind that the girl did know her, knew her in some intense and personal way, beyond time and place and condition"? How do the attack and this assertion set up what unfolds eventually on the farm?

4. Mary Grace is more than merely an unhappy girl with bad manners. What does O'Connor mean the reader to understand about this character, and how does O'Connor convey this to the reader?

5. It is a while before we begin to suspect what might be at stake for Mrs. Turpin in this story. What would you say the stakes are, and why? When do those stakes begin to present themselves to you? How would you answer the question of what Mrs. Turpin *wants*, what she *fears*, and what stands in the way of her having her desire fulfilled, or of her avoiding that which she fears?

6. One of the ways O'Connor activates the reader's sense of recognition in "Revelation" is through a particular extended metaphor. What is that metaphor, and where does it appear? How does O'Connor deepen our understanding of what's at stake in the story each time that metaphor is revisited?

2

BEGINNINGS (PART II)

The great majority of men are bundles of beginnings.

—Ralph Waldo Emerson
Journals, 1828

Often as you write stories, you'll find that because so much depends on your making a good beginning, the beginning is the most difficult part of the story to shape properly, and the part of the story you find yourself revisiting and revising most frequently as the story unfolds.

Evoking the World of Your Story

For examples of why good beginnings are so crucial, let's look at the openings of two of the stories included in this book, Jorge Luis Borges's "The Aleph" (p. 248) and Wallace Stegner's "The Traveler" (p. 258).

Let's look first at the opening paragraph of "The Aleph":

On the incandescent February morning Beatriz Viterbo died, after a death agony so imperious it did not for a moment descend into sentimentalism or fear, I noticed that the iron billboards in the Plaza Constitución bore new advertisements for some brand or other of Virginia tobacco; I was saddened by this fact, for it made me realize that the incessant and vast universe was already moving away from her and that this change was the first in an infinite series. The universe would change but I would not, I thought with melancholy vanity; I knew that sometimes my vain devotion had exasperated her; now that she was dead, I could consecrate myself to her memory, without hope but also without humiliation. I thought of how the thirtieth of April was her birthday; to visit her house in Calle Garay on that day and pay my respects to her father and Carlos Argentino Daneri, her first cousin, would be an act of courtesy, irreproachable and perhaps even unavoidable. I would wait, once again, in the twilight of the overladen entrance hall; I would study, one more time, the particulars of her numerous portraits: Beatriz Viterbo in profile, in color; Beatriz wearing a mask, during the

Carnival of 1921; Beatriz at her First Communion; Beatriz on the day of her wedding to Roberto Alessandri; Beatriz a little while after the divorce, at a dinner in the Club Hípico; Beatriz with Delia San Marco Porcel and Carlos Argentino; Beatriz with the Pekingese which had been a present from Villegas Haedo; Beatriz from the front and in a three-quarter view, smiling, her hand under her chin. . . . I would not be obliged, as on other occasions, to justify my presence with moderate-priced offerings of books, with books whose pages, finally, I learned to cut beforehand, so as to avoid finding, months later, that they were still uncut.

Notice how in the space of the story's long opening sentence, Borges manages to set us down in a very particular world. Through the words he chooses and their rhythms, the attachment of sadness to a change of cigarette advertisements on billboards facing a public square, the recitation of names and gifts, and the description of his dead lover's many portraits, we begin to know what it feels like to be him (or, rather, what it feels like to be the persona he takes on for the telling of this story—that of a self-impressed Argentine aesthete, pining overdramatically in the long shadow of his lover's harrowing death). With subtle choices—the decision, for instance, to have the narrator-Borges refer to the world now slipping away from Beatriz Viterbo as "incessant and vast"—the author tells us important things about this narrator, and about the world he looks at. Word choices like these are vital, and whole stories can turn on the writer's choice of the apt words to convey the scene, the character, and the action.

Now read the first three paragraphs of "The Traveler":

He was rolling in the first early dark down a snowy road, his headlights pinched between dark walls of trees, when the engine coughed, recovered, coughed again, and died. Down a slight hill he coasted in compression, working the choke, but at the bottom he had to pull over against the three-foot wall of plowed snow. Snow creaked under the tires as the car eased to a stop. The heater fan unwound with a final tinny sigh.

Here in its middle age this hitherto dependable mechanism had betrayed him, but he refused to admit immediately that he was betrayed. Some speck of dirt or bubble of water in the gas line, some momentary short circuit, some splash of snow on distributor points or plug connections—something that would cure itself before long. But turning off the lights and pressing on the starter brought no result; he held the choke out for several seconds, and got only the hopeful stink of gasoline; he waited and let the flooded carburetor rest and tried again, and nothing. Eventually he opened the door and stepped out onto the packed snow of the road.

It was so cold that his first breath turned to iron in his throat, the hairs in his nostrils webbed into instant ice, his eyes stung and watered. In the faint starlight and the bluish luminescence of the snow everything beyond a few yards away swam deceptive and without depth, glimmering with things half seen or imagined. Beside the dead car he stood with his head bent, listening, and there was not a sound. Everything on the planet might have died in the cold.

Notice how tangibly Wallace Stegner evokes the snow-cloaked countryside and the lonely road in which he sets the beginning of his story. Within a few sentences, we are given an entire landscape, and within three paragraphs we have a clear sense of the unnamed traveler's sensibility and the loneliness of his situation. The reader's mind is the writer's partner, and because Wallace Stegner is able, quickly and economically, to provide luminous details that present our imaginations with sufficient material, we, the readers, paint the rest of the picture, and are happy to do it. The story's first paragraph sets a tone for the rest of the story, and after we've read it, we can begin to speculate usefully about what might unfold in the world the author has conjured.

Notice how the story beginnings above answer the questions posed in the previous chapter, or how they subtly offer the promise that the story will provide answers to these questions further on. This is work that is done without the reader even knowing it; the story's magic happening right before her eyes, in the way a good magician unfolds a trick, making it visible and keeping it hidden, both at once.

Beginning in the Middle

As a reader, you'll often notice that events are already in motion as you arrive in the world of a story. It is as though you've walked into a conversation that has been going on for some time, arrived at a dinner party already in full swing, or sat down at a table just after a couple has had an argument. Writers refer to this as beginning in medias res—"in the middle of things." Movement is already occurring in the narrative that will carry the reader forward into what happens next.

You may be worrying that, in beginning your own story, you won't be able to manage the subtle interplay of sensory information, thought, and conception the way that Borges and Stegner do in "The Aleph" and "The Traveler." Don't be too concerned, though. Many fiction writers are a good distance into their stories' early drafts before they begin to see what the story they're telling might be about. This being so, you should consider this beginning to be provisional, and you should allow yourself to revisit it many times in light of what your subsequent exploration tells you about the story you're writing. You may even decide to discard your beginning in favor of another. Ultimately, the most important function of a beginning is to sufficiently inform the reader about the characters and conditions in play as the story opens, and to compel a feeling of tension in the reader, so she moves forward into the narrative, asking, And *then* what happened?

> "*I* write for a couple of hours every day, even if I only get a couple of sentences. I put in that time. You do that every day, and inspiration will come along. I don't allow myself not to keep trying. It's not fun, but if you wait until you want to write, you'll never do it."
> —DAVE BARRY

ॐ ॐ ॐ

Progressive Writing Exercise #2:
Writing Your Opening Scene

For this assignment, you'll be writing a *scene* that will serve as the opening for your story. A scene is a portion of the story in which things are *dramatized*—that is, in which settings, events, physical movements, conversations or other interactions between characters are used to portray action that explores the central themes so vividly that this exploration seems to the reader to be happening before her eyes. There are two parts to this assignment, and you should give yourself at least two days to do it.

DAY ONE

Carve an hour or two out of your schedule and settle in with your pad and your pen, your typewriter, your computer—whatever it is you compose on. Take out the cloud diagram you completed for the last exercise. You'll be using it now to try to get your story off the ground by writing a beginning scene. The scene you're going to write should *involve an element from each level* of the cloud diagram—your **central character**, a particular **emotional state** which dominates the scene, a **situation** in which your primary character interacts with a **secondary character**. As you may have surmised from reading the commentary on the story clouds created by Jeremy and Sarah, it may be possible for you to develop ideas for several scenes—maybe your entire story—from a meditation upon connections that might exist among elements present in the three clouds. If it seems possible, you could arrange the situations listed in the second cloud in the rough order they would assume in your narrative (leaving yourself the option to drop situations, add new ones or come up with a different order if it should seem necessary at some point). It may also help you to consider the following:

One of the first things most journalists learn is that a good news story delivers essential information up front. The lead—the first sentence or the first paragraph, generally—answers the questions: *Who? What? When? Where? Why?* and *How?* As a way of getting you started on your short story, let's use these questions to tease some narrative order out of the cloud of possibilities you've conjured. Write out your responses and save them.

WHO . . .   are your characters? Who is your *main* character, and what identifies him/her as such for you? What is it that makes him/her appeal to you as a main character?

WHAT . . .   are the circumstances bringing your characters together as your story begins?

WHEN . . .   is your story beginning? Time of day? Time of year? Is the story set in a specific historical time? How is this time crucial to your character(s) and (his/her/their) situation(s)?

WHERE . . . is your story opening? In a kitchen? In a cave? In the Black Forest? What is it like in this setting? How does this setting and situation present itself to your character's or characters' senses? How might this setting function as both *place* and *metaphor* (i.e., what does this place *mean* to your character/characters)?

WHY . . . are your characters in this situation? This is tricky; you may not *want* your reader to know the whys of the situation too soon. In-deed, as you begin writing, *you* may not yet have a firm grasp on the story's "why." But you should be able—and after reading your opening, your *reader* should be able—to begin to speculate usefully about it.

HOW . . . will your story proceed? The beginning should propel your reader deeper into the story. It should convey a sense that things will get more complicated, that the action will rise, and it should offer a sense of the arc along which your reader will move as she reads fur-ther. This doesn't mean that after you've written the beginning, you ought to know everything that's going to happen in the story; rather, you ought to have a notion of what happens *next*. A good beginning leaves the reader thinking: *Something interesting is going on here, and I'm willing to invest in finding out what that is, in finding out how things come out.*

As you answer these six beginning questions, do it in as much detail as you can. Imagine a schematic of the beginning's events, the connections it might set up among the elements of your cloud diagram. You might begin to write your opening scene by making an appeal to your reader's senses: What are your characters wearing? Are they inside or outside? If outside, is there wind? Sunshine? Rain wet on their skin? If inside, is there a smell—from cooking, for instance, or from a fire or flowers? Who is the secondary character you've imagined as being present? What is her face like—shape, shade, color of eyes? Is her face lined or smooth? What emotions does it convey? How do your characters' voices sound? Are the voices sorrowful, quivering with suppressed excitement, shaky with rage? Where and how do your characters stand, or do they stand at all?

Keep pushing, and as you work, try not to edit. Set these details down as they come—in pieces, in tatters. Use incomplete sentences, single phrases, colors, sounds. Get them down on the page and don't tell yourself: *This isn't a story* . . . It doesn't have to be—not yet. You are only explor-ing, poking around in a dark cave; you don't know what you'll find, but you must catalog everything you come across.

> "*Be regular and orderly in your life, so that you may be violent and original in your work.*"
>
> —GUSTAVE FLAUBERT

Stop there, and promise yourself you'll come back the next day to what you've just produced. It's often best to allow newly produced writing to cool off for a bit be-fore you try to be objective about it, so you should do anything you can to push the story from your mind. This would be a good practice for you to establish now: new writing, a bit of rest that allows you to gain perspective on what you've written, then revision, then new writing again. The writing of a story can be usefully conceived as a climbing spiral that involves each of these steps, each mounting on the other. It might help your process if you were to establish a regular writing time at which you take up your writing; do this now, and resolve to look again at what you've written tomorrow at that hour.

DAY TWO

Take a look at what you wrote yesterday, resisting the urge to judge whether it's "literature." It isn't; not yet. Just read. You have pieces of character and situation before you—like memories your body has held, gathered by your senses. Now you can bring your brain on board to order these scattered pieces, orchestrate them like notes, begin making them into the music of the story you want to tell.

Work now to bring the opening scene you've imagined—a primary and secondary character, a particular emotional state and the situation in which they come together—up out of the murk in which it has rested. Set your reader down in the place where you yourself began—ignorant, curious, puzzled, interested. Try to keep your reader in mind as you work, and remember the basic questions he's asking as he reads: Who's telling this story? Who does this story belong to? Who am I with? Why does the story begin at this moment in the character's/characters' life/lives, and no other? Where am I as the story opens? Why am I here? What do I see? When—what time, what year, in what part of life—is this story unfolding? Why now and at no other time? Why does the story present this sequence of moments in the character's/characters' life/lives, and no other? What will this sequence of moments add up to? What's at stake for my character or characters? What do they want? What stands between (him/her/them) and (his/her/their) having what (s/he/they) want(s)? What does/do (s/he/they) fear? As you work to answer these questions with an opening scene, you might keep in mind another of the journalist's lead-writing guidelines: put the important facts first. The order of the elements in the "who, what, when, why and how" formula isn't arbitrary: this is the order of importance usually assigned to the facts which make up a story. The reader is concerned first with who the story concerns, followed by what happens, the time frame of the action, the location and (ultimately) the reason for things happening as they did.

What you'll learn: The "Who? What? When? Where? Why? And How?" formula is a simple tool journalists use to focus their minds on the facts their stories ought to convey up front. As you work to answer these questions in their modified form for your short story's beginning,

> "*Writing is harder than anything else; at least starting to write is. It's much easier to wash dishes. When I'm writing I set myself a daily quota of pages, but nine times out of ten I'm doing those pages at four o'clock in the afternoon because I've done everything else first. . . . But once I get flowing with it, I wonder what took me so long.*"
>
> —KRISTEN HUNTER

you're capturing the state in which your narrative might begin, giving us the story's exact and particular characters, setting and situation, and so you are establishing your story's *frame*. Like the foundation, the load-bearing walls, and the roof of a house, this frame must be sufficient to support, contain and protect the world you hope to create within it.

STUDENT EXAMPLES

Jeremy's Response

David was on his way. After twenty-one years of simple rural Midwestern existence, David was making the journey to start a new life, a new job, to find a new home, and live a dream in the city that never sleeps: New York.

He'd long ago lost count of how many hours he'd been riding the Greyhound bus. The passing cars on the interstate, the bright green blankets of freshly cut summer grass, and the brilliant warmth of the mid-July afternoon sun through the window on his face were enough to make him forget all about the passage of time. David knew he had left the bus station in Topeka the day before and that he would be in New York by nightfall. The journey itself, be it a minute, hour, week, whatever, was one unit of time. It was the beginning—the first lap of a long and hard-fought race, or the pistol shot that would start a sprint that was over before it began. To David, the journey would be everything.

And so how long had it been since he had left his parents in the tiny Topeka bus station, amid a flurry of hugs and goodbyes? The memory had grown vague already in David's mind, but he thought back pleasantly on those moments. He came from a loving family. Not necessarily close or dependant, but very loving all the same. When David had decided to leave the family farm and move to the city, his parents had been more than supportive, emotionally. David knew everything else—money, clothes, food, a place to live—would be his responsibility. The Midwestern farm mentality was "We'll be here for you, but you have to do it on your own." In fact, David felt that somehow his parents had been expecting this moment. They assured him of their love and emotional support and reminded him that he could call home any time, although David knew that wouldn't be very necessary; he was out on his own now both in his eyes and his parents'. They had bought his bus ticket for him and promptly left on a cruise vacation in the Bahamas.

David had packed light for his new trip. Everything he owned was in the small duffel stuffed under his bus seat. There were a couple of changes of clothes, a book or two, a toothbrush, a few hundred dollars, and a picture of his family. Everything else would fall into place eventually, he thought. He had a job lined up with a small publishing company. He had been going to classes at a community college in Topeka when he saw the sign on a bulletin board in one of the academic buildings. When he had called, the man on the other end of the line had seemed very pleased with David's experience and his college class work. He had immediately offered David the job. It wouldn't be much, the man had told him: just mundane office tasks for a while. But David couldn't have been more thrilled. He made a few more calls and found a cheap, one-bedroom apartment that he thought he could afford, near what would soon be his office. He had mailed the security deposit months before.

David had every reason to be optimistic as he gazed out the window of the bus. He watched the cars going the other direction, away from the city, and asked himself why anyone would want to leave such a lively, busy, and exciting place. David was an innocent, uninitiated, flying down the highway toward a new life.

Commentary As with the situations in Jeremy's second cloud, the beginning for his story presents us with some fairly familiar situations. Not surprisingly, then, this beginning suggests a fairly familiar story: a farm boy leaving home for the bright lights of the city. Jeremy places David on the bus to New York City, suspended between home and his destination. Starting us out with David's bus trip may be a good choice: it gives Jeremy a long stretch in which David might muse about his hopes for his destination and his memories of the place he's leaving behind.

Concerns As was also mentioned in the previous commentary, the fact that the story line laid out in this beginning is a familiar one isn't necessarily a problem: good stories can be and are still written that freshly visit familiar themes: love, loss, growing up, growing old, the struggle of identity, to name just a few. Jeremy might have problems, though, unless he's able to find a way to make his story feel new. The best way for Jeremy to proceed is by offering fresh, particularly observed detail and action that will convince the reader this is not the story she's all too familiar with. Phrases like "twenty-one years of simple rural Midwestern existence" are problematic, though, because they don't really tell us much about David. A few points of fact are a bit worrisome, too: David seems to have gotten his job very easily; was it too easy? Also, anyone who's ever looked for an apartment in New York City knows finding a place can take weeks, and that "a cheap, one-bedroom apartment" is a relative term. "Cheap" to someone who actually lives in New York might seem ruinously expensive to someone coming from the small town Midwest.

⟨ᴈ⟩ *Sarah's Response*

Mint's mother drove them downtown to the show, Lindsay in her lime green tank top and cut-offs, Mint in a yellow flowered halter dress cut too low, so she had to hold her shoulders back and her hands kept flying to her throat, wrists pressing the fabric up against her chest. Mint's mother bravely ignored the spike-jacketed punks and smoky-eyed daytime receptionists frowning against the fenders of their rusty Chryslers as she turned into the parking lot. She didn't say anything about drugs when the girls climbed out of the car in front of the Red Room steps. She could feel their shame like a release of heat as they slammed the doors shut and slipped away into the anonymous throng pushing toward the loaded darkness of the doorways. Mint's mother tried to listen to NPR on the way home, but she couldn't get her mind off that yellow halter dress, just hoping and hoping that it would stay up, that Mint had kept the receipt, that the daringness of it would somehow make her happy.

Lindsay forged a path through the crowd inside the Red Room, Mint close behind with one hand on her shoulder so she couldn't be lost. The first band was already playing, something loud and thrashy that made Mint think of animals and dirt. It was stirring up the boys, though. Mint wouldn't meet their eyes as she climbed through the jungle of bodies, slid across fleshy backs prickling with the first dew of concert sweat. She could feel the anticipation in taut shoulders, the trembling of the ones who would be dancing crazy before the night was over. Lindsay stopped in a little knot of guys in pop-punk band shirts and Abercrombie hats—older guys, maybe eighteen or nineteen—who pretended not to notice them. Mint was startled by the sudden permanence of this. She kept her right arm across her chest. Lindsay leaned back to scream in her ear that it looked like she was saying the pledge of allegiance, but Mint couldn't hear over the music.

The second band came on, but Mint didn't know them either. Lindsay was really into it, entranced and rocking back and forth. The Abercrombie boys kept looking at her. She had become, while Mint blinked, one of those untouchable concert demigods, enlightened, in control, the symphony conductor of the collective breathing of the crowd. Mint was jealous, had always been jealous, of people with passion.

And then, through the color and thrash, over the heads of petite trendy girls and through the momentary spaces between dancing kids, Mint recognized a face. It was there for one second, suspended, ghostly, for one long freeze-frame second. It was Claire Danes. Claire Danes, film star, actress, heroine of the 1990s *teen!* Star of "My So-Called Life," Juliet in Baz Luhrman's *Romeo and Juliet,* icon of a generation! Mint spun around, frantically searching for someone else who had seen what she had seen. No one. Instinctively, she dropped her arm and dove into the crowd, kicked, burrowed awkwardly toward the space where Claire Danes was. The crowd didn't understand her urgency, and they flipped her off, muttered angrily. Mint couldn't explain it, but she knew she had to find Claire Danes. Claire Danes would know things, be able to tell her things. She was right over there, *so close,* just in the crowd, standing there, knowing.

But she couldn't find her. Mint was the last person to leave the Red Room that night, her dress drenched in other people's sweat, sort of beaten down and confused, an ache in her right arm. She lay awake in her house in the suburbs and felt an emptiness, or an *almost,* or perhaps a new sense of quest.

Commentary The thing that is most immediately appealing about Sarah's opening scene is the freshness of its observation. There are numerous instances of vivid and original description ("The first band was already playing something loud and thrashy that made Mint think of animals and dirt"; ". . . the first dew of concert sweat . . ."; ". . . the trembling of the ones who would be dancing crazy before the night was over") that, in their aggregate, deliver the sense of a very particular world. Sarah sets the reader down in medias res, in a place of excitement and tension: the moments before a concert begins. It eventually develops that Mint is looking for something, hoping for something, and the undefined *something* expresses itself like a lightning bolt when Mint thinks she sees Claire Danes's face amid the crowd.

"Writing is like meditation or going into an ESP trance, or prayer. Like dreaming. You are tapping into your unconscious. To be fully conscious and alert, with life banging and popping and cuckooing all around, you are not going to find your way to your subconscious, which is a place of complete submission. Complete submission."

—CAROLYN CHUTE, "HOW CAN YOU CREATE FICTION WHEN REALITY COMES TO CALL?"

Concerns What is it that Mint's looking for or hoping for that finds its focus in her sighting of the actress? Given what's currently on the page, it's impossible to tell. This is a problem because it seems as though Mint knows what Claire Danes represents to her, but the reader is not let in on this knowledge. Because the reader isn't being taken into the story's confidence at this point, it's difficult for her to see into or experience the sense of urgency it seems Mint feels.

This is not to say that what's needed is an explicit declaration of the "problem" this story is going to set out to "solve." Such a story would be didactic, and anyway, would work against the appealing sense of mystery in Mint's emotional response. Readers find it pleasant to speculate, to wonder about the causes of things. They like trying to see into characters' hearts. However, if a character seems too opaque—as Mint currently does—the reader may become frustrated. It would be good if the beginning provided a bit more information about what Mint wants and/or fears, so that leaning figuratively closer to the story, trying to understand what the story is attempting to convey, will seem rewarding.

One technical problem that seems worth pointing out: Sarah's opening paragraph is set in Mint's mother's point of view. This leads the reader to begin the story assuming that it's Mint's mother's story. This red herring creates a temporary pause in the reader, during which the story's spell is broken because the technical hitch interrupts its flow. If it's not Mint's mother's story, Sarah probably shouldn't begin with her. If it's Mint's story, it seems more expedient to put us right in Mint's head.

QUESTIONS FOR REVISION

1. After completing your response to this assignment, did you see a need to add to or delete from your cloud of possible emotional states? Do any of the emotional states in your diagram's first cloud need to be altered, or rendered in additional detail?

2. Now look at your cloud of situations: Has writing this scene made you consider additions, or changes to or deletions from it?

3. Do any of these situations seem too familiar? Can they be imagined in fresher or more compelling ways?

4. Have you seen a need to add to or delete from your character cloud?

5. Are there details about or characteristics of any of your characters it now seems necessary to add or alter?

6. Each story offers a universe of possible choices as we begin it—a universe that begins to shrink as the story evolves. The possible connections among the emotional, situational, and characterological levels of your cloud are one way of thinking about the various directions your story could go. Has writing your beginning scene moved you to consider new connections among the various levels of your story cloud, or shown you connections you now won't need to consider?

Alternative Writing Exercises

Note: if you decide to do one of these alternative exercises rather than the linked assignment above, remember to give yourself the same two-day time frame for your work. Begin with messy, exploratory writing, then come back on the second day to order, cut and polish.

1. **How bad (or good) was it?** Reach back into your memory for **the best or worst thing that ever happened to you.** Where and how—under what circumstances— did this event begin to unfold? Making use of the full range of sensory information, render the setting and situation in which this wonderful/terrible event took place. *What you'll learn:* Memory holds all the details necessary to a narrative's construction. With sufficient practice, you can mine your memory for everything you need to create stories. Vivid experiences—such as the best and worst things that have happened to you—generally have strong sense memories attached to them, and may be a good place to experiment with how you can assemble the elements which make up a story's beginning.

2. **Make up an adult fairy tale.** For this exercise, you're going to avail yourself of an old beginning-of-the-story gambit. Your assignment is to complete the phrase: "Once upon a time . . ." three times, and in three different ways. First, you'll write the opening of a story about a stranger coming to a small town or neighborhood; second, you'll open the story of someone who must leave home on a journey; third, you'll begin a narrative that unfolds in the aftermath of a death. *What you'll learn:* There are very few entirely unique human experiences, and one of the things we enjoy in reading stories is the way they bring our common human experience freshly to life. Stories often emerge out of our fresh contemplation of old story lines, and the three story lines suggested above are among the oldest.

3. **To sleep, perchance to dream . . .** Another old dodge: keep a notepad beside your bed for a while, and when you wake—in the morning, in the middle of the night, whenever—jot down as much as you can remember of the dreams you've had. Don't try to make them cohere—write them down in the hectic, bewildering and disjointed form in which they arrive. After you've done this a few times, see if you can't mine one of the dreams for a story beginning. In framing the scene you write, you should concentrate not so much on presenting the dream's *events* as you should on coming up with a coherent narrative frame for presenting the emotional and characterologic implications of those events. *What you'll learn:* In terms of art, the unconscious mind has shown itself time and again to be smarter than the conscious mind, and it can open important doors for you as a writer if you allow this assumption to guide your practice. Your contact with your unconscious is seldom as sharp as when you're dreaming, and you can take advantage of this contact by mining your dreams for story ideas. Of course, dreams very seldom provide coherent narratives; instead, you should pay attention to the suggestions they contain—resonances, intriguing juxtapositions of object and event, seeming discontinuities that

make a weird kind of emotional sense. Wherever dreams particularly bother or frighten you, there is often a narrative lurking, waiting to be released.

4. **Be a busy-body.** Go to your favorite bar, restaurant or coffee house and sit somewhere where you can deliberately eavesdrop on a conversation without being detected. Take down a transcript of the conversation. Odds are, you won't have enough details to completely understand what these people are talking about—so much the better, as this will give your imagination some room in which to work. After you've completed your transcript, as a way of beginning a narrative, try to make up the details that are missing from this conversation. *What you'll learn:* A variation on the read-a-newspaper exercise from the last chapter, this exercise sends you directly to life for your material. You're surrounded by story ideas—all day, every day. All you have to do is open your ears, cultivate your curiosity, take dictation.

Reading Exercise:
Beginnings in Judith Claire Mitchell's
"A Man of Few Words"

Archimedes said that, given a well-placed lever and a firm place to stand, he could move the world. Good story beginnings function in much the same way, providing the firm footing and fulcrum the writer needs—not to lift the world, but to lift the reader, moving her out of skepticism and into full involvement with the narrative. With its opening challenge to the reader's willing suspense of disbelief—a challenge she makes it worth the reader's while to meet—Judith Claire Mitchell's "A Man of Few Words" gives us a powerful illustration of how and why this works.

QUESTIONS

1. What is the "middle" into which Mitchell's story drops us?

2. What does the story's beginning lead you to think the story will be about? Do you end with the same notion of its intentions as the notion you began with? If not, how or why does this notion change?

3. We learn immediately that Ike will be permitted to relive one pleasure from his life, and the first pleasure that's suggested to us is Yonah Schlissel's knishes. What purpose, then, is served when Mitchell follows this with a catalog of *other* pleasures he might choose?

4. How much of the ending of Ike's story is contained in its beginning?

5. After you've finished reading the story, go back and read forward again until you can identify a place where you feel the story's ending is foreshadowed. Where is that place, and what does it convey to you of that ending?

6. Does the ending seem like a plausible answer to the questions the beginning seemed to pose?

3

POINT OF VIEW

*I present myself to you in a form suitable to the
relationship I wish to achieve with you.*

—Luigi Pirandello
The Pleasure of Honesty

When you created your cloud diagram, you made a decision about who you were
going to put at the story's center—the person you could offer as the answer when
your reader asked: *Who does this story belong to?* It may be useful now for you to come
up with an answer for the second question in the list proposed in the first chapter—
that is, *Who's telling this story, and why?*

The answer to this question is considered **point of view**. As the term suggests,
point of view is the perch the writer provides for the reader to see into the heart of
the story. Just as different vistas would be provided by observation platforms placed at
various spots along a mountain trail, so different points of view will provide readers
with varied experiences of the narrative.

One Story, Three Beginnings

By way of illustrating what point of view is and how it affects a story, let's extend the
mountain-climbing metaphor by positing a short story about a rock climber making a
solo ascent of a very difficult rock face. We'll give this story three possible beginnings: one with the story told by the climber herself; a second with the story told by
her father, who's there to support her effort; and a third told by a journalist who likes
the father/daughter angle and is watching the climb from the top through powerful
binoculars, taking notes toward a story he will file after the climb.

Let's start with the opening of the story told from the climber's point of view:

> The first pitch is the easy part. A crack runs straight up the face for fifty feet, and
> I barely have to think about what I'm doing as I pull myself toward the little
> ledge I saw in the pictures I took with the long lens. I reach into the crack; wedge
> my fist in; test the hold; contract my biceps, my lats, my abs; find a toe-hold;

reach with my other hand; reach again. The ground falls away, further and further. My body works automatically, and my mind is free to roam.

That's a problem. My thoughts turn to Dad on the ground. I can feel his attention like a weight tied down there behind me, his anxiety like a stone swinging on a rope, throwing me off balance. I should never have agreed to let him watch.

I let myself hang for a moment, resting. With my free hand I dip into the rosin bag. Get your head right, I tell myself. I concentrate on the feel of the stone where it rasps against the knuckles of my wedged hand, the blood leaving the arm: good. Then I force my mind up, up.

Now the opening of the story told from the father's perspective:

You ascend ten feet, twenty, thirty, and I can't see how you're able to cling to the face. *Rock climbing:* it sounds like something you would have done when you were six, scrambling over a pile of boulders in the park, getting your knees skinned. Not this. You reach high, put your hand into the crack and hang there from it, and it is so beautiful and awful I can barely watch. A hawk drifts across the face of the rock; soon it will be flying below you. I raise the binoculars, and you jump into focus. I can see sweat shining on your shoulders; a wisp of hair that has escaped from your hair tie. It bobs like a spring, and I automatically reach out to tuck it in again, but my hand touches air. I lower the binoculars, then raise them again. The muscles in your back flex, like something in an illustration from *Gray's Anatomy*. When did you become so strong, and how did I miss seeing it? I want to shout advice, but what do I know about what you're doing? You hang from one hand, and half turn your head. You're not thinking, afraid, about the ground; I know you're thinking about being watched.

Finally, here is the story's opening, told from the journalist's perspective:

The climber's father is near the two tents at the face's base. He is heavy, wide, and solid, standing in the ragged shade of a Ponderosa pine, chewing on his beard. Near him are the scattered gear: the breakfast dishes, the basin of water, the packs, the ropes, the pitons, the bundles of carabiners the climber decided at the last minute not to use, making this a free ascent, nothing holding her to the wall but her muscle, her understanding of the stone. Beside him is a camp chair that has fallen, forgotten, on its side. He lifts the binoculars with metronomic regularity to his eyes, and when he lets them hang from the strap around his neck again, the lines around his eyes seem to deepen, his mouth folding into a sharp line. Above him, she is only looking up, creeping along the vertical, and as she climbs, whatever weight she carries seems to lighten, the emptying serenity of what she is doing growing greater the further she gets from the ground. She hangs a minute, easy, her right hand wedged into a crack, and reaches back with her left hand to her waist, whitening the hand in a bag filled with rosin. Below, he looks as if he wants to call something out to her; if he did, she looks as if she would pretend she hadn't heard.

Types of Point of View

The three beginnings above demonstrate the fact that a story concerning the same sequence of events can have a very different character, depending on the point of view used to frame it.

The story set up by the first beginning, which put us directly in the head of the climber, would be filled with the images of the climb, the effort it involves, the desire, perhaps, to escape the bonds and boundaries of the ground below. Because the story would be strongly rooted in the immediate experience of the narrator/protagonist as she climbed, the pronoun *I* would be the one most often used.

If the story were told from the worried father's perspective, because he is watching and not doing anything other than steering his thoughts toward his daughter as if in conversation with her, the story's focus would be directed away from the self of the narrator, concentrating more on the climber as she ascends the face. In a story framed this way, *you* would be dominant pronoun, rather than *I.*

The story told from the journalist's point of view would be more comprehensive and objective than the other two stories, taking on the portrayal of both the father's and daughter's experience of the climb. In the story set up by this beginning, the self of the narrator has no part in the story, except as the means to deliver information to the reader. Using this point of view, it might be possible to tell a story that had *both* the father and daughter as main characters, with the narrator inferring the experience of each, what they think and feel as the climb progresses. The pronouns used most often would be *he, she,* and *they.*

> *"Nobody outside of a baby carriage or a judge's chamber believes in an unprejudiced point of view."*   —LILLIAN HELLMAN

One story, three possible point of view approaches to telling it. There are many, many other point of view approaches we might have taken to frame the story. To gain a clearer picture of what considerations might go into choosing the point of view for the story you're working on, let's look more closely at the strengths and limitations of the main types.

FIRST-PERSON NARRATION

The story told in the climber's voice provides an example of *first-person narration.* A story is said to be in first person when a character in the story narrates it, as with the story narrated by the climber. *Moby Dick* provides another example of first-person narration. Melville telegraphs the book's status as a first-person story with one of the most famous opening sentences in literature: "Call me Ishmael." In this way, the reader is immediately placed in the head of an extremely articulate sometime-teacher who signs on for sea journeys periodically to clear his melancholia. Ishmael's voyage ends up giving him much more than he bargained for, and because we learn about the journey of the whaling vessel Pequod through Ishmael's own words, we are set on very, very close terms with him. His sensibility—his feelings, thoughts, and habits of mind—colors everything we come to know of the tragedy as the novel unfolds.

There can be tremendous intimacy in the relationship a first-person frame enables the reader to establish with the story. Most often, a first-person narrator brings the reader close to his view of the story's action, telling the reader, in effect, Here is a thing that happened to me or Here is a thing I observed. The inevitable result is a narrow focus on the experience of a single consciousness, filtered through its prejudices, fears, desires, and concerns.

While this intimacy can make for a vivid story, the first-person mode also has limits. The narrow focus of one person's experience can also limit the amount of information the story using it can present.

Why Is Your Narrator Telling the Story?   The question asked at the beginning of this chapter wasn't just Who's telling this story?; it was Who's telling this story, *and why?* If you're using the first-person narrative in your story, it can be helpful to think through the narrator's stake in telling it. Beginning writers sometimes write first-person stories whose narrators are only observers—recounting the action without being affected by it. This may seem all right, but consider this: when you tell a story to someone about an experience you have had, it's usually because the experiences you recount—even if you weren't at the center of events—affected *you* in some way or taught you something about *yourself.* Nick Caraway in *The Great Gatsby* is a wonderful onlooker and narrator. One of the reasons *The Great Gatsby* is such a poignant story is that we come to understand how much Nick Caraway's witnessing of this story has affected him. The full tragedy of Jay Gatsby's life becomes clear because it is a *personal* tragedy to Nick, as well as a tragedy he witnessed.

Reliable and Unreliable Narrators   In stories whose narrator is a character in the story, consider whether your narrator is *reliable* or *unreliable.* An unreliable narrator can't be entirely trusted to tell the whole truth. She may be hiding something, may be lying, self-deluded, ignorant of important details, or limited in some other way. Unreliable narrators, however, can be used to good effect. Benjy, the mentally handicapped character in William Faulkner's *The Sound and the Fury* is one example of an interesting unreliable narrator, and Jorge Borges's story "The Aleph" depends on his narrator's unreliability to achieve its effect; but, such characters have to be handled carefully. The reader has to be able to see around the unreliable narrator, to pick up vital details that will help her to know more than the narrator knows or is telling, so she is able to figure out what's important.

> *"A definite purpose, like blinders on a horse, inevitably narrows its possessor's point of view."*
>
> —ROBERT FROST

In reading "The Aleph," for instance, much depends upon the reader's understanding of the relationship between two poets, the fictional Borges who narrates and Carlos Argentino Daneri, the cousin of a dead woman whom Borges tells himself was the love of his life. Borges hates Daneri, a fact made clear to the reader by this passage, in which he describes a conversation he has had with Daneri:

His ideas seemed so inept to me, their exposition so pompous and so vast, that I immediately related them to literature: I asked him why he did not write them down. Foreseeably he replied that he had already done so: these concepts, and others no less novel, figured in the Augural Canto, or more simply, the Prologue Canto, of a poem on which he had been working for many years, without publicity, without any deafening to-do, putting his entire reliance on those two props known as work and solitude. First, he opened the floodgates of the imagination; then he made use of a sharp file. The poem was titled *The Earth*; it consisted of a description of the planet, wherein, naturally, there was no lack of picturesque digression and elegant apostrophe.

It's clear this narrator-Borges doesn't much like Daneri or his poetry; more subtly, this passage also helps lead the reader to wonder whether Borges's disgust with Daneri is entirely literary, and whether Borges can be trusted to speak reliably about Daneri. As becomes clear as the story unfolds, the reader is justified in holding back from trusting Borges-the-narrator's view of things. His motivations are fueled as much by professional and romantic jealousy as they are by aesthetic judgement. He is *unreliable*.

The Limits of the First-Person Narrator's Charm   If you've ever had a conversation with a con man—all style and very little substance—you know another pitfall of first-person narration. If your narrator has a beguiling voice, it can be tempting to allow the narrator to talk on and on, rather than pushing him to do the hard work of presenting compelling action or believable characters to the reader. Don't let your narrator exercise his wit to the extent that he forgets to tell a story.

SECOND-PERSON NARRATION

Another narrative strategy—not often used—is *second-person narration*, where, by speaking through the story's narration to "you" (e.g., "You go to the store and buy the morning paper"), the author is either talking or writing (in the case of the *epistolary* story, which is told through letters) to another character to whom the story is addressed, or is asking the reader to imagine himself experiencing events as a character in the story. The father's version of our story above provides an example of second-person narration of the first type, as does Tillie Olsen's story, "I Stand Here Ironing" (p. 312). In the father's story, the "you" being addressed is his daughter, while in Olsen's story, the narrator speaks to a social worker or teacher who's come to talk to her about her troubled eldest daughter. Jay McInerney's first novel, *Bright Lights, Big City*, provides an example of the second type of second-person narration, with the reader invited to imagine himself as the book's club-hopping protagonist.

Because second-person narration can pull the reader into the action and invite him either to stand in the shoes of or become a character, it can create an intimate bond between the reader and the story. Anyone thinking about using the second person in his story should be aware, though, that unless he uses this strategy very skillfully, the reader can start to resent the story's presumption. Who, after all, likes to be told *You* feel this . . . and *You* do that . . . , especially when the "you" of the story makes choices the reader wouldn't make himself, or (more to the point) has feelings or reactions he wouldn't have or can't believe in?

THIRD-PERSON NARRATION

In stories using third-person narration, the narrator is what we will call an *informing intelligence*—the teller of the tale, who (like the journalist watching the woman climb the rock wall) is not a character in the story, but manages the story's unfolding. The story you read as part of the first chapter, Flannery O'Connor's "Revelation" (p. 217), provides a good example of well-managed third-person narration. The reader knows immediately that Mrs. Turpin is the main character; she is an imposingly self-assured figure whose rock-ribbed prejudices—and their transformation—are the subject of the story. O'Connor would have lost quite a bit if she had allowed Mrs. Turpin to narrate the story. O'Connor, as the story's informing intelligence, is able to bring her considerable powers of observation and description to bear on the other characters as she follows Mrs. Turpin closely through the story's scenes, giving the reader a picture of Mrs. Turpin's world that Mrs. Turpin herself—gazing as she must through the hazy film of her bigotry—would not have been able to provide.

There are other approaches to third-person narration. In some stories—James Joyce's "The Dead" from his *Dubliners* collection provides a notable example—rather than attaching the reader to one consciousness within the story (as Flannery O'Connor did in "Revelation"), the author allows his reader access to the consciousnesses of the story's other characters as it suits his purposes. It is as though, with this narrative strategy, the author makes the reader telepathic. Standing to one side and watching as things unfold, he is able to listen to different characters' thoughts as the author needs him to, always following where the author leads and concentrating on whatever is important to the story. This movement from consciousness to consciousness is known as *third-person narration with shifting points of view*.

In another third-person approach, the author may give the reader access, via a godlike informing intelligence, to all consciousnesses in the story, at all times. This is known as *third-person-omniscient narration*. This approach suspends the reader further above the story's events and characters than any other form of narration, and can be tricky to use in a short story. It's important for writers using the third-person-omniscient approach to manage the story's unfolding in a way that clearly establishes who the main characters are.

In another, often-used third-person narrative approach, the author may give us access to the world of the story *only* through the consciousness of the protagonist or other character, a strategy known as *close third person* or *third-person-limited narration*. The reading assignment for this chapter is Tobias Wolff's story "Bullet in the Brain," which provides a good example of close third-person narrative. Yet another third-person narrative stance is the *third-person-objective* approach that puts the reader in the place of a "fly on the wall"—able to observe the details of physical action and conversation, but without access to the characters' inner lives. Such stories leave the reader to draw his own conclusions about what characters think and feel. A

> *"Let observation with extensive view
> Survey mankind, from China to Peru."*
>
> —SAMUEL JOHNSON,
> *VANITY OF HUMAN WISHES,* LINE 1

number of Ernest Hemingway's short stories—most famously "Hills Like White Elephants"—take this approach.

Third-person narration may at times lack the intimacy that first-person narration makes possible, but it can offer the writer greater control than first- or second-person narration. Third-person narration can enable you to present more detail, and make it possible to shift more easily from the point of view of one character to another, an ability that can allow you to render a richer and more varied narrative.

The Dangers of Shifting Points of View You should, however, be careful about shifting your point of view too much. As we've said, one of those unspoken questions your readers bring to your stories is: Who does this story belong to? As readers, we generally expect a story to contain a person on whom we can focus our attention most closely—someone whose realization, change, achievement, downfall (etc., etc.) we identify as the story's heart. If you move your reader around too abruptly or too often from consciousness to consciousness over the length of your story, you run the risk that she will stop reading in frustration (imagine sitting in the middle of a group of people, all of whom are trying simultaneously to tell their version of the same story).

VARIATIONS

There are variations on all of these types of narration. Though first-person stories typically root us in one consciousness, it is possible—as in *Moby Dick*—to create a first-person narrative in which the narrator presumes to be able to move omnisciently from consciousness to consciousness of the other characters in the story. William Faulkner framed his story "A Rose for Emily" as a narrative in first-person plural, with the story's narrative "we" being the collective consciousness of a town. Though first-person stories often feel very intimate, it's also possible to write a first-person story in which the narrator is reserved, cool and reluctant to reveal himself, like the protagonist in Kazuo Ishiguro's "A Family Supper" (p. 284). It's possible to write third-person narratives that provide tremendously intimate contact with a character or characters, as in Joyce's "The Dead."

> *"Nothing's beautiful from every point of view."*
>
> —HORACE

The "Surface" of the Story

It should be clear by now that each point of view dictates a different reader relationship with the events and characters in the story. It may be useful to think about this relationship in terms of the reader's contact with what we will call the story's "surface." What's meant by "surface" here is that conceptual place in which your characters live and breathe, and where the events of the story seem to be happening in real time. Think of the story's surface as you would think about the surface of a planet. The closer your reader is brought to this surface (as in the opening of the story told from the climber's perspective), the more direct his contact will be with the thoughts, feelings, actions, and imperatives of the character or characters, and with the situation in which she is/they are embroiled. With more distance from this surface (as in the journalist's version of the story's opening), the reader will have more perspective on the characters, their movements, and the scenes through which they move. The father's version of the story, with its focus directed away from his own immediate experience and toward his daughter's experience, could be said to fall somewhere between these two polarities.

Katherine Mansfield's "A Married Man's Story" provides an example of how the reader can be brought very close to the story's surface. Here is the opening paragraph:

> It is evening. Supper is over. We have left the small, cold dining-room, we have come back to the sitting room where there is a fire. All is as usual. I am sitting at my writing-table which is placed across a corner so that I am behind it, as it were, and facing the room. The lamp with the green shade is alight; I have before me two large books of reference, both open, a pile of papers. . . . All the paraphernalia, in fact, of an extremely occupied man. My wife, with her little boy on her lap, is in a low chair before the fire. She is about to put him to bed before she clears away the dishes and piles them up in the kitchen for the servant girl tomorrow morning. But the warmth, the quiet, and the sleepy baby, have made her dreamy. One of his red woollen boots is off, one is on. She sits, bent forward, clasping the little bare foot, staring into the glow, and as the fire quickens, falls, flares again, her shadow—an immense Mother and Child—is here and gone again upon the wall.

The story's protagonist is at the center of his universe. We are given a deeply intimate view of the room in which he sits; we know what his physical world looks like and what he thinks and feels, and from this understanding we may begin to infer his emotional state as well.

In narratively proximate stories like Mansfield's, the writer brings the reader very close to the story's surface, most often by locating the narrative in the consciousness of a single character or of a few characters in series. Because Mansfield roots us in the consciousness of her title character, the story's focus is tighter, the scale of its setting and its events is obviously reduced, more intimate.

In contrast, here are the opening two paragraphs of Charles Dickens's A *Tale of Two Cities*:

> It was the best of times, it was the worst of times, it was the age of wisdom, it was the age of foolishness, it was the epoch of belief, it was the epoch of incredulity, it was the season of Light, it was the season of Darkness, it was the spring of hope, it was the winter of despair, we had everything before us, we had nothing before us, we were all going direct to Heaven, we were all going direct the other way— in short, the period was so far like the present period that some of its noisiest authorities insisted on its being received, for good or for evil, in the superlative degree of comparison only.
>
> There were a king with a large jaw and a queen with a plain face, on the throne of England; there were a king with a large jaw and a queen with a fair

face, on the throne of France. In both countries it was clearer than crystal to the lords of the State preserves of loaves and fishes, that things in general were settled for ever.

In Dickens's opening the reader is lifted high above the world the novel contains. There is no declared protagonist, nor even yet a concrete reference to the time period in which the story will be taking place. The reader is set up for a journey not just into one life, but into multiple lives, and a journey that will acquaint him not just with the small and limited settings of one person's experience, but with the experiences of a cast of characters amid the broad and teeming settings provided (as will be revealed further on) by London and Paris at the time of the American and French Revolutions.

Think of the intimacy of a reader's encounter with the story as existing on a continuum. At the near end, where Mansfield's story is located, is what we will call *narrative proximity*, while at the far end, where *A Tale of Two Cities* is located, is *narrative distance*. In stories that are narratively distant, the reader often gains access to the story's action and characters through the agency of the story's informing intelligence. In *A Tale of Two Cities* it is this informing intelligence that takes the reader into the world of the story, eventually leading her to an overview of the confusion and tumult of the year 1775 that no single character—embroiled in that year's events as he would have been— could have given her. In the book's early going, the informing intelligence of the narrator uses this narratively distant perspective to steer the reader into and out of various characters' experiences, thus helping her to understand the full context of the story unfolding before her. There is often a certain coolness to stories told this way—a remove from character and event that serves quite well the telling of a story like Dickens's, in which multiple characters have something necessary to add to the story, and where the ability to move fluidly from setting to setting and consciousness to consciousness is important to the establishment of the reader's understanding of the subtleties of human motive and interaction at work within the book. The informing intelligence of the narrator is strongly present in Dickens's story, responsible for much of its poetry, and almost a character in its own right. This narrative voice comments upon the action, stops to observe the characters in important moments, and in this way brings the very different worlds of late-eighteenth-century London and Paris vividly to life.

> "We do not receive wisdom, we must discover it for ourselves, after a journey through the wilderness which no one else can make for us, which no one can spare us, for our wisdom is the point of view from which we come at last to regard the world."
>
> —MARCEL PROUST

It's important to add that the reader's proximity to, or distance from, the surface of events in the story can change—often multiple times—within a given story. In a passage that contains important action, the writer may set the reader right in amongst events; then, in a passage where a long stretch of time goes by during which relatively little of importance happens, or in another passage where it's important to stop the action to explain something, the reader may be lifted away from the story's surface.

Tobias Wolff's story "Bullet in the Brain" (p. 000) provides a good example of how this can work: the story begins with a rather distanced third-person-limited narration, focused on the protagonist, Anders, as he waits impatiently in line at a bank. He's a rather effete and unlikable character when he's first introduced, and it's not until later in the story, when a robbery begins in the bank, that Wolff takes us close to the surface of his story, to a minute examination of a single instant in time. In this instant, Anders' full depth and complexity as a character is revealed. This sort of movement—changing the distance from, or proximity to, the story's surface as the needs of the story dictate—is one of the ways the writer can introduce a feeling of rhythm or *pacing* into her telling of the story.

There are no hard-and-fast formulas—nor should there be—for what point of view you should use in framing a given type of story. The only real rule is the most obvious one: whatever narrative approach you choose, the first consideration is that it give your reader the best possible view into the heart of the story.

Progressive Writing Exercise #3:
Choosing Your Point of View

You've already written the opening scene for your story; have you taken the best approach to point of view with it? It may take some experimentation to find out. That's what you're be going to be doing in this next exercise.

Go back to your cloud diagram again, and use it to help you to imagine the scene that comes right after your beginning. Now write this scene you're imagining three times—once as a first-person narration, once as a second-person narration (addressed either to another character in your story or to the reader), and once as a third-person narration (limited, omniscient, objective—your choice). You should also take into account what has been said above about the contact you're providing your reader with the surface of your story, and make at least one of your scenes *narratively distant* and at least one other *narratively proximate*. Also—and this is important—be sure to change more than merely the pronouns you use in each version. Remember that different points of view argue for different types of contact with the details and characters in your story. Use the scene you write for each point of view as a method of meditating on this fact.

What you'll learn: Different approaches to narrative offer different levels of intimacy and control; writing these scenes should illustrate this for you.

STUDENT EXAMPLES
৩৩ *Jeremy's Response*

FIRST PERSON

I was so absorbed in the brilliance of the city as I was riding on the bus that I hardly noticed the fact that we were already pulling into the bus station. The city was incredible, so huge and massive, just amazing. Even though I'd seen cities before,

Topeka, Salina, even Kansas City, they couldn't even begin to compare with the aura that possessed New York. There was something beautiful and artistic about this city.

In fact, the city was so breathtaking that I hardly even noticed the guy beside me jump up and run out the door as soon as we arrived until I reached down for my duffel bag and couldn't find it. By this time the aisle was packed full of people and there was no way for me to run after him. I even saw the little punk cross the street and disappear around the corner from out of the window. There was just no way to get around everyone in the aisles to chase him, so I pretty much just resigned myself to a passive, almost debilitating, state of shock.

I got off the bus fine, although I really can't remember how, and stumbled to a bench just inside the door of the station. I was out of breath, my stomach had sunk to my feet, and I couldn't really see very clearly. After about fifteen minutes of just sitting and trying to stabilize myself, I somewhat absently began to sort through what was in my pockets. It was an odd sensation, discovering what was in my pockets. I had put the items there at some point, but the whole bus ordeal had caused me to completely forget what was there. For all I know these items had been slipped into my pocket by some stranger at a rest stop along the way. I found myself left with about $15 in cash, a pen, a lighter, the last remains of a package of mints, and a tiny notebook where I found all the names, addresses, and phone numbers that I had thought would be important on my arrival to the city. I had recorded the info for my apartment building, my job, the police, fire and hospitals, plus a few restaurants, cafés, and bookstores I'd found in a guidebook. Seeing all of this information seemed to snap me out of the daze I was in. Something needed to be done; I couldn't just sit on the bench forever. So I looked for a pay phone.

There was a phone at the end of the hall by the restrooms and I was very happy to find a few loose coins on top of it. Any other day I would have considered that very lucky, but today had already proven itself unbecoming of luck. I used the coins to call my landlord. I'm not sure why exactly; I didn't have the rent anymore now that my bag was gone, but I needed to call someone and he was obviously the first person I should call.

He picked up on the third ring.

"Yeah?" He had a slightly harsh, yet warm and smoky old man's voice that comes from years of smoking cheap cigars and drinking too much. I could almost smell him on the other end.

"Hi, my name is David. I'm calling about the apartment I'm supposed to be moving into today. 7b?" I went on to explain that I was in the city, and how my bag and money had been stolen. I told him I couldn't pay the first month's rent yet.

"Ah, well, my my, that is a problem," he said with an odd detachment characteristic of the landlord kind enough to make sure his tenants don't move out, but who quite honestly doesn't even care.

"Well, I'm starting a new job tomorrow. Maybe I could get some sort of advance for the rent."

"Listen kid, I'll tell you what, because you're new in town and I'm such a nice guy, find out about this job of yours, give me some assurance that you'll pay soon—a letter from your boss or something—and I'll let you move in. Although I guess you really don't have much to move, do ya kid?!"

Over the old man's hearty chuckles I tried to say thank you, trying to focus on what I wanted to see as a very kind act on his part.

"Thanks so much," I said again, "I'll call you tomorrow once I've found out about my job."

"No problem kid." I hung up the phone to his full belly laugh. And suddenly I realized that I had nowhere to stay the night.

SECOND PERSON

All around you see the massive structures of New York City, the wide expanses of concrete and the busy life of the urban world. You hardly notice the bus pull into the station. You're somewhat brought back to the world of the bus when the guy sitting next to you jumps up and runs through the door, almost before the driver can even open it. Ok, you think, the guy must be in a hurry. And then your thoughts drift back to the paved world outside and your eager hopes for the new day in the city. First, you have to get off the bus.

As everyone else in the bus grabs their bags and begins to crowd into the aisle, you reach down to grab your duffel. But it's not there! You search around your seat and then you remember the guy beside you who rushed off the bus. Out the window, you see him cross the street and disappear around the corner, holding your bag, your every possession. With the aisles as crowded as they are, you find it impossible to give chase to the thief and so you regress into a state of mild shock. Somehow you make it off the bus and stumble to a bench just inside the door of the station.

You need to sit down for a little while to calm your nerves and figure out what to do next. The whole world seems turned upside down now. With your duffel bag, the kid seemed to steal all of your confidence, optimism, and energy for this first day in the city. The only things you have left are what is in your pockets, but you can't even remember what is there. Slowly you take a complete inventory. You have $15 in cash, a pen, a lighter (although you don't smoke), the sad remains of a package of mints, and a tiny notebook where you've recorded the names, addresses, and phone numbers you'd thought would be helpful when you arrived in the city. Your apartment building, your job, the police, fire, and hospital plus a few random restaurants, cafés, and bookstores are all listed. Seeing these listings is just enough to bring you back into the real world and you realize that you need to do something besides sit on the bench. You begin to look for a pay phone.

A phone happens to be at the end of the hall by the restrooms and you head straight for it as soon as you see it. You notice some loose change on the top of the phone as you walk up. You manage a faint grin. Any other day and this would be lucky, you think. You drop a couple coins in the slot and dial the number for your landlord. You know you can't pay the first month's rent that's due before you move in, but you've got to call someone and he seems like the best option. You need to talk, to connect with someone right now.

He picks up on the third ring.

"Yeah?" His voice is the slightly harsh, yet warm and smoky old man's voice that comes from years of smoking cheap cigars and drinking too much. You can almost smell him on the other end.

"Hi, my name is David. I'm calling about the apartment I'm supposed to be moving into today, 7b?" you say. You go on to explain how you are now in the city, and how your bag and money were ripped off on the bus. You tell him that you can't pay the first month's rent yet.

"Ah, well, my my, that is a problem," he tells you with an odd sort of detachment characteristic of a landlord kind enough to make sure his tenants don't move out, but who quite honestly doesn't even care.

"Well, I'm starting a new job tomorrow. Maybe I could get some sort of advance for the rent."

"Listen kid, I'll tell you what, because you're new in town (and I'm such a nice guy), find out about this job of yours, give me some assurance that you'll pay soon—a letter from your boss or something—and I'll let you move in. Although I guess you really don't have much to move, do ya kid?!"

You try to say thank you over the old man's hearty chuckles, focusing on what you interpret as an act of kindness. In another moment the laughter dies.

"Thanks so much," you say again, "I'll call you tomorrow once I've found out about my job."

"No problem kid." You hear his full belly laugh as you hang up the phone. And suddenly it hits you that you have nowhere to stay the night.

THIRD PERSON

As the bus pulled into the station, David was still eagerly trying to absorb the massive sea of urban culture that he had ridden into. He had seen cities before, big buildings, freeways, never-ending expanses of concrete and steel—man's greatest achievements and his greatest impression on the earth—but New York City, unique and full of character, presented David with something beyond his wildest imagination. NYC was, to the Kansas farm boy, a work of art that represented the epitome of what farmland, or any land, might become if only someone would take the time, if some artist of progress would choose to paint on that cornfield canvas.

It was while David was daydreaming about the magnificence of the city that the boy sitting next to him—who had slept, or pretended to sleep, almost the entire journey and hadn't even talked to David—made a mad dash to the door as soon as the bus had stopped. David thought passively about why the boy might be in such a hurry, but didn't think twice about it until he reached for his bag underneath his seat and found it missing. Suddenly, the boy's quick dash out the door made perfect sense. David was now trapped behind a busload of puttering old ladies and unhurried youth, making any sort of chase after the thief impossible. Out the window, David saw the boy run across the street and disappear.

Once outside of the bus, David began to try and make sense of his situation. He was in an unfamiliar city, which was anxiety inducing enough, but now that his bag had been stolen, a good part of his optimism and confidence had left him. He still knew where he was supposed to go and had a vague idea how to go about getting there, and yet he now felt lost and confused, as if his entire future had been packed somewhere in the bottom of his duffel.

A quick inventory of his pockets showed around $15, a pen, a lighter (although he didn't smoke, David took great pride in always being of service to those in need of a light), a couple mints, and a tiny notebook in which he had written down the names, addresses, and phone numbers for his apartment building and his job. David, in desperate need to make some sort of contact in the city, if for nothing else than to settle himself down, decided to call his landlord. He knew that he didn't have the first month's rent that he needed to pay before he could move in, but he needed to talk to someone, and he would have to sort out the apartment situation at some point.

David had been sitting on a bench just inside door of the bus station and could see a pay phone down the hall to his left, near the restrooms. He walked over to the phone and managed a grin when he found some loose change sitting on top of the phone. Any other day I might call this lucky, he thought. But the change was enough to make a phone call and he was glad about that at least. He dialed the number and a smoky, harsh old man's voice answered after the third ring.

"Yeah?"

"Hi, my name is David. I'm calling about the apartment I'm supposed to be moving into today . . ." From there he went on to explain how he had arrived in the city and the situation where his bag, and money, had been stolen so that he could not pay the first month's rent today.

"Ah, well, my my . . ." the voice on the other end said with a distinct sort of detached sentiment, "that is a problem."

"Well, I'm starting a new job tomorrow. Maybe I could get some sort of advance for the rent."

"Ok kid, I'll tell you what, because I'm such a nice guy, find out about this job of yours and give me some sort of assurance that you can pay soon, a letter from your boss or something, and I'll let you go ahead and move in. Although I guess you don't really have much to move, do you?!"

David ignored the old man's chuckles to focus on the fact that he was being incredibly kind at the same time. "Thanks so much," David said. "I'll give you a call tomorrow once I've found out about my job." He hung up and suddenly realized that he needed to find someplace to spend the night.

Commentary In considering the three versions of Jeremy's scene, it's useful to consider which one seems to draw the reader most completely into the action. Each version has its attractions. The first scene, set as it is in first person, offers the reader access to David's immediate experience of having his possessions stolen and finding himself nearly destitute in New York City. Because David is the scene's narrator, the language of this version sounds most like everyday speech, and this may make it easier for the reader to identify with what happens. The second-person version invites the reader to imagine what David's situation feels like, and in this version Jeremy provides some additional detail that makes this experience more palpable to the reader. The third-person version most obviously dovetails with Jeremy's third-person opening scene, and this may make it the most immediately appealing of the three versions. There are some other reasons to like it as well, though. For one thing, it gives Jeremy, as the story's informing intelligence, a bit more latitude in interpreting David's experience for the reader, and enables him to use rhetorical devices like simile ("...he now felt lost and confused, as if his entire future had been packed somewhere in the bottom of his duffel") that it might have felt out of character to have David himself use. Because of this latitude, Jeremy is able to use the third-person version to suggest a more comprehensive view of character and action. Having a third-person narrator on board assures the reader that no matter what kind of crisis David might undergo during the story, there will be a steady, clear-eyed narrative presence to tell her about it. This makes the third-person version of the scene the "winner" here, if only by a hair.

Concerns Jeremy could have gone a bit further in using his three versions of this scene to explore the differences in detail and contact with the surface of the story that rendering the scene from different points of view could have made possible. Though there is some difference in the tone of the narrative (particularly between the third-person version and the first- and second-person versions) and in the ability the third-person version gives Jeremy to interpret the scene's action for the reader, there's little appreciable difference in the amount of contact Jeremy enables his reader to have with his story's "surface" in these scenes.

> "*[O] ur history now arrives on the confines, where daylight and truth meet us with a clear dawn, representing to our view, though at a far distance, true colours and shapes.*"
>
> —JOHN MILTON,
> *THE HISTORY OF ENGLAND, BOOK I*

Sarah's Response

FIRST PERSON

I barely spoke on the ride home that night. Lindsay sat in the front with my mom, but that was fine because I wanted to look out the windows and think as we drove through the city. The silence pounded in my head, you know, how it does after you've been up close to the speakers at a show like that. And I remember we passed this old grizzled black man on the street, actually stopped at a stoplight right next to the corner where he was sitting on an orange crate. My window was down, and I could hear him chanting, over and over, "God's salvation is your only hope today," only he slurred it like, "Gods All Vation Isher Only Hope Tuh Day." I'm not religious, or anything, but it struck something in me. We looked at each other through the window, and I know this is weird, this whole night was weird, but I felt like we had this deep connection in that moment. I felt like if I got out of the car and told him I'd just seen Claire Danes, he would have understood how much that meant. Lindsay and Mom were just talking in the front, no fucking clue.

We dropped Lindsay off and got home. I went to the kitchen to get a quick drink so I could get right into the shower—I hate sitting there all sweaty and gross, sticking to the kitchen stools—but Mom came with me. It's so hard to talk to your mom after a concert, especially after *this* concert, when I had just lost Claire Danes and all I wanted to do was cry into my pillow. But Mom made up a pitcher of pink lemonade for me, and got out two glasses, and sat down with me, sort of desperate and sad. I can't take her like that, or something, so I stayed downstairs and we talked. She asked what was wrong, but she asked it all annoying, like, "Honey, why are you *distraught?*" And I said, "I'm not *distraught,* I'm thinking," and I tried to tell her about seeing Claire Danes. She asked if that was a rock star. *God.*

"No, Mom, she's an actress. You know that show I used to watch, "My So-Called Life"? She's the girl with the red hair."

"Ohhhh. Was she *with* one of the rock groups?" Mom looked at me earnestly, trying so hard to understand, like a puppy listening to people talk.

"No, I just saw her in the crowd, but then I couldn't find her." I realized about here that I couldn't explain it, that there was no way I could make Mom understand this feeling in my gut. I didn't understand it myself. I went upstairs without finishing my lemonade, and I could hear Mom sigh after I left the room.

SECOND PERSON

You get into the car distraught, and your silence pains me as we start the drive home. I ask Lindsay how the concert was, but I only half listen to her descriptions; my thoughts are in the back seat with you. Your pretty dress is all wet, and I hope to God I'm not being too relaxed letting you go to a concert like this. I really don't know what goes on in places like the Red Room. You'd never in a million years let me come in with you. They say that's normal, for a teenager.

I drop Lindsay off, you say goodbye in a too-loud voice, and we wait to make sure she gets inside okay. I turn on one of your mix tapes as we head home. I don't mind it, really, though you think I do. I ask you if you want it louder, but you don't answer because I have called you Amanda instead of Mint. It's so hard for me to remember to call you Mint. Why would you throw away the beautiful name your father and I chose for you? It's almost as if you have been acting a part since you changed it last year. But you're still you, sweet girl. You can kick and scream, but you're my Mandy, and I don't understand how to pull you back toward me. You're off like a shot as I park in the driveway.

I find you in the kitchen, holding the refrigerator door open too long. I don't need to ask you, I just find a pitcher and make up some pink lemonade. I know what you want before you do. You drink it tentatively, and I am amazed by how beautiful you are. Your hair shines a warm black in the incandescent light from the table lamp, and the delicate crook in the bridge of your nose, a lovelier version of mine, gives you a certain exoticism. I ache to be able to tell you, but you are a fortress. I'm not allowed inside, but sometimes you will open a window and throw something out for me to study, to tuck into a pocket near my heart.

I know I may do more harm than good, but I can't keep myself from reaching out to you. "Honey, why are you distraught?" I ask.

You speak to me as though each word wearies you. "I'm not distraught. I'm thinking." But then you reconsider, because you *are* clearly distraught, and you have to get this thing out of your system, whatever it is, even if it means telling your mother something about your life. You tell me that you saw an actress named Claire Danes at the rock concert tonight, but that you couldn't find her to talk to her. You wait for me to say the right thing, but I don't understand and I'm no good at subtlety.

I want so badly for you to tell me why this is important. You are looking at me hopelessly, and you get up amidst my uninformed questions. You switch off the lamp instinctually as you leave the room, and I sit in darkness asking silent questions over and over. Why did you need to talk to an actress? What have you invested in this, Mandy? Who is this person, this actress, that is so desperately much more important to you than I am?

THIRD PERSON

Mint was too lost—lost in thought, lost in a vague despair that reminded her of missing the last train out of the city at night—to be embarrassed about climbing into her mother's blue Acura outside the Red Room. A pins-and-needles rain was just beginning to come down. A few of the smokers pressed against the front of the building, sheltering under the gutter, noticed her dress, wet and a shade darker, hanging half open. No one laughed.

Lindsay took the front seat and politely answered Mint's mother's questions about the concert, though they were obviously directed at Mint. The quiet in the car reverberated in Mint's skull, and when Lindsay turned the radio on, it sounded distant and unimportant. They coasted through the inner city, doors locked. Mint stared out the window at the dirty city speeding past. Bulky men in NFL jerseys slouched outside of bars, women in skintight jeans and bustier tops leaned into the traffic. The people of the world seemed dingy and unkempt: sad, common people with skin imperfections and alcoholic spouses. They did not even exist in the same night as Claire Danes.

Mint shut her eyes until they pulled into their driveway, having dropped Lindsay off at her house. She went straight to the kitchen for a glass of water, and her mother followed her in and sat down at the kitchen table.

"Was the band any good, Amanda?"

Mint turned on the water violently in response. "Do you even *try* to remember my name?" She had thrown away the name Amanda almost six months ago, and every time her mother said it, she felt a shudder of childhood.

"Honey." Her mother's voice was self-consciously soft, pained. "Why are you distraught?"

Just hearing her mother use the word *distraught* made Mint squirm. She took her water and sat down at the far end of the table. "I'm not distraught, I'm thinking," she said. But it wasn't true, and they both knew it wasn't true, and maybe it would help if she could tell someone about tonight.

Mint decided to talk, and her whole body showed it. She turned towards her mother, and shifted so that she was backlit by the table lamp. Her hair shone a warm black in the incandescent light, and the delicate crook in the bridge of her nose, a subtler version of her mother's, gave her a certain exoticism. Her mother wanted to tell her how pretty she was, but she was almost holding her breath, waiting for Mint to let out whatever she was going to let out.

"Ok," said Mint. "I saw Claire Danes tonight at the concert, but then I went look-ing for her, and I never found her." Her mother's face was blank. Did she understand? "Claire Danes, you know, from 'My So-Called Life'?" Mint thought of the star's face, the golden glow of celebrity that she had radiated through the crowd. How could she explain the need she had felt, intense and stomach wrenching, to learn the secret? How could she explain the allure of magazine spreads, *Seventeen* interviews, musician boyfriends? "I wanted to talk to her because I think she knows how to. . . ." The soft-ening around her mother's mouth meant she didn't understand; she thought Mint had wanted an autograph or a handshake. Then Mint understood that this wasn't something she could share. She left the room midsentence and slept dreamlessly until the morning.

Commentary To help in judging the success of the three versions of Sarah's scene, it's useful to coin a variation of the Who's telling this story, and why? question, opting instead for Who *ought* to be telling this story? On first reading of Sarah's scenes, it doesn't seem as if it will be an easy question to answer. What's surprising and gratify-ing about Sarah's scenes is how faithful each seems to be to the sensibility at its cen-ter, how persuasive the scenes seem to be that it presents the "right" point of view for the telling of this story. The scene written using Mint's point of view is very sharply drawn, and vividly captures Mint's frustration with herself and her mother. The second-person version, which takes the reader into the mother's consciousness, offers such a compellingly different view of Mint's experience that this scene could be from an entirely different story—a story equally worth reading, at whose heart might be the mother's attempt to bridge the growing gap between herself and her daughter. The third-person version, connecting as it does with the first scene, is the most logi-cal follow-on.

Concerns While the third-person version of this scene connects most immediately with the first scene, it's also the most problematic of the three, largely because of sev-eral missed opportunities. In the second paragraph, Sarah tells us that "Lindsay took the front seat and politely answered Mint's mother's questions about the concert, though they were obviously directed at Mint." It might have given the reader better access to an understanding of Mint's mother, Mint herself, and her relationship with Lindsay if Sarah had rendered a few of these questions and replies, and registered Mint's reactions. Similarly, the final sentence of the scene, "She left the room mid-sentence and slept dreamlessly until the morning," seems a bit thin, and isn't quite in keeping with what came immediately before it—a conversation that it appears was vexing and uncomfortable for both Mint and her mother, which could provide fodder for Mint's thought as she abruptly ends the conversation and retreats to her room. Having her sleep "dreamlessly" so quickly after leaving the kitchen seems a narrative move that's not in keeping with the scene's emotional content. Finally, there is a mechanical problem in the eighth paragraph: it presents an observation about Mint's appearance without attributing that observation to anyone. The implication is that it's the mother's observation (especially given the previous scene, which contained a nearly identical observation set in the mother's point of view), but this is not clear. It could be made so quite easily.

QUESTIONS FOR REVISION

1. Reconsider your beginning in light of the assignment you just finished: Does the point of view you used in your opening scene give your reader the clearest possible view into the action with which the story begins?

2. If the narrator who begins your story is an informing intelligence, would there be any benefit in making him or her a character in the story instead? If your narrator is a character, would your story benefit from the objectivity brought by having an informing intelligence as narrator?

3. If you wrote your opening in first person, is your narrator the main character or a secondary character? Would it help your story if you switched from this narrator to the other? Can you say how reliable your narrator is? If your narrator is unreliable—a liar or self-deceiving—how will you enable your reader to see around him or her?

4. If you wrote your opening in third person, might rewriting it in first person help you to know more about the narrating character, or about what's at stake for this character?

5. How close to the "surface" of your story would you say your beginning places your reader? Is this the best proximity to the story's surface, or would your story benefit from either more proximity or more distance from the story's objects, characters, and events?

6. Is there a sufficient transition between the two scenes you've now written? Do the scenes, considered together, begin to suggest your story's narrative arc? Does it feel as if energy is starting to build that will move the reader to ask, And *then* what happened?

Alternative Writing Exercises

1. **Just the facts, Ma'am ...** In this exercise, you're a police officer who's at the scene of a purse snatching. Your job is to take statements and then to write a report that offers your conclusions. The first statement is that of the victim, and you should record your transcript of this woman's statement in her voice, in first person. The second statement is that of a witness, and this should be written in third person—the voice of the witness, relating what he saw (i.e., "The man ran up 3rd Avenue . . ."). The third statement will demonstrate the objective narrative voice of an official report, in which an "informing intelligence" correlates the information gathered from both the victim and the witness, drawing conclusions which are then duly related for the record. *What you'll learn:* as above, to explore the levels of control and intimacy rendered by the different narrative stances.

2. **Be a busy-body (part two): change the mood.** Go to your favorite bar, restaurant or bookstore. Now describe a transaction—the purchase of a cup of coffee or a

novel or the ordering of a meal—twice. The first time, do your description using an *angry* and *intimate* point of view that brings your reader close to the surface of the scene; the second time using an *ironic* and *distanced* point of view that holds your reader away from the surface of the scene. *What you'll learn:* to give you a feel for the fact that different emotional states provide the reader with different experiences of your narrative.

3. **Combatant and non-combatant.** Imagine an argument. Now write that argument twice—once as an observer and once as a participant. *What you'll learn:* to demonstrate how the level of a character's involvement in the events of a scene affects the reader's experience with that scene's depth of occupation.

4. **One story, several versions.** Your mission with this exercise is to describe a holiday dinner that's taking place right after a family argument. Write your description twice—the first time from a single point of view, the second time by shifting point of view from person to person, around the table, and in doing so make clear in each scene the causes of the argument. *What you'll learn:* to give you a feel for the differences in control in scenes written with either steady or with shifting points of view.

Reading Exercise:
Point of View in Tobias Wolff's "Bullet in the Brain"

The more skillfully you manage your reader's relationship with your story, the more complete will be her experience of that emotion Aristotle called *recognition*. In "Bullet in the Brain," Tobias Wolff provides a very good example of an author using point of view to control the intimacy of contact his reader is able to have with the story's surface, changing it as the story unfolds, intensifying the impact of events, moving the reader from the relatively cool and ironic experience of the outer world the protagonist has as the story opens, and into a passionate and intimate experience of the last moments of his inner world.

QUESTIONS

1. After reading the story's first paragraph, how close do you feel to the surface of events? What creates that feeling for you?

2. How do you feel about Anders as the story opens? Do you feel invited to develop a sense of sympathy for him? What kind of relationship does it seem the author is encouraging?

3. Where does your sense of contact with the surface of this story begin to change? How does Wolff effect this change?

4. After Anders has been shot, what does the mosaic of things he *doesn't* remember do for your understanding of his character? If this information changes your feeling for him as a character, how would you describe that change?

5. How does Wolff's choice of a third-person narrative frame enable him to tell the reader about all that Anders *didn't* remember after he'd been shot? Could he have conveyed the same information to the reader if the narrative had been framed in the first person? In third-person objective?

6. Speculate for a moment about the effects of the past tense framing of this story. How would the story have been affected if the story had been set in present tense? Would this change have hurt it? How so? Would it have helped it? Again, how so?

4

TONE OF VOICE

The voice is a second face.
—Gérard Bauër
Carnets inédits

What do we mean by "tone of voice" in fiction? The human voice, certainly—the sound of the dialogue within your story. That's part, but not all of it. Tone of voice also refers to a story's *diction*, the cadences in which it's told, the rhythms present in the sentences that are *not* dialogue. Tone of voice is how you know you're reading Ernest Hemingway and not F. Scott Fitzgerald, Katherine Mansfield and not Virginia Woolf, Toni Morrison and not Don Delillo. Tone of voice is how you know to laugh at a line of James Thurber's or Lorrie Moore's that's delivered straight. It's how you know there's sadness, bile, and disappointment with the human race laced through the humor in Swift's *Gulliver's Travels*, Voltaire's *Candide*, and John Kennedy Toole's *A Confederacy of Dunces*.

Tone of voice, as Janet Burroway says succinctly in her book, *Writing Fiction*, "can match, emphasize, alter, or contradict the meaning of the words." It is there in the way characters and the details of the story's physical world are presented; it is in the color, emotion, and pacing of the language itself. It is each writer's individual poetry. Aristotle believed voice—or, as he referred to it, the "metrical arrangement of the words"—to be one of the basic components of a good narrative. If voice weren't given sufficient attention in a narrative, Aristotle believed it would fail just as surely as a narrative with flat characters or a flawed plot fails.

This is true because of one glaringly obvious fact about fiction: it's not actual experience, in which we have a hundred cues that guide us to an understanding of meanings that flow, like underground streams, beneath the surface of the spoken word. In the real world, we can conclude that a person is lying by reading his

"One day, as [Richard] Wright and I walked together to the elevated station, he turned to me and said, "Margaret, if a voice speaks within you, you can live." —MARGARET WALKER

body language, listening to the inflections in his voice, even by making inferences from the way he's dressed, from the way he drinks his coffee, or the fact that he can't keep direct eye contact. We have no such guides in fiction, unless the writer finds a way artfully to convey them. Tone of voice is one tool she can use to do this.

Every writer has his or her characteristic ways of using tone to paint a full picture of character and action, and—depending on the needs of the story—a good writer can change that tone, much as, in the real world, our tone of voice changes to match our emotions. As you consider the best way to do this in the story you're writing, it might help you to think about tone of voice this way: a skilled car mechanic can often tell if an engine is functioning well—or can even tell what's wrong with it—by listening to it as it runs. You may be able to do the same thing with your story. Let's illustrate by presenting more of the climbing story we began in the previous chapter; one section is from the first-person story as narrated by the climber, the second section is from the third-person version written by the journalist.

First, the climber's version:

Sounds change as I move higher. This always happens. There are sounds that come only from the ground: animals in the underbrush, hikers arguing on nearby trails, radios playing in tourists' cars, stream water pouring over rocks. I leave this world as I move higher. I climb into the middle world, where the sounds are fewer, and come from the birds and the trees' limbs being pushed around by the air. Then, finally, I climb into another world far above the trees where the sounds are fewer still, coming from the wind, the hammer *pinging* on the pitons, the carabiners clicking into place, the ropes creaking.

On this climb, I wanted the sounds to be even fewer. That's why I left the gear behind. This time I wanted only to hear the air hissing over the rock face, my breath, my blood like a tide in my ears. This is the world I truly live in.

The wind drops, then dies entirely, and I hold still. I feel the sweat rise on my skin like a blush. Faint, like a memory I will soon lose, I hear Dad's voice come into the stillness: Be careful, sweetheart. For God's sake . . .

Now here's the journalist's third-person version:

Finally, unable to restrain himself, the father calls to her, "Be careful, sweetheart. For God's sake . . ."

It is a cri de coeur; nonsense, of course, for what else can she be but careful, without the web of pitons, ropes, and carabiners, woven to reduce danger to near security? *For God's sake* is really *for my sake*. It is really *Whatever would I do, if I saw you fall? How could I live afterward? What could I tell your mother, and what could she say to me?* Her father lifts the binoculars again.

She gives no sign she has heard him. She's reached the top of the crack that brought her up from the ground, and the ledge that was her first objective. Her face is pinched and still, and she breathes in short gasps, her face tilted up, toward the top. There is only *up; down* has faded into a mathematical mist behind her, the origin of the gravity she must defy if she is to live.

These are very different versions of the same event. Obviously, some of this difference comes from the point of view used in each section, but the difference is also a product of tone of voice. Notice how, in the climber's version, the tone of voice is much more matter-of-fact, much more grounded in the physical specifics of the climber's experience and more personal, while tone of voice in the journalist's section is more impersonal and pitched higher, rhetorically. Given the tone of voice—the *diction* or way of talking—which was established for the climber in the beginning of the story featured in the last chapter, it would have sounded false to have the climber call her father's admonition a cri de coeur, or to have her refer to "down" as "a mathematical mist." That wouldn't have been how *she'd* express it, and so it would have been "out of diction."

> "*One* must *avoid ambition* in order *to write. Otherwise something else is the goal: some kind of power beyond the power of language. And the power of language, it seems to me, is the only kind of power a writer is entitled to.*"
>
> —CYNTHIA OZICK

In the journalist's version, however—because of the more distant third-person point of view, the more elevated language used in that beginning—the tone of voice created by these rhetorical flourishes seems more in keeping with the *sensibility* that version of the story expresses.

Who's Telling the Story?

As is implied above, a story's tone of voice is often a function of who is narrating it. If a story is narrated by a limited or unsophisticated character in the story (think of Celie in Alice Walker's *The Color Purple*), or an inhuman character (as in James Tiptree, Jr.'s story "Love Is the Plan, the Plan Is Death") then the tone of voice must reflect this narrator's sensibility. To use *The Great Gatsby* as an example again, much of the book's solemn, melancholy beauty is there because Nick Caraway is its narrator. He is an outsider to the world of casual wealth and glamour through which Gatsby and Daisy move, and his outsider status gives the reader a perspective on this world that Gatsby or Daisy themselves wouldn't possess. Even when the narrator is an informing intelligence and not a character, the tone of voice may present a particular sensibility, as in Judith Claire Mitchell's story "A Man of Few Words," where the narrative voice is colored distinctly by the Jewish culture from which its main character springs.

What's Your Narrator's Relationship to the Story or Its Characters?

Whether your story's narrator is a character in the story or an informing narrative intelligence, the attitude of that personage toward the story and the characters it contains will be a large consideration in determining the voice in which the story is told.

Part of the joy in reading Dickens comes from the sensibility conveyed by his authorial/narrative voice—deeply humane, interested in even the most despicable of his characters, by turns vastly moved or amused by the dramas set in motion on the page. The voice of Sandra Cisneros's narrator in "Mericans" (p. 291) also has a large effect on how the reader receives the story. Here are the first two paragraphs of the story, narrated by Cisneros's main character:

> We're waiting for the awful grandmother who is inside dropping pesos into *la ofrenda* box before the altar to La Divina Providencia. Lighting votive candles and genuflecting. Blessing herself and kissing her thumb. Running a crystal rosary between her fingers. Mumbling, mumbling, mumbling.
>
> There are so many prayers and promises and thanks-be-to-God to be given in the name of the husband and the sons and the only daughter who never attend mass. It doesn't matter: Like La Virgen de Guadalupe, the awful grandmother intercedes on their behalf. For the grandfather who hasn't believed in anything since the first PRI elections. For my father, El Periquín, so skinny he needs his sleep. For Auntie Light-skin, who only a few hours before was breakfasting on brain and goat tacos after dancing all night in the pink zone. For Uncle Fat-face, the blackest of the black sheep—*Always remember your Uncle Fat-Face in your prayers.* And Uncle Baby—*You go for me, Mamá*—God listens to you.

"The first stricture of [English A at Harvard in 1939] was a wise one: writing is an extension of speech, we were told. So we were instructed to write with something of the ease with which we might speak, and that is a good rule for beginners. . . . The best writing comes, obviously, out of a precision we do not and dare not employ when we speak, yet such writing still has the ring of speech."

—NORMAN MAILER,
"WRITING COURSES" FROM *THE SPOOKY ART*

The narrator's voice—its pitch, its tempo, the use of sentence fragments and expressions in Spanish, and the word choice, the honorific "awful" she has given to her grandmother and the dead-on caricature she offers of the grandmother's martyred, self-serving devotion—all these combine to ground us in an immediate understanding of who is talking to us, and of what the world of her story is like.

Try Writing the Way You Talk

Many beginning writers, thinking that stories must *sound* like stories, make the mistake of straining to sound "literary," and write using a high-flown or artificial diction that lifts them above regular, everyday speech. It's an understandable impulse: some of the best, most memorable writing—*Moby Dick*, for instance, or Cormac McCarthy's *Blood Meridian*—makes use of a voice that is decidedly not the type you hear every day in class or at the office or in the grocery store. However, straining after this voice is not always the best choice.

Think of it this way: we've all known someone who we would say is a born story-teller. She knows how to use pauses, facial expressions, hand gestures, and different intonations and timbres to spice up an anecdote and make it into a full-blown story. On the other hand, there are people who muff the recounting of even the juiciest incident. These people may be fine in casual conversation, but the minute they have an audience they become stiff, unnatural, dull. They sound awkward and artificial because they're so conscious of the fact that they're telling a story.

This happens for many of us when we begin trying to write stories: we stop sounding like ourselves and start sounding like someone else entirely, someone who's trying to sound like a writer. Stop when you feel this happening, and ask yourself whether you're really adding anything to the telling of your story by using this voice. Instead, try to act naturally on the page, telling the story as if you were talking to a friend.

Make Sound Match Sense

This is not to say that all writing should sound like people standing on a street corner chatting. In framing "The Aleph" (p. 248), which you'll be reading in conjunction with this chapter, Jorge Luis Borges obviously used anything but an everyday voice. When you read the story, notice the way this voice helps Borges tell a very particular tale. His narrator is a vain and pompous poet who is competing with an even-more-pompous fellow-poet. For the character who narrates the story, a highly stylized, overblown diction *is* the right voice. He wouldn't be a convincing character otherwise, nor would his encounter with the Aleph be as poignant. In writing a story, then, you should use the voice the story and the characters call for.

Deciding on this voice is a delicate business, though, and requires great care. In trying to capture a voice, you can very easily slip into caricature and your characters can become clichés or cartoons. This happens often when a writer uses dialect or nonstandard spelling to capture the quirks of a character's speech or her regional accent.

Tone of voice is affected, too, by the way a writer sets a scene, the details she chooses to record. If you work hard to see through your narrator's eyes using your narrator's sensibility, tone of voice will come as it ought to: naturally, because your narrator seems real in the way she's noticing things, the way she's telling the reader: *Here. Look at the way his mouth turns down when he listens to what his wife is saying. Observe the slow way the girl has of describing for the blind grandfather what she sees through a window. This is what's important.* No one else will notice things, tell things, in quite the way your carefully managed narrative persona or your meticulously imagined characters will.

Your Way with Words Is Not the Subject of the Story

You should avoid writing that calls attention to you, the writer, and calls it away from your characters and the story you're telling through them. James Joyce once said (in the person of Stephen Dedalus, in *A Portrait of the Artist as a Young Man*) that the author ought never to enter the mind of the reader, that he should be standing off to the side like an indifferent god, paring his fingernails—a face in the crowd, never center stage. Often good fiction writing calls for a type of humility that doesn't come naturally to everyone. The story you're writing isn't about you, even if you're drawing directly from life experience in framing it, and it's not about your large vocabulary. The story should excite recognition in your readers; it's about your characters, the piece of the human experience you get to see through them, which your readers get to see through your efforts. Your readers want engaging characters, a solid narrative. They don't want authorial grandstanding. It's fine if the reader comes away from a story thinking, I like listening to this writer tell a story. But it's bad if the reader comes away thinking, For this writer, the story was just an excuse for him to talk at me.

> *"If, while writing, you must always be proving that you write well, the writing will suffer. If you must be establishing something about yourself that is not yet established, you will tart up the writing in some way or other, and do pyrotechnics rather than the particular work of fiction, which, because it is commitedly local—about these specific characters, this particular place—runs the risk of seeming inconsequential."*
>
> —BONNIE FRIEDMAN,
> "GLITTERING ICONS, LUSH ORCHARDS"
> FROM *WRITING AFTER DARK*

Imitation—Its Uses and Abuses

Most writers have a chorus of other writers who've influenced them that lives in their heads. We're often powerfully affected by the writers we've read, and may be first prompted to write by our love for these writers' work. Indeed, trying to match the example other writers have set for us—experimenting to figure out how they write the way they write, how they manage to sound the way they sound—can teach an apprentice writer valuable lessons. When it comes time to craft your own stories, though, however much you may have been influenced by another writer's way with words, it's a good idea to try to expunge that influence from your writing. You don't want to end up sounding as if you're *trying* to sound like one of your favorite writers, or worse, like an untidy and unsteady amalgam of all of them.

A Few Thoughts on Precision

This chapter on tone of voice is the right place for a brief discussion of precise use of language. Most writers are interested in how language works, not only because words are the material with which they build their stories, but because of the music present in words and the interplay of that music and meaning in the story's voice. If meaning is neglected in favor of music, though, the story suffers.

To balance sound and sense in your stories, you must develop a mania for precision. You have to be sure your words mean exactly what you intend, avoiding, for instance, saying an unused room smells *musky* if what you really mean is that it smells *musty*. If your reader ever has to stop and argue with word choice—either because he can't understand your meaning or because he gets a different meaning than the one you've intended—your story is failing. What's written doesn't signify to the reader. This is a language problem at its most basic level.

Overdependence on Adjectives and Adverbs

In trying to make their characters, action, and settings more vivid, many beginning writers will pile adjectives and adverbs into their stories by the scoopful. Paradoxically, this often bogs their stories down and renders them murky, predictable, and uninteresting. This is because adjectives and adverbs lack the precision to convey movement, atmosphere, and character that careful assemblies of verbs and nouns offer. Compare the following two passages, in which adjectives and adverbs are in bold:

Sergeant Jones, an **obese** policeman, breathed **heavily** on his way up the **crumbly** steps that went into the **dilapidated old Victorian** house. None of the streetlights on this **impoverished** block worked and it was a **moonless, dark** night, with only the stars to see by. He stepped on a **loose** piece of concrete on the top step and **clumsily** staggered to the side into the **rusty** railing, where he cut his hand.

"Damnit," he said **exasperatedly** as he looked at his **bloody** palm. He pulled out his **glossy ebony** flashlight and pounded with its butt on the **peeling** and **punky** wood of the front door. It was **inky** dark on the stoop, so Jones clicked his flashlight on.

"Anybody in there?" he called, and his voice sounded **trembly** and **thin**. He **reluctantly** decided to go in.

Now read this passage, from which the adjectives and adjectives have either been removed or used more precisely to support the sharper, more concrete nouns and verbs:

"I listen attentively in bars and cafés, while standing in line at the checkout counter, noting particular pronunciations and the rhythms of regional speech, vivid turns of speech and the duller talk of everyday life. In Melbourne I paid money into the hand of a sidewalk poetry reciter to hear 'The Spell of the Yukon,' in London listened to a cabby's story of his psychopath brother in Paris, on a trans-Pacific flight heard from a New Zealand engineer the peculiarities of building a pipeline across New Guinea."

—ANNIE PROULX,
"INSPIRATION? HEAD DOWN THE BACK ROAD, AND STOP FOR THE YARD SALES"

Sergeant Jones waddled up the steps of the brownstone, wheezing as he went. Near the top, a **head-sized** chunk of concrete gave way under his foot and clattered down the steps behind him. He lurched to the side and caught himself on the **rusted** iron railing, which squealed and bent as it took his weight.

"Damnit," he said, and looked at his palm, cut by the scale. So much for the element of surprise. He reached the top step and looked up and down the street. Though the bulbs of the block's streetlights had been shot out or shattered by stones long before, the starlight showed him most of the houses were like this one, or worse. **Dark** as the inside of a pocket, he thought. He pulled his flashlight out of the holster on his belt and pounded on the door with its butt, grimacing as he thought of the finish. He'd spent thirty bucks on it the week before. The sound of the concussion was **dull**;

the door's wood must be **rotten**. No lights came on. He pushed the button on the flashlight.

"Anybody in there?" he called, the words seeming to disappear into the air, as if he'd never spoken. He reached out to try the doorknob, hoping it wouldn't turn. It did. Jones started to sweat.

Twenty-two of the first passage's 136 words—about sixteen percent—were adjectives and adverbs, while the second passage, despite using 96 more words, used only five adjectives, or about two percent. Not only does the second passage yield a much more vivid and precise picture of the neighborhood and the policeman's situation, it also takes the reader more deeply into Sergeant Jones's character. This is because well-chosen verbs and nouns *deliver* action and atmosphere while adjectives and adverbs can only *interpret* action and atmosphere. In the second passage, the reader is able to intuit the fact that the policeman is overweight because of the verbs used to convey how he climbs the stairs: he "waddles" as he ascends, and wheezes with what, for a thinner person, would be a relatively modest effort. The house's condition is conveyed by action rather than by adjective or adverb, and the darkness of the street and the poverty of the neighborhood are registered with the reader as observations the sergeant makes about the setting ("Though the bulbs of the block's streetlights had been shot out or shattered by stones long before, the starlight showed him most of the houses were like this one, or worse"), rather than more abstract observations made by the third-person narrative voice (i.e., "None of the streetlights on this impoverished block worked . . .").

Progressive Writing Exercise #4:
Finding the Right Tone of Voice

Consult your cloud diagram again. This time, you're going to use it to write two versions of the next scene in your narrative, **using different voices**. First write the scene using the voice of your main character, then write the scene again, using the voice of one of your secondary characters or the voice of a third-person narrator.

What you'll learn: The object is to work in awareness of the advantages and disadvantages of—and the different narrative textures rendered by—the voice in which you've chosen to work.

STUDENT EXAMPLES
☜ *Jeremy's Response*

Jeremy's Note: *I should explain the differences between these two scenes, because without explanation the differences might not be clear. The first scene is a section of the story as it would be told by a first-person narrator (having reframed my beginning to introduce a character that*

tells David's story). The second scene keeps the basic third-person-omniscient narrator that
tells the story, beginning with David as he leaves the bus station.

FIRST-PERSON VERSION

David left the bus station confused and frustrated. The worst isn't over yet, he
thought. His apartment was still at least a day away, he didn't have enough money for
a hotel, let alone know where to find one, and he didn't know another soul in the city.

As he walked down the crowded sidewalk amid the tidal wave of people crashing
into and swirling around skyscrapers and city streets, David wondered if any of these
other people were lost or alone, if any felt the same way he did or if everyone *did* and
yet they all ignored it or had somehow adapted. Evolved, as it were, into Modern
City Man. No one looked at each other, no one spoke, no one pretended to care.
Each being was autonomous, completely separate from all others in mind and purpose. And yet David felt himself moving with the biggest herd in the world, millions
strong, fenced in by concrete and steel and traffic lights and crosswalks, raised for the
business industry, for Wall Street instead of the sale barn, to crunch numbers rather
than chew cud.

These realizations didn't make David feel more alone, or frightened, or lost or
anything like that; in fact he later told me that "for one of the only times in my life I
felt completely safe in that moment. I was a part of something great and uncontrollable, something, as odd as this might sound in the city, natural. It was like swimming
with a school of fish or running with the pack—I wasn't going to get eaten up by
whatever predators were out there to get me (many of which it took me years to discover) and even if I did it was for the good of the group. I wasn't worried." The streets
were primal, instinctual, a constructed habitat for double-breasted males and skirted
females. New York City was, and still is, the human house extension of the Central
Park Zoo, constructed by the animals for their own amusement and protection, but
no one takes notice, they've never even seen the bars. We're on display for some gods
or devils. And who knows, even they might have gotten bored and went home.

"It was shallow though; it was a cold comfort," he said, "Colder 'n hell," and I told
him he wasn't far off. A city with so many people, so many institutions, ideas, con-
structions, lives, deaths, all of that can't help but be organic. Cities live, breathe, and
die. Cities have a soul. So does the country, of course, but in a much different way.
Like the Garden of Eden before and after the Fall, but in our infinite, godlike knowledge the city spends all of its time trying to find ways to make us all forget that we
still exist.

David ducked into a McDonalds to escape the confused drive of the sidewalk and
figure out what to do for the quickly approaching evening. He hadn't eaten since
breakfast and his stomach began to call for attention. He ordered a cheeseburger and
a coffee, nearly $1.50 of his last $15 now gone, and he sat down in a booth near the
front window so he could watch the movement outside while he studied his options.

Fifteen minutes later, David had finished the cheeseburger, half of the coffee, and
ruled out any sort of hotel or hostel (too expensive), finding someone to stay with
(he didn't know anyone and, at this point, trying to meet someone would be a ridiculous and scary proposal), or sleeping on the street (besides being dangerous, this was

still somehow beneath his dignity). He wasn't left with much and now he was puzzling out what might be left for him to try.

He looked up from the brightly colored tray liner he had been studying just in time to see a slightly past middle-aged priest, in traditional collared black garb, walk in the door and head toward the counter. Of course, he thought, a church! He was certain that a church would be safe, quiet, comfortable, and welcoming. After all, if you can't trust in God, in whom else can you trust? And obviously there was a church around here, or else where did the priest come from? David got up from his seat, dumped his tray, and approached the priest where he stood in line. The man seemed more than happy to talk to David, and after he had been through the line and gotten his meal they sat down at a table to discuss the situation. David quickly explained why he was in the city, how his bag had been stolen, and his need for a place to spend the night. David's story was either quite convincing, or the priest just incredibly kind, for he immediately offered a spare room in the rectory for David to spend the night. David couldn't have been more thrilled and the two men left the restaurant to walk to the parish a few blocks down the road.

THIRD-PERSON-OMNISCIENT VERSION

David left the bus station confused and frustrated. The worst isn't over yet, he thought. His apartment was still at least a day away, he didn't have enough money for a hotel, let alone know where to find one, and he didn't know another soul in the city.

As he walked down the crowded sidewalk among the tidal wave of people crashing into and swirling around skyscrapers and city streets, David wondered if any of these other people were lost or alone, if any felt the same way he did or if everyone *did* and yet they all ignored it or had somehow adapted. Evolved, as it were, into Modern City Man. No one looked at each other, no one spoke, no one pretended to care. Each being was autonomous, completely separate from all others in mind and purpose. And yet David felt himself moving with the biggest herd in the world, millions strong, fenced in by concrete and steel and traffic lights and crosswalks, raised for the business industry, for Wall Street instead of the sale barn, to crunch numbers rather than chew cud.

These realizations didn't make David feel more alone, or frightened, or lost or anything like that. He felt comfortable and safe in the moment. For one rare occasion in his solitary and lonely life, he was part of something great and uncontrollable, something natural and organic in the middle of a concrete jungle. Like swimming in a school of fish or running with the pack, David was safe from any predator that might lie in wait around the corner. The streets were a primal, instinctual, constructed habitat for the double-breasted males and skirted females of the wild human species. New York City could be seen as the human house extension of the Central Park Zoo, constructed by the animals themselves, yet no one notices, no one has even seen the bars. Everyone on display for some god or devil; and who knows, they might have gotten bored and went home.

David's comfort was short-lived, shallow, and cold. The city is a being with no sense of commitment. One moment for you, another against; the city is organic, ever changing, growing, decaying, living and breathing. To David, the soul of the city suddenly stood out as a dark cloud on the bright blue sky that was the rural soul he had always known. Like the Garden of Eden before and after the Fall, but in humanity's infinite, godlike wisdom, the city spends all of its time trying to find ways to make itself forget its own existence.

Commentary Jeremy's experiment—using the voice of a somewhat distanced first-person narrator in the first scene and that of a fairly standard-issue third-person-omniscient narrator in the second—raises some interesting questions, in the first scene particularly. In this scene, the question of who's telling the story and why arises almost immediately. This narrative approach introduces the notion that David's story is possibly being told by a friend of David's, at some unspecified future date when whatever drama the story contains has come to seem like ancient history. Because it introduces a retrospective, this-was-all-a-long-time-ago tone, this tactic takes some of the emotional heat out of David's situation, and it invites the reader into a more relaxed relationship with character and situation.

The second scene, in third-person-omniscient point of view, uses a somewhat elevated and philosophical narrative voice to put even more distance between David, the story's events, and the narrative informing intelligence. It's interesting that through the very simple expedient of removing the relaxed and cordial persona of a flesh-and-blood narrator from the story, Jeremy manages to reintroduce the tension of David's situation. The ultimate solution to David's problems seems less assured in the second scene—a feeling that's heightened because in this version, the scene ends without the priest coming to the rescue.

Concerns As so often happens, the advantages of a particular narrative tactic are also its potential limitations. In the first scene, the first-person narrator—removed in space and time from the events of the story he's relating—lends the story an emotionally cooler and more relaxed atmosphere. But this narrator also raises questions about the narrator's stake in the telling of the story, and his or her relationship with the (presumably) older and wiser David. And while Jeremy takes the omniscient third-person version of the scene as an opportunity to use a more elevated rhetorical tone and so creates some pleasing effects ("The city is a being with no sense of commitment. One moment for you, another against; the city is organic, ever changing, growing, decaying, living and breathing"), it gets a little out of control from time to time, and the narrative gets a bit sticky and over-grand ("To David, the soul of the city suddenly stood out as a dark cloud on the bright blue sky that was the rural soul he had always known. Like the Garden of Eden before and after the Fall, but in humanity's infinite, godlike wisdom, the city spends all of its time trying to find ways to make itself forget its own existence").

⟨⟩ *Sarah's Response*

THIRD-PERSON VERSION

Claire Danes lived in Mint's mind all the time after that. Mint slogged through days of high school distractedly, labeling her x and y axes, skipping seventh period to smoke behind the art building, holding her secret out of view like a firefly in cupped hands. She was thrilled by the privacy of her compulsion to study Claire Danes, dissect her charm. She made up excuses to get out of Lindsay's after school get-togethers—sorry, her mom made her clean the house, or take the cat to the vet—and she holed herself up in the basement with old taped episodes of "My So-Called Life."

Breathless, she'd push in a tape, press play, and there was Claire Danes, with that crimson hair, yearning for Jordan Catalano and delivering voice-over monologues all shivery with meaning. There she was, soft-faced and thoughtful and important. Mint rewound and fast-forwarded, excavating scenes to try to understand the source of all this wisdom and passion. Here was high school, here was *life*, grasped firmly and molded into something beautiful. Her mother brought her fruit and iced tea, and lingered in the doorway a few seconds too long each time, trying to think of the right thing to say. Mint appreciated her silence.

Mint felt crazy even admitting it to herself, but she was preparing for another meeting. This was training for some kind of second chance. She didn't know when it would come, or where, but she knew that there would be an opportunity—an astral convergence that would give her a window into Claire Danes. It would only last a moment, and if she didn't know the words of her question by then, she would never get to ask.

FIRST-PERSON VERSION

After that, I thought about Claire Danes all the time. It wasn't something I could tell Lindsay, or anyone. I mean, if Lindsay out and told me she was spending a lot of time contemplating Julia Roberts, I'd think she was weird, maybe a lesbo. It was a secret, and it almost felt like a dirty, shameful secret, maybe because I couldn't explain it away. I started watching old episodes of "My So-Called Life" every day after school. It was the only thing that seemed important to me, and I lost myself in it.

I'd get home and put in a tape, and Mom would always bring me a snack. She wouldn't say anything, just look at me wistfully and then leave. I wish there was some way she could have helped me, because it would have made her happy, I think.

I'd seen all the episodes a hundred times before, but now I was looking for something. It's strange but I almost felt like I was training for something. I had the irrational idea that I would see Claire Danes again, and that rewatching all the episodes would teach me what to ask her. So I watched closely, how Jordan Catalano's eyes changed when he saw her, how Rayanne felt her specialness and scrambled to be a part of it, how everyone tried to fit as closely as they could into her life. Watching, I was never jealous of Claire Danes. I *was* her. I never wanted to go back.

Commentary It's interesting to note the differences the shift in tone of voice brings to the reader's experience of these two scenes. For instance, the third-person version registers the fact that Mint is ducking her friend Lindsay, while in the other version Mint only implies that Lindsay wouldn't understand her obsession. Also, when Mint's mother brings her a snack in the third-person version of the story it is framed as an act of concern. When Mint notes the same action, she puts a slightly different spin on it, registering that it would make her mother *happy* if she could help Mint figure out what it is Mint is struggling with. The voice used in the third-person version also seems a bit more even-handed in identifying Mint's emotions (i.e., "She was thrilled by the privacy of her compulsion to study Claire Danes, dissect her charm")—an objectivity Mint herself would lack.

Concerns Sarah leaves very little to be concerned about here. Both of the approaches she used are effective for different reasons. As was discussed earlier, a story told using one voice would result in a story very different in character from a story told using another, largely because of the different relationship it would dictate for the reader to the story's events. In the version of the scene in Mint's voice, Sarah takes good advantage of the opportunity to put her reader on intimate terms with Mint, rendering her voice almost as a conversation she's holding with the reader. The third-person version offers the cooler, more objective tone noted above—a narrative tone that might be useful in helping the reader gain a more balanced view of Mint's story. One difference between the two scenes that is dictated by tone is the third-person version's final line. It offers a very succinct statement of what's at stake for Mint in this story—a statement that would have been hard to make (and have it sound authentic) in Mint's voice.

QUESTIONS FOR REVISION

1. Look back over your beginning scene and the response you made to the point of view exercise. How natural does the diction seem in these scenes? How natural do you think the diction *needs* to be?

2. What details establish voice in these scenes? What details tell you the most about the speaker? What is it that these details tell you? Do these details need to be sharpened or rendered more exactly?

3. If you're using a first-person narrator, does this narrator's voice feel like it's trying too hard anywhere? Does it seem like a caricature at any point?

4. If you're using a first-person narrator, do you feel you've sufficiently established your narrator's stake in telling the story? Would any other character in the story make a *better* narrator?

5. If you're using third-person narration, does the voice feel too elevated or too self-consciously "literary" at any point?

6. Have you allowed a love of verbal pyrotechnics to get ahead of your obligation to tell a story? Have you been as *precise* in word choice as you need to be, and have you avoided relying too heavily on adverbs and adjectives to make the world of your story tangible to your reader?

Alternative Writing Exercises

1. **What's your narrator's IQ?** Your assignment in this exercise is to write two first-person narrations of a scene in which a character is being evicted from his apartment. When you've finished writing the scene the first time, write it again, this time imagining that your narrator is either more intelligent or educated or *less* intelligent or educated than he was in the first scene. *What you'll learn:* The work you do for this exercise will illustrate how the decisions you make about who a character is will inevitably affect the narrative's voice.

2. **Look who's talking . . .** Write two versions of a scene in which a student and a professor have an argument. In the first version, have the scene narrated by either the student or the professor, and in the second version, have the scene narrated by a secondary character in the story who's looking on objectively as the argument plays out. *What you'll learn:* Working on this exercise should illustrate for you the fact that the speaker's level of involvement in a scene's action also has an effect on voice.

3. **What's your diagnosis?** Write a scene in which a frightened main character is talking to her relaxed doctor. Now switch the roles, with the doctor functioning as the main character, talking to a frightened secondary character. *What you'll learn:* This exercise will demonstrate for you the ways in which a character's emotional state and role in a scene have an effect on the diction of the narrative.

4. **The battle of the sexes.** Your narrator is looking on as a man tries to pick up a woman in a café. Write the scene once with your narrator feeling sympathetically toward this man, then rewrite it with your narrator standing in judgement of him. *What you'll learn:* This exercise should show you how voice can be colored by the narrator's attitude toward a character or characters.

Reading Exercise:
Tone of Voice in Jorge Luis Borges's "The Aleph"

Jorge Luis Borges's "The Aleph" is a strange story; the pitch of its diction places it purposely above the realms of everyday conversation. You may find that it tries your patience in the early going, but stick with it. Few stories provide us with a better object lesson in the ways tone of voice can add to a story's narrative power, giving the retelling of events a spice, a character, a strangeness and particularity that makes it seem, as poems were once described, like a "letter from another world."

QUESTIONS

1. Based on a reading of the first paragraph, what kind of a world would you say it is that Borges is inviting us into? Is this world emotionally cold or warm?

2. Examine Borges's word choices and the feeling tones these word choices convey. Using these cues, what can you infer about how the narrator feels about himself? About Carlos Argentino? About Beatriz Viterbo? What passages in the text would you use to support each of these opinions?

3. How would you describe the voices of Carlos Argentino and Borges the narrator? How are they the same? How are they different?

4. Within the story, where do you notice changes in voice? What purpose do you think these changes in voice serve?

5. If you're reading carefully, you'll notice one place where tone of voice changes dramatically. Where is this place, and what is the effect of the change on how you receive the story?

6. What emotion is the narrator feeling at the end of the story? What tone of voice cues convey this emotion to you?

PART TWO

BUILDING THE SCENE

Drama is action, sir, action, and not confounded philosophy.

—Luigi Pirandello
Six Characters in Search of an Author

In the writing assignment accompanying the second chapter, we defined the scene as that part of the story in which things are *dramatized*—that is, where events, physical actions, conversations, or other interactions between characters are described so vividly that it seems to the reader to be happening before her eyes. The scene is one of the basic components from which every story is constructed, and in this section we'll be examining the ways the writer can build it using some combination of three main elements: *setting* (the physical world of the scene), *characters* (which the writer renders through a process known as *characterization*), and *dialogue*, which the writer uses (often, but not always) to allow characters to interact. You've already written several dramatized scenes to get to this point in your story; in the next three chapters, to build your understanding of what makes a good scene, you're going to examine setting, characterization, and dialogue as the parts of two disassembled scenes. Then—in the section's fourth chapter, on dramatization—you'll reverse the process, putting these scenes together and dramatizing them fully.

How Action Becomes Praxis

In his *Poetics*, Aristotle touched on what makes the action the dramatized scene brings to the story so important. He defined tragedy as an "imitation [of life] that works through action," and held that if the actions making up a tragedy are dramatized with sufficient craft, the audience will be purified through the process of *catharsis*, purging negative emotions by exciting pity and fear. Good tragedy, he believed, is the highest form of Art.

Of course, modern conceptions of narrative include comedy as well as tragedy, but for our purposes, it's useful to emphasize Aristotle's belief that the emotional response he believed to be the goal of a narrative could only be achieved through the portrayal of action. As an example, let's look at Sophocles' play *Oedipus Rex*, which was Aristotle's favorite tragedy.

Here's a synopsis of events: in response to a prophecy, a boy is exiled as an infant. He is raised by a stranger, returns to his home as a man, unknowingly kills his biological father, the King, on the road and, equally unknowingly, marries his biological mother, the Queen. Then, on learning the truth and finding out that his acts have offended the gods and brought a plague on the city he rules, he tears his own eyes out and goes into self-imposed exile. Summarized this way, the story just seems outlandish, and so has little impact on us. If we are *shown* these events in dramatized scenes, however—if we see the full tragedy of King Oedipus's life acted out before us—his story presents us with a profound examination of character and fate that informs us anew every time it is staged.

> *Give up trying to explain. Fiction must convince our bodies for it to have any chance of convincing our minds.*
>
> —BONNIE FRIEDMAN,
> "THE STORY'S BODY:
> HOW TO GET THE MEANING IN"

Why should a collection of scenes have this effect? Aristotle said it was because when well-dramatized scenes are related as a narrative, what the audience experiences is not merely action, but *praxis*. Praxis (as Francis Fergusson defines it in his introduction to the Butcher translation of Aristotle's *Poetics*) "[is] not . . . events, or physical activity: it means, rather, the motivation from which deeds spring." Praxis, then, is *internal* movement or *motive* that comes before *external* movement or *action*. Each new scene plays a part in building the reader's understanding of this internal movement, and the story as a whole presents the reader with the working out of praxis to its necessary ends.

Exposition, Summary, and Jump Cuts

While the dramatized scene is indispensable to the story, few stories are all action, and one dramatized scene doesn't often flow into the next. Instead, scenes usually alternate with *jump cuts* and passages of *exposition* and *summary*, which act as transitions between them.

> *Before a thing can be a symbol it must be a thing. It must do its job as a thing in the world before and during and after you have projected all your meaning all over it.*
>
> —BONNIE FRIEDMAN,
> "THE STORY'S BODY:
> HOW TO GET THE MEANING IN"

Jump cut is a term adapted from film. In fiction, it identifies a place in the story where the action stops at the end of a scene, then picks up again at another point, in another place and/or time. Where a jump cut occurs, the action that takes place between one scene and the next is implied rather than summarized.

A jump cut is generally used when the action that *would* take place in the stretch of time is unimportant—the space, for instance, between the time two characters set for a lunch date and the date itself. It can also be used as a way to create tension—when, for example, what happens between one scene and the next will be revealed later in the story rather than being dramatized between those scenes.

Exposition is that part of a play or narrative in which the writer conveys the background information the reader needs in order to understand characters and action. The first paragraph of Judith Claire Mitchell's story "A Man of Few Words" provides an example of exposition:

> Only minutes after he died at age seventy-eight Ike Grossbart had come to understand he could enjoy, one more time, a pleasure from his life. It was up to him to choose which pleasure that would be. Ike was surprised and grateful. He had been expecting earthworms and dirt. Instead, or at least, first—here was a squirt of whipped cream to top off his time on earth.

This statement—offered to the reader before any action takes place in the story—gives the reader the context necessary to her understanding of the brief dramatized discussion of knishes that comes immediately after.

Summary is a description of events and their outcomes, rather than their dramatization. Immediately after the brief scene in which Ike and his family talk over who made the best knishes, Ike's death is offered in summary:

> It was a few hours later—the brother-in-law gone home, the daughter in the cafeteria having a late-night snack, the Grossbarts asleep—that death came for Ike. *Yitzchak ben Moshe,* death sang like a rabbi honoring a congregant by calling him to the pulpit to bless the Torah. Ike left the hospital room quietly, obediently. He was thankful he hadn't been asked to say good-bye to his wife; he could not imagine anything more difficult.

Objects, action, what was felt, what was said—these are the beakers of meaning, these are the little pots and vessels which catch the dew as it forms.

—BONNIE FRIEDMAN,
"THE STORY'S BODY:
HOW TO GET THE MEANING IN"

Though the fact of Ike's death is of central importance in the story, it is not as important as what happens *after* it. Therefore Mitchell doesn't linger with it, instead offering the event in graceful synopsis, using the summary as a transition that takes the reader into the story's *real* action—Ike's pilgrimage to Yonah Shlissel's.

The Parts That Make Up the Parts That Make Up the Whole

Taking it as a given that scenes, helped by exposition, summary, and jump cuts, build on one another and have different functions in the story as a whole, let's talk a bit more about how individual scenes are shaped. We'll do this by looking at the components that make up a dramatized scene.

One way we can conceive of the essence of a dramatized scene is by using a very simple equation: *Situation + Character = Action*. "Situation" we can define as the physical details of setting (which we'll talk more about in the next chapter), combined with the circumstances that bring the scene's character or characters into this setting. The "character" part of the equation refers to more than merely the people who populate your story; it refers to your representation of those people so that the ways they act and speak and think seem real and recognizable, or at least plausible, to your reader. The process through which believable characters are created is captured under the rubric *characterization,* and we'll be examining it in the second chapter in this section, after we've examined setting. Dialogue is another important element of many, if not most, well-wrought scenes, as it is one of the clearest, most illustrative, and economical ways of expressing character and exploring relationship and conflict between characters. We'll address this aspect of scene in more detail after we've explored character.

Add a carefully drawn situation to a fully realized, deeply imagined character and the result is plausible action, which—because of its plausibility, its "reality"—will engage your reader and flow naturally into the other scenes of the narrative.

Let's follow up this rather abstract formula with an illustration. We'll begin with the merest schematic of a scene—that is, a statement of a character and a statement of a situation.

> Character: A boy
> Situation: He eats his breakfast in the kitchen of the house

Offered this way, the pairing of character and situation doesn't provide a very promising beginning for a scene that is supposed to take us deeper into a story and add narrative momentum to it. At best, we have a picture of a generic boy eating his morning meal. Given these bare facts, it's tough to imagine what significant action would come out of their combination. He eats breakfast; what are we supposed to learn from this? How will this help make his story worth reading?

Now let's add some nuance to character and situation and see what happens to our feeling about the possibilities that bringing them together might have for the scene:

> Character: A skinny, red-haired, seven-year-old boy named Robert. He is rather dreamy, and he'd rather draw pictures than do anything else. He had an older sister, Nancy, whom he loved very much, who died of leukemia two years before.
>
> Situation: Robert is eating breakfast on a bright, cold Monday morning just before Christmas vacation. The kitchen in which he's eating is very clean and modern, and the highly polished table is set with white dishes and gleaming flatware. Robert is hiding from his mother the fact that he's failing most of his classes in the second grade. Over the weekend he was supposed to have given his mother a note from his teacher about his grades, but he couldn't face the shame. His mother knows he's troubled about something, and she's

fixing his favorite breakfast—French toast and sausages—to make him feel better.

With these new details, if we think about bringing character and situation together here, it's much easier to imagine a complex and interesting action emerging as the result. We know more about the character than the fact that he's male: We can picture him (skinny, red hair, seven years old), he's got characteristics (dreamy, maybe a budding artist), and he has problems: a grief he's carrying around inside him, unresolved; trouble at school; and an inability to tell his mother. The situation makes a much more immediate appeal to our senses (a cold, bright winter morning, Christmas and vacation hanging like a charge in the air, the smells of cooking sausages and French toast perfuming the spotless kitchen), it provides another character (the mother), and holds within it the seeds of conflict (he has to tell his mother what's going on and is not certain how she'll react). As we think over actions that might come out of the combination of character and situation, questions emerge: Does Robert's trouble at school come from his dreamy nature? Is it tied to unresolved grief over his sister's death? How does the fact that his mother is fixing his favorite breakfast affect him? Does it make him feel better, or more miserable because he's deceiving her? Will he tell her about his grades or not? How will she react if he does tell her? Will she be angry? How will it affect Robert if she is? Will she be sympathetic? Will that make Robert feel better or worse?

Whatever the answers to these questions might be, one thing is certain: in dramatizing them, the writer of Robert's story would tell the reader more about him, and the action that emerged from this deeply imagined pairing of character and situation would be more likely to be plausible and to produce energy—energy that would carry over into the scenes that follow.

Making the Action Plausible

Plausibility deserves further examination here. Plausibility doesn't mean that the action produced when character and situation come together has to conform to our everyday experience with reality. Rather, it means that the careful combination of character and situation should produce action that supports the story's *own* reality—i.e., what it leads the reader to expect of the world it contains. Readers have enormous tolerance for confusing or bewildering action, as long as they feel that it's rooted in a believable character and in understandable circumstances, that things will cohere at some point, that the action is working to some purpose. If, though, at any point your reader begins to think: Hmm. I don't think the writer is in control here, you've lost that reader, and the spell of the story is broken. By all means make your story's action strange, but make it strange in a way that makes sense in the context of the story's other action, and makes it possible for your reader to stay engaged.

Show, Don't Tell: Right or Wrong?

Flannery O'Connor once said that "fiction writing is very seldom a matter of saying things; it is a matter of showing things." Too often, this admonition gets oversimplified into *show, don't tell,* and is used as a club on apprentice writers to make them do everything with action. Scene is only appropriate, though, when summarizing action rather than dramatizing it would rob the story of the power present in what the Irish writer and folklorist Marie Heaney has referred to as "the music of what happens." Don't write a scene unless the action it contains tells the reader something absolutely critical and adds momentum. When it stops informing the reader, stops pumping necessary energy into the narrative, stop the scene.

5

SETTING

*The axis of the earth sticks out visibly through
the centre of each and every town and city.*

—Oliver Wendell Holmes, Sr.
The Autocrat of the Breakfast Table

There are places so intrinsic to our understanding of the world and of ourselves that
we will remember them for as long as memory lasts. These are the places where we
were nursed as infants or where we lay paralyzed by our fear of the dark as toddlers.
They are schoolrooms in which we learned the limits of the world, learned to write
our names, and sang for our grandparents at Christmas. They are the places where we
wrestled with belief and unbelief, where we first made love, where we first encountered death. The drama of being begins its unfolding in these first rooms, these first
houses, amid these first landscapes—new for each of us, the world created anew as
each person grows to encompass it. This anchors our particular worlds within us. We
do not think to separate place from memory any more than we thought in childhood
to separate the mountain, streetscape, or meadow from our view of it from front
porch, kitchen, or bedroom window.

Many writers find that as they begin to work at writing fiction, images they hadn't
thought of for years, sometimes for decades, begin to return, presenting themselves as
settings. A writer who left a country childhood behind for the city long before may
begin to find that her stories are set amid the features of the landscape where she
grew up: fields of corn, five-mile prospects the harvest opened to her view from
school-bus windows, the slow progress of storms across wide-open country. She remembers the way she learned to read the coming of the fall in the color of weeds in
roadside ditches, or the progress of winter in the condition of ice in farm ponds or in
the quality of light that came obliquely in through a window. As she frames her fiction, it is inevitable that these fields, these views, these storms, these colors, that
light, and those original landscapes should be among the tools she uses as she tries to
deliver meaning to her readers. Each writer is challenged to explain the world, and
the world as it lives in her memory—original, intrinsic, and pure—is often her best
argument.

This isn't to say that you ought always to write about the place where you grew up, nor is it to say that you can only create legitimately from what you have known personally and intimately. More, this is to support the point that setting affects us profoundly. Because this is true in life, it is also true in fiction. You don't have to have grown up amid the settings your story features, but you have to write about them with such vividness, such faithfulness to the settings' truth, that your reader is convinced you did.

Ernest Hemingway began his story "Big Two-Hearted River: Part I": "The train went up the track out of sight, around one of the hills of burnt timber." His setting comes before he even introduces his character, Nick Adams. This is because setting is vital to our understanding of Nick's shattered condition and the cure Nick is seeking for it. In his telling of this story and "Big Two-Hearted River: Part II" Hemingway gives us the larger meaning Nick searches for in the woods of northern Michigan— the communion and healing he finds there that he could find in no other place, no other way. By making his way through the precincts of his former, innocent happiness, Nick rejoins the world. In Cormac McCarthy's novel *All the Pretty Horses*, the southwest is an enormous stage on which the author sets the small, terrible drama of his hero John Grady Cole's coming of age: "Dark and cold and no wind and a thin gray reef beginning along the eastern rim of the world. He walked out on the prairie and stood holding his hat like some supplicant to the darkness over them all and he stood there for a long time." This opening gives us the landscape as a wide proscenium on which John Grady Cole's destiny will be played out. The spareness and scope of this setting help McCarthy shape a diction inevitably different from that he used in telling the Tennessee-set stories of his earlier books.

These examples are arbitrary—two chosen from among dozens, scores of stories produced by writers at work during any period of literature's history. The point would have been the same if the examples had been excerpted from Jane Austen's *Mansfield Park* or Henry Roth's *Call It Sleep* or Marjorie Kinnan Rawlings's *The Yearling* or Toni Morrison's *Beloved*: narratives that are rooted strongly in the particulars of place are the rule rather than the exception. Rooms, houses, and landscapes are our larger bodies. The heart is fixed in them, attached to the rituals, the views, the habits of seeing and being we developed there. Such a deep truth has an inevitable place in our fictions. We judge the work that lacks these connections as flawed. It floats above the page, unmoored.

> "*H*ow do you write? My answer is that I start with the trees and keep right on straight ahead. I start with these companions of this place, each fixed into the soil of where it is, and sometimes the rock or rocks and very little else, and after that the going is not only easy, it is very nearly rollicking, for the tree is a thing of great attachments, and it puts forth all manner of leaves, abundantly, and each leaf is the same, but not precisely so, so that noticing this repetitive imprecision leads to everything else, especially life, especially speculation and especially the last act of life, the unknown abandoment of tree, branch, twig, leaf, bud, flower, fruit and self."
>
> —WILLIAM SAROYAN,
> "STARTING WITH A TREE, AND FINALLY
> GETTING TO THE DEATH OF A BROTHER"

Creating a Setting

So, where does this leave us in more concrete terms—that is, in a chapter on setting? Some elaboration on the brief definition for setting given in the introduction to this section seems in order. "Setting" refers most obviously to place, but it is more than this. *It is the physical, emotional, economic, cultural, even the spiritual ecologies within which our stories are constructed.* It is the air your characters breathe, the neighborhoods they live in, the food they eat, the parties they get invited to, the churches they attend, the offices they work in, the stores where they find the clothing they like, the way they decorate their homes for the holidays they observe. In all its moods and lights, all its atmospheres, your characters interact with their environment, their setting, much as if they were interacting with another living being. Setting affects their moods, guides their actions, narrows their choices or widens them. It can be cast as malevolent, benevolent, or any state in between. Your story must reflect your awareness of this. To help you begin to prepare this foundation, let's examine some questions you should ask yourself about your setting.

WHAT'S GOING TO HAPPEN IN THIS SETTING?

Think about what you want to have happen after the scene you wrote in response to the last assignment on tone of voice. As you think about your next scene, think also about *where* you want that action to take place. If your main character is arguing with someone, what would be the best setting for that argument? Would it be a kitchen? A garden? A dorm room? A nightclub? If your main character is going to be struggling with grief or loneliness, what would be the best setting for this struggle? Think of your scene's setting the way you would think of the setting for a stone in a ring: what setting will display your character to best advantage—the way a ring's setting displays a diamond or sapphire?

WHAT IS YOUR SETTING'S "EMOTIONAL TEMPERATURE"?

Will your scene be a cool, retrospective depiction of the conflict that arises between a pair of pool hustlers? Are you going to be writing a close and stifling account of a character's humiliation by a bully in high school? Your description of your setting can serve to support the release of emotion in your scene. It can also serve to damp emotion down, or to make it stand out in stark contrast (think of a screaming argument that takes place in a hushed museum). Whether your setting itself is hot or cold or somewhere in between, you should put some thought into how your setting will be appropriate to a framing of the scene's events.

WHERE AND HOW DO YOU WANT YOUR READER TO ENTER THE SETTING?

What will show your characters in the proper light, the light that will help your reader to see these characters as *real* and *complete*? Think of it as though you were a set designer for a play. Set designers consider the metaphoric weight of every assemblage of objects and the way these assemblages prepare the audience for its encounter with characters and events. This is also what you should do. Naturally, you're not going to describe every setting in exhaustive detail. That would quickly become tiresome, and anyway would lead to your reader losing contact with the scene's action. However, your description of each scene's setting should, in one way or another, be appropriate to your reader's encounter with the truth, the part of praxis, that this scene in your story presents.

HOW WOULD YOU SHOOT THIS SETTING IF YOU WERE MAKING A MOVIE?

You also need to think about helping your reader to navigate the setting. Many beginning writers present setting in a bewildering welter of objects, furnishings, and characters appearing in no particular order. This can make it impossible for the reader to figure out what the writer is trying to accomplish with the scene. The next time you watch a movie, pay attention to how the filmmaker handles setting. Filmmakers, if they know what they're doing, bring the viewer carefully into critical scenes, and they keep the camera focused on the scene's important action. The camera doesn't wander all over; it takes in information that's necessary to the viewer's understanding of the scene's mood and the characters' relationships with one another, then focuses on the action.

ARE YOU APPEALING TO THE FULL RANGE OF THE SENSES?

Humans process information using five senses, not just one, and if you describe setting in your story using only sight—the first sense through which most of us experience an environment—you may be missing an opportunity to add tremendously to the vividness of your scenes. By all means, appeal to the reader's eyes, but use sound, smell, texture, and taste to register your characters' experiences as well.

HOW MUCH DETAIL IS NECESSARY?

Just as you should take care that you don't present the details of setting in a confusing way, you should also make sure you don't overwhelm your reader with the volume of detail you present. In a scene where your character is just going to walk through a grove of trees, stop to light a cigarette, then move on, it won't be necessary for you to catalog all of the grove's physical details—the types of trees growing there, the species of birds on the limbs, the exact color and strength of the moonlight falling through the boughs, the smell of the decaying leaves, the sound of a distant barking dog. A detail or two will suffice. On the other hand, you should linger and provide meticulous setting detail in a scene where that setting's atmosphere is important to what you want the scene to accomplish. A woman waiting, terrified, in a doctor's office for the results of a biopsy might drink in every detail, turning them obsessively in her mind, sensing in them the gathering of some malign force. You can bog your reader down with too much detail, or leave her starving for it. Be careful to do neither.

Something ignoble, loathsome, undignified attends all associations between people and has been transferred to all objects, dwellings, tools, even the landscape itself. —BERTOLT BRECHT

DOES YOUR DESCRIPTION OF SETTING SUPPORT THE SCENE'S ACTION?

If you've ever read Charles Dickens's "A Christmas Carol," you may have noticed how hard Dickens worked to suit the atmosphere in each section of the story to the characters and events it contained. Dickens was an avid theater-goer and an enthusiastic amateur thespian; he learned a lot from the dramatists of his time. One could imagine him as the manager of a prop department, making sure all the furnishing and appurtenances were precisely right for each play. He seems, in his prose, to have been *that* particular, and his particularity makes the worlds of his stories among the most physically vivid and clearly evoked in our canon. Here's one example from "A Christmas Carol"—a description of Scrooge's room remade into a stage for his meeting with the Ghost of Christmas Present:

> It was his own room. There was no doubt about that. But it had undergone a surprising transformation. The walls and ceiling were so hung with living green, that it looked a perfect grove, from every part of which, bright gleaming berries glistened. The crisp leaves of holly, mistletoe, and ivy reflected back the light, as if so many little mirrors had been scattered there; and such a mighty blaze went roaring up the chimney, as that dull petrifaction of a hearth had never known in Scrooge's time, or Marley's or for many and many a winter season gone. Heaped up on the floor, to form a kind of throne, were turkeys, geese, game, poultry, brawn, great joints of meat, sucking-pigs, long wreaths of sausages, mince-pies, plum-puddings, barrels of oysters, red-hot chestnuts, cherry-cheeked apples, juicy oranges, luscious pears, immense twelfth-cakes, and seething bowls of punch, that made the chamber dim with their delicious steam. In easy state upon this couch, there sat a jolly Giant, glorious to see; who bore a glowing torch, in shape not unlike Plenty's horn, and held it up, high up, to shed its light on Scrooge, as he came peeping around the door.

Because of the richness and intricacy of Dickens's description of the room and especially of the tremendous throne of food, the fact that the ghost is a "jolly giant" isn't that great a surprise, and the description sets the tone for the business he will transact with Scrooge. The description of setting functions as a foundation for the scene that follows it. See if you can use setting as vividly—and as appropriately—in your own work.

HOW DO YOUR CHARACTERS' EMOTIONAL STATE AND THE SETTING AFFECT EACH OTHER?

Think about the narrating or point of view character in the scene you're trying to write. What kinds of emotions is she feeling? What are her circumstances as she enters the scene? A character's emotional state will have an effect on what she sees and how she sees it, and this is an important consideration if you're telling a story using a first person or a close-third-person point of view. A woman standing in the

Courage is nine-tenths context. What is courageous in one setting can be foolhardy in another and even cowardly in a third.

—JOSEPH EPSTEIN, *WOMEN'S QUARTERLY*

doorway of a room and looking in would have a much different experience of the setting she sees if she had just won the lottery than she would if she'd just squandered her last dime. The effect can run the other way, too: a surgeon who fancies himself king of the world might have a hard time supporting his inflated opinion of himself if he were to find himself marooned (for instance) by the unexpected failure of his expensive Land Rover's engine on a vast savanna, in the middle of a pride of lions. Setting and situation affect character and character affects setting and situation. It is a dialogue.

Progressing Writing Exercise #5:
Writing Where Things Happen

After completing the writing exercises in the first four chapters, you have a possible beginning and a few proto-scenes for your story. What happens next? To open your exploration of some possible answers, you should consult your cloud diagram again. Take a look at the second cloud—the one made up of possible situations. From this situation list you should work now to extract a number of possible settings for these situations. The settings you choose should have some conceptual link to what you've written so far, however tenuous that link might seem at this early stage.

Now consult the first cloud—the emotional states cloud—which you arranged around your protagonist—and from this create a list of possible emotional states. The two completed lists might look something like this:

Setting	Emotional state
1. An abandoned chapel	1. Pained regret
2. The lot of a Christmas tree farm in the middle of June	2. Foolish hope
3. The killing floor of a slaughterhouse	3. Anger after betrayal
4. A showroom for caskets	4. Incredulity
5. A dog kennel	5. Religious awe
6. An art museum	6. Confused grief
7. A canyon in a western national park	7. Ashamed penitence
8. A truck stop restaurant at 3am, somewhere in the empty country along I-80	8. Bewildered fear
9. An empty apartment, newly cleaned and painted, ready for moving in.	9. Frustrated greed

Next you should choose two emotional states and two settings from each column, pairing each emotional state with a setting, like so:

Setting	Emotional state
1. The lot of a Christmas tree farm in the middle of June	1. Religious awe
2. An art museum	2. Confused grief

Now imagine looking at each setting through the eyes of a character whose emotions are dominated by the emotional state you have linked it with. This setting should also contain one other character beside your observer character. Using these givens, write a description of each setting. One restriction, and it's an important one: however much you might want to, *don't have the character do anything, or say anything to the other character*; just have him or her *observe* the setting.

What you'll learn: Characters are affected by their environment much as they are affected by other fully realized characters. Ideally, this exercise will illustrate this for you, and you will be able to use each of these settings in scenes you'll write as you move your story forward.

STUDENT EXAMPLES

↺ *Jeremy's Response*

THE RECTORY

David and Father McLaughlin walked up the steps onto the porch of the priest's home. Outside, David was struck by the otherworldly appearance of the house; it seemed to belong to another era, in another place, not in the bustling concrete and steel of New York City. The Gothic style house reminded him of old pictures he had seen long ago in history textbooks describing life more than a century before. As he looked at the house, David felt the city behind him disappear. For a while, at least, he wouldn't have to deal with that wild world anymore.

The two men walked through the big oak wood door into the rectory. Directly inside was the living room. The room was warm and inviting, with rose-colored wood paneling covering the walls and plush dark red carpet under foot. On the far wall of the room was a fireplace out of use during the warm summer months. Beside the fireplace sat a series of pokers and tools as well as a small rack holding a few stray logs left over from the previous winter. The mantle held a series of particularly cherished trinkets and religious items that Fr. McLaughlin's parishioners had given him throughout the years. A large framed image of the Virgin Mary hung on the wall above, an image of her David knew he had never seen before and yet still instantly recognized as vaguely familiar. She looked David straight in the eye, peering directly into his soul, crying softly with a tear in her eye. He shuddered and looked away quickly. A moment later when he looked back she gazed to the sky with tearless eyes.

"Can I get you anything?" broke in Fr. McLaughlin, bringing David back to the present. "Something to drink, perhaps?"

"Um, sure," said David, "anything would be great, really."

"Why don't you have a seat and I'll be back in just a moment," Fr. McLaughlin said as he ducked down the hall on the right toward the kitchen.

A leather couch and loveseat combination furnished the living room, along with matching end tables and two beautiful brass lamps. David sat down on the loveseat that faced the fireplace, with his back toward the big picture window looking out over the street. He noticed the bookshelves on his left and browsed through a few of the titles, mostly religious texts with a few mystery novels and random self-help books thrown in. He looked around the room again and started to look outside of it for the first time. He noticed the staircase directly across the room from the front door. Somehow he had missed seeing it when they came in earlier; the living room had completely monopolized his attention. My bedroom must be up the stairs, he thought, and yawned.

Father McLaughlin came back into the room with two cold glasses of lemonade.

"This is a very nice room," said David, accepting the drink. It was quite sour.

"Thank you, I'm glad you feel comfortable here. Would you like to see the upstairs?"

"Yes, very much."

Father McLaughlin led David up the stairs and into the long hallway. Along the corridor were a series of photographs that David thought must be the priest's family. As they moved along the hall, the priest pointed toward a couple of closed doors—saying one was his office, another his bedroom—before they came to a door he opened and encouraged David to enter.

"This will be where you can sleep tonight," said Fr. McLaughlin.

The guest room was nearly full with the enormous bed covered by a beautiful, hand-sewn quilt. A bible sat open on the bedside table and a small crucifix hung on the wall just above the bed. David walked slowly toward the bed, "Thank you very much," he said absently to Fr. McLaughlin, who stood silent in the doorway. David set his lemonade on the bedside table and lay down on the bed. He felt himself sink in and knew it wouldn't be long until he dozed off. The last thing he noticed before he fell asleep was the painted portrait of a man and woman, presumably husband and wife, on the wall across the room. Fr. McLaughlin shut the door gently and left David to dream. In his dream, David grew up in this house with his parents, parents he had never known in real life, parents he only knew from the portrait on the wall across the room from his bed.

THE CITY

Outside the bus station, David encountered the New York City he had been dreaming about for years. Only today, after having nearly everything he owned stolen before getting off the bus, the city was still not entirely real. David looked at the people, the cars, and the world with the same surreal bewilderment that had always accompanied his dreams while still at home in rural Kansas. David grew more frustrated. The city and he were being thrown together under the worst possible circumstances, without compassion or introduction. They weren't meeting as friends like David had always imagined. David knew that, as soon as he walked out of the station, the city was not going to go easy on him.

The bus station opened onto a crowded sidewalk where a sea of people swam by David, picking him up and forcing him along. Having little choice, and not knowing where to go or what to do regardless, David all too willingly joined the group. From his place in the crowd moving along the sidewalk, he was able to get his first experience of the city, to be taken on an anonymous tour, guided by those who knew the city best. To his left was the busy street full of traffic. Hordes of yellow cabs going in every direction, a few other cars, and a couple buses filled the road. David remembered how there was a time that he didn't believe that yellow taxis actually existed;

he had only seen them on TV, of course, and they seemed as much an invention as cars that could fly. He looked up at the buildings rising above the street toward the sky.

Suddenly he felt small, even smaller than he had before at the bus station, although he hadn't thought it possible. Billboards covered the sides of the buildings and store fronts comprised the ground floor as far as David could see, people moving in and out, buying and selling, more commerce than a small Midwestern town would see in a lifetime in every minute of every day. The thought proved too much for David and he tore his eyes away from the stores. Plenty of time for that later, once I have some money again, he thought.

David gazed into the crowded sidewalk where he moved among the virtual tidal wave of people crashing into and swirling around the buildings and streets. Were any of these people lost and alone like he felt? Would they admit it if they were? Or had all of these people adapted, evolved, into the Modern City Man who could survive in this environment. Each being was utterly individual; no one looked around or at each other, no one spoke, no one cared. All had mind and purpose apart from all others. Yet, at the same time, David felt a strange comfort as he moved with this great herd of people, millions strong, fenced in by concrete and steel and traffic lights and crosswalks, raised for the business industry, for Wall Street instead of the sale barn, to crunch numbers rather than chew cud. David began to understand the city in this brief moment of relative clarity. The sidewalk drive was something great and uncontrollable, something natural in the city, like swimming with a school of fish or running with the pack. The people moved as much for protection as for comfort, even if they didn't understand—they were moving by instinct. The city was full of predators of all shapes and sizes. These streets were primal, instinctual, a giant constructed habitat for double-breasted males and skirted females. New York City became the human house extension of the Central Park Zoo, constructed by the same animals it was meant to enclose, for their own amusement and protection. And no one could even see the bars. On display for some gods or devils that had long ago gotten bored and gone home.

David ducked out of the moving crowd and rounded the corner. He nearly ran into a hot dog vendor. David was hungry, but he realized how little money he had left. The commercial city again tapped him on the shoulder and whispered in his ear that he couldn't last long on the measly $15 he had left. David looked around again at the giant concrete and steel structures surrounding him, at the people walking by, and the traffic in the street. Where had all the space gone? He pined briefly for the wide-open fields of the Midwest, where he at least knew how to live. The city leaned over him, stared down at him, seemed to be taunting him and drawing him out for a fight. David heard laughter.

"Hey kid, if you're not gonna buy nothin', beat it, willya?" David looked up at the hot dog vendor, shook his head dejectedly, and walked on down the street.

Commentary As exercise has succeeded exercise, it seems Jeremy has gotten more comfortable working within this frame, and has been able to push past his story's more familiar particulars (a small-town boy goes to the big city and is robbed on arrival) and into fresh territory. The details he uses to conjure the rectory are quite well imagined:

the rack that still held a few logs left over from the previous winter; the bookcases that held mystery novels and self-help books in addition to the religious texts one might expect; the lemonade that was "quite sour." The description of the city made it seem as if it was being seen through eyes that hadn't seen its like before. For all his naïveté, though, David still seems intelligent and self-possessed enough to form a fairly sophisticated metaphor to describe the life he finds surging along the streets; this takes us into who David is as a character, as all good scene-setting does.

Concerns   The first thing to notice is the obvious: in having his characters move, speak, and interact, Jeremy broke the rules of the assignment. That consideration aside, there were also a few missteps ("Gothic" architecture, for instance, is from a period quite a bit further back in time than a century), as well as places where Jeremy missed opportunities to use elements of setting to provide his reader with more salient information about his characters. For instance, when David noticed "a series of particularly cherished trinkets" lining the mantle, Jeremy might have let us know what a few of those trinkets were, and what it was (a high state of polish? a careful arrangement? artfully directed track lighting?) that conveyed to David the objects' value to their owner. Also, in a few places (although in many fewer places than in his previous exercises) Jeremy lapsed into abstractions, which end up being opaque and uninformative to the reader. For instance, in the city setting, he told the reader that David looked at the street scene with "the same surreal bewilderment that had always accompanied his dreams while [he was] still at home in rural Kansas." It's the phrase "surreal bewilderment" that is most troubling—first because it's an unintentional inversion ("the same sense of bewildering surreality that had accompanied his dreams" would be more appropriate). Second, and more importantly, "surreal bewilderment" is an abstraction—it tells us nothing about what David sees that he identifies as surreal, nor does it convey to us what was surreal to David about the dreams he had back home, nor, finally, does it convey to us how the dream and the reality are similar. The phrase asserts something without giving the reader the *concrete* means—i.e., illustration—that would enable him to understand it.

✄ *Sarah's Response*

FILMING OF A CLAIRE DANES MOVIE; MINT IS OBSESSED WITH CELEBRITY

At 6:00 A.M., Mint and Lindsay were among the earliest extras to arrive. Mint's mother handed them bagged lunches as they got out of the car, and they waited until she was out of sight to throw them away. They spoke to the guard and passed under the giant stucco arch that proclaimed AMAZO-LAND! They found themselves alone, and stopped short to take it all in, to appreciate the shivers of anticipation coursing up and down their spines. In the foreground, they faced trinket shops, candy shops, old-fashioned-photo shops, not yet opened for the day. Their window displays shone darkly. Beyond that, rides rose like giant metal skeletons from the trees and building tops. Mint blinked her eyes to regain depth perception, because it looked to her as she squinted into the distance that everything converged at one point; the epic rollercoasters, strange spherical vehicles, tubes, swings, inexplicable towers, and the Ferris wheel, the crowning image of Amusement, all sprouting from the same square foot of cement. That was where she would find Claire Danes. The paved walkway before them was clean and empty, like a yellow brick road leading them to adventure, promising, promising, promising. They started walking, and as they passed *La Chocolaterie*, a waft of chocolate scent hit them hard. Mint's acute sense of smell wouldn't let her enjoy it, though. She couldn't ignore the underscents: the sourness of last night's hot dogs, dropped popcorn kernels, cotton candy tubes festering behind trash cans where the janitorial staff didn't care to reach.

MINT'S POSTER-COVERED ROOM AT 2:00 A.M. ON TUESDAY; MINT HAS INSOMNIA

Sarah's Note: This scene doesn't have a second character yet, but it will soon, when Mint's mother comes into Mint's room.

It was 2:00 A.M., and the moon had just risen high enough or sunk low enough (Mint wasn't sure) to enter the square of the window at the head of her bed. Frustrated almost to tears by three hours and twenty-eight minutes of longing for sleep, Mint surveyed her room. There was something foreboding about the space right now; familiar objects made foreign by the cold moonlight. Her black corduroy armchair, shredded by some long-dead cat, hulked in the corner menacingly. The bookshelves that flanked the door opposite her bed sagged under the weight of former books—last week, Mint's mother had donated everything marked Young Adult to an inner-city school. Her old wooden bureau had grown a face in the moonlight, knot-eyes and a jutting top-drawer jaw. Mint looked away, embarrassed that she still saw monsters in the dark. The new posters gleamed in a minor key, as if the optimistic neons of smirking pop stars were revolted by the grittiness of dark childhood things. Mint wanted so badly to sleep.

Commentary The features of the physical world are one of the best tools writers can use in giving the reader access to the story's characters and the conflicts in which they find themselves embroiled. You can tell your reader quite a bit about the inner life of the least articulate or least self-revealing character by letting that character make a simple visual sweep of a neighbor's living room, and can simultaneously tell us everything we need to know about the neighbor, too. Each of Sarah's settings was richly physically described, and a real pleasure to read for that reason. Readers love reading about worlds they feel they could walk into, and each of these scenes offers such a world.

Concerns The most important question, in considering these two settings, is their navigability. For the reader to get the full benefit of contact with the physical environment of a scene, the writer must make it an environment the reader feels he can enter. Using this measure, the scene in which Mint and Lindsay enter the amusement park could use a bit of work. Sarah presents some arresting images, and the notion of finding her idol amid the park's created landscape is metaphorically apt, but it's a bit hard to visualize the park's layout, given Sarah's description.

Also, the experience Sarah presents of these two settings is (except for Mint's experience of the early morning smells of the amusement park) primarily visual. This begs the question of how much more effective both the scenes might have been if

Sarah had made more of an appeal to the other senses as well. Was the air cool in the morning? What sounds did Mint and Lindsay hear as they made their way along the street into the heart of Amazo-land? Was the window open in Mint's room, and could she hear sounds from the street, crickets loud in the bushes, night birds, a neighbor's stereo? Were there textures in her bedclothes that annoyed her? Could she catch a whiff of the popcorn her mother was microwaving down the stairs? One or two of these sorts of details from other sectors of the sensorium might round these settings out, giving the reader a more informative experience with the scenes' physical world.

QUESTIONS FOR REVISION

1. How well have you rendered the setting in your previous scenes? Are there any places you should do more to increase the reader's contact with the story by providing additional detail?

2. Conversely, have you *over*described your setting at any point, giving more detail than is really needed to support the action in any of your scenes?

3. Is your setting "cinematic"? Can your reader navigate the physical world of your scenes, or have you rendered scenes in a confusing or chaotic manner?

4. Do the details of your setting give the reader a window into your character's or characters' emotions and moods, making it unnecessary for you to name those emotions and moods?

5. Conversely, does setting contrast interestingly with your character's or characters' emotions and moods, in a way that makes emotions and moods stand out in relief?

6. Do you make sufficient use of all your characters' senses in describing their experience with setting?

Alternative Writing Exercises

1. **Rich man/poor man.** Two situations: in the first, you've just hit the lottery and you're coming into your bank to deposit your winnings; in the second, you've been called in by the loan officer at your bank because you've missed two car payments. In each case, imagine you've just walked into the lobby and describe the setting. *What you'll learn:* Our emotions act as lenses through which we see the world, with whatever we're feeling at any given moment having a profound effect on what we see and how we see it. Your characters' reactions and perceptions should reflect this truth.

2. **Good room/bad room.** First imagine walking into a room in a good mood. Write a setting that could spoil that mood. Now imagine walking into a room in a really foul mood, and describe a setting that could make you feel better. *What you'll*

learn: While our moods color our perceptions, we are not emotionally imperme-able. Everyone has had the experience of a bright and cheerful environment clearing off a foul mood (or vice-versa). Because this happens in life, it can also happen in your fiction, and this exercise should reflect this truth.

3. **Name that emotion.** A woman sits alone at kitchen table. Giving your reader no cues other than setting, write two separate descriptions of setting that convey two different emotional states. *What you'll learn:* A skillful writer can make the reader understand a character's mood by using the character's perceptions of the setting in which she is located.

4. **What's in the package?** Your job in this exercise is to walk into a room where a box wrapped in brown paper rests on a table. Describe the box once looking at it through the eyes of a police bomb squad member sent to defuse the bomb the box contains. When you've finished this description, do it again, this time looking at the box through the eyes of a lonely or depressed student who's been expecting a care package from home. *What you'll learn:* Our perceptions of objects and settings are intimately affected by what we know (or don't know) about them. This exer-cise focuses on that fact.

Reading Exercise:
Setting in Wallace Stegner's "The Traveler"

Wallace Stegner does many things well in "The Traveler": his characterization is subtle and humane; the situation is at once admirably simple in its presentation and richly complicated in its possibilities; and the relationship the author establishes between his protagonist and the lonely farm boy is compelling and psychologically complex. For our purposes in this chapter, though, it's interesting to look most closely at Steg-ner's masterful treatment of the physical world in which the story is set. Without his rich rendering of the nighttime winter landscape, the other elements of his story—character, situation, and interaction—would not have come to us with such clarity or vividness. Few writers can match Wallace Stegner in making a setting seem *inhabitable* as if the reader could step right into it. He makes sharp and economical use of the objects of the physical world, rendering landscapes that are rich, originally observed, and thematically appropriate.

QUESTIONS

1. How does Stegner use the features of his setting to establish a mood for the story? What would you say that mood is?

2. How does Stegner use the features of his setting to help him characterize his pro-tagonist? Describe the salesman's character, and point to those places in the text where his actions in the face of the setting would seem to support your conclusions.

3. Do you think Stegner wants us to believe the traveler is in danger? What features of setting or landscape does he use, and how does he use them to convey the impression that he either is or isn't in peril?

4. There are several places in the story where the traveler's interaction with setting effects a change in his and the story's mood. Identify these places, and describe the changes that take place.

5. How would the story have been affected if Stegner had had the traveler's car break down at the top of the second long rise, where the risen moon is bright and clear? How would the story have been affected if he had broken down right at the farm?

6. How does Stegner establish for us the connection between the traveler and the boy? List the visual cues he gives us that make the connection clear.

6

CHARACTERIZATION

As he thinketh in his heart, so he is.

—Proverbs, 23:7

Although it's appearing here in the sixth chapter, characterization is actually a primary consideration in story writing. Stories often arise out of a deep consideration of how character is formed and how it is pulled apart. Chances are the work you've done so far has had a fair amount of characterization in it.

Characters Are What They Do

What does *characterization* mean? It's one of those terms of art that gets tossed about pretty liberally in fiction-writing classes, but that is too often insufficiently defined and thus poorly understood. We offered a simple working definition in the introduction to this section; Aristotle—as usual—offers one that's a little more complete.

In *Poetics* he calls character in narrative "that which reveals moral purpose, showing what kinds of things a man chooses or avoids." Further, Aristotle says that character is "that in accordance with which we say that the persons portrayed have a defined moral character," i.e., those features of soul or psyche which make them what they are, and lead them to do what they do.

So, how is the writer to accomplish this portrayal? Characterization is one area where showing is usually preferable to telling, because character emerges more immediately and vividly for the reader when presented in the frame of action that a scene provides. For example, compare the following two examples of characterization:

He was angry.

and

He pinched what was left of the cigarette between his fingers and brought it to his mouth. He drew on it so sharply I could hear the tobacco crackle as it burned.

Then with a quick movement he threw it down on the sidewalk and stepped on it, grinding his toe on the butt like it was the head of a snake that had tried to strike him.

The first example—"He was angry"—is just a naked statement, an *assertion* or *abstraction*. It doesn't conjure a picture, so it doesn't do much narrative work. The second example provides enough closely observed physical detail to allow you not only to know the character is angry, but to *see* him, and to picture how he expresses that anger in a way that begins to tell you who he is. Because this description shows you the character in motion, in action, it opens a door for you into who he is. It *shows*.

Imagine a friend, an enemy, a family member, and imagine describing him or her to a stranger. Your job is to render this person real—using basic details of height, weight, color of hair and eyes, skin tone—but carrying your description further still, to depths of subtlety that pass the physical—taste in music, for instance, or sense of humor, favorite meal, the fashions she favors, the cadences of his speech. Does your sister have a way of smiling that tells you she's embarrassed and another way of smiling that tells you she's angry? How would you convey to a reader these different smiles? Does your best friend have a way of clearing his throat that tells you he's lying? Can you convey your uncle's basic kindness, your boss's arrogance, by describing the way one stands, the way the other buys a pack of gum? Can you convey the crippled woman's sadness at the death of her dog not by naming her emotions, but by showing how she sees the evening light that strikes the furnishings of the room in which she sits? This is the work of characterization. In fiction writing, character emerges through the author's skillful presentation of the emotional meaning present in what the character does, says, and sees or responds to the situations, events, and other characters in the story.

> "*I spend a lot of time working on characters. I start off with a resume—a job application form that I have extended a little bit. I fill that out and sort of force myself to think about the characters. Then, if I am lucky, I will find a picture of my character in a magazine. I will go through hundreds of pictures to find pictures of my characters and pictures of their houses.*"
>
> —WALTER DEAN MYERS

The obvious implication is, as Aristotle says, that character unfolds best "in a setting of action," i.e., a scene. Aristotle says that the character expressed must be *appropriate* (the right kind of character to carry off the action portrayed), *possessed of recognizable human nature* (i.e., behaving in ways that don't strain our belief), and *consistent* (that is, not brave in one scene and cowardly in another—at least not without sufficient explanation).

Conflict is an important part of this action. Aristotle applauded the powerful instances of conflict that were so often a feature of Greek tragedy because, as he believed, character is revealed most deeply when it is being challenged or even pulled apart.

When you're reading a story and characterization is going right, you know it: you believe in the people the author puts before you. When the characterization is going wrong, you argue. You think to yourself: Would the bus driver really say that? Would a little girl know that? I don't understand why the waitress threw that plate at the cook. I don't believe the priest would lose his temper that way. When a reader starts asking these kinds of questions, the tell-me-a-story contract between writer and reader has been broken. The reader has grown suspicious because the writer has lost the reader's trust.

Avoid Types

Often a writer breaks his contract with the reader when he relies on *type*. The writer does this when he uses stock characters—the tough-guy private eye, the whore with a heart of gold, the mad scientist, the absent-minded professor, the bubble-headed blonde, the drunken Irishman, the lecherous old man, the mean and dried-up old woman. We could go on and on with these examples, but the main point is this: don't use them or any other cliché-ridden characterizations in your fiction. Because they do not take any energy in the writing, they do not *give* any energy in the reading. They're dead air in the stories they occupy and are an unmistakable sign of a lazy writer.

Treat Characters Respectfully

Connected to this caveat is another difficult but essential thing to remember: you as writer do not have the luxury of looking down on your characters. Even when you're writing stories that have nasty, abusive, reprehensible characters in them, you must avoid denying these characters their humanity. Everyone can agree that domestic violence is bad, and it's easy to despise someone who indulges in it, so it's quite easy to write a story in which the reader is encouraged to dislike a wife beater. While this is true, it's unlikely a story set in such black-and-white terms would be interesting. It's much harder—but much more rewarding for your reader and, ultimately, much truer to life—if you write a story in which the wife beater is rendered, through skillful characterization, as a man who is not merely evil, but whose evil is mixed with regret, sorrow, even flashes of real kindness. The first man is a *type;* the second is a fully realized character, complex and fascinating to watch, more representative of the people we meet in the real world. Even the person who seems most simple and uncomplicated on the surface is *infinitely* complicated beneath the surface. Stories populated with shallowly drawn characters almost invariably end up being moralizing, dead, inert.

> "*T*he question becomes: what is the appropriate behavior for a man or a woman in the midst of this world, where each person is clinging to his piece of debris? What is the proper salutation between people as they pass each other in this flood? These are the things that concern my work today."
>
> —LEONARD COHEN

Humor is another area where characterization can go wrong. You can write a funny story, but you should avoid laughing *at* your characters. The reader's deepest laughter arises from feelings of *sympathy* with the characters—not from watching them humiliated and made small.

Round and Flat Characters

As was suggested in the definition of characterization above, good characterization comes out of the author's strategic consideration of the role each character plays in the story. Those who play relatively minor roles in the story are more simply rendered, while more careful characterization is saved for those whose role in the narrative demands deeper and more subtle depiction.

British writer E. M. Forster addressed this in his essay "Flat and Round Characters." Flat characters, he said, "are constructed round a single idea or quality: when there is more than one factor in them, we get the beginning of the curve towards the round." Flat characters, he says "can be expressed in a single sentence." Round characters are the only ones "who are fit to perform tragically for any length of time and [the only characters who] can move us to any feelings except humor and appropriateness." To use characters from Forsters's own work as examples, Cyril Vise—Lucey Honeychurch's suitor in *A Room with a View*—provides an example of a relatively flat character, while Leonard Bast, the doomed bank clerk in *Howard's End*, is round.

You should keep the usefulness of flat characters in mind as you write. Some will walk onto the story's stage, speak a line or two, transact the brief business the story assigns to them, then exit. Much of the art of characterization consists of carefully balancing depth of detail against narrative necessity.

Allow Characters to Declare Themselves

You should be ready for your characters to surprise you. It's one of the appealing strangenesses of fiction writing that, while you may begin with a very solid idea of a character's role in your story, it may develop that, as the story unrolls, the character has very different ideas. That's great—or it can be. The character may be a messenger from your unconscious, telling you that this story is meant to be more, deeper, different than you thought it would be. You may start out writing a solemn story about a funeral. Then the corpse's crazy Uncle Mike shows up, and the somber proceedings quickly become a drunken party. You may think the person standing behind your protagonist in line at the convenience store is a nobody—someone who is supposed to utter one sentence and then disappear. She may not consent to do what you want her to, though. She may want to have a complete conversation with him. She may ask him to hold the lottery ticket she's just bought, to keep it safe from her controlling boyfriend who . . .

> "Can the novelist entirely control the ideas in her text, or conceal herself among them? There's the phenomenon well known to writers whose characters, given their head, take off and do or say things the writer did not foresee. The writing has a Ouija board will of its own."   —DIANE JOHNSON

You get the picture. If a character seems to be taking the story in a direction different from the one you started out with, just go with it, see where it leads. You can always cut it out later if it doesn't end up helping your story. *Don't decide with too much certainty who your characters are. Instead, as you characterize, let them tell you.* Just as people often surprise you in life, so your characters can surprise you in fiction. If you're surprised and pleased by what you discover, chances are your readers will be too.

Build a Foundation for Characterization Early On

Characterization is one of those paradoxical things in fiction: hard for the writer to do well but which, when it *is* done well, seems effortless or even transparent to a reader. It maintains the spell that the good story casts, and keeps the reader enthralled, convinced that she is listening to real people speaking, watching real events unfold.

One way beginning writers can err in trying to write convincing characters, ending up instead with characters that seem artificial, is by trying to pack all their characterizing efforts into the character's first appearance. This feels unnatural on the page because it's not the way things happen in real life. In the real world, we very rarely exchange full biographies when we're first getting to know each other; we start off by sharing a little bit of information, then a bit more the next time we meet, then a bit more, and come to know even more about each other in settings where we can see each other in action—talking with our spouses or throwing balls at a carnival, telling a story about a coworker, discussing politics, cooking steaks on a grill, or dealing with a child who's pitching a tantrum. Stories are built from strings of such observations and, as has been implied, it is this kind of examination of character that makes clear the reason the story is being told.

In more practical terms, what this means is that, instead of offering characterization to the reader in a hard-to-digest lump, you should build a foundation for the character by rendering a single salient detail or two on his first appearance in the story, then let the events of the story build the reader's understanding of that character as the story unfolds.

Add Characterizing Detail Like Layers of Lacquer

The process of applying lacquer to a surface provides a useful metaphor for the characterization process. Successive layers of lacquer, applied to a piece of furniture or an object over time, give the surface a feeling of depth. The same thing happens with a character who is built detail by detail, scene by scene, in your story.

As you give your reader information about your characters' thoughts and actions, you should also resist the urge to explain things too much, instead trusting the details you use—the things you have your characters notice, do, and say, and the way they notice, do, and say them—to tell your reader what she ought to know. As Francine Prose has said in her essay, "On Details," "[a] single true gesture obviates pages of psychological exposition."

> "A *writer begins by breathing life into his* *characters. But if you are very lucky, they breathe* *life into you."* —CARYL PHILLIPS

Progressive Writing Exercise #6:
Building Your Characters

In the previous exercise, you showed what two different settings looked like when seen through a character's eyes. An obvious question remains unanswered by the descriptions of setting you've done, though: *Why does your character feel as she feels? Why is she describing this setting in the way she is describing it?* For this exercise on characterization, you're going to be trying to provide some answers, and in doing so move from *observation* to *action*. You'll build on the work you did in the previous exercise by bringing your character into each of the two settings you've imagined and having him or her *do something* in each setting that is in some way consonant with mood and character. **One complication:** though you have another character in each of these settings besides your observer character, you should hold off on having them talk to each other yet. See how much work you can do, how much character you can expose, *without* resorting to words.

What you'll learn: To illustrate within your story Aristotle's assertion that character is presented best and most vividly to the reader in a context of action.

STUDENT EXAMPLES

Jeremy's Response

THE RECTORY (CONTINUED): FATHER MCLAUGHLIN'S POINT OF VIEW

Father McLaughlin shut the guestroom door as quietly as possible so as not to disturb his sleeping guest. He then walked down the hallway and down the stairs back into the living room. The boy had been so impressed with the room and the priest wondered why. He knew little about the boy's past, only about his recent arrival and troubles, so he could only venture to guess what was on David's mind and at this point there seemed little reason to worry about the boy so peacefully asleep upstairs.

The priest walked over to the bookcase and spent a couple minutes gazing at the titles. He had read every book on the shelf, a feat he often took silent pride in because there appeared to be a sizable number of books on the shelf. Frankly, the reason he had read all of those books was quite simple and practical. Because he often had visitors from the parish in his living room and because they often would peruse his bookcase and ask questions about the books, he had made sure that he would never have to tell someone he hadn't gotten around to reading that book yet. Upstairs in his den, where outsiders only visited for the occasional confession, he had at least twice as many books he had yet to read. But no one ever asked about those.

He pulled out a Raymond Chandler mystery and sat down on the loveseat in the same place David had sat earlier. Fr. McLaughlin took a drink of his lemonade. Sour, just how he liked it. Then reached over to set it on the end table, but the absence of a coaster made him set the book down on the seat for a moment and cross the room to grab one off the other end table. Now, he placed the lemonade on a coaster on the table beside him and picked up his book. The book had spent a good number of years occupying a place in the downstairs bookcase and he had lost count how many times he had actually read it. He didn't own a television and rarely went out to movies—usually only ones recommended strongly by parishioners or those movies based on books he had read and enjoyed—so he spent most quiet evenings at home in the company of great literary figures like Philip Marlowe or Jesus Christ. Once upon a time he had wanted to be a private eye like Marlowe, all of his childhood dreams for the future had been based on literary characters, and it was Jesus that made him decide on the life he was currently living.

The first chapter of the book went quickly, but Fr. McLaughlin had trouble keeping his mind on the story. David's presence in the house made the priest think about his youth and how his decision to become a priest was made in a situation not entirely unlike the boy's current one. Years ago when he was nineteen and was wandering alone in the city one night, he met a priest in a cafe, they began talking and he had stayed the night in the rectory . . .

Fr. McLaughlin shook his head and stood up trying to get the thoughts to go away. He crossed the room to the fireplace and picked up a small tin off the mantle. A family had given him the tin when they had moved away, as a remembrance. The tin was brilliantly hand painted in reds and golds with angels all around and the Agony in the Garden scene on top. He opened the tin and from inside pulled out a precious pearl rosary. He looked up at the picture of Mary on the wall, crossed himself and kissed the crucifix on the rosary, then knelt where he was standing and began to pray.

THE CITY (CONTINUED); FATHER MCLAUGHLIN'S POINT OF VIEW

Early in the morning of the day David arrived, Father McLaughlin left his house wearing his Newsie cap and a thin windbreaker since the air was just a bit brisk for a summer morning. He walked down the street toward the coffee shop he frequented most mornings around 8:30 or so. Along the way, an occasional familiar face would appear in the crowd on the sidewalk—many people in the neighborhood knew Fr. McLaughlin, if only in passing, and most liked him very well—he tipped his cap to each of them with the pleasant demeanor and bright smile on his face.

At the coffee shop, he got his usual coffee, cream no sugar, and a bear claw. He jokingly gave the girl behind the counter a hard time for the tepid coffee, the same subpar brew served across the city, probably across the country, in little places like this. But she had grown to expect this sort of behavior from the man and played it off with the same halfhearted scowl in his direction that she used at least a couple times a week, when she didn't tell him just to go drink his coffee and be quiet. He laughed heartily and sat down in a booth nearby a group of other morning regulars, mostly retired old men who enjoyed talking about nearly anything, with strong emphasis on politics, the weather, and the changing (deteriorating) face of the world and youth. Fr. McLaughlin had never become a part of this group but they fascinated him endlessly with their banter. He would, occasionally, throw in the odd comment or two if he felt moved to do so or if it would stimulate the conversation. The group was all too willing to indulge his fancy.

He stayed at the coffee shop for almost an hour, listening to the conversations, watching people on the street outside the window and the workers inside doing their jobs. He would have been content to sit and watch people move in and about the shop all day long, but the church called him to his duty. So he walked back to his church, just beside the rectory, and there he performed the morning mass, another part in his daily routine.

The grandfather clock in the upstairs hallway was just striking noon when he returned to the rectory from his morning out. He went into the kitchen and made himself a quick sandwich, nothing fancy, just a bit of ham with some lettuce and mustard, and made a fresh pitcher of lemonade. He put the sandwich on a plate with a few potato chips, grabbed a glass of lemonade, and went out on the porch to eat his lunch. The porch had a swinging chair, something Fr. McLaughlin had built himself and installed years ago, and he ate his lunch slowly swaying with the breeze in the porch swing. A few people passed by, sometimes stopping a moment or two to chat about the weather or to ask how the church was doing, but mainly Fr. McLaughlin enjoyed sitting on the porch to watch the birds in the trees across the street and flying around in the sky. He had a book on bird watching somewhere, but had never read it, he wasn't all that interested in knowing the names or anything else about the creatures, he just loved to watch them fly and perch and sing.

Commentary The thing to notice first is that Jeremy has changed point of view characters for this exercise. He explains his decision this way: *David has been a difficult character to work with so far. When I started the story I had a plot and a bunch of ideas I wanted to explore, and I've tried to force David to conform. He has refused. However, the character of Fr. McLaughlin, whom I originally thought of as secondary, has started to take on an incredibly interesting life. He now seems to me a more natural and intriguing character. Since I don't think there's any point in forcing what isn't working, I'm letting him take over.*

Jeremy appears to have had an experience that's familiar to most writers who've been working on stories for a while: his story decided it didn't want to go in the direction he wanted it to, and in fact has decided—through the person of Father McLaughlin—to strike off in an entirely new direction. While it isn't necessarily common for a secondary character to displace the main character with whom the writer began a story, it is, at least, not surprising. This obviously returns the story to beginning territory, where the reader's basic questions (p. 14) float, as yet unanswered. The most important question—at least in terms of this lesson—is: What's at stake for my character or characters? For David—now a secondary character—that question has been answered: he needs Fr. McLaughlin's help. But what about the priest? Why is his story being told? And do these scenes, engaged as they are in the delineation of the priest's character, convey any clues?

Although these questions aren't entirely answered in these two scenes, the scenes nevertheless do some admirable work in establishing the priest's character. The rendering of Fr. McLaughlin's parlor and his relationship to his books is smoothly presented, and the scene closes with the revelation of the remarkable parallel between David's situation and his own past, the suggestion of a shadow cast across it by McLaughlin's concluding gesture. The coffee shop scene presents the reader with a kindly man of settled habits, going quietly through his morning routine.

Concerns A few details—particularly in the first scene—raise questions. First is the assertion that, as he grew up, Fr. McLaughlin's heros had all been literary figures "like [Philip] Marlowe or Jesus Christ." It seems odd to assert that Christ would be merely a literary hero to a priest, even when he was a boy. This begs the question of what, precisely, he found heroic in Christ (His self-sacrifice? His compassion? His wisdom? His sanctity?) and when McLaughlin's admiration changed, and became the conviction that led him to become a priest rather than an admirer of Christ's "story."

The parallel between David and himself is also a fairly startling thing to assert—something (one would think) McLaughlin would have noted earlier, something that would have been looming large in his mind, as he helped David get settled and thought about the boy's situation. Also, what was it that made McLaughlin shake his head to "get the thoughts [of the episode from his youth in which he was helped by a priest] to go away"? Something dark seems to be suggested, whether this was intended or not.

Finally, though the second scene is plausible in its rendering of how McLaughlin spent a pleasant morning, and though it offers some nicely characterizing gestures, it never really develops much momentum, nor does it seem to deepen the reader's experience with what's at stake for the priest. This may be solved with the addition of dialogue to the scene, in the next exercise, but given what's on the page now, things seem a bit flat. The priest's celebration of the morning Mass presents one possibility for making this action do a bit more. Framing the Mass—which one would assume is a signal event in a priest's day—as an event that has become *only* a part of his routine may have larger implications about McLaughlin's character than the scene currently seems to acknowledge.

Sarah's Response

THE SET OF CLAIRE DANES'S MOVIE

At 6:00 A.M., Mint and Lindsay were among the earliest extras to arrive. Mint's mother handed them bagged lunches as they got out of the car, and they waited until she was out of sight to throw them away. They spoke to the guard and passed under the giant stucco arch proclaiming, AMAZO-LAND! They found themselves alone, and stopped short to take it all in, to appreciate the sharp shivers of anticipation, or was it cold? In the foreground, they faced trinket shops, candy shops, old-fashioned-photo shops, not yet opened for the day. Their window displays shone darkly. Beyond that, rides like giant metal skeletons rose from the trees and building tops. Mint blinked her eyes to regain depth perception, because it looked to her as she squinted into the distance as if everything converged at one point; the epic rollercoasters, strange spherical vehicles, tubes, swings, inexplicable towers, and the Ferris wheel, the crowning image of Amusement, all sprouting from the same square foot of cement. That was where she would find Claire Danes. The paved walkway before them was clean and empty, like a yellow brick road leading them to adventure, promising, promising, promising. They started walking, and as they passed *La Chocolaterie,* a waft of chocolate scent hit them hard. Mint's acute sense of smell wouldn't let her enjoy it, though. She couldn't ignore the underscents: the sourness of last night's hot dogs, dropped popcorn kernels, cotton candy tubes festering behind trash cans where the janitorial staff didn't care to reach.

It was too early to talk, but Mint could feel her senses sharpening one by one as she drew nearer to the filming site at the base of the Ferris wheel. This is it, she thought. This is it. I'm here. I have arrived. Just around the next airbrushed-shirt stand, there were camera crews and wardrobe mistresses. Claire Danes would be sitting in a director's chair with her name on the back, Mint thought. There would be two beautiful gay men dressed in black combing her hair. Mint glanced over at Lindsay, but she couldn't tell what she was thinking. Lindsay was like that, stoic and hip in a denim jacket, gray tube top, and gray GAP slacks. Mint looked down at her body and wished she had worn a dress. These capris made her ankles look fat, and her strappy sandals were making ugly red imprints on the top of her feet. She had on a yellow flowered t-shirt with translucent cap sleeves, and she realized she was shivering almost convulsively. It was cold for October.

They rounded the bend—the last bend—and they had arrived at the filming site. It was sparser than she had imagined it, but still thrilling, still Hollywood. There were more ugly people than she had predicted, pimply tech guys in black t-shirts trotting back and forth with monstrous loops of wire hung on their shoulders, yelling things across the courtyard to people named Dave or Mike. The Ferris wheel was the center of the action, hulking above them like a giant white Christmas tree, the cars shiny Christmas balls swaying in an invisible air current. There weren't trailers, only tents, which surprised Mint. She couldn't tell which of the people milling about were important and which were just crew members. She looked furiously for Claire Danes, but she wasn't there. Had she arrived yet? What if she were sick, or dead?! Oh my God. Mint turned to Lindsay, but she was gone and it took a second to spot her across the way in a tent, signing a clipboard and speaking eagerly to a bored-looking woman in a black turtleneck. Mint took a deep breath and walked over to sign in.

MINT'S ROOM

It was 2:00 A.M., and the moon had just risen high enough or sunk low enough (Mint wasn't sure) to enter the square of the window at the head of her bed. Frustrated almost to tears by three hours and twenty-eight minutes of longing for sleep, Mint surveyed her room. There was something foreboding about the space right now; familiar objects made foreign by the cold moonlight. Her black corduroy armchair, shredded by some long-dead cat, hulked in the corner menacingly. The bookshelves that flanked the door opposite her bed sagged under the weight of former books—last week, Mint's mother had donated everything marked Young Adult to an inner-city school. Her wooden bureau had grown a face in the moonlight, knot-eyes and a jutting bottom-drawer jaw. Mint looked away, embarrassed that she still saw monsters in the dark. The new posters gleamed in a minor key, as if the beautiful airbrushed pop stars were revolted by the grittiness of dark childhood things. Mint wanted so badly to sleep.

The door opened a crack, letting a sliver of light fall across Mint's folded hands like a cut-down tree. A tall, dark strip of her mother materialized in the crack as

Mint's eyes adjusted to the light. Mint squinted, trying to look asleep, but intrigued by the idea of watching her mother watch her. It should have made her mad, but it felt comforting tonight—someone looking in on her, making sure she was still there.

Her mother looked pathetic, standing there. Not pathetic-sad, but pathetic in the Greek tragedy sense of the word, English-class pathetic. Evoking pathos. Mint appraised her. What a sad end, she thought. To live out life as a divorcée in the suburbs, working late nights to afford vacations to colonial Williamsburg, vaccinations for the cat. The lines in her mother's face spoke to her of failure. She had looked beautiful in her wedding pictures, seventies-belle with long, blond feathered hair and two little girls holding the white silk train on her wedding dress. And from there, somehow, she had eroded into this frumpy middle-aged woman, spying on her daughter at 2:00 A.M. in bunny slippers, with undereye circles like bruises. What did she have? Mint realized her breathing had changed as the door opened wider and her mother padded over to her bed. She had given herself away.

Commentary These two scenes do quite well in bringing into sharper focus the picture of Mint conveyed by previous scenes. Mint in the amusement park is giddy with image, excited by a glamour she thinks must somehow be attached to substance, her desire playing out ironically against the somewhat tawdry created world of the amusement park. She has dressed as if for a date, but doubts she has created the right effect; she doesn't seem to have the natural acumen for moving through this world that her friend Lindsay has. Lindsay provides an interesting contrast: she seems to be looking on this with a mercenary eye, while Mint seems to want much more from it than to be "discovered"; she seems to want access to the wisdom she thinks beauty must possess. The anxiety her desire provokes is palpable throughout the scene.

The second scene is equally effective. Few spaces are more deeply characterized (and characterizing) than a teenager's bedroom, and the details of Mint's bedroom scene subtly fill in more important details of what might be at stake in this story: the bookshelf now emptied of "young adult" books tells the reader she has only recently crossed over the hazy frontier that stands between early adolescence and adulthood. The fear Mint feels as she imagines a face for her dresser conveys the fact that she has by no means completed this transition. In this equivocal moment, her mother's checking on her is both welcome and an intrusion, and Mint thinks—fearfully, judgmentally—about the seemingly bleak place her mother's choices have led her to. The unspoken questions hang in the air: Is this what happens? Will this happen to me?

Concerns Mint seems fairly passive in these scenes—an observer (albeit a very sharp-eyed observer), rather than an actor. The most she does in the first scene is walk into the amusement park, and in the second scene she lies in bed, reflecting. If it weren't for the fact that Mint also seemed fairly passive in the previous scene, it might be possible to conclude that this was an artifact of the assignment. This passivity may be a part of Mint's character; she may just be a quiet girl, one of life's observers rather than one of its actors, like her friend Lindsay. Certainly the contact Sarah is able to give her reader with Mint's character is deepened in these scenes. However, a bit more action might make it possible for the scenes to convey even more of Mint's character.

QUESTIONS FOR REVISION

1. Look back over the scenes you've written so far, with an eye toward the characterization you did in these scenes. Have you characterized in enough detail? Too much?

2. Are there details of character that now seem clichéd to you, steering your character or characters toward *type*?

3. Have you treated your characters respectfully, avoiding oversimplification?

4. Are there any characters in your previous scenes who're *flat* when they ought to be *round*? Round when they ought to be flat?

5. Do any of the characters you introduced in earlier scenes now seem to require more development?

6. Have you depended too heavily on a block of characterizing exposition in your characters's first appearance? Could your early scenes benefit from a characterizing gesture or two instead that you'll be able to build on in later scenes?

Alternative Writing Exercises

1. **Mad, sad, lonely, tired.** Conceive of separate characters who're feeling each of these emotions, one emotion per character. Do four brief pieces of characterization, each one featuring one of these mad/sad/lonely or tired characters as they walk down an urban sidewalk and encounter someone who asks him or her the time. Represent that walk and that encounter so that your reader knows your character's emotional state *without your ever naming it explicitly. What you'll learn:* In terms of characterization, showing is nearly always better than telling.

2. **Don't talk with strangers.** Two characters are throwing a frisbee in a park. They're strangers who've only just met. Write two passages of characterization, one from each character's point of view, as they watch each other and speculate about what kind of person they're playing catch with. *What you'll learn:* We're very visually oriented creatures, and we derive quite a bit of information about others merely from watching them move.

3. **Can I trust you?** You meet a man in a bar who is telling you about his relationship with his wife. Write two scenes. In the first, he's lying, in the second he's telling the truth. Your task is to convey the truth or falsity to your reader through careful characterization. *What you'll learn:* Experienced poker players watch other players to see if they'll reveal a "tell"—a physical mannerism, verbal tic or other cue that reveals whether they have a good or bad hand. Whether we're aware of it or not, as we weigh what people are saying to us, most of us watch for these tells much of the time. Here, you'll be making this normally unconscious process conscious.

4. **He's not your type . . .** For this exercise, pick one of those character clichés referred to above as "types"—the cold-hearted career woman, for instance, or the Irish priest who's a secret drunk. Now write a passage of characterization that *explodes that type*, and shows that all is not as it first appears. *What you'll learn:* While you should avoid character clichés in your fiction, it can be useful to take them on as challenges to help you to sharpen your character-writing skills. Inside every cliché there's a real person screaming to get out.

Reading Exercise:
Character in Kevin Brockmeier's "These Hands"

Memorable stories often arise from authors taking novel paths in their exploration of character—the ways character is built, how it's pulled apart, how human beings come to do the outlandish and seemingly inexplicable things they do. With "These Hands," Kevin Brockmeier puts us on notice almost immediately that he is going to do just this: on the story's first page he tells us Lewis Winters, a thirty-four-year-old man, has fallen in love with a baby, and that he has lost his love. To convince us this could happen, to make us care for Lewis and see his plight with sympathetic eyes, the author must do a masterful job of characterization. Brockmeier uses the tools of characterization to take us deeply into his protagonist, giving us the means to feel what Lewis feels, to know what Lewis knows, and to believe in his suffering. In doing so, Brockmeier breaks through the surface tension of our conventional ideas about love, bringing us to a larger understanding of the human heart.

QUESTIONS

1. "These Hands" uses an unconventional narrative stance: Lewis Winters tells his own story as a third-person narrative. What does this suggest to us about his character?

2. The conflict in which Lewis is caught is fairly typical: he is suffering in the throes of recently lost love. How do you react to the *atypical* facet of his affliction: the fact that the object of his affection is eighteen months old? Does the author address this reaction? Does he make use of it? How?

3. What role does Lewis's description of the physical world in which his story takes place play in unfolding his character for us?

4. In several places in the story, Lewis abandons his third-person narrative stance and drops briefly into first person. How does this affect your deepening understanding of character?

5. Can you say of Lewis that he fits Aristotle's criteria for character—that is, that he is *appropriate, possessed of recognizable human nature,* and *consistent*? If yes, how does

Brockmeier shape his characterization of Lewis to fit these requirements? If no, how does Lewis fail to meet these requirements?

6. Using E. M. Forster's definition, we can confidently say that Lewis is a *round* or complex character. Would you say this complexity is *declared*, or *accreted*? How would you define Caroline?

7

DIALOGUE

Speech is conveniently located midway between thought and action where it often substitutes for both.

—John Andrew Holmes
"Wisdom in Small Doses"

Most writers love to listen to people talk—*real* talkers especially; the raconteurs who know that talk is not merely a means of communication but an art form, a kind of spell they can throw over listeners enabling them to feel or see nearly anything. There's something rudely alive in a really good talker—someone who loves the sound of words rolling out of his mouth, who's happy to be a teller of tall tales, a spinner of yarns. He gets our devotion early, and seldom, if ever, loses his power over us.

Literature began with talkers. The earliest stories—Homer's epics, the Icelandic skalds, the recitations of the Welsh and Irish bards—were memorized and delivered by the poets directly to their audiences. The spoken word is drama's basic building block, and in fiction, dialogue—as speech's simulacrum—has long been one of the storyteller's most important tools. The care we take with the sound of the human voice as it appears in our stories should reflect our awareness of this fact.

It would be possible to write a satisfying story that didn't use dialogue—Jack London's "To Build A Fire" comes immediately to mind—but such stories are the exception rather than the rule. Unless you're going to be writing exclusively about characters who are Trappists, mutes, or hermits living on the tops of columns, there will generally be some dialogue in your stories.

Dialogue's Dual Nature

In a story, speech always means more than it says. This is true for two reasons: the first has to do with how dialogue functions as one of the gears that makes a story run; the second has to do with how speech functions in the real world.

First—like point of view, tone of voice, setting, characterization, and scene—dialogue has to help the machine that is the story generate the story's motive energy. If dialogue is just spinning along, not connected to anything else—a long, involved

105

conversation between two rookie cops about sports teams, for instance—and doesn't deepen the reader's understanding of the characters or of what's at stake in the story, then there's no reason for the dialogue to take place.

Second, when we speak in the real world, everything we say is backed by both the imperatives of the present moment (we're hungry, we're frightened, we need to catch a train, etc.) and our life experience (what we have come to believe or disbelieve; what we desire, deplore, or fear; what we've been taught or told by others; what we've experienced firsthand or what we've merely heard about). It's as if every spoken word were the hub of a wheel at the center of an infinite number of radiating spokes. The hub—the things we say—we might call *text*, while the spokes—the things supporting the things we say—are *subtext*.

As an illustration of how *text* and *subtext* work in fiction, imagine a scene in which one character asks another "What time is it?" That question—the text—is fairly straightforward, but if we consider the subtext, it can become quite a bit different. For instance, the character asking the question might be asking because she's dreading the approach of the hour at which her now-dead child was born, twenty years before. She might be taunting the character of whom she's asking the question, knowing he had his watch stolen in a previous scene. She might be a suspect waiting in an outer office for an interview with a police detective that is to happen precisely at 9.00 A.M., or a mother sleepily asking her husband whether it's time to feed their newborn.

The fact that subtext lives beneath text makes carefully managed dialogue a very keen tool you may use to characterize the speakers, to outline for the reader their relationships, to vividly present their motives and emotions and so make clear the part they play in the rising or the falling of the story's action.

> *Be a craftsman in speech that thou mayest be strong, for the strength of one is the tongue, and speech is mightier than all fighting.*
>
> —MAXIMS OF PTAHHOTEP, 3400 BC

When you have a character speak, if your reader has been sufficiently prepared by what has come before in the story, the way your character responds to something as simple as the question Do you want a cigarette? can tell your reader volumes, and can convey it gracefully, through implication, more pleasingly and with more complexity and subtlety than you could manage with pages of exposition and interior monologue.

Use Dialogue to Characterize and Convey Information

As Edith Mirrielees says in *Story Writing*, "To cause the figures in a story to talk is not merely to make them speak as, under the circumstances given, they probably would. It is also to make their speaking forward the action, or display the speaker's temperament or character, or elucidate the characters or temperaments or relationships of other figures in the story—or, even, to do all three. It is along with doing one or all of these that the dialogue must also carry on the tune of the story."

As an example of how a writer addresses these considerations in rendering dialogue, let's take a look at an excerpt from Ernest Hemingway's story, "A Way You'll

Never Be." Notice how much the author is able to tell the reader in the following excerpt from a story set mostly in a command post on the Italian front during World War I. In the story, Nick Adams—a frequent protagonist in Hemingway's older stories—is visiting a friend, an Italian captain in command of a battalion, just after an attack has gone forward. Nick, who had previously been serving as an American volunteer in the Italian army, is recovering from a wound he received in an artillery barrage. During his convalescence he has been put in an American military uniform as a public relations gesture. As this excerpt opens, Nick is talking with his friend about the attack.

"I came from Fornaci," Nick said. "I could see how it had been. It was very good."

"It was extraordinary. Altogether extraordinary. Are you attached to the regiment?"

"No. I am supposed to move around and let them see the uniform."

"How odd."

"If they see one American uniform that is supposed to make them believe others are coming."

"But how will they know it is an American uniform?"

"You will tell them."

"Oh. Yes, I see. I will send a corporal with you to show you about and you will make a tour of the lines."

"Like a bloody politician," Nick said.

"You would be much more distinguished in civilian clothes. They are what is really distinguished."

"With a homburg hat," said Nick.

"Or with a very furry fedora."

"I'm supposed to have my pockets full of cigarettes and postal cards and such things," Nick said. "I should have a musette full of chocolate. These I should distribute with a kind word and a pat on the back. But there weren't any cigarettes and postcards and no chocolate. So they said to circulate around anyway."

"I'm sure your appearance will be very heartening to the troops."

"I wish you wouldn't," Nick said. "I feel badly enough about it as it is. In principle, I would have brought you a bottle of brandy."

"In principle," Para said and smiled, for the first time, showing yellowed teeth. "Such a beautiful expression. Would you like some Grappa?"

"No, thank you," Nick said.

"It hasn't any ether in it."

"I can taste that still," Nick remembered suddenly and completely.

"You know I never knew you were drunk until you started talking coming back in the camions."

"I was stinking in every attack," Nick said.

"I can't do it," Para said. "I took it in the first show, the very first show, and it only made me very upset and then frightfully thirsty."

"You don't need it."

"You're much braver in an attack than I am."

"No," Nick said. "I know how I am and I prefer to get stinking. I'm not ashamed of it."

"I've never seen you drunk."

"No?" said Nick. "Never? Not when we rode from Mestre to Portogrande that night and I wanted to go to sleep and used the bicycle for a blanket and pulled it up under my chin?"

"That wasn't in the lines."

"Let's not talk about how I am," Nick said. "It's a subject I know too much about to want to think about it any more."

This passage, which is nearly bare of physical description or information about Nick's thoughts, nonetheless manages to convey quite a lot of information about him, his relationship with his friend, and their attitudes toward battle, the war, and the military in which they serve. As was said above, dialogue always means more than it says, and the dialogue in "A Way You'll Never Be" bears this out: there's quite a lot said in the speech of Hemingway's soldiers that's not being stated explicitly, but is present as subtext.

Let's look at text and subtext as they are represented in this passage. On the surface, the scene seems set up to convey Nick's explanation to the captain of what's brought him to the battalion and provides a context as they talk over their memories of the actions they've been in together. The subtext of the scene—conveyed by what the two men seem to avoid saying—tells the reader quite a bit more.

Neither Nick nor the Italian captain are military zealots; this becomes clear as they chat about the fact that Nick has appeared in an American uniform. Irony and bitterness are at play in what they say to each other. The captain finds it odd that the powers that be have sent Nick up to show the uniform in the trenches; he suggests that civilian clothes would have been "much more distinguished"—an opinion that itself seems to contain an oblique jab at politicians. The irony becomes more explicit when he says, "I'm sure your appearance will be very heartening to the troops," and Nick's reply is, "I wish you wouldn't." It is clear the Italian is being sarcastic, and Nick winces at this. In the hands of a lesser writer, it might have been hard to convey all this, but Hemingway has chosen the words he puts in his characters' mouths so precisely that the reader doesn't become lost, even though Hemingway rarely uses dialogue tags—the "he said/she said" clauses that identify who's speaking when characters are talking to each other. Nick and the captain have very different voices, and it's easy—using only the syntax of their speech as a guide—to tell them apart. Hemingway even conveys the captain's Italian-inflected English. The author then uses a simple, polite exchange—the captain's offer of a drink—to introduce the information that Nick had formed the habit of getting drunk before every battle. The subtext? Both men know about the terror of war, and each has had to come to terms with it in his own way.

It seems important to note that using dialogue this way to move the scene along is not only vivid and economical, it

> *Speak properly, and in as few words as you can, but always plainly; for the end of speech is not ostentation, but to be understood.*
>
> —WILLIAM PENN

is also characterologically and situationally appropriate. It makes sense that battle-hardened soldiers who have quite a lot of experience in common—much of it horrible—would prefer not to say certain things to each other. It makes sense, too—as friends who've fought together and denizens of a very particular and specialized world—that there would be much they would find it unnecessary to say. Hemingway manages these conversations between the soldiers so skillfully, though, that the reader never feels left out of the conversation: she knows everything that must be known, and the conversation conveys important particulars about these characters and their situation. Learning salient information this way, rather than being filled in by the author's or a character's narrative voice, feels very authentic.

Make Your Dialogue Fit Your Characters

Remember Aristotle's admonition that characters ought to be consistent throughout your story? Dialogue is a part of this effort. You have to be sure that your characters' speech matches what you've told your reader about them—their background, their character, their desires, and fears—through other means. If you've shown a character to be fussy and meticulous in action, for example, it wouldn't do to have him be sloppy and imprecise in speech—at least not without proper explanation. You have to develop the ability to listen to an episode of dialogue you've written and to be brutally honest with yourself about whether or not you've gotten it right. When you read your dialogue to yourself, do the words you've put in your character's mouth sound as if they fit with what you "know" about him? If not, you may not be presenting him—his motivations, his personality—well enough yet.

Make Speech Sound Natural, Even Though It's Artificial

It's not enough merely to represent speech as it would sound "in the real world," spoken by a real person. If you've ever looked at a faithful transcript of an average, everyday conversation, you know it's filled with "ums" and "ers"; verbal tics; long, awkward silences; coughs; sentences that end in the middle or that ramble on forever without establishing point or destination; inappropriate laughter; repeated clauses; cheerful non sequiturs. Everyday conversation is a mess but it shouldn't be in fiction. In rendering dialogue, then, it's important to remember your loyalty should go first to good storytelling, and second to verisimilitude. Dialogue is artificial because we expunge most of what makes it awkward, stumbling, unclear. We clean it up to make it signify, to make sure it does the work we set it to: moving the narrative, delineating character, conveying information we can't convey with wordless action or with exposition.

Well-rendered dialogue seems natural in part because—as was said above about Hemingway's story—it's appropriate to character and situation. If you've imagined your character deeply enough, if you've represented setting and situation carefully enough, it's more likely the right dialogue will occur to you and your characters' speech will fall naturally on the reader's ear.

This also seems an appropriate place to talk for a moment about dialect—the rendering into dialogue of the regional peculiarities of your characters' speech. For the most part, you should avoid using nonstandard spellings to indicate dialect—substituting "gonta" for "going to," for instance. A very, very little of this goes a long way, and too much of it quickly becomes annoying for the reader. Some particularly skillful writers—Faulkner springs to mind—can pull this off, but too often the results are clumsy and artificial-sounding. Try it if you feel moved to, but remember the bar is set pretty high here. Instead, you might try to capture the cadences of a character's speech—her particular word choices, expressions, the pauses she makes, the rapidity or slowness with which she expresses herself, the physical details and gestures that accompany speech. Through the strange alchemy that takes place in reading, your reader's mind will work with these cues, and he will hear your character talking in precisely the accent you intend.

Make Characters Sound Different from Each Other and from the Narrator

Hemingway was able to avoid using dialogue tags because he was careful to render his characters' speech in a way that differentiated them from one another. This points up the need that you follow an injunction so basic that it has become one of the most-often-cited bits of writing workshop instruction: *When your characters talk, be sure they don't all sound alike.* Even people from the same neighborhood, the same ethnic group, the same family, should be sufficiently differentiated in their speech. Otherwise, you run the risk of confusing your reader or—worst of all—boring her with characters that seem interchangeable. Identical-sounding characters rob the story of the energy their differentness can bring to it. This is the energy of *synthesis*, which (as the philosopher Hegel defined it) is produced by the collision of different energies (which he called "thesis" and "antithesis"), with this collision producing a new and higher level of truth. Dialogue can usefully be conceived of this way: as differing (if not always opposing) forces that you bring together, combining their individual energies to create a new energy. If the characters sound too much alike, synthesis can't take place.

> *The opposite of talking isn't listening. The opposite of talking is waiting.*   —FRAN LEBOWITZ

Nor are the characters' voices the only ones you need to worry about. You should also be sure that, in third-person narratives, the narrative voice is sufficiently differentiated from the characters' speaking voices in your story. A certain remove from the characters is necessary to preserve the integrity both of the characters themselves and the narrative distantness the third-person narrative makes use of.

Weave Together What Characters *Say* with What They *Do*

Although Hemingway was able to employ dialogue that was almost bare of physical description, you can do a lot of the work of differentiating your characters from one another by carefully weaving speech together with observations of their physical actions. Take note of what they do while they're talking—render what their hands do as they speak, describe their expressions, or let a hesitant sip of a drink or an abrupt decision to get up from a chair serve as a subtle mark of punctuation. These actions are as much a part of dialogue as the words themselves; make sure you avail yourself of them to render the complete picture of your characters' conversation.

An allied point: you should use these details to color your characters' dialogue rather than trying to do it with a dialogue tag. It's generally a good idea to avoid conveying any more information than "he said" or "she said"—saying, for instance, "he whined," "she blathered," or "he said angrily." Most often context, the dialogue itself, and accompanying physical description do much more (and function much more vividly) to tell your reader who's speaking, and give what's said the necessary emotional coloration. Try to convey too much information with a dialogue tag and your characters' speech will usually end up seeming unnatural or ham-handed, and this will spoil the flow of your scene.

Find the Right Mix of Speech, Description, and Action

When do you write action without spoken words? Speech without action? When should you use exposition that involves neither? When should you *summarize* what characters say (known as *indirect discourse*), rather than delivering it line by line? Balance is an important consideration. It's possible to tell a story that's all dialogue, just as it's possible to tell a story that's nearly all exposition. There are scenes where no one speaks, and scenes where talking is practically all anybody does. There's no rule governing this except utility: *The right time to use dialogue is when only dialogue will work.* "Work" in this instance is "work" as physicists define it: the transfer of energy from one system to another. Dialogue that works is ergs, or calories; it's fuel burned to move the story forward. There will be times when having characters speak would only bog things down. Silence is part of good storytelling's equation, and it's important to use it occasionally. You can convey as much with what's *not* said in a late-night gas station robbery as you can with what's said.

Well-rendered dialogue forces the reader to pay a very particular type of attention. It fixes his attention firmly on your characters' interaction with one another. Because of this, it should be used at times when that fixing-of-attention is desirable: when drama is required, when a deeper and more subtle understanding of character and motive is needed. Dialogue can be used to deliver the moment of a character's change or realization in a way that's crystalline in its aptness.

Written speech has rhythms and moods. It conveys those rhythms and moods in the story, contributing importantly to your efforts to give the story its particular color and temperature. You should take pains to render atmosphere meticulously, fully, and so convincingly that it almost becomes another character in your story. Like breath misting on a cold day, dialogue enters this atmosphere, manifests it, gives it weight, shape, heft.

> *The face is the mirror of the mind, and eyes without speaking confess the secrets of the heart.*
>
> —SAINT JEROME (AD 374–AD 419), LETTER

Keep the Swearing to a Minimum

It may seem to you that in the real world obscenities have almost become a part of speech—used as conjunctions, adjectives, amplifiers of emphasis, punctuation marks. This may be true in real life, but it's not in fiction. In fiction, obscenities quickly become cloying and awkward, impediments to the flow of your narrative, and you should avoid overusing them. This isn't a puritanical injunction; more, it arises because of the difference between a spoken word and a word on the page. The spoken word is ephemeral, while the written word stays before the reader's eyes and lodges in the reader's consciousness more persistently. This gives an expletive in a story more weight, more permanence, than it does in actual speech. You ought to measure out the obscenities you use in your stories with a teaspoon rather than with a fire hose.

Progressive Writing Exercise #7:
Putting Words in Your Characters' Mouths

In the two previous chapters you created two proto-scenes as you explored setting and characterization. Now you're going to add dialogue to these exercises and in the process render them into more-or-less fully formed scenes.

In the previous two exercises, you had to keep the characters from speaking to one another; now that injunction is lifted. Complete the framing of the two scenes by having the characters in each of them hold a conversation. Be sure the dialogue in each scene adds energy and characterizing detail to the scene.

What you'll learn: Dialogue is one of the ways you can characterize economically and add to or alter the story's narrative momentum. Here, you should notice the change in energy and the different level of contact with character which comes through the addition of dialogue to your scenes.

STUDENT EXAMPLES
🔊 *Jeremy's Response*

FIRST SCENE

Father McLaughlin knocked softly on the door to David's bedroom. Inside, David slowly opened his eyes and, through the window, saw the bright sunshine and clear blue sky of morning. In the distance, birds chirped over the hum of the city.

He still wore his clothes from the day before, having fallen asleep so suddenly and soundly the night before. He hadn't even crawled under the sheets.

Another knock. This time a bit louder.

David slid off the bed, now fully awake, and opened the door.

"I wondered how long I might have to knock before you woke up."

"I must have been more exhausted than I thought."

"Well, after the nap you've just had, you should be good to go. After a good break-fast, that is."

Suddenly the smell of bacon became overwhelmingly apparent to David. He hadn't even thought about food for so long, and with a heavy lurch his stomach told him it was time to start thinking about it again.

"That sounds wonderful. Thanks."

"My pleasure. Why don't you just wash up a bit, then meet me downstairs in the kitchen."

"Great. Where's the bathroom?"

"Just across the hall on your left. I've got to go see about that bacon. See you in a minute."

Fr. McLaughlin turned and walked off down the hall. David crept across the hall to the bathroom. He thought about the night before and the strange comfort he had felt in this house. The bathroom was simple and straightforward. The priest had laid a towel and a new toothbrush out on the sink for David to use.

After cleaning up, David made his way down the hallway and stairs, and then took a left into the kitchen. Fr. McLaughlin was just pouring a couple of glasses of or-ange juice that he set on the table beside two plates that were covered with bacon, eggs, fried potatoes, and toast.

"That looks delicious," said David.

"Thank you. I hope everything was in order for you upstairs?"

"Yes. The toothbrush was nice, thanks."

"Well, sit down and eat. Is there anything else I can get you?"

"No, everything looks perfect," David said as he sat down at the table with the priest.

After a minute of satisfied silence as the two began to eat the meal, Fr. McLaugh-lin spoke. "You're very lucky, I hope you realize. I don't cook my famous home-style breakfast for just anyone. I'm actually quite fond of a little donut shop down the street myself, but I thought you would need something good to start your day."

"It is very good," David said in between bites of bacon, "and it's very kind of you to feed me like this. Maybe I could return the favor one day."

"What are your plans for today?"

"I really must find the company I'm supposed to start working for. Hopefully they can give me an advance on my pay and then I can pay the rent on my apartment. Maybe then I can start over, you know."

"Just in case, you are welcome to stay here until you're able to get on your feet."

"You're too kind. I think I must be lucky to have met you last night."

"Yes, perhaps we both were. Can I get you some more eggs, or bacon?"

"Please."

As Fr. McLaughlin scooped more food onto David's plate, the phone rang and the priest walked into the living room to answer it. David sat and finished his meal with a great deal of contentment. If the rest of the day went as smoothly as this beginning, everything would get worked out and his worries would be over. David knew he should get moving; the clock on the stove already read 9:00 A.M. He heard the phone conversation end and Fr. McLaughlin came back into the room.

"One of the elderly women from my parish fell down her front stairs this morning and broke her hip. That was the family; they want me to come visit this afternoon. They are quite nice people, they only live a few blocks away from here."

"I hope she'll be alright."

"I'm sure she will be. She's a very . . . strong-minded lady, I'm sure she won't let a broken hip slow her down much."

"Well, I must be going, I have a lot to do today."

"Right. Oh, let me give you my phone number," he ducked into the living room and grabbed a notepad and pencil from the phone stand. "If you have any trouble, give me a call. And like I said, you are perfectly welcome to stay here another night."

"Hopefully I won't have to stay here, but I'll certainly be in touch. Thank you again for everything."

"It was nothing. Take care of yourself and good luck."

David made his way out the front door and he was once again confronted with the streets.

SECOND SCENE

When Father McLaughlin had finished his sandwich and lemonade and sat for a bit just watching the world go by, he stood up from the porch swing and took the empty plate and glass into the kitchen. Just as he began to wash the dishes, the phone rang. He grabbed a towel and hurriedly dried his hands as he moved into the living room to answer the phone.

"Hello?"

"Hey, Mike."

"Oh, hi, Charlie, I should have known it was you."

"What's that supposed to mean?"

"I had just started doing the dishes and you always call just when I'm in the middle of starting something."

Father Charlie Mullins worked at a parish across town. The two men had gone to seminary together years before and had remained close friends ever since. They liked to think of their relationship in terms of the Bing Crosby movie *Going My Way*, and of course, each claimed to be the Bing Crosby in the relationship. Just like the priests in the movie, the two real men were both great baseball fans.

"I'll make it up to you. Ditch the dishes and come out to the Yankees game with me this afternoon. I'll buy you a hot dog or something."

Both of the men had held season tickets for as long as they could remember.

When both had been kids growing up in different neighborhoods, they had bought their first tickets with nickels and dimes saved up from entire summers of running errands and carrying groceries for their neighbors. After they met in seminary, they had started buying their tickets right next to each other.

"I'll tell you what, I have to go see somebody this afternoon, but then I'll head over to the game. Starts around 2:30 right? I should be there by the bottom of the third."

"That sounds good. Who are you going to see? Somebody sick?"

"No, not sick. Irma Wallace fell down her front steps early this morning. The family called and told me she'd broken her hip. Doesn't look terribly bad, they said, but they would still feel comforted if I came and sat with her a while."

"Is that the Mrs. Wallace that, oh what was it? Something about your potluck dinner last October?"

"Ah, yes. You know, I'd nearly forgotten about that until you mentioned it. I guess I was too busy thinking about the poor woman's hip. What happened was that she and Florence Grayson ended up bringing the same dish, I don't even remember what now. Not that it bothered anyone else there, including Florence, but Irma was outraged. First, she accused her of stealing her recipe, which she claimed had been passed down through the family for generations and, of course, no one else knows it unless they've stolen it."

"Sounds just like my mother."

"Sounds like everyone's mother, or grandmother at least. Anyway, she then proceeded to declare that Florence should take her dish elsewhere (using stronger language of course) and if she should like to participate in the potluck she should run around the corner to the store and get some potato chips or something, since they would probably taste better than Florence's cooking, she said."

"I bet she didn't take that well."

"Not at all. You can't just insult another woman's cooking in front of her parish and expect her to just let it go. Florence was definitely not taking her dish anywhere else and was not afraid to let Irma know it. Of course, Irma didn't react to that well and before anyone could do anything to stop her, she had grabbed Florence's dish—ah, now I remember what it was, some sort of creamy green bean casserole, quite delicious actually—anyway, I remember because then Irma grabbed Florence's dish and dumped it all over Florence's head and dress. Needless to say, Irma didn't stay long after that. A couple of her friends dragged her out of the hall and took her home. Luckily Florence's casserole had been sitting on the table cooling for a while so that there were no burns, despite all of her yelling otherwise. I don't think I've seen the two women in the same room since, I believe they have even settled into going to different Sunday masses in order to avoid each other."

Charlie had laughed heavily through the story. "As much trouble as they may cause, you've got to admit, they sure are entertaining."

"Yes, you know, I probably shouldn't say it, but the whole event was something straight out of a movie. Two crazy old ladies just going at it, and they fit the roles perfectly."

"Why don't you send one or two of those over here to my place, just to liven things up a bit?"

"Listen, they're here if you want them, but I'm not going to bring them over for you. Hey, that's smart, I'll just market all these ladies here to boring parishes like yours. I'd even deliver if the price were right. What do you say?"

"I'd say you're a pretty crazy old fool yourself."

The two men laughed.

"I should probably go, Charlie."

"Sure, see you at the game, Mike."

Commentary The dialogue in these two scenes is of two different types. The first conversation is slightly stiff and polite, as one might expect a conversation to be between new acquaintances, especially when one owes a debt of kindness to the other. The second scene gives the reader a conversation between two very old acquaintances, and it features the easy banter in which two old friends would quite naturally engage. These are not just any old friends, however; these men are priests, and the dialogue must be convincing on that level as well. Jeremy manages this tonal requirement quite nicely. One can well imagine two middle-aged priests laughing over the foibles of their parishioners, as Charlie and Mike do.

Concerns In the note accompanying Jeremy's response to the characterization exercise, he said he was moving Fr. McLaughlin to the center of his story. In the first of these two scenes, however, David is once again his point of view character. This doesn't necessarily preclude Fr. McLaughlin from being the story's protagonist—as was said in the third chapter, it *is* possible to switch point of view from character to character within a story—but it's tough to pull off in a short story, and so this raises the specter of confusion here. Also, since this scene is in David's point of view, Fr. McLaughlin—his feelings, thoughts, and motives—end up being a bit more obscure than is useful to a story that has him at its center. What, for example, does he mean when he responds to David's assertion that he was lucky bumping into the priest: "Yes, perhaps we both were"? This lack of clarity, in this context, seems problematic rather than intriguing.

As for the second scene, the reservations raised concerning it in the previous exercise hold here as well: though the scene is gracefully and naturalistically written, it's hard (at this point, anyway) to see how it adds much to the reader's ability to speculate about what may be at stake for the priest in this story.

〰 *Sarah's Response*

FIRST SCENE

At 9:00 A.M., Mint and Lindsay were among the last extras to arrive. Mint's mother handed them bagged lunches as they got out of the car, and they waited until she was out of sight to throw them away. They spoke to the guard and passed under the giant stucco arch proclaiming, AMAZO-LAND! They were surprised to find themselves alone, and stopped short to take it all in, to appreciate the sharp shivers of anticipation, or was it cold? In the foreground, they faced trinket shops, candy shops, old-fashioned photo shops, not yet opened for the day. Their window displays shone darkly. Beyond that, rides like giant metal skeletons rose from the trees and building tops. Mint blinked her eyes to regain depth perception, because it looked to her as she squinted into the distance as if everything converged at one point; the epic rollercoasters, strange spherical vehicles, tubes, swings, inexplicable towers, and the Ferris wheel, the crowning image of Amusement, all sprouting from the same square foot of cement. That was where she would find Claire Danes. The paved walkway before them was clean and empty, like a yellow brick road leading them to adventure, promising, promising, promising. They started walking, and as they passed *La Choco-*

laterie, a waft of chocolate scent hit them hard. Mint's acute sense of smell wouldn't let her enjoy it, though. She couldn't ignore the underscents: the sourness of last night's hot dogs, dropped popcorn kernels, cotton candy tubes festering behind trash cans where the janitorial staff didn't care to reach.

Mint could feel her senses sharpening one by one as she drew nearer to the filming site at the base of the Ferris wheel. This is it, she thought. This is it. I'm here. I have arrived. Just around the next airbrushed-shirt stand, there were camera crews and wardrobe mistresses. Claire Danes would be sitting in a director's chair with her name on the back, she thought. There would be two beautiful gay men dressed in black combing her hair. She glanced over at Lindsay, but she couldn't tell what she was thinking. Lindsay was like that, stoic and hip in a denim jacket, gray tube top, and gray GAP slacks. Mint looked down at her body and wished she had worn a dress. These capris made her ankles look fat, and her strappy sandals were making ugly red imprints on the top of her feet. She had on a yellow flowered t-shirt with translucent cap sleeves, and she realized she was shivering almost convulsively. It was cold for October.

They rounded the bend—the last bend—and they had arrived at the filming site. It was sparser than she had imagined it being, but still thrilling, still Hollywood. There were more ugly people than she had predicted, pimply tech guys in black t-shirts trotting back and forth with monstrous loops of wire hung on their shoulders, yelling things across the courtyard. The Ferris wheel was the center of the action. At its foot was a crowd of people who Mint surmised to be extras, listening to a young man with spiky black hair and a clipboard. There weren't trailers, only tents, which surprised Mint. She couldn't tell which of the people milling about were important and which were just crew members. She looked furiously for Claire Danes, but she wasn't there. Had she arrived yet? What if she were sick, or dead?! Oh my God. Mint turned to Lindsay, but she was gone and it took a second to spot her by the Ferris wheel, signing the young man's clipboard. Mint took a deep breath and walked over.

The spiky-haired man looked her over curtly before handing her the clipboard. "Ok honey, there's a release to sign here, and then I need you and your friend riding the Ferris wheel, ok?" Mint took the clipboard and hunched over it, scrawling her name on the bottom line without reading the text. It didn't matter. Nothing mattered, if she was about to see Claire Danes.

Mint and Lindsay let themselves be ushered into a red car on the Ferris wheel, and hoisted into the air. They hung ten feet above the ground as the next extras were loaded in, then rose ten more feet, and ten more. There they stopped, inexplicably. There was no one to ask what was going on, so they settled in for a wait, peering down at the miniature scurrying of Hollywood below them. Lindsay was picking at the old red paint on the car's safety bars, and she got a piece lodged underneath her fingernail.

"Damn it," she hissed, fussing with her hand. "That's hideous, it looks like my fingernails are bleeding! I guess if I just hold it in my lap . . ."

"Lindsay?" said Mint anxiously, "What if we get stuck up here? I mean, I'm sure they want the Ferris wheel turning for the movie, but what if Claire Danes is down there, and we're up here?"

Lindsay gave her a calculatedly scornful look. "Mint, goddamn it, what's your hangup? I mean, I'm a fan too, or whatever, but could you please look at the bigger picture?" She paused for just long enough to make Mint wonder what the "bigger picture" was. Her dark hair fell perfectly across the white of her neck as she leaned toward Mint. She was wearing berry lipstick and natural brown-toned eye makeup. She looked like a star should look the day she is discovered. "We're in a *movie*. I could just die."

Yes, said Mint's inner monologue. Please.

SECOND SCENE

It was 2:00 A.M., and the moon had just risen high enough or sunken low enough (Mint wasn't sure) to enter the square of the window at the head of her bed. Frustrated almost to tears by three hours and twenty-eight minutes of longing for sleep, Mint surveyed her room. There was something foreboding about the space right now; familiar objects made foreign by the cold moonlight. Her black corduroy armchair, shredded by some long-dead cat, hulked in the corner menacingly. The bookshelves that flanked the door opposite her bed sagged under the weight of former books—the week before, Mint's mother had donated everything marked Young Adult to an inner-city school. Mint's wooden bureau had grown a face in the moonlight, knot-eyes and a jutting bottom-drawer jaw. Mint looked away, embarrassed that she still saw monsters in the dark. The new posters gleamed in a minor key, as if the beautiful airbrushed pop stars were revolted by the grittiness of dark childhood things. Mint wanted so badly to sleep.

The door opened a crack, letting a sliver of light fall like a cut-down tree across Mint's folded hands. A tall, dark strip of her mother materialized in the crack as Mint's eyes adjusted to the light. She squinted, trying to look asleep, but intrigued by the idea of watching her mother watch her. This should have made her mad, but it felt comforting tonight—someone looking in on her, making sure she was still there.

Her mother looked pathetic, standing there. Not pathetic-sad, but pathetic in the Greek tragedy sense of the word, English-class pathetic. Evoking pathos. Mint appraised her. What a sad end, she thought. To live out life as a divorcée in the suburbs, working late nights to afford vacations to colonial Williamsburg, vaccinations for the cat. The lines in her mother's face spoke to her of failure. She had looked beautiful in her wedding pictures, seventies-belle with long, blond feathered hair and two little girls holding the white silk train on her wedding dress. And from there, somehow, she had eroded into this frumpy middle-aged woman, spying on her daughter at 2:00 A.M. in bunny slippers, with undereye circles like bruises. What did she have? Mint realized her breathing had changed as the door opened wider and her mother padded over to her bed. She had given herself away.

"Mint," whispered her mother with a conscious tact that was so much worse than being called the wrong name. Mint didn't move. "Faker," said her mother. An involuntary smile twisted the corners of Mint's mouth. Mint's mother, surprised, seized the opportunity behind the smile and slid into long-abandoned routine. "I know how to wake up sleeping girls . . ." she intoned, and bent down to kiss Mint's forehead gently. Then she leaned away as if expecting an explosion. Mint opened her eyes and her mother saw the same stale resentment there, but also a gratitude, a vulnerability—a silent admission that tenderness at night was allowed.

Mint's mother knelt by the bed, reckless at the opportunity to be heard. "Honey, I'm sorry I called you Amanda tonight. I'm sorry for all the times. It's just so *hard* for me to remember your new name. Why . . ." She paused, gazing at the silvered blankness of her daughter's face, before she resolved to just say it all, while she was listening. "Why would you throw away the beautiful name your father and I chose for you? It's almost as if you've been acting a part since you changed it. You're—you're like a fortress."

Mint propped herself up on her elbow and said weakly, staring at her hands, "Mom, don't. I'm fine."

Mint's mother had to get this out, and just went on talking as if she were reciting something she had memorized. "A fortress. I'm not allowed inside, but sometimes you open a window and throw something out for me to study, to tuck into a pocket near my heart."

Mint rolled onto her stomach, facing the dark other side of the room. "Mom," she protested tonelessly. She didn't want to acknowledge the guilt that rose like a lump in her throat when she heard her mother talk like this, earnest and pained and late-at-night.

Her mother touched her shoulder. "But you're still you, sweet girl." The old epithet hung in the air for a second, and Mint savored it secretly. Her mother stood up. "You can kick and scream, but you're still my Mandy. And if you ever need anything, *ever*, I'm here." She lingered in the doorway for a few moments, watching the rise and fall of Mint's back. She closed the door behind her, and her slippers made scuffing noises as she walked down the hallway to her room. Mint turned onto her back and watched the words that she wished she had said escape from her forehead like steam.

Commentary As with Jeremy's response to the exercise, there are two types of dialogue in Sarah's responses, but rather than the difference being in how the dialogue is pegged to the relationships of the people who're talking, here the differences proceed from the work each instance of character conversation does within the scene.

In the first scene, the dialogue functions mostly as a species of action: one of the movie people tells Mint where to go, and in the way he does this, manages to let the reader know what kind of world Mint has walked into. Mint's vulnerability stands out starkly against the backdrop of his hard-edged efficiency. Next Lindsay gets exasperated about getting loose paint from the Ferris wheel under her nails and further exasperated with Mint when it's clear Mint is worried about the wrong things— meeting Claire Danes rather than getting discovered.

In the second scene, the dialogue functions to sketch in the mother's character, her relationship with Mint, and tells the reader indirectly about Mint herself—that her mother sees her acting a part, no longer her natural self—a "fortress" sealed off in herself and in the privacy of her thoughts. As happens with so many of us when a nerve is touched, Mint draws further into herself, but not without Sarah's giving the reader a view into her conflictedness, the longing she still feels for her mother's love.

Concerns These now-completed scenes sharpen the reader's desire for contact with the imperatives that drive Sarah's story—what Mint is running *toward* in the person of Claire Danes and what she's running *away from* by changing her name. That what Mint wants and what she fears remain obscured here may be characterologically apt.

Mint doesn't seem to know what she longs for, aside from the wisdom she seems to associate with the actress's beauty, and what she fears seems to have gathered itself in her view of her mother's life: the mother's options gone and her beauty dissipated by middle age and suburban living. This is very satisfying, as far as it goes, and what follows is more speculation than criticism, but the question of Mint's relative silence—particularly in the second scene—rears its head. It feels plausible that Mint wouldn't want to engage in the embarrassingly earnest conversation her mother seems to want to have with her, but one wonders what might have happened if Mint had said the words to her mother that she imagines at the end of the scene "escap[ing] from her forehead like steam." Might this conflict have been useful to the unfolding of the story?

QUESTIONS FOR REVISION

1. Read over the instances of dialogue you've written in previous scenes. Based on what you've learned in this chapter, can you say this dialogue deepens your reader's contact with what's at stake in your story?

2. Do you think you gave sufficient thought in these scenes to the subtextual meaning present in characters' words?

3. Do you think the dialogue in these scenes is sufficiently characterizing? Have you used it efficiently to convey information to your reader, and is it the best way of introducing that information into the story?

4. Does the dialogue in these scenes create a consistent picture of your story's characters? Have you avoided giving the characters a clichéd diction?

5. When they speak in these scenes, do your characters sound sufficiently different from one another and from your narrative voice (if you're using a third-person frame)?

6. Have you balanced dialogue with action and with characters' gestures and expressions, silences, and passages of indirect discourse and exposition?

Alternative Writing Exercises

1. **Your silence speaks volumes ...** Write a scene where one character talks and the other remains silent. Work to convey the sense of what the silent person *would* say if he were talking, by filling in facial expression, body language, etc., and by having the speaking character react as if she knew what the other character would be saying if he *were* talking. *What you'll learn:* Dialogue is not merely the words your characters utter; it is the subtle interplay of speech, gesture, expression, attitude and even silence. This exercise will help you to explore this fact.

2. **Break up to make up.** For this exercise you should use dialogue in writing two scenes. In the first an argument should take place, while in the second a reconcil-

iation takes place. *What you'll learn:* As was said earlier, dialogue is synthesis—it is two different and sometimes opposing energies that come together to produce a third, different energy, a movement in a new direction. This exercise will explore dialogue's utility as a tool for dramatizing conflict and resolution, bringing a changed and changing energy into the narrative.

3. **It's not what you said, it's how you said it . . .** One roommate gives another roommate a phone message. Write this exchange twice, with the roommate passing on the exact same information, with this difference: in the first passage of dialogue, you have to make it clear to your reader—through use of word choice, syntax, gesture and physical description—that the roommate who's delivering the message is secretly in love with the roommate receiving the message. In the second passage, you have to use the same means to make it clear that the roommate who's delivering the message is furious with the roommate who's receiving the message, and is struggling unsuccessfully to hide it. *What you'll learn:* We've all had the experience of revealing our true feelings accidentally, or of being unable to hide what we feel as we talk, however much we might want to. As was said above, dialogue always means more than it says. Rendering speech in all its subtle and equivocal glory—using gestures, facial expressions and other types of body language as well as the spoken word—is one of the quickest, clearest and most economical ways you have of giving your reader access to a character's complex emotional states.

4. **What're you in for?** Two men are seated at a table in a prison cafeteria. One is a car thief who never made it out of elementary school; the other is an M.B.A. imprisoned for embezzlement. Neither character knows anything about the other's background, and nothing about their disparate educational or social backgrounds enters into the conversation. Your task is to make it clear who's who through what they say to each other and how they say it. *What you'll learn:* The assumptions you make about character and the situation in which the reader encounters it will inevitably affect the choices you make concerning dialogue.

Reading Exercise:
Dialogue in Kazuo Ishiguro's "A Family Supper"

Few contemporary writers make dialogue do more work in a short story than Kazuo Ishiguro. When his characters talk, we can be sure that passage of dialogue is functioning at multiple levels: as a tool of characterization, as a conveyance for dramatic tension, as a means of making the character's situation clear to the reader. What an Ishiguro character says is every bit as important as what he or she does, and in this story, what the characters *don't* say is a very important part of the story. "A Family Supper" provides a very vivid object lesson in the interplay of text and subtext in dialogue.

QUESTIONS TO CONSIDER

1. How do the initial paragraphs of exposition regarding death by fugu poisoning and the narrator's mother's death equip us better to understand what occurs in dialogue—at first between the narrator and his father, then between the narrator and his sister?

2. The narrator and his father talk briefly after they arrive home from the airport. Ishiguro manages this conversation skillfully to reveal some critical information about the father's situation. How does what we learn from the chat set up the narrator's chat with his sister, and the dinner itself?

3. How does the difference in the characters' voices enhance our understanding of what is going on in this family?

4. How would you say Kikuko's speech differs in character from the narrator's? How does that difference affect your picture of the narrator?

5. Ishiguro injects moments of nonverbal business into the conversation that takes place in the kitchen. In the first, the narrator notes that, after the father has asked Kikuko to help, "For some moments my sister didn't move." The second bit of nonverbal business comes a few lines later, when the narrator notes that his father, after making a few observations about his cooking, ". . . looked up and regarded me strangely for some seconds." How do these instances of physical observation provide subtext for the text of the dialogue?

6. There is an interesting exchange between father and son in the father's study. How do the interplay of text and subtext add to the sense of unease that began in the kitchen? What, specifically, is the impression you're left with as the men move into the dining room?

8

DRAMATIZATION

How many ages hence
shall this our lofty scene be acted o'er,
In states unborn and accents yet un-known!

—William Shakespeare
Julius Caesar, Act II, Scene 2

In the previous three chapters, we addressed setting, characterization, and dialogue as if they were individual components of the two scenes you were writing. In reality, though—in fully functioning scenes—these elements of scene can't really be separated from each other; they work together to form the action that characterizes a scene through a process known as *dramatization*.

The Story within the Story

It is useful to think of the dramatized scene as a small-scale story. Like the story itself, each scene has a beginning, a middle, and an end, and presents an unfolding event that changes or deepens the reader's understanding of the main character or characters and what's at stake in the larger world of the story.

Just as every story must eventually present the reason it's being told, every dramatized scene must have a role in the telling of the larger story—unfolding character, illustrating conflict, suggesting a path into the story's heart. Each scene must build on what has come before it, and provide a necessary bridge to what comes after it.

Balancing the Scene's Elements

Most writers have favorite tools they use in dramatizing a scene; you may find this is true for you as well. As should have become clear over the previous three chapters, though, while setting, characterization, and dialogue are powerful conveyors, individually, of the scene's drama, they have their greatest effect in combination. Wallace Stegner's setting, Kevin Brockmeier's characterization, Kazuo Ishiguro's dialogue—

each was supported in its effectiveness by the other elements of the scene. Don't deny your scene the power that can derive from using measured doses of each element as appropriate when you're creating your scenes' action.

The Necessity of Conflict

"Hell," as writer Charles Baxter has said, "is story friendly." Stories almost invariably involve things going wrong, things breaking down, characters struggling amid the trillion varieties of trouble to which human beings are subject. If there's no trouble, then generally speaking, there's no story. This being true, the writer is called upon to develop her skills of dramatization as a way of bringing this trouble to life on the page.

> *In this world without quiet corners, there can be no easy escapes from history, from hullabaloo, from terrible, unquiet fuss.* —SALMAN RUSHDIE, "OUTSIDE THE WHALE"

In his essay, "Dysfunctional Narratives, or: 'Mistakes Were Made,'" Charles Baxter frames the utility of conflict in this way: "We have to nudge but not force [our characters] toward situations where they will get into interesting trouble, where they will make interesting mistakes that they may take responsibility for. When we allow our characters to make mistakes, we release them from the grip of our own authorial narcissism. That's wonderful for them, it's wonderful for us, but it's best of all for the story."

Trouble, trauma, conflict, "interesting mistakes"—these are the instruments the writer uses to tease apart the twisted fibers that make up his characters' souls, laying bare the exploration of praxis which is the story's goal. If, as Aristotle suggested, praxis is the soul's deep urging which finds its expression in your characters' acts, then the scene in which conflict is carefully dramatized is one of the primary tools you can use to enable your reader to experience this deep urging in your stories. Scenes in which characters are embroiled in conflict take the reader deeper into an understanding of what the characters want or fear, how they may overcome (or why they are overcome by) the obstacles they face. When conflict is embodied in the dramatized scene, it presents the reader with the sort of landmark moment that will serve as the answer the writer provides to the reader's question (p. 14) about why the story offers a particular sequence of events. Presenting conflict—and what it's possible to learn from it—is quite simply the reason the story exists.

> *The first glance at History convinces us that the actions of men proceed from their needs, their passions, their characters and talents; and impresses us with the belief that such needs, passions and interests are the sole spring of actions.* —GEORG HEGEL, THE PHILOSOPHY OF HISTORY, "INTRODUCTION, SCT. 3"

Internal and External Conflict

There are as many types of conflict in fiction as there are in life. There are conflicts between characters, of a character or characters with the environment or with soci-

ety, conflicts with technology, relationship conflicts, conflicts at work, spiritual conflicts. Literary theorists have come up with still more taxonomies of conflict that are
as complex as the genealogy of the British royal family. To keep our examination of
the topic manageable, though, it may be useful to use Jesse Lee Kercheval's division
of the types of conflict into *internal* and *external*. In her book *Building Fiction*,
Kercheval illustrates her concept this way: "Cinderella's external conflict is that she
wants to go to the ball, but her stepmother won't let her. Her internal conflict is that
she wants love but doesn't think she deserves it." Kercheval goes on to say that external conflicts are always resolved by what she calls a *crisis action* that happens at the
critical moment and is always visible in the exterior world of the story—the inter-
vention of the fairy godmother that permits Cinderella to go to the ball, for instance.
Internal conflicts are solved through *internal* action—characters' realizations, in-
sights, epiphanies. In Cinderella's case, we might say this would be her realization
that she is better than her humble condition—that she in fact deserves the prince's
love. The resolution of external conflicts happens best in a dramatized scene (the
scene where the fairy godmother arrives and transforms Cinderella); the resolution of
internal conflicts through exposition (the narrator giving us, perhaps, the stream of
Cinderella's thought that leads to her new understanding of herself).

The Danger of Miracles

Cinderella notwithstanding, if you're resolving a conflict, you shouldn't create a
miraculous event that solves your characters' problems. You should also avoid having
the answer to all a character's problems come to him in a blinding flash of inspiration. You'll often hear this referred to as a deus ex machina solution to a conflict. Literally, this means "god from the machine" and refers to the practice, in Greek and
Roman drama, of lowering a god onto the stage by means of machinery to unsnarl a
tangled plot or extricate the protagonist from a difficult situation. In modern stories,
solving problems by miraculous means not prepared for by the unfolding of plot is
most often seen as authorial cheating, and it will leave your reader feeling unsatisfied,
even duped. Problems and conflicts seldom have neat and tidy solutions in real life,
so they shouldn't in your fiction.

The Right Action, in the Right Amounts,
at the Right Pace

While dramatized action increases the reader's sense of involvement in the scene,
more action is not necessarily better. In working out what you will put in scene, you
should avoid wasting time detailing your characters' simple and mundane movement:
trips down stairs, travel through rooms, the ascent of ramps leading into planes, etc. If,
on your return home in the evening, a
friend asked you how your day went, you'd
only hit the high points and leave out the
stop you made at the post office for
stamps, the half hour you spent waiting in

The secret of being tiresome is to tell everything.

—VOLTAIRE

line at the Department of Motor Vehicles. Your friend's eyes would glaze over quickly if you launched into an exhaustively detailed account of such trivia. So will your reader's.

Don't repeat yourself. Don't write a scene and then write another later on that does the same work, covering the same characterologic or thematic ground. Do the work once and trust your reader to carry an awareness of the information provided, the characterologic nuance added, into what comes after.

Do *slow down*, especially when you're writing a scene that contains fast action—especially violence. This may seem a bit counterintuitive, but you'll find it's apt. Film director Sam Peckinpah's signature move in violent scenes in his movies was to put the action in slow motion. This increased the drama of the scene, and made the action much more affecting. You should describe the events in your scenes as though you were carefully choreographing the steps of a ballet, and pay scrupulous attention to the appeal you make to your reader's senses with your description of setting. You must resist the urge to match the speed of your writing to the speed of the action the scene delivers, lest you leave your reader bewildered, unsatisfied, and—worst of all—uninformed.

Progressive Writing Exercise #8:
Making Everything Happen at Once

In this exercise, you're going to write another scene that will propel you further down the narrative road in your story. Revisit your story cloud and pick another character/situation pairing. Rather than creating this scene piecemeal—writing the setting, then adding characterizing action, then adding dialogue and character interaction, as you have so far—you should dramatize this scene as a piece. Your scene should contain each of the elements—an evocation of setting, characterization and dialogue—on which you focused over the previous three assignments.

What you'll learn: Setting, character and dialogue come together in the process of **dramatization** to create action in the functioning mini-narrative of the scene. In this exercise, you'll concentrate on striking the proper balance of all these elements.

STUDENT EXAMPLES
Jeremy's Response

Father Mike McLaughlin and Father Charlie Mullins walked out of the baseball game a bit sad but not disappointed. The Yankees had lost, 3–2 to the Twins, but it had been a good game and that was what the two men cared about most. Both teams had played tough, but a late-inning triple deep into the right field corner scored one for the Twins and put another in position to score. The next pitch was a solid single and there was nothing the Yankees could do.

Often, after the games, provided there was not evening mass to attend to, the two priests would walk a couple blocks from the stadium to a little diner where they could eat dinner and chat.

"I don't know if I feel like going out to eat right now Charlie," said Mike, "I think that hot dog you bought me made me a little sick to my stomach. Maybe I should just go home."

"Are you sure? I mean, if you're sick maybe you should go, but you know that cute little waitress is going to ask me where you are when I get there."

"You can tell her I'll see her next week, on the condition she do one favor for me: give you the worst service possible."

"Oh, thanks Mike!" and the two priests laughed, then went their separate ways.

Clouds had started to drift overhead in the bottom of the sixth inning. As Fr. McLaughlin walked toward the bus stop, he looked up to see the gray clouds now covered the sky except for a small patch of deep blue just above the eastern horizon. The sun was trapped behind the clouds and the air felt as if it might begin to rain soon. The day had become quite suddenly very dreary.

On the bus ride home, it began to rain, slowly at first and then steadily gathering speed into fine constant drizzle. Fr. McLaughlin's bus ride was a long one and he sat quietly in his window seat gazing out at the rain and the people on the sidewalk, many of them caught unawares by the rain and now frantically trying to cover themselves with newspapers, run quickly to where they were going, or wait calmly or angrily under awnings and in doorways for the shower to end. Funny, he thought, how something as natural and expected as rain can still be such an interruption to people's lives.

Fr. McLaughlin's bus finally reached his stop. He jumped off and ran quickly under the awning of the building there, joining a small band of people waiting for the next bus or just trying to get away from the sudden strong burst of rain that had accompanied his exit from the bus. The building he was standing next to happened to be a McDonald's and he suddenly realized that he was now hungry. While waiting out this shower, he reasoned, I might as well get something to eat.

He walked in the door and brushed as much wetness as he could off his clothes. The rain he liked, the dampness of his clothes he did not, unfortunately he didn't think to bring his rain jacket to the game.

There was a line at the counter, and Fr. McLaughlin moved into it. He didn't need to look at the menu, he got the same thing every time he came here, just another one of his routines that happened on those nights he didn't feel like cooking (and there were a suprising number of those).

Before he got to the counter to order, however, a young man approached him. He said in a voice of false confidence, assured out of necessity but shaky, "Excuse me Father, I, I'm in trouble, could I talk to you? I mean, I'm Catholic and everything, if that makes a difference."

Fr. McLaughlin saw the confusion on the boy's face, he tried not to show his true concern but rather said with a large smile, "Sure, just let me get my dinner and I'll be with you in a moment."

The boy's eye twinkled ever so slightly at this good news—probably the first he's heard in a while, thought the priest—and the boy walked back to the booth near the window where he had been sitting, watching people on the sidewalk deal with the rain.

Commentary Clearly this scene constitutes Jeremy's rethinking—in light of his decision to make Fr. McLaughlin his protagonist—how the priest and David met. It's a solid scene, showing Fr. McLaughlin in a lightly pensive mood, and it serves as a good setup for the meeting that follows.

Concerns While this is a good setup for the meeting between Fr. McLauglin and David, without the meeting itself this can't, strictly speaking, be called a scene. It's all setup, with very little that is important to the story actually happening. More dialogue covering the conversation between David and Fr. McLaughlin after the priest has gotten his meal could presumably fix this.

Another thing that seems worth noticing is that, for all the compassionate attention Fr. McLaughlin seems capable of paying to the world, he actually seems to register very little detail about David beyond the nervousness David seems to be covering with false confidence, and the fact that David's eyes "[twinkle] ever so slightly" when the priest tells him they can talk. One would think a priest—whose life is dedicated to helping his flock—would be able to offer a somewhat more comprehensive and insightful description than this. This could be an opportunity for Jeremy to build a foundation for whatever further characterization might happen after this scene—characterization both of David (by what the priest observes about him) and of the priest (by what he observes about David and how he observes it).

> *A*ction is character.
>
> —F. SCOTT FITZGERALD,
> "HOLLYWOOD, ETC.," NOTES FOR
> *THE LAST TYCOON*

🎬 Sarah's Response

Sarah's Note: *My dramatization exercise is a continuation of the amusement park scene I've worked on for the last few exercises. This exercise picks up right where that scene left off.*

THE AMUSEMENT PARK

At 10:20, the Ferris wheel started turning again. There was less movement on the ground—something was happening. In their rusty red car, Mint and Lindsay swayed past the highest point of the wheel, skybound and alone for one last minute, and began arcing downward. Mint felt that she was being inexorably drawn toward something; the gravity that dragged her down toward resolution was stronger than any desire she had known. People below grew larger and larger, standing in clusters, clipboards clutched to their chests, watching some action unfold on the ground. The wheel groaned to a halt when Mint and Lindsay's car was just two cars up from the ground, exactly the height where they had waited on the way up. Mint stood up and pressed her head against the top of the safety bars to see what was going on just below them.

There, without warning, without a change in background music or an introductory voiceover, stood Claire Danes. Mint couldn't see her face from above, but she could tell it was her by the way people were fluttering around her, and by the part in her strawberry-blonde-dyed hair, almost perfect, but just irregular enough to be cute. She was standing still, and someone was adjusting a brown scarf around her neck, making it look unplanned. She was living, breathing in and out, just twenty feet away from Mint. They were probably recycling each other's carbon dioxide. Look up, thought Mint. Just look up, now! Look up and see me here. Now. Now.

Lindsay was standing now, too, breathless, and the two of them watched as Claire Danes was carefully placed in a yellow car, two away from their own. Some tech people were working on affixing a giant camera to the outside of the car, and Mint wondered how they could be so calm in the face of flawlessness.

"Mint," said Lindsay, "stare much?" She laughed, but it was a conspiratorial laugh, because she was staring too. "It's so weird how movie stars are people, you know? They, like, brush their teeth and have doctor's appointments."

"Yeah," said Mint, but it didn't make any sense to her. As if Claire Danes had to brush her teeth. What a stupid idea. "Weird."

Lindsay was coming out of the initial stun and starting to get excited. "When they start filming, do you want to be talking to each other? Or fighting? Or what?" Mint tried to process this.

"I mean, because, we should *try* to act. Who knows, the director could notice us."

"Sure, uh, let's be talking," said Mint, hoping Lindsay would stop talking so she could stretch this moment to infinity.

Claire Danes sat facing them in her accidentally mussed scarf and a jean jacket like Lindsay's. She wasn't speaking, and her eyes were closed. She glowed, ethereally pale and blond, like a lit candle in a dark space. Mint tried to shake the surrealism that blurred the edges of her sight. Here she was, here was Claire Danes, and what had she wanted to ask her? She tried to remember, but just ended up staring. This was Angela from "My So-Called Life," this was a goddess, this was passion and beauty. This was how Mint could be, how she *knew* she was, beneath the mess of her life. This was her secret self.

A handsome actor was ushered into the car next to Claire Danes, and they smiled at each other. The Ferris wheel creaked into motion, and somewhere, somebody yelled "Action!" Reality slid away and Mint was watching a movie, except on mute, because she couldn't hear what they were saying over the mechanical hum of the Ferris wheel. The man was talking, and then Claire Danes was talking, and laughing, and then they were near the top of the wheel, and looking out over the park, and then the man reached over and kissed her, and someone yelled "Cut!" They did this over and over. Mint was fixated. She strained to catch the words, but the wind snatched each one away.

"You realize," Lindsay interrupted, forcing Mint into the present, "that there's no way we're in this shot? Why the hell did they have to put people in *every* car? The camera isn't even facing this way. It doesn't make any sense."

At that exact moment, while Lindsay was saying, "sense," Mint and Claire Danes looked at each other. Straight at each other, without question. Beauty for beauty, secret for secret, they saw each other. Claire Danes began to open her mouth—she was going to say something! Mint strained forward desperately. It seemed like everyone was waiting, everyone was listening in that one second. Then Claire Danes yelled, "Can I get down now?"

And then she looked away, and they got her down to her tent dressing room and her life, whatever that might be. Everybody got down, and left, one by one, and there would never be another film shot at this location. Mint was numb—not happy or unhappy, but something else entirely. She called her mother from a pay phone and they waited for her on a bench outside the park gates, watching the crew pack up their vans and drive away. It was 1:00.

Commentary There's a lot to like in this scene. Sarah's gift for pleasingly original observation of detail is amply in evidence here. As with her other scenes, Sarah is able to present the ironic tension created by Mint's vivid inner world and her inability to share it within anyone else. Here, Sarah is able to point up this tension by locating a moment of important conflict at its center: Mint is experiencing (or, rather, hoping to experience) her moment close to Claire Danes, as a kind of epiphany, while simultaneously conducting a rather superficial conversation with Lindsay. Sarah's careful observation of the physical world of the scene supports the reader's experience with this moment's strain and drama. Then, when Mint's big moment comes and goes without providing Mint with any of what she hoped for—Sarah allows the scene to collapse quickly at its end. This feels just right.

Concerns One working definition of sentimentality in fiction is when the emotion represented in the writing seems to be out of proportion to its apparent causes. In a few critical moments, Sarah's writing in this scene steps across this line: first, when she tells the reader that "Mint felt that she was being inexorably drawn toward something; the gravity that dragged her down toward resolution was stronger than any desire she had known"; and second, when she says Mint wishes to "stretch [the moment of her proximity to Claire Danes] to infinity." In these places the writing seems sentimental because the origins of these strongly expressed emotions are obscure, neither sufficiently set up in this scene nor sufficiently supported by what was conveyed in previous scenes. It may be—as often happens—that Sarah's overstatement of emotion comes here because she doesn't trust that the action she has portrayed has enough meaning for the reader, and so she feels compelled to intercede on the reader's behalf, explaining what is (or what should be) clear because of the picture of the action Sarah was able to provide.

Drama is life with the dull bits cut out.

—ALFRED HITCHCOCK, QUOTED IN
LESLIE HALLIWELL'S *FILMGOER'S COMPANION*

QUESTIONS FOR REVISION

1. Does the "story" represented by each of the scenes you've written so far do work that is necessary to the story—deepening the reader's understanding of your character(s) or increasing her understanding of what's at stake in the story?

2. Does each scene build on the scene(s) that came before it, and does each scene offer a path into the scene(s) that follow(s) it?

3. Do any of your scenes offer action that's too similar to action presented in other scenes? Do any of your scenes cover characterologic or thematic ground you've already covered previously?

4. Have you struck the necessary balance of setting description, characterization, and dialogue in each of your scenes?

5. Have you made good use of dramatized internal and external conflict to deepen the reader's understanding of the story's characters and themes?

6. Have you used the pace the action in your scene calls for, avoiding (for instance) making violent action unfold too quickly?

Alternative Writing Exercises

1. **Inside-out or outside-in?** A handyman is cutting wood at his employer's cabin, trying to get ready for a winter the *Farmer's Almanac* has said will be particularly brutal. Write a scene in which you represent both *internal* and *external* conflicts. An example of an external conflict might be a coming snowstorm or an argument the handyman has had with his employer over his pay; his internal conflict might be his loneliness and his lack of skill in establishing human connections. *What you'll learn:* You decide what the internal and external conflicts will be; the main purpose is to explore their expression in action and in thought, and to set action and thought in conversation with each other.

2. **How important is it?** In this exercise, you'll be writing two versions of the same scene—a character pulling into a convenience store parking lot, getting out of the car and going in to buy a bag of chips for a party he's going to. In the first version, the important action happens in the car as he pulls into the parking lot; in the second version, the important action happens inside the store. *What you'll learn:* In framing these two scenes, you're going to have to balance summary and dramatization so the reader's attention is drawn to the proper place.

3. **Speed things up . . . No, slow them down . . .** Let's stick with the scene above— a character pulling into a convenience store parking lot, getting out of the car and going in to buy a bag of chips. You're going to be writing this scene twice again, with this difference: in the first scene, after your character has bought his chips, he has to do something he dreads. In the second scene, after your character has bought his chips, he has to do something he looks forward to. Write each scene so that it reflects your character's emotional state. *What you'll learn:* Your characters' various emotional states will dictate different depths of occupation and time senses for the scenes you write.

4. **Show and/or tell.** A character waits on a street corner, anxiously checking her watch in anticipation of a meeting with a second character. The second character

rushes up, late for the meeting. Write this scene twice. In the first version, the reason for the second character's lateness should be important, while in the second version the reason for that character's lateness should be trivial. *What you'll learn:* Some types of action should be exhaustively detailed in your story, while other types can profitably be summarized. Your task here is to illustrate these two types of action.

Reading Exercise:
Scene in Sandra Cisneros's "Mericans"

What makes a scene work as a scene? Often, it's easier to answer that question by examining a scene that *isn't* working. We can point to those things that keep us from being involved in it—usually imbalances in setting, characterization, dialogue, and action that make it seem unreal, awkward, contrived, not a representation of life as we know it. When a scene is working well, we tend not to worry about such considerations, and instead fall willingly under the story's spell. Let's hold ourselves back from falling under the spell Sandra Cisneros casts with her quite short story, "Mericans," at least long enough to permit us to see how she brings the disparate elements of scene together to make her story work.

QUESTIONS

1. Setting often functions in short stories almost like another character. How does the "character" of this setting—the environs of a church in Mexico—function here? What kind of "character" would you say it is? How would the story be different if the children were waiting for the grandmother, say, outside a market or a political rally?

2. How are the protagonist and the secondary characters presented to us as the story opens? What is it that makes the "awful grandmother" awful?

3. Now that you've defined the characters above, how would you define the situation—the physical details of setting, combined with the circumstances—that brings the scene's character or characters into this setting?

4. If *Situation + Character = Action*, how would you say situation and character come together in "Mericans" to produce action? How does the story's action present us with this story's central conflict? What do you think that conflict is?

5. There is a tension in "Mericans" between two varieties of dialogue—what is said in Spanish and what is said in English. How does Cisneros convey this tension, and how does she use it to unfold her story?

6. How is our understanding of situation and character deepened when Michele goes into the church? How is this understanding further deepened when she comes out again?

PART THREE

MOVING FROM
SCENE TO STORY

The prologue is the grace,
Each act, a course, each scene, a different dish.

—George Farquhar
The Inconstant, Prologue

Imagine for a moment that you are the head chef in a fine restaurant. People come to your establishment not just to eat, but to *dine*. As the person in charge, you know that you are not just putting food before them; you are orchestrating an experience. The courses, the wines, the sauces, the breads, the cheeses, the desserts you offer are the complex and interlocking parts of a complete work, with rhythms, resting places, sensations that contrast with and complement one another. When the last dish is cleared and coffee is served, the experience will remain vivid in your customer's memory.

As the epigram from Farquhar suggests above, we can extend this metaphor to play and story writing. Your story must first whet, then engage, and finally sate the appetite—the hunger for narrative—your reader brings to the page. As you write your story, each of its parts—its beginning, its ending, and everything that comes between—must relate to the other like the courses of a meal. Each scene must build or release tension, must add to or slow down the story's momentum. Everything you put on the page must deliver essential information, building your reader's understanding of character and situation. If a story element doesn't do any of these things, it doesn't have a part in the story. It's a simple formula—a contract, as we've said; unspoken but ironclad: *I will provide you with something that satisfies*. How are you to set about delivering this meal, balancing its dishes?

For an answer, let's turn to a schematic for narrative art called the *Freytag Pyramid*, devised by the German playwright and novelist, Gustav Freytag. Like many other such illustrative devices, the pyramid

> *"Imagination is a good horse to carry you over the ground—not a flying carpet to set you free from probability."*
>
> —ROBERTSON DAVIES

oversimplifies the thing it examines. Note that, in this illustration, the leg of the rising action is relatively gradual, while the leg of falling action shows a steeper grade of descent. Though stories are often structured this way, this isn't invariable, nor do stories always contain only one crisis point or a single conflict. It's more useful to consider this an illustration of *a* story, but not of *all* stories. With those caveats registered, let's look at the diagram:

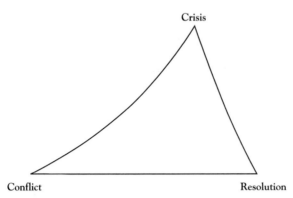

Freytag said a piece of narrative art most often begins with a *conflict*, leads through a period of *rising action* to a point of *crisis*, which is followed by a period of *falling action*, and concludes with a *resolution*. Now imagine these two legs—the rising and the falling—being intersected at several points by vertical lines, like so:

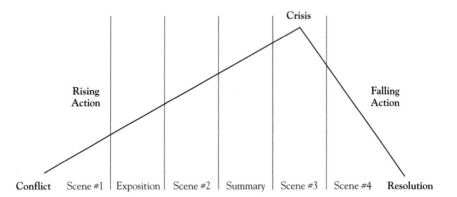

Between each of the vertical lines in the illustration above, you'll notice that something happens to advance the narrative. If you're writing a story that covers fifty years of your protagonist's life, you obviously can't *dramatize* that person's entire life—that is, put every part of it in a scene. Some of the story's work will have to be done using exposition, summary, and jump cuts. These elements must be balanced, the transitions between them smooth. Each element links with elements preceding and following it, and—like the courses of the aforementioned banquet—they should be in conversation with one another, so they add up to a whole and integrated experience.

John Gardner captured the process of arriving at this "integrated experience" very well when he said in his book *The Art of Fiction:*

> What Fancy sends, the writer must order by Judgement. He must think out completely, as coolly as any critic, what his fiction means, or is trying to mean. He must complete his equations, think out the subtlest implications of what he's said, get at the truth not just of his characters and action but also of his fiction's form, remembering that neatness can be carried too far, so that the work begins to seem fussy and overwrought, anal compulsive, unspontaneous, and remembering that, on the other hand, mess is no adequate alternative. He must think as cleanly as a mathematician, but he must also know by intuition when to sacrifice precision for some higher good, how to simplify, to take short cuts, keep the foreground up there in front and the background back.

What Gardner seems to be doing above is applying Ockham's Razor to the process of creating a narrative. Ockham's Razor is the rule propounded by William of Ockham, a fourteenth-century thinker, which has since guided scientists and logicians in the design of experiments and the formation of hypotheses. It states (in part) that entities should not be multiplied needlessly, and that the simplest theory is the preferable theory. Applied to story writing, we can take this to mean that *everything on the page must have a role in advancing the narrative, and the writer should take the most direct path to the telling of the complete story.* As the story moves through its rising-then-falling course and draws toward its conclusion, the writer must make sure there are no characters, scenes, passages of description, exposition, or summary that have been "multiplied needlessly," making no absolutely necessary contribution to the telling of the story. Bits of unnecessary decoration, flash, and dash should be hunted down ruthlessly and cut.

This is not, it's important to say, an argument for fiction that's stripped to its bones; it is an argument for fiction that is, above all things, dedicated to the best possible telling of the story. By all means, write complex, strange, baroque fictions that explore every nook and cranny of language; let a hundred narrative flowers bloom. But at the bottom of things, never forget your obligation to the reader: to assemble each story with the exactitude of that four-star chef.

9

PLOT

I guarantee you that no modern story scheme, even plotlessness, will give a reader genuine satisfaction, unless one of those old-fashioned plots is smuggled in somewhere. I don't praise plots as accurate representations of life, but as ways to keep readers reading.

—Kurt Vonnegut, Jr.

Aristotle defined plot in his *Poetics* as the "first principle and heart and soul of tragedy." It is the "structuring of incidents" that enables an audience to appreciate the unfolding of praxis in a character or characters. Aristotle emphasized that plot has a beginning, middle, and end and should be of "a length which can be easily embraced by the memory."

What that beginning, middle, and end are, what they add up to, and how they arrive at that sum, is a complex matter. Plot is a difficult thing to discuss, encompassing as it does definitional spaces as broad as the steppes of Russia. A story's plot can be built from causality that is as intricate as a pond's ecosystem, or can emerge from the ebb and flow of simple conversation between two friends in a café.

It Takes a Plot to Describe "Interesting Trouble"

Some writers will tell you they don't think about plot at all—that they write "character-driven" fiction. What they're really telling you is that they *begin* with character, and that their meditations on character—the way it moves us to do the unique things we do in the unique ways we do them—allow the story to unfold in its particular way. Heraclitus said "character is destiny," and in the context of our discussion of plot, Heraclitus was 100 percent right. Our fictions are shaped as are the characters contained within them. *Situation + Character = Action*; and action, adding up scene by scene, leads to changes in character. In fiction as in life, it is an endless loop.

Let's look a bit more closely at how this process proceeds and how plot is constructed. Another word for *action* in the *Situation + Character = Action* equation is *scene*—the portion of the story in which things are dramatized. The writer brings scene, summary, and exposition together so that by story's end a whole—the plot—is yielded that is greater than the sum of its parts. Thus, to build on Aristotle's definition a bit, plot is *the structure through which the writer brings the story's parts into conversation.* This "conversation" among parts is more than mere causality—more than event flowing from event—as we shall see.

In his essay, "Dysfunctional Narratives, or: 'Mistakes Were Made,' " Charles Baxter says something that may be useful in deepening our discussion of plot:

> "Sometimes . . . we have to talk to our characters. We have to try to persuade them to do what they've only imagined doing. We have to nudge but not force them toward situations where they will get into interesting trouble, where they will make interesting mistakes that they may take responsibility for. When we allow our characters to make mistakes, we release them from the grip of our own authorial narcissism. That's wonderful for them, it's wonderful for us, but it's best of all for the story."

This captures a few important ideas: first, the notion that characters must enter situations where they get into "interesting trouble." The notion of interesting trouble presupposes two things: complex characters (since cardboard-cutout characters can only have cardboard-cutout problems) and an unfolding of this trouble through time (i.e., through scenes), since the authorial "nudging" that accompanies the dramatization of interesting trouble is almost invariably more process than event. A car that bashes accidentally into a post in a parking lot is trouble that can be described in a second or two; a car that crashes intentionally through the front of the driver's boss's house is *interesting* trouble, and it takes a little more setup (i.e., more than one scene) if it's going to be believable, if it is going to answer the reader's natural question, Why would the driver do such a thing? As scene succeeds scene and the story's action gathers momentum, satisfying short stories deepen the reader's understanding of the circumstances that propel people into the unfamiliar territory of crisis, and the ways they survive (or don't survive) this journey.

> *"Being a trial lawyer has improved my writing. A trial is basically a problem in narration. Every witness has his or her story to tell. A trial lawyer's function is to help shape that story so it gets across to the audience."* —SCOTT TUROW

The Necessity of Change

The fact that characters travel in unfamiliar territory and commit rash but interesting deeds calls to mind a writing shibboleth one will hear often if one attends enough fiction workshops: *almost always in a short story, the main character or characters will change in some way, or the reader's understanding of that character or those characters will change.*

Let's take Shakespeare's *Hamlet* as an example of how this sense of conflict and complexity builds, deepens, and gathers momentum in a narrative, eventually yielding a sense of change. Hamlet has been performed for more than 400 years precisely because his conflicts—both internal and external—are so knotty and only grow increasingly so as the play unfolds. Things are relatively static at the beginning: Claudius and Gertrude have married, and Hamlet has been consigned to the life of the perpetual student, never to be king. Then Hamlet meets his father's ghost, which leads to the soliloquy, the mounting of the play-within-the-play, Polonius's accidental murder, Hamlet's near escape from Claudius's plot to have him killed in England, Ophelia's suicide, and the fateful encounter with Laertes at Ophelia's graveside. As the play proceeds, the audience's sense of the internal and external conflicts Hamlet faces deepens. Tension mounts, a sense of pressure builds, until the sword fight occurs—the outcome of which is terrible and tragic, but comes nonetheless as a *release*. By the time Horatio gives Hamlet his famous, final blessing and Fortinbras, the Norwegian prince, enters the hall, the audience has come to understand that what was truly at stake for Hamlet was more than Denmark's throne or vengeance for his father's murder, and because of the change in understanding the play has created through its unfolding, the audience sees that the change Hamlet has undergone as the play closes is deeper than mere death.

Remember Why People Read Stories

In her nonfiction book, *Journal of a Solitude*, the poet and novelist May Sarton said: "I have written every poem, every novel, for the same purpose—to find out what I think, to know where I stand." As readers we come to stories with similar, though unstated, feelings. Of course we want to be entertained; we may want to while away a few hours on a dull Sunday or pass the time while we wait in an airport for a delayed flight. As we said in Chapter 1 (p. 12), at a deeper level, we also want the story we're reading to excite in us the emotion Aristotle called *recognition*. Aristotle believed that if a story didn't hook this emotion, its plot was a failure. To excite recognition in your reader, you'll need to give her more than mere facts.

Fiction is actuated by, and acts upon, a conviction that lies in each of us: that being conscious means more than merely being awake. Life is an intensely strange, magical, and funny text we struggle to read each day of our lives. In moments of heightened awareness (moments of terror, wonder, desire, surprise, hilarity, hunger, love, suffering, shame, exaltation, rage—those moments which most often become the nuclei of short fiction), we can come closer to understanding why we want what we want, why we do what we do, what the source is of the larger forces we feel constantly moving within and outside of ourselves. We are drawn to that in art which holds out the promise of answering such questions, and it is fiction's business—as an art form—to frame these questions for us and—sometimes—even to attempt answers. Plot as we have defined it is one of the short story writer's most important tools in this effort, as surely as a brush or palette knife is important to the painter.

> "*There's a dialogue in my mind with a sort of ideal reader who would deeply respond to everything I express, but is much more intelligent and demanding than I am.*"
>
> —DEBORAH EISENBERG

Plot Is More Than a Sequence of Events

"Life," as John Gardner said in *On Moral Fiction*, "is just one damn thing after another." Not so fiction. Recall what Kurt Vonnegut, Jr. said in the epigram that began the chapter: readers come to stories expecting more than "an accurate representation of life"—they expect that an author has something to say with her piece. The reader expects, at some point, to learn the author's intention, expects the events of the story to add up to something, teach something, deliver something, ask a question. Why else tell a story, unless you hope to convey something particular?

If the story doesn't give the reader more than mere events, it won't convey that "something particular," and instead will most likely end up being a piece of *abject naturalism*—a phrase coined by memoirist and fiction writer Frank Conroy to describe fiction in which the writer merely sets down a plausible sequence of events. Abjectly naturalistic stories are dull. They seem pointless, lack life. When such a story is criticized, its writer will sometimes respond: "But everything in it could have happened!" And the reader's invariable response is: "So what?" Mere plausibility does not a story make.

Writers attempting to write too closely from their own lives often run into the problem of abject naturalism. Abjectly naturalistic stories may recite facts, but they don't convey the mysterious life inside facts. They do not move the reader because they do not convey a story's *soul*. This soul is the thing you're working to penetrate. It's what you should be trying to get a sense of, the mysterious whole that is greater than the sum of its parts.

> "Is it constantly on my mind when I'm going clickety-clack on the machine that this is somehow going to enlarge the scope of human comprehension? I would have to say no, that's not what I'm thinking about. I'm trying to get the line done."
>
> —ROBERT STONE

The reader wants more than Here's a thing that happened. He wants Here's a thing that happened, and here's what it did to the characters, what it made them feel, what it made them think, how it changed them, and changed our understanding of them.

Don't Put *Ideas* Ahead of *Story*

Too often, in early drafts of their stories beginning writers will give their idea of what ought to happen, what a reader ought to learn from the story, too much prominence. When this happens, the story can feel overdetermined; the reader can feel the presence of the author, bossing his characters around, ordering action and emotion in ways that can seem at odds with situation or plausibility. Ideas are fine, and they're often expressed movingly and elegantly in the best stories. This expression is *earned*, not forced. The expression of your ideas in your story ought to feel *organic*, as if it grew from the root stock of the story, not vice versa.

Verisimilitude

One way to develop this feeling of organicity is to pay close attention to verisimilitude in your presentation of your characters, the physical world of your story, and its events. Verisimilitude is a complicated-sounding word for a simple concept. What happens in your story should be true to the lives you are trying to capture. As the writer, you must show the reader you are sensitive to all the implications your story contains. If the eight-year-old girl in your story talks like a twenty year old with no explanation, your reader may begin to shift uncomfortably in her chair, wondering if you really know what you're doing as a writer. If the clergyman in your story works as a stevedore on the docks and you never explain why, this may also cause discomfort, create a drop in the level of trust your reader feels for you.

This concern with accuracy and appropriateness extends to all the objects and encounters that, in their interweaving, make up the fabric of our stories: furnishings in houses, music that plays on radios, the fashions characters wear, the directions streets run, the sound the wind makes through the trees, the operation of tides, the way two teenagers greet each other in a high school hallway, the way a fight unfolds, the causality that leads to a declaration of love or of hatred. All of these things and more are the materials from which we build our stories, and we must choose those materials carefully, make sure they're the

> *"By the time the imagination is finished with a fact, believe me, it bears no resemblance to a fact."*
>
> —PHILIP ROTH

right materials. If your readers ever have cause to question the skill or understanding with which you build the worlds your stories contain, you have failed. All details—individually and in combination with one another—must ring true. What you write must feel like *life*—not an approximation, but the genuine article.

Your Story's Landscape

Every story has its own geography, made up of the physical and psychological space through which your characters move in the rising and the falling of the story's action. Managing this geography properly is part of what will ensure a sense of verisimilitude. If your reader is to navigate this space effectively without feeling lost, you'll need to provide a map. That means you'll need to provide cues that allow the reader to follow characters as they move in and out of rooms, through the blossoming and dying of emotional states, and amid the intricacies of motive and event. This can mean something as simple as providing enough furniture to accommodate all your characters during a scene in which they're playing Monopoly, or making sure there are no physical impossibilities, such as a mug of steaming coffee that materializes in your protagonist's hand without anyone ever bringing it and vanishes just as mysteriously. It can be as complex as establishing a chain of emotional and situational causality over a number of scenes to support your contention that a solitary cab driver goes from being passively resigned to his loneliness as your story opens to resolutely acting to change his life at story's end.

Keep Track of All Your Story's Implications

Another of the old chestnuts of advice you will hear in almost every fiction-writing class is that if you show the reader a gun on the first page of your story (as Chekhov does in the early going of his play, "The Seagull"), you'd better be sure it fires by the last page. Or, if the gun doesn't go off by story's end (to make this bromide a little more subtle), you'd better have demonstrated a very good reason for that gun *not* to have been fired, not to mention having made good narrative use of the tension created by the not-firing.

Many beginning writers will make the mistake of not considering the implications of all the elements of their stories. These elements (to quote Frank Conroy again) are "tracks." If you establish a track for your reader—an interesting character, for instance, or a metaphorically significant object or event—the reader automatically assumes it's important to the story and will try to follow it, looking for further development. You jump the tracks when you introduce the gun that never goes off, or if you introduce a character who never really *does* anything, an object or event that ultimately seems to serve no narrative purpose. A single line of dialogue that implies something the story never bears out is a jumped track, as is a foreshadowing that has several implications, some of them (unintentionally) very misleading.

Progressive Writing Exercise #9:
Linking Scene to Scene

With the scenes you've been writing and the contemplation of your story cloud you've been doing, odds are good that you have some idea of where your story is headed—that is, its *plot*. You're going to do a bit more work on plot as part of this exercise. Of course, it would be too much to ask you to convey a complete plot in a single exercise. Instead, your goal in this exercise will be to do some writing that may serve to illustrate for you the way plot can begin to emerge from a deep meditation upon *character* and *situation*, the ways they meet to produce *action*, and the use of *summary*, *exposition* and *jump cuts* as a way of bringing scenes together.

Consult your story cloud again to identify the next situation in which it would be useful for you to set your main character. Now you're going to write two scenes, linked by a passage of exposition or summary which is necessary to the reader's full understanding of character, situation and outcome. You might also use a jump cut to imply the passage of time between the scenes, but only if this usefully creates tension or usefully lets you out of the the obligation to dramatize action that would have no real role in the story (i.e., a night's sleep, a boring concert, a walk from one part of town to another during which no interesting action happens).

In the first scene, your character will begin an action which he will have to complete later, in the second scene. For example, in the first scene you might detail a man's preparation of a gourmet meal for his girlfriend. In the second scene, he might share that meal with her—with positive or negative results. In the passage between these scenes, you would convey necessary information in summary (what he did while the meal cooked, for example) or in exposition (maybe some information about his being a dedicated carnivore who's gone out of his way to learn to make something his vegetarian girlfriend would like). A further desirable result would be that these two scenes would combine to convey some change, either in your character himself or in the reader's understanding of the character. Following through on the example above, for example, the cook might discover that his girlfriend doesn't appreciate his efforts—a circumstance which provides him with a defining metaphor for their relationship.

As always, try to move beyond the scenes you've already written. Try not to cover dramatic, situational or characterologic ground you've already covered in previous exercises.

What you'll learn: Consider this exercise to be a thought experiment whose aim is to instruct you in the ways that scenes "talk to" one another, and in the ways exposition and summary can create transitions between scenes. If you like, you can write scenes that you don't think will have a place in the story as you envision it now. Stay open to the possibilities in what you write though: your efforts may surprise you, yielding a result which you hadn't imagined yet, but which advances the story.

STUDENT EXAMPLES

Jeremy's Response

SCENE ONE

Charlie stood staring out of the second-floor classroom's window onto the student parking lot below. School had just let out five minutes before and the lot was crawling with scores of students eager to be out of the building and away from authority. Some jumped straight into their cars and drove away; others stood around in groups chatting and laughing, while still others tried to sneak a cigarette behind someone's van, out of sight from the parking lot monitor whom Charlie knew was standing in the doorway beneath the window where he stood. At the far end of the lot, he noticed a couple leaning against a car making out.

"Charlie?" Ms. Lonsdale said as she walked into the room and set the book she was carrying on her desk. She was an attractive woman, tall and slender with shoulder-length, straight brown hair and bright, penetrating blue eyes. Boys at the school would have made her quite popular if she hadn't been such a good and dedicated teacher. She was a stickler for rules and didn't let anyone get away with anything. She dressed conservatively, long skirts and long-sleeved blouses, and wore no makeup. Ms. Lonsdale had two loves in her life: reading poetry and teaching poetry. That left little time for anything else, but Charlie was a good student whose poetry showed a lot of promise. She always tried to make time for Charlie.

"I came to turn in the homework for tomorrow. I'm going to be gone for a college visit."

"Well. You do realize that a college visit is an excused absence, so you have until Monday to hand it in?"

"Oh yes," Charlie had crossed the room to the desk that held his backpack and he was rummaging through it for the right paper, "but I had a burst of inspiration, you could call it, last night so I went ahead and wrote something. I think you might like it."

He found the paper and handed it to her. "Let me get my glasses and I'll give it a quick once over, how about that?" She circled around her desk, took her glasses out of the top drawer and slipped them on. Had Charlie been one to notice such things, he would have realized at that moment that Ms. Lonsdale's glasses fit her face better than any glasses have ever fit a face and performed the impossible task of making her even more beautiful.

"I'm impressed, Charlie; this is quite good. I'd like to ask you, though, what inspired the line, 'Heightened senses sense little/In a small world of false fronts.'"

Charlie looked at his shoes. There was nothing interesting about his shoes. "It just sounded poetic, I think, that's all."

"Can we talk freely for a minute, not as teacher and student, but as friends?"

Charlie looked up. He later hoped his face had looked adequately surprised to cover up his joy at her words. "I suppose so."

"What do you want to do with your life?"

"Well, my parents want me to go to college and medical school, then move back here and work with my dad until he retires so I can take over his practice."

"No Charlie, what do you want to do? If there is anything of you in this poetry, you don't want to be a doctor, and you certainly don't want to move back here. Something inspired this poem in you. It wasn't the college visit tomorrow and it wasn't your parents. There is something trapped inside of you looking for a release, and whether it be through poetry or another way, you need to let it out."

Charlie could not speak. He looked back at his uninteresting shoes. He knew all of the things she had said before she had said them, but from her they all meant more. His poetry was about him. He didn't want to be a doctor and the last thing he wanted was to stay in the suburbs all his life.

After a few minutes of silence, Ms. Lonsdale spoke, "I'm not trying to tell you what path to take in life, Charlie, I'm just telling you to find your own. I teach poetry as a means of self-reflection and meditation. Your poetry says you have a greater calling than that of taking over your father's practice."

He looked up and began to open his mouth as if to speak.

"No. Now I'm going to be a teacher again. I've got some work to do so you had better go."

"Thank you." The comment was equal parts gratitude for what she had said to him and for her not allowing him to respond. He grabbed his backpack and headed for the door.

"Oh Charlie," Ms. Lonsdale said before he was out of the room, "I want to hear about your college visit when you get back. Why don't you come by after school early next week and we can talk some more. Until then, think about what I said so you'll have a response. Write it down if you have to, in iambic pentameter, then you can turn it in for the assignment Wednesday."

She smiled. Charlie smiled back and they both began to laugh. In that moment, a lifelong friendship began.

"See you soon, Ms. Lonsdale."

SCENE TWO

Father Charles McLaughlin stood looking out the waiting room window on the second floor of the hospital. Below was the hospital parking lot. Fr. McLaughlin remembered a day nearly twenty years ago when he looked down on a parking lot, waiting to see Ms. Lonsdale. He watched the bodies of people below scurry to cars and leave. No one stood about chatting or laughing, smoking or making out.

The call had come the night before. Eveline's, as he had grown to call Ms. Lonsdale, sister had been the one to call, saying simply "It's cancer. You know Eveline; she refused to take a single day off from teaching to go see a doctor and now it's out of control. She doesn't have long. She wanted to see you." He hadn't seen her in nearly three years, but they wrote each other often. He booked the first train from the city he could, 4:30 A.M. the next morning, and arrived at the hospital midmorning. Eveline, however, was not fit to see him until after lunch. An orderly came to him at the window to tell him he could see her now.

"Father McLaughlin? You may see her now."

The information took a couple seconds to process and by the time he had broken himself from his thoughts to say "thank you" the orderly was already halfway down the hallway. Fr. McLaughlin followed. The orderly stopped and pointed at a door near the end of the hallway on the right, "You can go right in, she's feeling relatively well at the moment," he said.

The room was spacious, housing two patients, Eveline away from the door and a mystery patient behind a curtain just inside the door. As Fr. McLaughlin walked over to the teacher's bed, he noticed the massive amount of flowers surrounding her bed, all colors and shapes; he felt he had walked into a flower store. A window behind her bed let in brilliant rays of sunlight that, along with the flowers, made Eveline's corner seem more like a garden than a hospital room. In the center of the garden was Eveline's bed, and beneath a thin blanket lay the frail woman, still as beautiful and radiant as ever, with one exception. Her eyes, so vibrant and expressive in the past, were sunken and hollow; the only expression was an occasional one of intense pain, and recognition of her dire situation.

"Father McLaughlin?"

"Yes, do call me Charlie though, won't you, Eveline?" She was the one person in the world he would still allow to call him Charlie. She was the one person he had ever *wanted* to call him Charlie.

"Only if you call me Ms. Lonsdale." She had retained her sense of humor, probably an important reason why she had lasted so long. She was a remarkably strong-willed woman.

"How are you, Ms. Lonsdale?"

"The food could be better, but the service is pretty good here. I don't have much to complain about, but I probably won't recommend this place to friends who are in town." The two laughed. Then Eveline coughed and the mood turned serious. "I want to thank you for coming."

"My pleasure, of course."

Charlie pulled a chair up to the bed and the two friends talked nonstop for an hour until a nurse came into the room and interrupted them. "Now Eveline, don't you think you should get some rest? You've had enough excitement for one after-noon."

"Ah, I see I should go," said Charlie.

"Just a few moments, Lori, let my friend and me say our good-byes."

"Ok, Eveline; I'll come back to check on you in about ten minutes."

Once the nurse had left, Eveline said, "Nice girl, but she could stand to be a little more strict at times."

"Good old Eveline," said Charlie.

"Hush now and give me my bag," said the teacher.

Charlie grabbed her bag from the table across the room and brought it to her. She reached in and pulled out a small rectangular bundle wrapped in newspaper and a tiny blue ribbon. "I've been meaning to give this to you for a long time. Don't open it here, wait until you are out of the hospital at least."

"I don't know what to say. You're not the one who's supposed to be giving gifts and I didn't bring you anything."

"Yes, you did. But if you must insist on giving me something tangible, I could use a blessing Father."

Charlie suddenly remembered that he was, in fact, a priest. And as awkward as a blessing for Eveline might be, he felt compelled to honor her wish. He blessed her and prayed with all his soul for her good health and grace in the eyes of God.

"Thank you Charlie, but I'm going to have to be a teacher now. I've got some things to do, so you better go."

"When should I come back and see you again?"

"Not again Charlie. It was good seeing you, I'll write while I still can."

"But . . ."

She interrupted, "Think of me from time to time, will you?" The nurse walked into the room, clearly meaning to get Fr. McLaughlin out of the room. He looked at the nurse before turning back to Eveline. "Good-bye."

"Good-bye, Father."

Sitting in his car in the parking lot of the hospital, Fr. McLaughlin carefully un-wrapped the bundle Eveline had given him upstairs. It was a small book, pocket-sized, bound in leather and hand sewn. He opened to a random page and read a few hand-scripted lines, the same lines he had once written for a class in high school. Charlie began to cry.

Commentary The first thing to notice about Jeremy's two scenes is the amount of time that has passed between them. Clearly, much happens between these two meetings of student and teacher, and just as clearly, it would have been impossible to dramatize all of it. This makes a jump cut the obvious choice for moving from the first scene to the second. In the first scene, Charlie is struggling with the question of his vocation. His father wants him to be a doctor, and Eveline Lonsdale thinks his gifts argue for his trav-eling a different path. In the second scene it becomes clear that Charlie has traveled not just a different path, but a different path entirely—one that didn't seem to be part of the choices before Charlie in the first scene. Jeremy's use of the jump cut as a transi-tion between the scenes naturally begs significant questions: How did Charlie change? How did he move from loving poetry to entering the priesthood? Though the second scene in Eveline Lonsdale's hospital room doesn't answer this question, it hangs in that scene's atmosphere, coloring the reader's awareness as the scene unfolds. Given what we learn about the characters and their relationship in the first scene—they are student and teacher, they are budding poet and mentor, they are admirer and object of admiration (perhaps even a little worship), they are friends—the interaction in the second scene becomes even more poignant. Charlie's teacher has asked him to bless her before she dies. In return, she conveys her own blessing.

Concerns   Although these two scenes are powerful both in what they say explicitly and in what they imply, there are a few hitches.

When Eveline asks Charlie whether they can "talk freely for a minute, not as teacher and student, but as friends," the scene glides over this moment quickly. Given the moment's gravity, this seems both a sin against verisimilitude and a missed opportunity. Eveline has stepped from behind her veil of authority and spoken as a friend to Charlie about his talent as a poet, but Jeremy is very spare in noting Charlie's response: "Charlie looked at his shoes. There was nothing interesting about his shoes." It may be that Jeremy was reluctant to dramatize a larger reaction because Charlie is not an emotionally demonstrative character; still, this is a special and particular moment, and giving the reader a bit more contact with his reaction in this moment—when Charlie is truly seen by his mentor as perhaps no one else has ever seen him—would go a long way toward characterizing him, and might even give the reader some information that would help in understanding why Charlie makes the choice he makes (to become a priest rather than a physician or a poet). This contact could have come through physical description, through dialogue, or through a more comprehensive description of his and Eveline's body language, to name a few of the ways Jeremy might have approached things.

Another, similar moment comes a bit later in the scene, when Eveline has told Charlie that "[his] poetry says [he has] a greater calling than that of taking over [his] father's practice." Charlie reacts by "opening his mouth as if to speak," but Eveline doesn't permit him to respond, instead stepping back behind her teacherly veil again and dismissing him, something that, as Jeremy tells the reader, Charlie feels grateful for. What is it that moves Ms. Lonsdale to stop Charlie from speaking, and why does Charlie feel grateful for this? It's difficult to tell, given the context of the scene. This is problematic because this is another moment that, were it a bit more fully described, would have carried the reader closer to the characters, their motives, and Charlie's reaction at the end of the second scene.

Sarah's Response

During fifth period lunch, the cafeteria was mined with social perils. You needed either upperclassman status or a powerful friend if you didn't want to end up at the long, yellow tables in the middle of the room, where kids in sweatpants laughed quietly about BBC TV shows and frizzy-haired freshman French club girls unpacked their brown-bag lunches item by item. Milton High's elite gathered at the red, octagonal tables by the floor-to-ceiling windows at the far end of the cafeteria: the smokers, the stoners, the artists, the athletes, student government. Mint sat at the octagonal tables because of Lindsay.

"You guys will not believe what happened to me last night!" Lindsay called as she strode toward her table, breathless and bright. Mint moved her chair back so Lindsay could pull one up from another table. "Coolest thing to ever happen, ever!" She grinned around the circle, relishing the attention. These were Lindsay's friends, pretty, competent girls and mop-haired, back-of-the-classroom boys, all one or two years older than Mint and Lindsay. They were, indirectly, Mint's ticket to high school notoriety. A redheaded, fragile-looking girl laughed. "Yeah, so, what is it, Lindsay?"

Lindsay bit her lip dramatically. "I can't just, like, say it now. It's too crazy. I feel like there should be a drumroll, or something. God!" Lindsay's excitement was infectious, and everyone was smiling without knowing why. "I'm going to be in a movie, with Claire Danes!"

Mint felt the injustice of this like a hard push as Lindsay's friends started talking. "Whoa, an actual part? How did you get that? What movie?" Lindsay squirmed with excitement as she answered them. "No, I'm an extra—my aunt knows this Hollywood lighting guy—it's called *The Last Night*." Lindsay smiled at Mint with pointed kindness, and Mint smiled back automatically. She didn't care about being in a movie—that wasn't the rub—but to meet Claire Danes! Claire Danes, film star, actress, heroine of the 1990s teen! Star of "My So-Called Life," Juliet in Baz Luhrman's *Romeo and Juliet*, icon of a generation! Lindsay *knew* how big a fan Mint was. Congratulations, Mint thought bitterly. I hope you enjoy living out *my* fantasy.

The topic faded out of conversation after a few moments, since it was Lindsay-specific, and people had their own excitements to disclose. Lindsay didn't stop radiating joy, though. Mint sulked subtly. She could tell why Lindsay was so happy, anyway, she'd been talking about auditions and breaking into acting since they'd met. It made sense—she was beautiful and poised and talented. Mint couldn't hate that, not in anybody. She smiled when smiled at and tried as hard as she could to be happy for her best friend.

The next few days passed stiltedly between Mint and Lindsay. Mint consoled herself with imperceptibly catty comments and Lindsay seemed to be guarding something, waiting for something. It was just worked into their dynamic, like old mud is worked into a rug by footsteps, day after day.

Then, when Mint met Lindsay behind the art building to smoke before homeroom on Friday morning, came the news. Lindsay slapped a paper slip into her hand. "Your pass," she explained. "You can come, Mint. I found out I can bring a friend to the shoot." Lindsay inclined her head and grinned expectantly. "Yeah? You in, Mintyfresh?" Mint wanted to play it down, to make her worry for a second while she had the chance, but she couldn't control this elation. She realized she was beaming. Lindsay hugged her spastically and said, in a silly, high voice, "I choose yooooooouuuuu! Holy shit, we're going to be in a movie!"

Mint giggled uncontrollably. "A Claire Danes movie! Holy shit," she echoed. "Holy shit!" Somewhere inside her happiness, though, she sensed the uncomfortable presence of deeper meaning. It was the sensation she'd felt upon reading *Heart of Darkness* in eighth grade, when she couldn't grasp the whole, but only marvel at the complexity that was going on beyond her reach. She could tell, now that Claire Danes had entered her reality, that she was moving toward a significant life event.

Commentary For a teenager, one of the most potentially dramatic places in day-to-day life has to be the school lunchroom, site of constant battles, potential humiliations and triumphs, fateful encounters, and (of course) food. That makes the lunchroom an excellent setting for the business the first scene transacts: Lindsay breezes in to share her momentous news in the place where all the people she wants to impress are gathered. She uses theatrical flair to tell everyone what's going on, and a poignant moment passes during which she smiles at Mint "with pointed kindness."

This is a very subtle moment: Lindsay knows what this news must be doing to her friend—the notion that she's going to be in a movie with Mint's muse, Claire Danes, has got to be painful to Mint, and as Lindsay consults the running tally of power and influence that goes on constantly beneath the surface of high school life, she must know she has just scored major points.

Sarah elides this scene into the next with a passage of summary in which she describes how the next few days pass. Mint tries to be happy for her friend, and tries to console herself with "imperceptibly catty comments," but the days pass "stiltedly," with this new tension "worked into their dynamic, like old mud is worked into a rug by footsteps." The scene that follows is quick: Lindsay gives Mint the happy news that she, Mint, will be able to be in the movie too, and Mint looks forward to the shoot, seeing in it a significance that has nothing to do with becoming famous.

Concerns One of the important questions any writer must answer in dramatizing a scene is *what*, precisely, she is going to dramatize. By describing the way Lindsay delivers her news—in the middle of a group of the popular crowd of which she and Mint are a part—Sarah has complicated her reader's understanding of Lindsay and of Lindsay's relationship with Mint.

A few questions of dramatization arise, though, when we examine the passage of summary that links the scenes. There may be some missed opportunities for further dramatization here. For instance, Sarah tells us that, after Lindsay has shared her news, conversation goes in other directions because "people had their own excitements to disclose." What might these "excitements" have been? Might a sense of competition have been dramatized in the way other people expressed them? Would a bit more of this conversation have told the reader that much more about the social world through which Mint and Lindsay move? A few sentences later, Sarah tells the reader that it made sense that this opportunity had come Lindsay's way because she is "beautiful and poised and talented," and Mint "couldn't hate that, not in anybody." This seems a bit *too* nice, and raises a flicker of suspicion, especially when Sarah says a few sentences later that Mint "consoled herself with imperceptibly catty comments." Might there be some advantage in Sarah's doing a bit more dramatization in which Mint's struggle with these contradictory feelings is usefully illustrated?

Finally, there is a slight falling-off in Sarah's observation of Mint's emotional state when she says at the end of her second scene that Mint felt herself "moving toward a significant life event." This is a bit of uncharacteristically clichéd language—something Sarah could easily render more informative with a bit more effort.

QUESTIONS FOR REVISION

1. Is your story illustrating "interesting trouble"? Are the events you're describing in your scenes building on one another to take your reader deeper into the heart of this trouble?

2. Do you feel your scenes are set up in such a way that your story will deliver some change, either in the main character or charaters, or in the reader's understanding of them?

3. Does it seem as if your scenes, in their aggregate, are offering the reader more than merely a sequence of events?

4. Have you been allowing *ideas* to get ahead of *story*, at the expense of your characters and your accurate portrayal of them?

5. Have you made it possible for your reader to navigate all your story's physical and emotional landscapes, and is your portrayal of your story's action *plausible*?

6. Have you been following all the "tracks" your story has suggested to your reader so far?

Alternative Writing Exercises

1. **Are you coming or going?** The givens for this exercise are two characters and a room, and your task is to write two scenes using them. In the first scene one of your characters enters the room where the other character is seated; in the second scene one of your characters leaves the room. In the first scene, the fact of one of the characters' entering the room should be used to *increase* tension; in the second scene, the fact of one of the character's leaving the room should be used to *relieve* tension. You could reverse the order if you like, with leaving being the cause of an increase in tension and entering being the action that relieves tension. *What you'll learn:* Each scene has its own purpose in the formation of the narrative ecology the story represents, pushing the story up the slope of complication (*nouement*) or bringing the story down from its peak or turning-point and reducing complication along the way (*denouement*). For this exercise, you'll be writing an example of each type of scene.

2. **"Billy Pilgrim has come unstuck in time . . ."** So began the second chapter of Kurt Vonnegut's *Slaughterhouse Five*, which is the real beginning of the novel's action. It seems a pretty outlandish way to kick off a story, but before Vonnegut ends his book, he has explained the universe in his narrative in such a way that the fact of Billy Pilgrim's "unstuckness" makes sense to us. In this exercise, you should begin by stating something implausible—"A pig flew by the window . . ." or "She

turned on the faucet and the water poured up," for instance—and work to write a scene in which that outlandish event is made to seem plausible. *What you'll learn:* Plot can be made to support narratives that would seem flatly impossible in the "real" world. Even fantastic, unusual or implausible events can seem right in a story if they're given sufficient foundation in the facts and the logic that rule the story. Your mission here, should you choose to accept it, is to demonstrate that in brief in a single scene. Be economical.

3. **Well, I was in a good mood when I came into this joint . . .** An off-duty cop enters a diner in a good mood. Your job here is to write a scene where, by the time she leaves the diner at scene's end, a chain of *external* events will have taken place in the diner causing a change in her *internal* state. One caveat: You should avoid making recourse to obvious causes—like a robbery, for instance. Go for something subtler. *What you'll learn:* Things happen in our stories for reasons, and those reasons—usually reflecting the imperatives of character—need to be demonstrated in realistic, organic ways if our readers are to believe in them. Your job here is to avoid *assertion*, and to *demonstrate* a change in your character.

4. **You going to do something with that?** In this exercise you'll be writing two scenes. In the first scene, two characters enter a kitchen involved in conversation. There's an object on the table (a knife, a sandwich, a potted plant—you decide what it ought to be) that remains innocuous during the first scene, though it comes to notice. In the second scene—which may take place in the kitchen or in another room—that object attains some significance, and is brought into action or into conversation in a way that brings necessary energy into the scene. *What you'll learn:* No object or event should have a place in a story if it's not going to be significant in supporting or moving the narrative. This exercise will help you to illustrate this injunction with your treatment of the significant object you choose.

Reading Exercise:
Plot in Louise Erdrich's "The Red Convertible"

In the first alternative exercise suggested for this chapter, the phrase "narrative ecology" was used to describe the story. It's a useful idea: every story is like an ecosystem, with all its parts and pieces—its characters, its setting and situation, its passages of exposition and summary—working together like one of those sealed terrariums you sometimes see in catalogs: a bubble of glass that holds everything needed to keep the plants and animals it contains alive without requiring anything from the outside. If the elements making up this closed narrative world are in balance, the story works, and we can see the story gives us an instance of praxis. If there are imbalances—underdeveloped characters, for instance, or poor mechanics, implausible actions, or stiff and unnatural dialogue—the system can't work, and praxis never takes place. The story dies.

Happily, that's not a problem with Louise Erdrich's story, "The Red Convertible."

Scene by scene, it builds our understanding of character and situation so that we assent to its poignant ending, which seems both surprising and inevitable. Taking it as a given that each element of the narrative has a role in supporting the life of the whole, let's break Erdrich's story down into its components, and see if we can define what function each of those components has in creating a healthy and functioning narrative.

QUESTIONS

1. What does Erdrich establish with the first four paragraphs of the story? Would you classify this passage as *scene*, *exposition*, or *summary*?

2. Using the *Situation + Character = Action* equation, how would you describe the situation in "The Red Convertible," and how would you describe character? How do these two elements yield action? Does the action these two elements produce seem plausible to you? Why, or why not?

3. What information does the first scene—the purchase of the car and the brothers' summer road trip—give you that's necessary to your understanding of what comes after?

4. There is a long stretch of time that passes between the first fully dramatized scene and the next, which Lyman mostly accounts for through summary—a suggestion of the trauma of Henry's wartime experience and the way he was changed when he came back. What effect does Erdrich's summarizing of this stretch of time have on the story, and how does she use it to establish the story's conflict?

5. In the story's early going, Erdrich establishes the car as a symbol of freedom. How is this symbolism changed or made more complicated after Henry's return? What does Lyman hope to accomplish through what he does to the car?

6. If every story contains a statement of character and situation and a conflict or conflicts that must somehow be resolved, it might have been possible for Erdrich to offer Lyman's deliberate damaging of the car as a resolution: fixing the car gives Henry something, a task, that can reanchor him in his world, pull him back from the state of suffering and dislocation in which he returned from Vietnam. Would that have been a satisfying ending? What would Erdrich have had to do to make such an ending satisfying? How would such an ending compare to the ending that Erdrich does render?

10

TIME

. . . too soon, too soon. Already. Now.

—James Wright
"Two Horses Playing in the Orchard"

At every story's heart there is the sound of a ticking watch.

What does this mean? Time. Time of day or night; time of life; time passing, time stopping; time to begin something or end it; time to stop, to eat, to drink; time to take a pill; time to leave; time past, time *now*, time yet to come; time gone too quickly or time that drags like a sledge loaded with sandbags; the time it takes to drink a cup of coffee, to share a confidence, to fall six miles without a parachute. The swaying of the pendulum in a hall clock, the crumbling of a pyramid. Such are the increments we strive to capture in our fictions—each second, each minute, each hour like a room we must light, furnish, occupy.

Time has flavors, a character that differs when it is considered by a young girl dying of leukemia, by a middle-aged man graduating at last from college, by a bride drifting down the aisle, or by a long-retired cop who's just been placed in a nursing home. Time is eternity, an instant, and every length of measurement between, and every story holds some portion of it, glistening—if the writer works hard enough at his craft—with particularity, with life.

How much of that life ought a story to contain? A single day, an escalator ride—each can be fictionally telescoped, á la James Joyce's *Ulysses* or Nicholsen Baker's *The Mezzanine*—or an entire lifetime's experiences can be distilled into a single paragraph, as in Jamaica Kincaid's story "Girl." To answer the "how much" question, let's take a moment to consider our relationship to time, as people and as fiction writers.

Representing Time's Movement in Stories

As we frame our stories, time looms large because of its omnipresence in human consciousness. Like a bead slid along a string, the present is only a single point on the continuum of our lives. Behind us, the past is that long stretch of string along which we have already traveled, providing context for every instant of the present, informing our notions of beauty, truth, justice, pain, pleasure, sadness, joy, and so on. We call this context "memory" or "wisdom" or "experience," and we use it to measure and understand everything that happens in the eternal "now" of the present, and to project possible outcomes in the future. In our stories, we manage the expression of this fact by using *prolepsis, analepsis, jump cuts,* and *metalepsis.* We've already discussed jump cuts (p. 72), but we'll examine each of the other three terms below.

PROLEPSIS, OR FLASHBACK

What is the proper way to visit the past in fiction? One way is through the use of *flashback* or *prolepsis.* Most often, this means a fully dramatized scene, represented in the story as a character's memory of a situation or event that has bearing on something that's happening in the story's here and now. In his story, "Bullet in the Brain," which you read for the chapter on point of view, Tobias Wolff uses prolepsis at the end of his story to particularly powerful effect: at the moment his protagonist, Anders, dies, he returns to an afternoon in his youth long before his relationship with the English language had begun to pall, when he was struck with the simple beauty of the words "there is" spoken with a southern inflection.

ANALEPSIS, OR FLASH FORWARD

The future is always in our thoughts as well. Whether or not we are conscious of it, we are always prognosticating, thinking about what's *going* to happen—feeling afraid of the future, eager for the future, scheming, planning, running scenarios, thinking: What if . . . ? This constant juggling of possibilities—like the numbered balls bouncing inside a bingo machine—is another reality we can work into our representations of character and situation. It is possible to accelerate time, to use *analepsis* (also called *flash forward*) to jump the character or characters through time and into an altered reality for which the preceding story has amply prepared the reader. Jeremy's response to the plot assignment in the previous chapter can be considered an instance of analepsis: Jeremy jumps Father Mclauglin from his high school discussion with Eveline Lonsdale into a time years into his priesthood, when she calls on him for a blessing.

> "*You can't say certain things in the realistic form. You can't write a realistic story if you're going to take millions of years into account. And this is how we all think now.*"   —DORIS LESSING

JUMP CUTS AND METALEPSIS

We've already discussed the way the writer can move the story forward through periods of time—a day, a year, a decade, whatever period is appropriate to the narrative—by using *jump cuts.* Metalepsis is still another way of altering the time sense within a story. Metalepsis comes into play when there is an intrusion of one narrative level into another, which serves strategically to make the reader conscious of the story's various narrative levels and its fictionality. Kevin Brockmeier makes use of metalepsis in "These Hands" (which you read as part of the chapter on characterization) when he has Lewis stop the story's action to explain various things to the reader. This reminds the reader of one of the most unusual aspects of the story: Lewis is the narrator of a story in which he is the main character, and he talks about himself in third person. This seems apt, given Lewis's description of himself as an out-of-work fairy tale writer, and it also heightens the reader's understanding of Lewis's distress: his loss of Caroline is so painful to him, the only way he can recount it is to cast it as a fable.

Each Character Has His Own Relationship with Time

The first chapter included a list of unstated questions with which every reader begins her reading of a story. To that list, you should add another now: What is this character's relationship with time? The answer to this question will inevitably affect how you manage the unfolding of the story.

As an example, consider this: A man and a woman in a story have been dating for a few weeks. He's really enjoying the time they spend together, but that time always seems to end too soon. On the night he has decided to ask her if she will date him exclusively, as he is driving her home on the freeway he decides to stretch their time together out by driving more slowly. The needle falls well below the speed limit, but time still seems to race by.

Meanwhile, his date is having a *very* different experience. She can't wait for the date to be over; she finds him tedious, his stories boring, his choice of movies juvenile, the restaurants he picks pedestrian and too loud, his jokes offensive. She knows he's too self-absorbed to see that she's really not enjoying their involvement, or to suspect the truth: that she's only been going out with him because she's been lonely. To her, it seems this evening—which she has decided to end by telling him she doesn't want to see him again—will never end. As she watches the needle of his car's speedometer sink, she feels like screaming.

Clearly, these characters' emotional states—excited affection on one hand, boredom and antipathy on the other—have a profound effect on their experiences with time. If you were to write two stories that presented these characters and this situation, one using each person's point of view, how would the stories differ? Odds are, it would be the structural and characterologic choices you made that would accurately render their individual experiences with the evening's time.

You've heard the phrase, "Time hung heavy on his hands," and this has probably rung true for you at some time in your past. If you had to put into words what it was that made time seem so weighty, these words would probably include "dread" or "sadness," "anticipation" or "boredom." You could probably pick others that had an opposite effect on your sense of time: extreme fear can accelerate our sense of time, as can rapture. Whether emotions are positive or negative, they affect our experience with time, and stories have to reflect this essential fact.

There was a custom in classical Rome that can provide an illustration of another important part of our characters' awareness of time. Whenever a conquering general was returning to the city in triumph, a slave was always posted at his shoulder whose only task, as the adoring throngs surged along the path of procession into Rome, was to whisper continually in the general's ear: "Remember: you will die." This was to keep the general from imagining himself to be a god. We hear this slave's whispering ourselves—sometimes soft, barely audible; sometimes as insistent as the refrain of a song we don't want in our heads: life passes; our time is limited. Our characters will hear that voice, too. Because of it, human life is most often lived with some sense of urgency and anxiety. Let's keep it moving, that internal voice mutters, I've got a life to lead here . . .

> *"An hour is not merely an hour, it is a vase filled with perfumes, with sounds, with projects, with climates."* —MARCEL PROUST

Keep these considerations in mind as you work: as you articulate your characters, as you envision your story's situation, as your conception of possible scenes unfolds, your understanding of your characters' emotional state will also develop. This understanding will inform your characters' experience with time.

Time Is Context

In her book, *Story Writing*, Edith Ronald Mirrielees says that if you sit down with five or six people who are swapping stories, you will notice:

> . . . that at least five out of six, and more frequently the whole six, begin their recitals by the mention of time. "I was going over to the store yesterday . . ." "A funny thing happened the other night. It was just after I'd turned out the light; it couldn't have been more than eleven . . ." Even recapitulations of meditations and mental conclusions are given a time placing. "While I was getting breakfast this morning, I was thinking . . ." "I hadn't heard from him for a month, and I decided . . ."

As we write stories, it's important for us to pay close attention to this part of the basic human storytelling instinct. Whether we're telling the story casually or formally, time references are essential. The references we make to specific times and the duration of specific events provide important cues to states of consciousness, the significance of events, emotional shadings, the clarity or fuzziness of a character's thoughts, the emotions coloring the atmosphere in a room. When a writer sets a scene at midnight in the summer, or in the harsh, pure light of a winter morning, she establishes a set of crucial connections—between the reader's memory and experiences and the writer's and (by extension) those of the story's characters. The skilled use of this common experience with the passage and processing of time is as important to the construction of a sense of trust and rapport with the reader as characterization or the vivid presentation of sensory information in describing setting and action. When we've been listening carefully to the ticking at the story's heart, allowing our sense of time to guide us in the story's structuring, our readers take a scene's setting in, and unfolding through, time with a feeling of recognition: Yes. That's what it feels like.

Writing at the Speed of Thought and Experience

Readers also bring to the story their awareness of how long it takes to understand things, to really *feel* things. That's one of the reasons the deus ex machina ending rings so false, and why at times we find ourselves arguing with the *pace* at which a story is unfolding. Some part of us, the part that's always listening to the story's ticking watch, says in response: That trip across town was too quick. This seduction is going too slowly. She didn't really have enough time to figure that out. How could he love her so much, so soon? Recall the slopes of rising and falling action on the Freytag Pyramid: we know how fast bodies ought to move through space, the pace at which desire blossoms, the speed at which the mind operates, the heart's velocity, and we know when fiction is failing to approximate our experience. We say such fiction is *out of synch*—*synch* as in *synchronization*, as in *time*.

What Tense Should You Use?

At a mechanical level, the tense in which you set your story can dramatically affect your reader's encounter with the story.

PAST TENSE

Most stories are set in past tense, which enables the writer to convey a sense to the reader that the recounted events have been meditated upon, processed, their meaning distilled for presentation. This gives the story a retrospective flavor. The reader has the feeling throughout that the narrator or informing intelligence of the story knows how things are going to come out, is perhaps leading up to the moment when things changed, when the protagonist had an important realization, or to the moment when it becomes possible for the reader to achieve that realization.

Past tense stories recognize the fact that every human being compares each moment of conscious experience to similar experiences held in memory. Memory is the means by which we weigh the importance of everything that happens to us, significant and insignificant. Through this comparison we tell ourselves: I know what this means. I've been here before. I've had a similar experience. Because this process of comparative weighing and measuring is such a common component of human consciousness, it is inevitably one of the ways we convey in fiction the importance—and, ipso facto, the intimacy—of a moment of experience.

Past tense stories derive their power from the continuity of our experiences, the way we have of imbuing them with an importance that transcends the moment of their occurrence. The reader sees these moments with recognition: I know now what it means to the narrator when the light falls on the old woman's face as she sits at the picnic table. Because of what the narrator remembers and the clarity retrospective understanding brings to that memory, I know that face. I know that light. In conveying the way meaning arrives—the way a character's understanding of the story's events is synthesized—we create a powerful bond between character and reader.

For an example of how this works, let's look at the concluding two paragraphs of Wallace Stegner's story, "The Traveler," which you read as part of the chapter on setting:

> For half a breath he was utterly bewitched, frozen at the heart of some icy dream. Abruptly he slapped the reins across the backs of the horses; the cutter jerked and then slid smoothly out towards the road. The traveler looked back once, to fix forever the picture of himself standing silently watching himself go. As he slid into the road the horses broke into a trot. The icy flow of air locked his throat and made him let go the reins with one hand to pull the hairy, wool-smelling edge of the blanket all but shut across his face.
>
> Along a road he had never driven he went swiftly toward an unknown farm and an unknown town, to distribute according to some wise law part of the burden of the boy's emergency and his own; but he bore in his mind, bright as moonlight over snow, a vivid wonder, almost an awe. For from the most chronic and incurable of ills, identity, he had looked outward and for one unmistakable instant recognized himself.

Because this story is set in past tense, Stegner is able to adopt a higher rhetorical pitch than might have been possible had he chosen to set the story in present tense. As it is presented, the meaning of the moment at the story's end—the mysterious and beautiful recognition the traveler has of his kinship with the boy—would have been difficult, if not impossible, to render. Wordsworth once defined poetry as strong emotion recollected in tranquillity; the poetry in the traveler's "recollection" certainly seems to fit this bill.

PRESENT TENSE

Present tense stories carry the immediacy of the unfolding moment—things happening in the story's here and now. The reader experiences the story's events at the same pace its characters do. Present tense stories are a bit harder to manage than past tense stories; for one thing, retrospective narration lends itself much more easily to summary and exposition. When stories are set in present tense it can give their events a feeling of great immediacy and vividness, and less of a feeling that the reality the story contains is being mediated by the writer or narrator. The reader can be brought closer to character and story in this way, made to feel more responsible for summing and understanding the story's events, drawing conclusions.

Stories can mix tense elements, moving, for example, from present tense to past, to a flashback in deep past and back again, as the needs of the story dictate. James Alan McPherson's story, "Why I Like Country Music," which you'll be reading as part of this chapter, provides an example of how this can work. Please note, though, we're not talking here about *tense shifting*, which is a confusion of tenses within a sentence or paragraph, and which is almost always a flaw.

Progressive Writing Exercise #10:
Pacing, and the Uses of Time

For this exercise, you're going to write two scenes, each of which will present different action. As always, because you need to keep your story moving forward, you should use these scenes to convey action or characterologic information you haven't yet conveyed in your other exercises. Though by this time you may have a pretty good idea of what happens next in your story, if you're feeling stuck you might take another look at your story cloud. Each of the two scenes you'll write for this exercise must involve more than one character.

Now here are the variables that focus on the time sense your scenes will convey: each scene should be written in a different tense (i.e., past, present, future); the time of year should be different in each, as should the time of day and the point of view character's emotional state. One of the scenes should also contain an instance of flashback, flash-forward or metalepsis. It's important that these time elements not be merely incidental to the work these scenes do. The time sense you create should be important in helping the scene to do its work. For instance, a couple's argument might feel more urgent, tense and uncomfortable if you dramatize it with the couple standing outside, coatless, at 2:00 A.M. on a January night in Chicago.

What you'll learn: Time of day, time of the year, the time of your characters' lives, the tense in which your narrative is framed and the scene's relationship with the story's past, present or future—these represent the multiple levels at which time flows in our stories. The goal here is to work in awareness of the different effects it is possible for you to achieve when you vary the "time palette" of your story.

STUDENT EXAMPLES
ᢒᢔ *Jeremy's Response*

FIRST SCENE

Charlie had sat on the floor in front of the television in his living room. His mother on the couch directly behind him. His father off in his study, perhaps reading the daily papers, perhaps balancing his checkbook. Regardless, his wife and son cared little.

Thirty minutes until midnight. The pair in the living room had been watching the crowds in Times Square going wild in preparation for the ball to drop. New Year's Eve. Louise, Charlie's mother, thought about the dinner she would have to prepare the next day for friends of the family who were invited over to celebrate the holiday. She thought about how she wished her husband would leave his study and join the family for the ball drop. She thought about making popcorn.

"Charlie, would you go make me some popcorn?" she had asked with gentle command.

"Yes, Mother." She did not think about her son.

Charlie had gotten up from the floor and walked through the door into the kitchen. He had found the bag of popcorn kernels in the refrigerator and pulled the popper down from the top of the cabinet. He set the popper on the counter and plugged it in, added some oil and a cup of popcorn kernels. He put the lid on and waited.

Charlie thought about his mother sitting in front of the television. Charlie thought about his father working at something up in his study. He wished his father would join his mother at the television, he wished they could stand being in a room together, he wished they could talk to each other, he wished they could communicate. Charlie thought of what he needed to tell his parents. His stomach twisted. He tried to think of something else.

The popcorn, meanwhile, had finished popping. He poured it into a bowl and salted it with the shaker from the breakfast table. His mother liked lots of salt on her popcorn.

He walked into the living room and handed his mother the popcorn. He grabbed a small handful as he went to sit down; he knew she would not offer him any.

They sat in silence, with the exception of Louise's loud munching, until it was nearly time for the ball to drop. Charlie's mother began to yell:

"Bert!" her voice was shrill, "Bert, it's almost midnight! Come watch the TV!"

Charlie's father came ambling down the hallway from his study. He was a well-built man, stout; he might have been a football player in his youth if his parents hadn't forbidden it. He made sure to make a lot of noise coming into the room.

"I was almost done, did you have to interrupt?" He tossed a folded *New York Times* with the crossword facing up—almost complete—at Charlie's feet as if Charlie had been the one to yell.

"Sit down Bert, watch the TV."

"Same thing every year," he grumbled as he sat down on the couch.

Charlie had watched the TV screen as if, without it, he would have drowned in the sea of his own uncertainty. The ball was dropping. His mom was counting softly.

"3 . . . 2 . . . 1 . . . Happy New Year!" So very shrill.

"Great, now that's over . . ." His father had stood up to leave. His mother had reached out her hand with the popcorn bowl and asked Charlie to take it into the kitchen.

"Hold on a second, Dad." Charlie had decided to do it. "I need to tell you both something." There had been a brief moment of hesitation, Charlie thought of Ms. Lonsdale, "I've thought about things a lot and I've come to a decision. Next fall I'm not going to a regular college, I'm going to seminary. I want to be a priest."

The popcorn bowl had fallen out of Louise's outstretched hands. There had been a shrill scream.

SECOND SCENE

Father McLaughlin knocked softly on the mahogany door. The grotesque brass knocker looked at him and warned him to go away. The door opened. His mother let out a short gasp.

"Why, Charlie! You're the last person I expected. To what do we owe this honor?"

"May I come in, Louise?"

She moved away from the doorway and patronizingly waved an arm to the inside. "Our home is your home . . . at least it was once upon a time."

He took the pointed comment in silence, he was in no mood to get into a fight with his mother now, not the first time he had seen her in six years, not the day he had seen Eveline.

"Can I get you anything?" The question was obviously sarcastic.

"Some tea would be nice." Fr. McLaughlin didn't notice and Louise went into the kitchen, now bound by her insincere commitment.

Fr. McLaughlin looked around the living room. Nothing much had changed in the twenty years since he had lived here. They had bought a new TV a few years ago and it stuck out in the room as a futuristic contraption. All the furniture was the same. Apparently they had been content enough twenty years ago; they saw no need for unnecessary change. He sat on the sofa and picked up a copy of the *Times* from the coffee table. It had been folded, nearly completed crossword up. He wondered where his father was.

Louise walked in from the kitchen, handing him the tea. "I hope you like it."

"Thank you," he replied.

Silence. Fr. McLaughlin studied the lamp on the stand beside the couch. Louise straightened the *TV Guides* on the coffee table. A few tense minutes passed.

Suddenly, Louise was taken by an idea. She was quite proud of herself for thinking of such an idea and immediately put it into practice. She walked over to the hallway and yelled:

"Bert!" Fr. McLaughlin had never once missed that yell. "Bert! Come in here, we have a guest."

"Good God Louise, I'm trying to finish these accounts." Fr. McLaughlin heard the muffled voice of his father from his study down the hall.

"Come on then!"

Bert made his way into the living room, and made plenty of noise in the process. He still liked to make his movement through the house an event. Everyone should hear him coming. He stopped when he entered the living room. He stood silent a moment.

"What are you doing here?" It was not so much a question as a shocked response on the verge of angry tears.

Charlie looked at his father. He thought about disappointing him years ago, he thought about how hard his father had taken the news, but he also thought about how happy his life had been since he entered the priesthood. He thought about the dying Eveline and the preciousness of life. He had been thinking all day about his own life and he wasn't satisfied. Yet he still could not figure out why he had come to his parent's house.

"I don't know. Eveline Lonsdale is in the hospital dying of cancer. I came to town to visit her. I ended up here. I'd like to talk."

Commentary Time, when it's well handled in a scene, colors the scene much as a gel filter will color the illumination a stage light throws onto a set, casting a subtle and mood-creating color over the scene. So it is with Jeremy's scenes. Jeremy uses an admirable economy of language to illustrate the disconnect between Charlie and his parents.

To anchor the first scene in a season and a time of day, Jeremy chose New Year's Eve, a half hour before the turning of the year. Though it's a time of celebration and togetherness under the best of circumstances, this is clearly not the best of circumstances. Charlie's father is upstairs in his study, working a crossword puzzle, while his mother indifferently asks Charlie to make her a bowl of popcorn, then doesn't offer to share it with him. She shrewishly compels Charlie's father to come down to what can only ironically be called a "family moment" as the ball drops in Times Square. His father intends to stay only as long as it takes for this event to be over, and then he intends to go back to his den, but it is at this moment that Charlie announces he has decided to become a priest, which draws only a scream from his mother.

In the second scene, set just after Charlie has made his visit to Eveline Lonsdale's bedside, Charlie has followed an impulse and has dropped in on his parents after six years of silence. Begun with what seems to be a sly reference to Dickens's "A Christmas Carol" (the "grotesque" door knocker on his parents' front door "look[ing] at him and warn[ing] him to go away" recalling the knocker on Scrooge's front door), Jeremy seems to suggest in this scene that Fr. McLaughlin is visiting with ghosts. They are unquiet ghosts, clearly. It is as if the sense of wounded grievance they felt when he decided to enter the priesthood never abated.

Concerns   There are a few opportunities for further development in these two scenes, and a few questions of dramatization that have directly to do with these scenes' conveyance of time.

First, at the end of the first paragraph of scene one, Jeremy tells us that Charlie and his mother "cared little" what Charlie's father was doing in his study. This creates a fairly strong impression of indifference, which is almost immediately contradicted by the fact that Charlie's mother calls the man into the living room to share New Year's Eve with them. It may be that what Jeremy had meant to convey is that Charlie and his mother cared little about the *specifics* of what Charlie's father was doing in the study, but the wording makes it difficult to untangle Jeremy's explicit meaning here.

It seems a small point, but it's important: this flashback (presumably) is the first time in Jeremy's story the reader has been presented with Charlie's relationship with his parents, and if this true, then it is vital to the story that the reader understand this relationship clearly. The cloudiness in meaning at the scene's very beginning puts in doubt the precise nature of the relationships between family members and the business the scene transacts.

A slightly fuller dramatization of this moment—unfolding just a bit more of the scene's atmosphere and action through time—would make it possible to be more certain about what happens, and might make it possible for the reader to take clearer meaning from things that now seem a bit ambiguous, such as Jeremy's assertion that Bert McLaughlin "made sure to make a lot of noise coming into a room."

In the second scene, some questions of verisimilitude arise, brought about largely by Jeremy's economy in observation: first, when he says Fr. McLaughlin doesn't notice his mother's sarcasm when she asks if she can get him anything; second, when, after she brings tea, a few moments pass in tense silence; and third, when, after the priest's father finally appears, Jeremy tells the reader the man asks Fr. McLaughlin why he has come and is ". . . on the verge of angry tears." We'll take each of these instances in turn.

First, it's a bit difficult to know how Charlie could have missed the sarcasm in his mother's voice. One would think that, after six years of silence, he would be hyper-aware of his mother's tone and aspect, and would—as a priest, trained in ministering to people—have been fairly good at reading even veiled emotion. He has certainly seemed so in earlier scenes, with David and with Charlie's friend, Mike. Of course, it may also be that Charlie is so distracted by his own tensions and anxieties over the visit that he truly doesn't sense the ironic topspin on his mother's question; the point that seems worth making here is that this is a question it would be fairly easy to clear up if Jeremy were to linger a bit longer in this interaction, describe it a bit more fully, give it a bit more *duration*. The amount of time represented would be the same; the depth with which Jeremy would occupy it—representing Fr. McLaughlin's experience with it—would be what changed.

This deeper occupation of a single moment would also improve the reader's access to what happens in the other two moments mentioned above. If Jeremy were to more fully present the tense moments of silence that pass between Charlie and his mother before she calls Bert to come into the room, it might be clearer why Charlie never speaks. The same goes for the response Charlie's father has, which now seems oddly abrupt and out of synch with the boorish insensitivity Jeremy seems to have portrayed in the previous scene.

Sarah's Response

FIRST SCENE

Lindsay was keeping her pass under her pillow, but Mint worried that hers might get washed with her sheets, so she taped it onto her calendar over the third week of November. She slogged through days of high school distractedly, labeling her x and y axes, skipping seventh period to smoke on the fire escape in the art wing, holding her secret out of view like a firefly in cupped hands. Lindsay didn't tell people about it either—Mint was glad she understood that this was something that belonged to best friends. After school, Mint and Lindsay would walk the four city blocks to Mint's house, crushing crimson leaves beneath never-muddied shoes. Sometimes Mint would rescue the prettiest ones to press secretly in her mother's unabridged dictionary.

Today the leaves escaped notice in the rush to get indoors—an unexpected cold front had blown in from the east during the school day. Mint and Lindsay crossed their arms and leaned into the wind. Mint giggled at their awkward hurry, backpacks smacking against their backs in the near-empty street, and they broke into a run. At the halfway point, Lindsay grabbed Mint's shoulder to slow down, but Mint only put on more speed, and the run silently became a race. A few old ladies waiting at the bus stop turned to watch them sprint by, unsmiling girls chased by invisible pursuers.

Mint reached her street first, and slowed to a walk when, around the corner, her mother came into view, sweeping the leaves off the narrow steps of her brownstone house. Lindsay caught up, unphased. Mint's mother looked lumpy and oblivious, in a bright green house dress, waving laboriously at them with the bristle end of the broom. Lindsay waved back, and then began to laugh uncontrollably at Mint's hair, blown straight back away from her face as if she were a shocked cartoon character. Mint's mother ushered them inside, chatting brightly about how much she loved autumn, and something about stray cats, or the neighbor's cat. Mint glanced at the mirror in the foyer, and decided that her hair *was* pretty funny.

They dropped their backpacks, pried off their shoes, and dodged up a half flight of stairs to the TV room to watch taped episodes of "My So-Called Life." Mint's mother called after them "Do you girls want a snack?"

"Yes," yelled Mint as she closed the door.

Breathless, Mint fed a tape into the VCR. Lindsay settled back against the brown-and-white-striped futon in the middle of the room, opposite the television.

"Why is it always so bare in here?" Lindsay asked, surveying the plain white walls, the one framed picture of a sailboat, and the card table spread with the pieces of a barely begun puzzle.

"I don't know." Mint was fast forwarding through the opening sequence of the episode. "I mean, yes I do. Mom won't let me tape things on the walls in here because it's supposed to be a guest bedroom some day."

"Wouldn't she probably repaint it anyway? I mean, the paint is, like, cracked. Over there, and there." She pointed.

"Yeah, I think she just likes it boring or something. OK, ready." Mint pressed play and scrambled back to the futon.

There, on the screen, was Claire Danes, with that crimson hair, yearning for Jordan Catalano and delivering voice-over monologues all shivery with meaning. There she was, soft-faced and thoughtful and important. In this episode, the nerd, Brian, wrote a love letter to Claire Danes for Jordan to send her, when he was secretly in love with her too. Lindsay was leaning toward the screen with her elbows on her knees. She looked like she should have been taking notes. Mint watched her out of the corner of her eye. Does she really care about Brian? Mint wondered. Does she have any idea what it's like for him, not to be sure about things? She surprised herself by saying it out loud.

"Do you really care about Brian?"

Lindsay tore herself away from the screen to glance at Mint. "What do you mean?" There was a hint of danger in her tone, that edge that made people want to please her.

Mint tread carefully. "I just mean, because . . . you know that guy Danny? He's a lot like him. That guy who asked you out the first week of school?"

Lindsay spoke easily, disaster averted. "Yeah, yeah, Danny. Yeah. I like Brian, but if he asked me out, like, in *real* life, I'd say no. I mean, would *you* date Brian?"

Mint didn't have to think. "No."

Mint's mother knocked and brought in fruit and iced tea on a tray shaped like Noah's Ark. She lingered in the doorway a few seconds too long on the way out, trying to think of the right thing to say. Mint and Lindsay craned their necks back to see why she was still there, and they looked at each other for a moment, across an ocean of age and misunderstanding and worry. "Enjoy . . ." said Mint's mother helplessly, and she left them alone.

SECOND SCENE

Lindsay and Mint are running home from a school dance. They are running partly because it is late, almost eleven, and even this part of the city isn't safe in the dark, especially when it is hot like this. The air is still dense and warm, and the people on the sidewalks all seem uncomfortable, as if they're out looking for some way to get comfortable, or at least get angry. They are also running because Lindsay wanted to run, and Mint didn't see the point of walking by herself. As they pass the halfway point to Mint's house, Mint surges ahead, her annoyance translated into physical energy. It becomes a race. Mint feels the stretch in her quads, and her insides burn because she hasn't run like this since the mile in gym class last semester, but she's winning, and she loves it. She gets to her brownstone house first, and trots up the front steps to wait at the front door as if she's been here *forever*.

Lindsay is only a few steps behind, though, and she doesn't really care. The two of them, red-faced and distastefully sweaty, go inside. Mint signals to Lindsay because she can see that the kitchen light is on; her mother is probably in there, reading and baking like she does late at night. They try to steal noiselessly upstairs to the TV room where they won't be bothered. On the stairs, though, they freeze. Mint's mother is at the top, lumpy in a green house dress, holding a stack of books.

"Hi, girls!" she says. "How was the dance?"

"It was fine," says Mint, though it wasn't. There is a silence where her mother clearly wants some clarification on "fine" or else on what they're doing, or if Lindsay is sleeping over, or if there is anything they need. "It was fine," repeats Mint, "and we're going upstairs to watch TV."

"Oh, good," says her mother. "Do you want a snack? Water or lemonade? I bought more microwave popcorn, if you want it, or watermelon?" She is desperate to be of use. Lindsay imagines that if she weren't holding books, she would be wringing her hands.

"Yeah," says Mint as she and Lindsay brush by, up the stairs. "Lemonade and popcorn would be good." They turn into the TV room and close the door.

Lindsay throws herself down on the brown-and-white-striped futon in the middle of the room, opposite the TV. Mint grabs a tape off of a shelf by the door and walks over to put it in the VCR.

"Remind me never to go to another high school dance," moans Lindsay, stretched out on the couch in a mock swoon. Mint grimaces and thinks, Lindsay danced with, like, half the school. There's no way she'll *ever* miss a dance.

"Yeah, they really suck," she answers. Mint didn't dance with anyone, unless you count sort of swaying and bobbing your head in a tight circle of French club girls "dancing."

"I mean," continues Lindsay, "they're so *amateur*. And the music sucks. I . . ."

Mint presses play, and the sound of the TV cuts Lindsay off subtly. They settle back against the futon and the episode of "My So-Called Life" begins. There she is, there's Claire Danes, who, Mint thinks as she watches, she'll meet in under a week. There's Claire Danes, with that crimson hair, yearning for Jordan Catalano and delivering voice-over monologues all shivery with meaning. There she is, soft-faced and thoughtful and important. In this episode, the nerd, Brian, writes a love letter to Claire Danes for Jordan to send her, when he's secretly in love with her too. Lindsay is leaning toward the screen with her elbows on her knees. She looks like she should be taking notes. Mint watches her out of the corner of her eye. Does she really care about Brian? Mint wonders. Does she have any idea what it's like for the boys she won't dance with? She surprises herself by saying it out loud.

"Do you really care about Brian?"

Lindsay tears herself away from the screen to glance at Mint. "What do you mean?" There is a hint of danger in her tone, that edge that makes people want to please her.

Mint treads carefully. "I just mean, because . . . you know that guy Danny? The one you wouldn't dance with tonight? I think they look alike."

Lindsay speaks slowly, coldly. "Yeah, yeah, Danny. Yeah." She pauses, as if trying to decide whether she will give Mint ten years or fifteen for her offenses. "I like Brian, but if he asked me out, like, in *real* life, I'd say no. I mean, would *you* date Brian?"

Mint doesn't have to think. "No." This satisfies Lindsay, and they watch in silence.

Mint's mother knocks and carries in a bowl of popcorn and two glasses of lemonade on a tray shaped like Noah's Ark. She lingers in the doorway a few seconds too long on the way out, trying to think of the right thing to say. Mint and Lindsay crane their necks back to see why she is still there, and they look at each other for a moment, across an ocean of age and misunderstanding and worry. "Lindsay's sleeping over . . ." says Mint, and her mother nods, as if that were just the information she needed. She leaves, and soon they can hear the clatter of pans in the kitchen over Claire Danes' dialogue.

Commentary Sarah decided (with permission) to take a different tack with this assignment. The two scenes cover approximately the same narrative territory, and this recalls the earlier exercises on point of view and tone of voice, which involved writing the same scene several times as a way of exploring which approach yielded the best effect. As with these earlier exercises, having the different versions of this action dramatized side by side enables comparison, and the second version of the scene—set in the early fall versus the late fall—seems more successful. This has less to do with Sarah's representation of the season than it does with the fact that in the second scene Sarah may have been able to better develop her ideas about how to dramatize the business she wanted to transact with the interaction between Lindsay and Mint in the TV room.

As was said in this chapter, *causality*—the way characters' thoughts and actions lead to outcomes—is one of the questions that comes up in consideration of a scene's time sense. The second version of the scene seems more successful at making this connection because it sets up a chain of causality between the scene's events and Mint's thoughts that seems more plausible than in the first version of the scene. The second version provides a much more satisfying foundation for Mint's question about

Brian: Mint and Lindsay have just come from a dance at which Lindsay has refused to dance with a boy, and it seems natural for Mint to probe about this when the taped episode of "My So-Called Life" that they're watching presents a situation with similar dynamics.

Concerns While the second scene did a better job of connecting event to thought and to the leitmotif of "My So-Called Life," the scene might have benefitted from a more complete representation—maybe in flashback—of what happened at the dance. Who Danny is, and the precise nature of his relationship to Mint and Lindsay, is still a bit obscure. More information about this relationship might make it possible for the reader to get that much more out of what is dramatized in the TV room.

QUESTIONS FOR REVISION

1. Can you identify any places in your story's scenes so far where the story would benefit from exposure to a character's memories in flashback, or a representation of future events in flash forward? Is there any place where you might drop action that is not useful, instead substituting a jump cut to move the reader forward more quickly?

2. Can you identify any places in your story where you might sharpen the reader's understanding of your character's relationship with time?

3. Are you making sufficient use of time to provide context for your story's action?

4. Does the action in your scenes seem to be unfolding at the right pace? Do you need to speed the action up or (more likely) slow it down at any point?

5. If you've framed your story using past tense, would it benefit from the immediacy a present-tense frame would deliver? If you've been writing your story using a present-tense frame, would a past-tense frame help it by introducing a retrospective flavor, a sense that the story's events have been meditated upon and their meaning distilled?

6. Does causality feel as if it has been handled right in your scenes? Have you dramatized at the right pace? Do the emotions, events, and outcomes of your scenes seem out of synch at any point?

Alternative Writing Exercises

1. **I'm not a morning person . . .** Write a scene in which a night person is rousted out of bed by his friend, the morning person, on a brilliant, sunny autumn day at 7am—just the sort of morning that makes morning people so cheerful that night people would like to cut their throats. Make full use of the setting and sensory information, and of the characters' contrasting sensibilities. If the obverse appeals to you, you might dramatize a night person trying to hold a wee-hours

conversation with a morning person. *What you'll learn:* People of different temperaments have different experiences with time. Writing this scene will give you a chance to illustrate this.

2. **Is any time the right time?** The exercise takes its form from Edith Mirrielees' thoughts on how necessary a time frame is to narrative. Your givens for this exercise are three events: a character's confession of a crime, a character's departure on a trip abroad and a character's encounter with a loved one who had been missing. Think about each of these events, and come up with a time of day, season of the year, and tense that would best frame scenes in which each of these events should take place, and explain your rationale, then choose the situation/time frame that most intrigues you and write a scene. *What you'll learn:* As Edith Mirrielees says, "[e]ven recapitulations of meditations and mental conclusions are given a time placing." This is one of the ways we involve the reader in the setting, presenting mood, intensifying the reader's contact with the scene's events and the characterologic and situational truth they convey.

3. **In time or through it?** Some events are here and gone in an instant—the firing of a starter's pistol at the track meet, for instance. Other events have duration—for instance, the complex ballet of a surgical team doing an open heart surgery. For this exercise, write two scenes: the first presenting a fast event and the second presenting a protracted event. *What you'll learn:* Part of attending to verisimilitude in your stories is working with an understanding of the sense of time proper to each event.

4. **Whose time is it?** A robber is knocking over a convenience store. Write two scenes—one scene set in the point of view of a first-time robber, whose wife is waiting anxiously in the car with their sick child, the other scene set in the point of view of the clerk, who's been through three robberies in the last month alone. Be sure that each character's time sense is a prominent part of the scene you write, conveying time of day, season of the year, and a sense of time's passage within the scene that's dictated by their experience or circumstances. *What you'll learn:* A character's circumstances or history can also have a lot to do with his relationship with time. Your job here is to show how these influences play out in each of the two scenes, and to show how the characters' different experiences—in the scene's here-and-now and in their history—make for a very different experience of time.

Reading Exercise:
Time in James Alan McPherson's
"Why I Like Country Music"

Things fall apart; the centre cannot hold . . . Yeats told us this in his poem "The Second Coming," and it's true. Given sufficient perspective, though, a larger truth asserts itself: things may fall apart, but they also come together, only to fall apart again. History—whether of individuals or of civilizations—rises and falls like a sine wave, and *history* is one synonym for *narrative*, for *story*.

To bring another metaphor into play, we live in a web of causality. Events connect to other events, and kingdoms fall for want of a horseshoe nail. We are wound in this web of infinite connection, and as we struggle, we wind its threads more tightly around ourselves. We don't escape this truth in life, and we can't escape it in *art*. In writing stories, we pitch ourselves headlong into the enterprise and challenge of time—this leading to that, that leading to this other thing, all of it adding mysteriously to the sum of being that becomes *self*, becomes *consciousness*, the woven thing that represents our understanding of the world.

"Why I Like Country Music" addresses this imperative by creating a conversation between a ghostly and schematic *now* and an idyllic and carefully realized *then*. By allowing us to eavesdrop on this conversation, James Alan McPherson makes it possible for us to understand his narrator with great depth, and to understand something about how and why the past lives so vividly within him—and, by extension, us. Let's try to analyze how he does it.

QUESTIONS

1. "Why I Like Country Music" begins in the middle of an argument between the narrator and his wife, but it doesn't stay there for long. Most of the story takes place in the narrator's deep past, and is related as a memory. What effect does this introduction have on your entry into the story and your understanding of its themes?

2. What does the narrator tell you about his present? How would this story have been different if the narrator had not framed his story as something told to his wife, but had simply framed it as something told to *us*, his readers?

3. How would you describe the narrator's emotional state at the beginning of the story? Does the story's representation of this state affect your understanding of his relationship with the past? How?

4. McPherson occasionally makes use of metalepsis, having his narrator stop the narrative to speak directly to his wife in the story's here and now. What effect does this have on the story?

5. The narrator summarizes the fourth grade school year during which his infatuation with Gweneth Lawson takes place, sketching in his relationship with her and his rivalry with Leon Pugh in a few paragraphs. He saves full dramatization for the May Day ceremony. Why do you suppose the author chose not to give us more of this school year as fully dramatized scenes? Would the story be different if he had dramatized more? How?

6. The story closes with a return to the argument with which it began. How has the understanding of the narrator's past, conveyed to you by the story of his love for Gweneth Lawson, changed your understanding of this argument?

PART FOUR

ENDING AND REVISING

Logic takes care of itself; all we have to do is to look and see how it does it.

—Ludwig Wittgenstein
Tractatus Logico-Philosophicus, sct. 5:473

In the first chapter, we compared the story's course to the flight of an arrow, saying that it must rise above the target before falling toward it and finding its mark. Now your arrow is approaching that mark, and in this section you'll be considering the role played by your ending. You'll also be revising your story to make sure you hit what you aimed at.

Odds are, as you've written and rewritten scenes for the preceding chapters, you've begun to develop an idea of where and how your story might conclude. Trying to move your story toward its close forces you to reconsider everything you've done up to this point in your process. You may find that, as you have been writing, you've been veering toward a conclusion that's much different from the one you first considered—rather like shooting at one target and ending up hitting another. You may have started out thinking you were writing a comedy but, as scene succeeded scene and you worked to knit things together, you noticed things were moving steadily and inexorably into more serious territory, finally approaching a climax you hadn't anticipated—and a distinctly unfunny ending. Although that may have been surprising or even uncomfortable, it's all right, if you can permit it to be. As we've said, oftentimes the richest fiction emerges if you can hold the story loosely as you write, allow yourself to be surprised, take the story where it seems to want itself to go.

Consider the text you've accumulated—its strangenesses and inconsistencies, its implications: what will round this story out, bring the pieces together, making of them not necessarily a harmony, but a recognizable music, a unity? Finding an answer to these questions is what the final two chapters are about.

11

ENDINGS

The means prepare the end, and the end is what the means have made it.

—John Morley
"Carlyle" from *Critical Miscellanies*

As we've stated several times, ideally a story should add up to a whole that is greater than the sum of its parts. The ending is where this sense of augmented summing comes clear in most stories, where—hopefully—the reader receives what she came to the story wanting.

A story's ending should bring to account all the implications of character and event that have preceded it. By the ending, the guns you have shown the reader should have fired, important characters should have said their piece and done what it is in their natures to do, threats should have been carried out or diffused, questions posed or implied should have been answered. No unusefully loose ends should remain. Remember that readers come to stories wanting to know what's at stake, why this story is being told. They come expecting some change, some revelation. By story's end, they should feel they have gotten what they came for.

This is not to argue for an absolute clarity, a complete dispersal of mystery, everything tied up so neatly that the reader has nothing to wonder at. In fact, the endings of fine stories are more often *openings* than closings; they leave the reader with the feeling of the spaciousness, variety, and strangeness of human experience, and of how large human life and human consciousness are. They stay in the reader's mind and memory this way. They keep bothering him, becoming work he continues to do long after he's closed the book and put the story back onto the shelf.

Endings shouldn't be rushed, and rushing is a mistake many writers make in early drafts. When we write stories, we want to know how things will turn out as much as the reader does, and because our stories deal with that slippery and elusive thing, human truth, they're most often a struggle. We want struggles to end quickly, because who likes struggling? Stick with it though; *don't end before the end.* This is one of the places in story writing that requires the most patience and endurance.

The End Is the Beginning Is the End

As you work toward the ending of your story, keep the story's beginning in mind. Many times the impulse that began a story also contains hints of its ending. We've said that stories often begin by stating their arc. All that comes after the beginning follows this thematic, metaphoric direction.

For the most part, though, the determination of this arc isn't a conscious process. Most often, we find our way instinctively to the menu of implications that a beginning is, and—as we've said—we may be a good way through the story before we appreciate those implications fully. Maybe your opening scene is of a teenaged boy shooting baskets by himself in the driveway of his home, trying to perfect his jump shot. You're not sure at the beginning why this is significant, but as your story unfolds, as scene succeeds scene and you gain a deeper sense of the boy's personality, his problems, what he wants, what he fears, what he must overcome, you begin also to gain a deeper sense of how that opening scene functions as a metaphor for the boy's loneliness, his determination and focus. You may want to close the story with a return to your opening reference to basketball—changed and deepened by all that has preceded it.

> *The end may justify the means as long as there is something that justifies the end.*
>
> —LEON TROTSKY, QUOTED IN: THE PREFACE TO *ANTONIO GRAMSCI: AN INTRODUCTION TO HIS THOUGHT,* BY ALBERTO POZZOLINI

If you tried to begin well; if you've been scrupulous about exploring character and situation deeply, if you've worked to keep all the parts of your story meshing with all the other parts, you can generally trust your ending to present itself to you.

Endings *After* Rather than *at* the Climax

It would be useful here to examine the notion of **denouement**. Many writers mistakenly believe that this word itself means the story's ending. Actually, it means the unraveling of action that comes *after* the story's most climactic moment or realization. If a short story can be likened to a thunderstorm, then most often the ending is the place of comparative calm after the rain has stopped and the lightning has moved off, when it's safe to come out and assess the changes that have been wrought on the landscape.

Pacing is also an important consideration in endings, and this is where writing a story is closest to composing music. Think of symphonies: in each of them there are passages of energy and passion where the notes crowd and pile up on each other, and others of comparative quiet. If you think about the endings of your favorite symphonies, most do not come in great crashes of sound. More often they end in measured ways, with recapitulations of opening themes, or in dying falls. As a symphony moves into its final measures, the entire orchestra may fall silent, leaving one lone instrument sounding at the end, an echo that suggests infinity. Remember this as you approach your ending: what is the last sound you want to leave in your reader's ear?

Tricks and Traps to Avoid

One sound you should usually avoid leaving the reader with is the "bang" of the surprise ending. This is not a hard-and-fast rule of course—the writer O. Henry built a reputation on his ability to work pleasing surprises into his stories. These are very, very tough to pull off, though. Too often a surprise ending will leave the reader feeling tricked by the writer, like someone on whom a practical joke has been played. A practical joke is fun for the one who plays it, but it's most often a humiliating or even enraging experience for its victim.

In a similar vein, avoid the "it was all a dream" ending. This is the ending where the story's events are revealed at the end to have taken place in the protagonist's—or even worse, the writer's—sleep or fantasy. These almost invariably leave a bad taste in the reader's mouth.

The End Is Not the End

You should also avoid "purse-string" endings. These are endings that draw the story tightly closed at the finish, like a cord in the mouth of a sack. Remember the chapter on beginnings, in which we said that good stories begin in medias res—in the middle of things? Good stories often end this way too. Your story may narrow down, but it shouldn't be cinched too tightly closed when you write your last word. The reader should come to the story's last word with the feeling that life continues, that the truths the story released into the characters' minds or the reader's mind will continue to resonate.

Progressive Writing Exercise #11: *Writing Your Ending*

By this time you probably have a fair notion of how your story wants to conclude. Even if you're still unsure, in all likelihood your story's ending is floating before you in the sentences, paragraphs and pages you've written. You've worked through what makes a vivid setting, you've brought characters to life and worked to make their imperatives clear, you've written scenes that added narrative energy and layers of subtlety and nuance to the reader's understanding, and you've considered how your unfolding of your story's scenes might contribute to a sense of rising tension, change and falling tension. You've worked through how these tensions can be carried through a number of scenes, and how the scenes can combine to suggest the coherent movement of external and internal causality we call *plot*. Now you will reconsider the work you've done for the following exercise on endings.

Begin by looking again at your response to the exercise for Chapter Two, on beginnings. Consider each of the characters you introduced in this exercise. If you've characterized sufficiently in the work you've done since you wrote this beginning,

you should have seen interesting currents appear in your story—friction points, colli-
sions, resonances, ways your characters' desires and fears might work together or be at
odds. Now put yourself in each of your
characters' places. On a clean sheet of
paper, for each of your characters, sketch
out in a few phrases an outcome each
character would *want* and an outcome
each character would *fear*. This should
give you a goodly number of possible sce-
narios. Choose the outcome that seems most interesting to you, the one that seems
most appropriate to the events of your story, and write that outcome.

If I see an ending, I can work backward.

—ARTHUR MILLER,
NEW YORK TIMES INTERVIEW, FEBRUARY 9, 1986

What you'll learn: Oddly enough, beginnings are often good places to search for
ending energies, having as they so often do the seeds of the endings in them. By returning to your beginning, now that you've done so much exploration of the characters and situation you created then, you may be better equipped to identify these
seeds, and it may be possible to speculate your way into a plausible outcome/action.

STUDENT EXAMPLES

Jeremy's Response

Jeremy's Note: *I honestly do not know how my story should end. As of this moment,
I am not completely sure how my story should begin. Thus, for the purposes of this exercise, I am using one of the many directions in which I have envisioned my story going. Following the scenes from the previous couple of exercises, Fr. McLaughlin finds himself
confused and frustrated with the priesthood, or at least his perceived ineffectiveness. A version of the David character enters the story (I might change the name) and, playing up
the parallel experiences between the characters, helps Charlie rediscover why he became a
priest.*

"Thank you for everything," said David.

"Ah, it was my pleasure," replied Father McLaughlin generously. "I'm glad that I
was here to help you when you needed it."

The two men stood just inside the front door of the rectory. Fr. McLaughlin had
opened the door as they talked and held it open. Through the screen door on the
outside they could hear the neighbor children riding their bikes up and down the
sidewalk. A robin landed on the porch railing and began to sing. The two inside
the door looked at each other one last time. For Fr. McLaughlin the moment was
eerily similar to looking into the mirror of his memory and seeing a recently remembered version of himself. David looked up into the eyes of a man who understood him
better than anyone had ever before or would ever again.

By his side, David held a paper bag, rolled closed at the top, that Fr. McLaughlin
had packed for him. There were a few sandwiches, a thermos full of lemonade, and a
couple apples. Fr. McLaughlin thought that would be enough food to get him
through the day. Beneath all of that, unknown to David, was a small pile of cash, a
hundred dollars or so, wrapped with a paper note and paperclipped together. The
note read simply: "Thank *you*! Fr. Charlie. P.S. If you need anything at all, just call
me . . ." and he listed his phone number.

David walked out the door and down the steps. He turned as he walked toward the street and waved. Fr. McLaughlin smiled. David turned, saw one of the kids coming on his bike and raced him down the sidewalk. Fr. McLaughlin shut the door and walked into the kitchen where he poured himself a tall glass of lemonade.

He walked back through the living room, stopping for a moment to look at the picture of the Virgin Mary hanging above the fireplace. Fr. McLaughlin saw something in her eyes he had never quite noticed before. Under his breath he muttered a quick prayer, a simple, personal prayer of the kind not really worth repeating but generally saying, "Thank you for everything."

Fr. McLaughlin picked up the novel he had been reading, opened the front door and stepped out onto the porch. He sat back in the porch swing and relaxed. The robin that had flown away when David had left came back and landed on the railing, out on the sidewalk the children were laughing. As Fr. McLaughlin watched them he let out a deep, appreciative sigh. Then he opened his book and began to read.

Commentary Jeremy's reservations notwithstanding, this ending resonates mutedly with the energies Jeremy released in the previous scenes. What the scene seems chiefly to express is a resolution to the problems of identity with which Charlie has long struggled, expressed variously in the story through his relationships with his parents, his former teacher, his fellow priest, and David. The concluding moment in this ending has similarities to the concluding moment in Wallace Stegner's "The Traveler," with each person staring at the other in mutual comprehension that what he is seeing is his double. In Jeremy's story, Charlie sees in David someone at the beginning of the journey on which he set out long ago, and David sees in the priest "a man who [understands] him better than anyone had ever before or would ever again."

Concerns Stories are like closed hydraulic systems: pressure on one part of the system becomes pressure exerted on all parts of the system. An ending naturally generates pressure on the rest of the story to support it—that is, to make it feel organic, make it a plausible rounding-out of all the actions and implications the story has presented in the preceding scenes. One particular part of Jeremy's ending creates quite a lot of this sort of pressure, and it is the clause quoted above, from the end of the third paragraph, in which this pressure is most concentrated. The notion that David sees in Fr. McLaughlin "a man who [understands] him better than anyone had ever before or would ever again" implies a tremendous intimacy and intensity in their connection— something the story has not yet presented to us. If Jeremy decides his final story must express this implication, he must also be sure the story he has told supports it.

Sarah's Response

And then she looked away, and they got her down to her trailer and her life, whatever that might be. Everybody got down, and left, one by one, and there would never be another film shot at this location. Mint and Lindsay called their rides from a pay phone and they waited on a bench outside the park gates, watching the crew pack up their vans and drive away. It was 1:00.

They sat in silence, because Mint could tell Lindsay would be snappish if she talked—she hadn't been discovered. Mint herself was surprised by how normal she felt. Her moment had come and gone, and here she was, on a bench. Her shoulder hurt from leaning against the safety bars in the Ferris wheel. Where was the punch, or the letdown? It struck her that nothing had happened. In the big picture, nothing had happened today at all. They were not in the shot. Claire Danes was still Claire Danes, her secrets kept. Glancing sideways at Lindsay, this didn't seem so bad. Mint felt vaguely sorry for her, such beauty wasted into droopy petulance. Some day she will be discovered, Mint thought, and then she will rise away from all this and become an image on the screen. And I will not.

Lindsay stood up when her sister's jeep pulled into the parking lot. She called, "See you," without turning around as she walked away. The door opened wide as she climbed up into the jeep, and Mint caught a glimpse of her sister, the picture of Lindsay, but bone-thin, her face a mask of makeup. Music blared as they drove away.

Mint's mother was ten minutes late—she had run into an old friend at the supermarket. Mint thought she looked almost dreamy, as if she had just come out of a dark movie theater. She said, as Mint belted herself in, "I've got to do some errands on the way home—the post office, the market, you don't mind, do you? How was the taping?"

"It was great."

"And was the actress that you wanted to see there? Was she . . ." Mint's mother sighed, indulging in the memory of some thrill from her youth, "exciting and beautiful?"

Mint studied her mother, since she was driving and couldn't look back. She was smiling in a way that Mint had never noticed before, a slight, wistful smile that banished the new wrinkles from the corners of her mouth and made her seem centered and far away at the same time. Mint wondered what the memory was that gave her mother this grace and gravity, or if she always looked this way when she smiled.

They pulled into a parking spot in front of the post office and Mint's mother turned the car off. "Yes," answered Mint against the new quiet. "She was exciting and beautiful."

"Not like us." Mint's mother spoke quickly as she got out of the car. "We're real." Mint repeated this to herself softly as she watched her mother through the windshield. Not like us. Not like we are. Not like we are. Her mother was wearing a long, red, felt coat that swirled around her ankles as she receded toward the post office door. A breeze picked up the orange and red leaves from the sidewalk and danced them around her in loops and spirals. Red like lips, red like a heart. And Mint could see her beauty for a moment, see that there was something waiting for her at the other end of uncertainty.

Commentary Sarah's ending picks up just where her dramatization exercise left off: with the collapse of Mint's hopes that she might meet Claire Danes and learn something essential about her own life through the meeting. In this ending, the scene coasts gently down the slope of denouement toward a closing that, to use the music metaphor again, is minor key and melancholy. Afer so much hope for transcendence, what Mint gets instead is the realization that transcendence—which Mint had hoped would lift her up out of the trap she identified her mother's life as being—may not be all it's cracked up to be. It's interesting to notice how satisfying Sarah manages to make this realization. Mint doesn't get what she had wanted, but that isn't a bad thing; on the contrary, Mint's ability at story's end to assign a modest beauty to her mother—a beauty with which she is able to identify—is quite moving.

Concerns Sarah takes some risks with this ending. Most of them pan out, but one or two provide some slight cause for concern. The risks include the way she edges up on endowing Mint with telepathy—Mint surmising that her mother was "indulging in the memory of some thrill from her youth." What enabled her to reach this conclusion? It's not clear, and it seems important that it be so, since immediately after this Mint studies her mother, seeing in her an unaccustomed "grace and gravity," and this is the beginning of her mother's minor redemption in her eyes.

Sarah also pushes the envelope a bit with the imagery in the story's final paragraph, with Mint assigning emotional meaning directly to aspects of the setting. Is this pathetic fallacy—the suggestion that the natural world feels human emotions? Maybe. It's a very human impulse to make the world into a metaphor for itself and for us; the key in making it work within a story is to be sure that it is supported by what we as writers have helped the reader to understand of our characters. What this means in terms of Sarah's story is that she has to be sure that Mint has been characterized enough, by the time this ending comes to cap her completed story, that the reader believes that Mint herself would arrive at these conclusions.

QUESTIONS FOR REVISION

1. In writing your ending, have you discovered a need to rewrite your beginning? Does your ending function as an answer to the questions your beginning encourages your reader to ask?

2. How close does your ending come to a turning point or instance of climactic action within your story? Does the period of denouement feel long enough? Too long?

3. Does the pacing of your story feel right as it leads up to your ending? Using the symphony metaphor, are the story's closing phrases a fitting conclusion to the piece of "music" the story represents?

4. Does this ending represent a plausible outcome, a whole that seems greater than the sum of the story's parts?

5. Do you see a need to strengthen any of the dramatization in your previous scenes to support this ending more fully? Might you need additional scenes?

6. Do you think this ending helps the reader to feel the main character or characters has/have changed? Do you think this ending helps change the reader's understanding of the main character or characters?

Alternative Writing Exercises

1. **And then what happened?—An endings engine.** This exercise uses a modified list of the situations given in Chapter Five, on setting, making them into full-blown situations. Here they are:
   a. An estranged mother and son reconcile in an abandoned chapel.
   b. In the middle of June, a brother and sister play hide and seek on the lot of a Christmas tree farm.
   c. A theological argument takes place on the killing floor of a slaughterhouse.
   d. In a casket showroom, a couple becomes engaged to be married.
   e. The manager of a dog kennel decides to go on a long journey.
   f. A man breaks up with his girlfriend while they're walking through an art museum.
   g. While hiking in a canyon in a western national park, a father breaks the news to his grown daughter that he's terminally ill.
   h. In a truck stop restaurant at 3 am, somewhere in the wilds along I-80, a woman decides to return to college after having dropped out years before.
   i. As a couple carries boxes into an empty apartment that has been newly cleaned and painted, one partner's infidelity to the other comes to light.

   Now, look over this list and choose a pair of situations. One will serve as a story's beginning, the other will serve as that story's middle. Ponder the pairing you've come up with, considering how they might be set in conversation with each other, and see whether you can't then come up with a situation that could serve as an ending. This may seem strange or arbitrary at first, but try it. Let your instincts suggest to you which of these situations might be connected to each other. You may find that, as you puzzle over the list, trying to establish this connection, a narrative suggests itself to you. How might a story that features these two situations end? Your task is to come up with an answer and write the scene. *What you'll learn:* One of the things we said in Chapter Seven is that dialogue is synthesis: it is different characters bringing their own personal energies together to create a new energy. The same thing happens when different scenes are linked—they bring a particular energy to the meeting, and those energies meet in ways that may be complementary, contradictory or somewhere in between, but that produce new energy. Your job here is to speculate on what energy would come from the linking of beginning and middle scenes, and to figure out how this energy might best be captured in a story's ending.

2. **Loosening the purse strings—rewriting the fairy tales.** Often, fairy tales end with the phrase: "And they lived happily ever after." Think of three fairy tales—Cinderella, Sleeping Beauty and Rumpelstiltskin, for instance, or three others that appeal to you—and imagine endings for them that occur beyond the rosy outcome. Choose the story that interests you most, and write a full scene that carries some of the original ending's energy, but leaves things more open and equivocal. For example, Sleeping Beauty might awaken to her prince's kiss and enjoy a few moments

of happiness in his arms. Then she realizes that her kingdom has been overrun by brambles, and she faces the huge task of setting things to rights—a fitting metaphor for an awakening into full adulthood. *What you'll learn:* As children, we're very satisfied with the "happily ever after" endings. As adults, though, they seem like cheating. In our experience, even happy outcomes are followed by long stretches when things *aren't* so happy, or when struggle is necessary. This is really when stories become interesting and meaningful to us as readers, because this is when they excite the sense of *recognition* that Aristotle identified as present in our experience of good drama.

3. **Have a do-over.** Everyone has a piece of personal history they wish they could rewrite. Now's your chance. For this exercise, you should begin by writing out your experience as a brief narrative. Now rewrite that experience so that it has a different outcome. Here's the kicker, though: for history to change, three things would generally need to be different: 1) the feelings you had; 2) the actions you took or reactions you had; and 3) the actions or events over which you had no control. Before you do your rewrite, you should think about the circumstances, feelings or events that would need to be changed for you to make this different outcome seem *organic.* Write down a list of these necessary differences in the categories suggested above. *What you'll learn:* Everything that happens is part of a web of causality, and even outcomes that seem simple and clear-cut on the surface are the result of complex interweavings of emotion, action and events that originate beyond our immediate control. In real terms, this means that if you change one thing, you change *everything.* So it goes in stories. This exercise is aimed at helping you to see this, and to represent it in the fictional outcome you create.

4. **Here's (re)looking at you, kid . . .** Many of us have seen *Casablanca*—one of the greatest (if not the greatest)—date movies of all time. If you haven't seen it, go rent it as part of your assignment: you won't regret it. For this exercise, you'll be reconsidering the famous concluding moment in which Humphrey Bogart puts Ingrid Bergman on the plane with Paul Henreid. When Ilsa leaves and Rick walks off into the fog, we're left with the understanding that Rick has been redeemed by learning the truth about why Ilsa had abandoned him in Paris. The change is both in Rick and in we who have watched as he wrestled with both rage and love during the story's unfolding. This dramatized change gives us an ending that is both surprising and satisfying. What would have happened, though, if Rick had decided he wanted Ilsa to stay with him? What if Ilsa had said: "Not a chance, Rick; I'm staying right here with you," and had refused to get on the plane? Your mission is to imagine a different outcome for *Casablanca,* and to write it as narrative. After you've done this, you should go one step further and write a brief analysis of 1) how this outcome changed the characters, and 2) how this outcome changed your understanding of those characters. *What you'll learn:* As readers we almost always come to a story expecting some change. Sometimes that change takes place in the characters and we learn something deeper thereby; sometimes it is only our understanding of those characters that changes, not the characters themselves. Sometimes—as in *Casablanca*—we get both: Rick's redemption and our understanding that he is a deeper character than we had thought he was, arriving at the same moment. This assignment offers you an opportunity to play around with this

formula, to see what it teaches you about that delicate and critical moment of change, where that change is located, and how.

Reading Exercise:
Tillie Olsen's "I Stand Here Ironing"

Tillie Olsen manages one of the most enviable kinds of endings for her story, "I Stand Here Ironing"—the ending that feels both surprising and inevitable. Because this story also offers such a good illustration of the lessons discussed in other chapters—beginnings, character, plot, voice, point of view/narrative proximity and distance, setting, scene, and time sense—it's a wonderful story for us to consider as we think about the way stories unfold toward their endings. As you read the story, watch how Olsen manages these nine elements and leads us to the tenth—the ending—gradually, patiently, detail by detail, leaving us with a closing that is light, but profound—as true as true can be to the characters she has summoned to the page with such assurance.

QUESTIONS

1. The story's title is "I Stand Here Ironing." Identify the first place in the text where this action becomes metaphor, and where in the story this metaphor might be said to be most explicitly expressed.

2. The social worker or teacher to whom the narrator talks is an important character in the story, but not in a conventional sense. How is that importance expressed, and how does it play a part in setting up the story's ending?

3. What purpose do you think is served by keeping the social worker—the "receiver of the narrative"—from being physically present in the story or actually speaking, save for the brief instance at the very beginning of the story when the narrator lifts a line from what seems to be a note this person has sent? How might the story's outcome have been affected if this character *had* spoken, or had actually been in the narrator's apartment?

4. The bulk of the story is told using exposition rather than dramatization. How, then, does Olsen create a sense of mounting tension that propels the story toward its ending?

5. Emily's comic talents are as big a surprise to the reader as they seem to be to her mother, however Olsen does not portray this talent as a ticket out of Emily's problems. On the contrary, the reader's knowledge of it sharpens the story's sense that Emily's early childhood is a shadow from which she is struggling—perhaps unsuccessfully—to escape. How does this sense—coming as it does so close to the ending—help to set up the ending?

6. What would you identify as the "climax" of this story? Is it the same as the ending? Is it different? If different, how?

12

REVISING YOUR FIRST DRAFT

Revision is one of the true pleasures of writing.
—Bernard Malamud

A Story Is More Process Than Event

You may have responded to the quote above by thinking: Say what?! It may be tough for you even to consider dipping back into your story at this stage, when you've just written what seems to be its ending. That's no surprise. To begin to think about revision you must first admit there's something that needs revising—that is, that there's something that's not working in your story. If you've taken seriously the "Questions for Revision" sections at the end of most of the chapters, you've been revising your story right along, and after you've done so much to get your story to this stage, setting out on a revision of the *entire* story is probably an unpleasant prospect.

Still, that's the business you're in. The truth is—as you may have begun to suspect as you've unfolded your story—writing a story is more process than event, and it's a gradual process with many stages. Completing a first draft of a story is an important stage in its development, no mistake, but it *is* a stage. There's more work to do. Revising your short story is an intrinsic part of the process of writing it.

As we've said, stories seldom arrive as a piece of whole cloth. Their beginnings are often provisional, tentative, even slapdash—as though the writer were a surveyor marking out territory. Each day as she sits down to work on the story before her, the writer pushes it incrementally further: a scene here, a paragraph there, a couple of lines of dialogue or summary in another place. She is using the work as a lens through which to try to see more of whatever it is she's chasing, getting down its features as she shapes her characters, capturing a certain timbre in a voice, showing her characters moving through a particular setting, unfolding the plot that suggests itself as she meditates on what the characters need, want, fear. She keeps pushing, trying to see her way to a conclusion that organically presents itself—a satisfying outcome that answers the question or questions she began with. Considered in its totality, this process seems like nothing so much as a long game of blind man's bluff, played in a limitless room whose furniture is rearranged constantly as we grope our way forward.

In his foreword to John Gardner's influential work, *On Becoming a Novelist*, Raymond Carver (who studied with Gardner at Chico State College in the very beginning of his writing career) wrote:

It was a basic tenet of [Gardner's] that a writer found what he wanted to say in the ongoing process of *seeing* what he'd said. And this seeing, or seeing more clearly, came about through revision. He *believed* in revision, endless revision; it was something very close to his heart and something he felt was vital for writers, at whatever stage of their development.

So revision is the process of seeing and *reseeing* your story, always in hopes that the next draft will help you to see the story more clearly. When you're revising, all the considerations we've discussed to this point come into play. You ponder the story's beginning; the point of view you use; the voice in which it is told; the care you've taken with setting; the construction of believable characters. You try to make your dialogue functional and genuine-sounding; you think through the unfolding of the story's plot; your balance of dramatized scene, summary, and exposition; your treatment of time and tense; the appropriateness of your ending. You consider the story in its gestalt—the "conversation" you've set up among your story's elements, the transitions you must manage in moving from beginning, through middle and end.

> *"How do I work? I grope."*
> —ALBERT EINSTEIN

Before pitching into your first revision of a story, it's often best to let the draft cool off for a while if you can. It's very difficult, after you've gone through all the struggle usually attendant in finishing a first draft, to summon the energy a good revision requires. Ideally you should move on to another story and work at that for a while, but at least let yourself feel that sense of first-draft triumph for a day or so before you start to pull at the story's seams, looking for loose threads.

Honesty is crucial. You have to be able to admit when something is not working, and you have to be able to face the work it will take to fix it. It is always worth *trying* to fix a story's flaws, even if you conclude that the story is not fixable. This is because, as you push on in your writing, you'll find that trying to repair the flaws and solve the problems of the early drafts of stories will teach you more about how good fiction is written than any writing class could. If you look at fiction writing this way, you'll see that no effort is wasted, that everything you do, or try to do, deepens your understanding of your craft.

The Revision Process

This process may seem abstract, so let's make revision a bit more concrete. As you set out to revise a piece of your fiction, work your way through the following series of questions as a way of focusing on your story's mechanics.

DOES YOUR STORY BEGIN WELL?

How effective is the story's beginning? Is the story's opening declaration of character and situation too murky? Does it take too long to enter the action? No reader is going to stick with a story that is too difficult to enter, or that provides insufficient payoff for that difficulty. Does the story enter the action *too* abruptly, or does it seem too long before you begin to pick up a sense of what the story might be about? It's fairly common for a writer to spend a few paragraphs or even a few pages "clearing his throat" before he gets down to the nitty-gritty and really starts telling the story. It's important to recognize when this is happening with your story, and to learn to cut away the extraneous material.

> *"When you get into a tight place and everything goes against you until it seems that you cannot hold on for a minute longer, never give up then, for that is just the place and time that the tide will turn."*
>
> —HARRIET BEECHER STOWE

Beware, also, hitting your reader over the head with the story's themes. The reader comes to a story hoping in part to be challenged, and in rising to this challenge to gain a sense of discovery. A story that denies her this experience—that insults her intelligence with a blatant statement of its intentions—will also be put down, half-read.

DOES YOUR POINT OF VIEW HELP YOU OR HURT YOU?

Have you brought your reader close enough to your story's surface? Have you brought her too close? If your story is told in first person, would you benefit from the control over perspective that a third-person approach would give you? If you've framed your story as an omniscient-third-person narrative, would you gain intimacy and vividness by changing to third-person limited, or even to first person?

If you decide any of these changes are necessary, it will involve quite a lot of work to make them. Still, if you want your story to be the best it can be and you think a change of narrative approach would help you, you'll do the right thing and try it. Again, no effort is ever wasted.

IS THE STORY'S LANGUAGE WORKING?

Read your story aloud to yourself, listening for those places where rhythm falters, where the flow of the words clots, or where clarity suffers because you're straining too hard after sound and not concentrating hard enough on sense. Does the tone you're using in your narration blunt the effects you're striving to create, or does it sharpen it to shrillness? Have you relied *too much* on a beguiling voice, expecting it to do too much of the hard work of characterization, dramatization, and plotting? Have you used language with sufficient precision? Have you depended upon abstraction to do the work of conveying meaning, rather than using concrete language, illustrating with strong, active verbs and characterizing detail? Have you pitched the diction of your story too high, and is the story suffering because the language is overblown?

ARE YOU USING THE PHYSICAL DETAILS OF YOUR STORY EFFECTIVELY?

Remember what we said about setting: in a good story it functions almost like a character. Have you helped your reader see this character by appealing to his senses, and by helping him navigate your settings so that he doesn't become confused trying to follow the actions in which you set them? Be sure, too, that you're not overdescribing your settings, losing your reader in a welter of unnecessary detail.

DO THE STORY'S CHARACTERS FEEL REAL?

Are your story's characters fully realized? Do they move and speak, think and feel, in believable ways? Do they relate to each other in ways that not only feel actual, but move the story, create dramatic tension, lead you to a deeper and more subtle illustration of what's at stake? Is the effort you've spent fleshing out each character commensurate with his or her role in the story? Have you balanced delivery of characterizing information in exposition, dialogue, scene? Have you characterized well early on in the story, and avoided overcharacterizing later on?

Another question that belongs under this heading and that's worth considering: Are your characters sufficiently individuated—that is, different from each other—and in framing them have you avoided slipping into *type*? As we said when we discussed character, it is vital for you to avoid clichéd characters. Also, think about how much characterizing detail each character requires. You don't want a character to be flat who ought to be round, or vice versa.

IS THE STORY'S STRUCTURE HOLDING IT BACK?

When we've talked about how necessary it is for all the story's elements to be in conversation with each other, we've also been talking about the necessity of a well-coordinated **structure**.

How effective is your story's movement from the beginning into the body of the story? If a story begins in an intriguing way but its subsequent scenes don't create any sense of rising action, or deepen the reader's sense of the complication existing within character and situation, the story will be unreadable. This deficiency comes clear in the story's *middle*, after the beginning has pulled your reader in, attached her to the character and situation that you've evoked with your beginning. As you revise this part of your story, take your time and work carefully. Does the story's plot cohere? Do the events follow, and are they presented in such order and detail that it is relatively easy for the reader to follow the piece's unfolding?

Your story must also carefully balance showing and telling. If your story has cooled off sufficiently and you read the draft with sufficient honesty, you will usually find places where meaning and narrative momentum will be conveyed better through a fully dramatized scene, and other places where a scene isn't doing work that is necessary to the story, and can be cut.

"Discipline is the refining fire by which talent becomes ability." —ROY L. SMITH

HOW IS THE STORY PACED?

We're talking here about the story's time sense, certainly, but also about its rhythms, created through your skillful interweaving of all the story's various elements. If you've overdescribed an unimportant setting or dramatized where you ought to have summarized, the result may be a slow-moving story. *Rushing* is a more common problem in early drafts of stories. The reader gets a sense of being rushed through a story when there are scenes that ought to be lingered over (especially, as we've said, those containing violence or a lot of action) or when the story contains characters who require fuller fleshing. As you reread your story, see whether you can identify places where a more lingering attention to detail will lend your story that vital sense of verisimilitude and deepen your reader's experience with it, or where slimming things down will give it a necessary feeling of momentum.

DOES THE STORY END WHERE AND AS IT OUGHT TO?
IS THAT ENDING "EARNED"?

Remember that a story that resolves weakly or not at all will leave your reader disappointed. Does your story's finish feel satisfying? Does it deliver that sense of "summing" that we instinctively look for by story's end—that sense of change or realization? If you've been working with a sense in mind of the ending to which your story leads, remember that the story must *earn* that ending. Ask yourself—as always, being brutally honest—whether your story *does* earn that ending or not. Stories that render an ending that feels both real and appropriate are the most satisfying.

Another word we can use in describing an ending that seems appropriate and real is *organic*—that is, it seems to be a natural outgrowth of all the narrative work and detail that have preceded it. Does your ending provide an organic closure to the events in which you have embroiled your characters? Does it feel too abrupt? Does it leave questions unanswered to which it seems vital to have answers? Does it leave loose ends dangling in a frustrating way? Have all the guns you've shown to your readers been fired, or have you provided plausible reasons for them *not* to have fired?

> "*After finishing the first draft, I work for as long as it takes (for two or three weeks, most often) to rework that first draft on a computer. Usually that involves expansion: filling in and adding to, but trying not to lose the spontaneous, direct sound. I use that first draft as a touchstone to make sure everything else in that section has the same sound, the same tone and impression of spontaneity. I revise until I'm done, and then I am done with that section or scene. I don't often go back and change much after that. So when I finish the last chapter, having redrafted the last page sufficiently, I'm done with the book.*"
> —KENT HARUF

WHEN YOU REACH YOUR STORY'S END, CAN YOU SAY WHAT IT WAS "ABOUT"?

We began with a consideration of your story's possible themes; it's useful to end by thinking about that here as well. Does your story offer your reader more than *abject naturalism*—that is, more than just a sequence of events? Does it offer your reader a working out of *praxis*?

IS THIS THE FINAL DRAFT?

This is one of the toughest questions you'll have to answer. Most often each new draft of a story will require at least as much of a cooling-off period as the first draft did, and even after you're fairly satisfied that you've gotten all the necessaries into a story, if you're like most dedicated writers, you'll seldom feel that you're done tinkering with it. Save your drafts, and look back over them periodically to notice your progression from version to version of the story. This can be a very useful practice, and you may find you'll use material from earlier drafts in new ways, once you've done the work in successive drafts that enables you to be ready for the information.

Progressive Writing Exercise #12: *Rewriting Is Writing*

By this point, obviously, you've linked together a fair number of exercises. Review them now, with an eye toward figuring out where the snags and infelicities are—in beginning, in point of view, in tone, in setting, in characterization, dialogue, pacing or your ending. Pick one of the exercises and, using the original guidelines of the exercise and the revision guidelines above, do a revision of the exercise.

What you'll learn: Though it may seem a little odd to be asking you to do a revision of one of your exercises after you've already completed the ending for your story, the hope is that sending you through the revision process at a micro level will help you to gear up to do a macro-level revision of your finished story.

STUDENT EXAMPLES
🔊 *Jeremy's Response*

Jeremy's Note: *I have yet to decide exactly when this scene will fit into my story, but I know it should be there. Depending on where it falls, important details of the conversation might change. That, however, is a matter to be dealt with as I finalize the draft of my story, not for the purposes of this exercise. The important thing is the conversation between the two priests. Therefore, this new version of the scene is merely an attempt to make the tone and content of the scene consistent with the current direction of the story.*

I notice that at some point I switched the character names; this was unintentional but I plan to keep it.

ORIGINAL SCENE (JEREMY'S RESPONSE TO THE DIALOGUE EXERCISE)

When Father McLaughlin had finished his sandwich and lemonade and sat for a bit just watching the world go by, he stood up from the porch swing and took the empty plate and glass into the kitchen. Just as he began to wash the dishes, the phone rang. He grabbed a towel and hurriedly dried his hands as he moved into the living room to answer the phone.

"Hello?"

"Hey, Mike."

"Oh hi, Charlie, I should have known it was you."

"What's that supposed to mean?"

"I had just started doing the dishes and you always call just when I'm in the middle of starting something."

Father Charlie Mullins worked at a parish across town. The two men had gone to seminary together years ago and had remained close friends ever since. They liked to think of their relationship in terms of the Bing Crosby movie *Going My Way*, and of course, each claimed to be the Bing Crosby in the relationship. Just like the priests in the movie, the two real men were both great baseball fans.

"I'll make it up to you. Ditch the dishes and come out to the Yankees game with me this afternoon. I'll buy you a hot dog or something."

Both of the men had held season tickets for as long as they could remember. When both had been kids growing up in different neighborhoods, they bought their first tickets with nickels and dimes saved up from entire summers of running errands and carrying groceries for their neighbors. After they met in seminary, they started buying their tickets right next to each other.

"I'll tell you what, I have to go see somebody this afternoon, but then I'll head over to the game. Starts around 2:30 right? I should be there by the bottom of the third."

"That sounds good. Who are you going to see? Somebody sick?"

"No, not sick. Irma Wallace fell down her front steps early this morning. The family called and told me she'd broken her hip. Doesn't look terribly bad, they said, but they would still feel comforted if I came and sat with her a while."

"Is that the Mrs. Wallace that, oh what was it, something about your potluck dinner last October?"

"Ah, yes. You know, I'd nearly forgotten about that until you mentioned it. I guess I was too busy thinking about the poor woman's hip. What happened was that she and Florence Grayson ended up bringing the same dish, I don't even remember what now. Not that it bothered anyone else there, including Florence, but Irma was outraged. First, she accused her of stealing her recipe, which she claimed had been passed down through the family for generations and, of course, no one else knows it unless they've stolen it."

"Sounds just like my mother."

"Sounds like everyone's mother, or grandmother at least. Anyway, she then proceeded to declare that Florence should take her dish elsewhere (using stronger language of course) and if she should like to participate in the potluck she should run around the corner to the store and get some potato chips or something, since they would probably taste better than Florence's cooking, she said."

"I bet she didn't take that well."

"Not at all. You can't just insult another woman's cooking in front of her parish and expect her to just let it go. Florence was definitely not taking her dish anywhere else and was not afraid to let Irma know it. Of course, Irma didn't react to that well and before anyone could do anything to stop her, she had grabbed Florence's dish—ah, now I remember what it was, some sort of creamy green bean casserole, quite delicious actually—anyway, I remember because then Irma grabbed Florence's dish and dumped it all over Florence's head and dress. Needless to say, Irma didn't stay long after that. A couple of her friends dragged her out of the hall and took her home. Luckily Florence's casserole had been sitting on the table cooling for a while so that there were no burns, despite all of her yelling otherwise. I don't think I've seen the two women in the same room since, I believe they have even settled into going to different Sunday masses in order to avoid each other."

Charlie had laughed heavily through the story. "As much trouble as they may cause, you've got to admit, they sure are entertaining."

"Yes, you know, I probably shouldn't say it, but the whole event was something straight out of a movie. Two crazy old ladies just going at it, and they fit the roles perfectly."

"Why don't you send one or two of those over here to my place, just to liven things up a bit."

"Hey listen, they're here if you want them, but I'm not going to bring them over for you. Hey, that's smart, I'll just market all these ladies here to boring parishes like yours. I'd even deliver if the price were right. What do you say?"

"I'd say you're a pretty crazy old fool yourself."

The two men laughed.

"I should probably go, Charlie."

"Sure, see you at the game, Mike."

REVISED SCENE

Father McLaughlin arrived home exhausted from his visit with Eveline. After making the brief, ill-advised stop at his parents' house, he had taken a bus straight back to the city. When he walked into the house, he headed straight for the living room mantle and placed there the book Eveline had given him. He leaned it against the wall so it was easily visible; Fr. McLaughlin was proud of the book and he wanted to see it and remember Eveline.

The house seemed suddenly empty and Fr. McLaughlin looked for something to bide his time and occupy his mind. The image of his frail teacher, surrounded by such lovely flowers, and such little hope refused to leave his mind. He found a few dirty dishes, left from last night when he had received the call of Eveline's illness. He set about cleaning them. The phone rang.

He grabbed the towel that draped over the oven door handle and dried his hands. He moved into the living room and picked up the receiver.

"Hello?" Fr. McLaughlin said gruffly. He had yet to decide if he actually wanted to talk to anyone, but he supposed it was at least as good distraction as doing the dishes.

"Charlie? Did I catch you at a bad time?"

"Mike," there was a slight bounce in Charlie's voice. Fr. Mike Mullins was the priest at a parish across town and the two men had gone to seminary together years before. He could talk to Mike. "I should have known."

"Huh?"

"It's just that I had just started doing the dishes and you always call just when I've started to do the dishes." Some things would never change, thought Charlie, but so many things had already.

"Well, if you don't want me to call anymore, just stop doing the dishes." Charlie couldn't help but laugh. "You realize there's a Yankees game tonight, starting in about thirty minutes, and I haven't been able to get ahold of you all day?" The two held a pair of season tickets, good seats, just behind the Yankees dugout.

"I've been out of town," he hesitated a moment before going on, "I just found out a good friend of mine has cancer."

"Oh no, Charlie, I'm sorry," said Mike genuinely.

"Thanks."

A moment of silence. "Do you want to talk about it?"

"I feel like I could never figure out what to say. She did so much for me. I never would have become a priest without her support and what have I ever done for her?"

"Look Charlie, come to the game with me, you need to get out and do something, get your mind off this. Afterward, we'll go get some coffee and talk about things."

Mike had perspective that Charlie realized he had all but lost, being so close to the situation. "That sounds good."

"Ok, I'll meet you outside the gate in about forty minutes. We should make it by the bottom of the second, let's hope we don't miss anything too exciting."

Fr. McLaughlin hung up the receiver. He reached into the front closet and grabbed his lucky Yankees baseball cap. He was almost out the door when he had a thought, turned around, walked over to the mantle and slipped the little book into his pocket.

Commentary Jeremy's revision obviously shapes the original scene to a much different purpose than it had when he wrote it in response to the dialogue exercise. He has dropped the anecdote about the argument between Charlie's parishioners, instead beginning the scene just after his return home from his visit to Eveline Lonsdale and his parents. It's interesting to notice how much more satisfying the scene seems now; although the very entertaining bit about the argument between the two old women has been cut, the scene now seems to have acquired more of a purpose, and seems to be much more purposefully in conversation with the story's other events. In its first version, the scene's purpose seemed chiefly to be lighthearted characterization; the second scene seems more serious in its intentions, with the conversation between the two priests functioning as a bridge from the pain and difficulty of Charlie's visit back into the life of his vocation.

Concerns This revised scene works quite well, but one piece of information—part of what Charlie tells his friend about Eveline Lonsdale's influence on him—creates some pressure backward on the story. Charlie tells Mike that he "never would have become a priest without [Eveline's] support." This is not something that has been either dramatized or stated in previous scenes, and so Jeremy will have to do some work in dramatizing this fact.

Sarah's Response

ORIGINAL SCENE (SARAH'S RESPONSE TO THE BEGINNING EXERCISE)

Mint's mother drove them downtown to the show, Lindsay in her lime green tank top and cut-offs, Mint in a yellow flowered halter dress cut too low, so she had to hold her shoulders back and her hands kept flying to her throat, wrists pressing the fabric up against her chest. Mint's mother bravely ignored the spike-jacketed punks and smoky-eyed daytime receptionists frowning against the fenders of their rusty Chryslers as she turned into the parking lot. She didn't say anything about drugs when the girls climbed out of the car in front of the Red Room steps. She could feel their shame like a release of heat as they slammed the doors shut and slipped away into the anonymous throng pushing toward the loaded darkness of the doorways. Mint's mother tried to listen to NPR on the way home, but she couldn't get her mind off that yellow halter dress, just hoping and hoping that it would stay up, that Mint had kept the receipt, that the daringness of it would somehow make her happy.

Lindsay forged a path through the crowd inside the Red Room, Mint close behind with one hand on her shoulder so she couldn't be lost. The first band was already playing, something loud and thrashy that made Mint think of animals and dirt. It was stirring up the boys, though. Mint wouldn't meet their eyes as she climbed through the jungle of bodies, slid across fleshy backs prickling with the first dew of concert sweat. She could feel the anticipation in taut shoulders, the trembling of the ones who would be dancing crazy before the night was over. Lindsay stopped in a little knot of guys in pop-punk band shirts and Abercrombie hats—older guys, maybe eighteen or nineteen—who pretended not to notice them. Mint was startled by the sudden permanence of this. She kept her right arm across her chest. Lindsay leaned back to scream in her ear that it looked like she was saying the pledge of allegiance, but Mint couldn't hear over the music.

The second band came on, but Mint didn't know them either. Lindsay was really into it, entranced and rocking back and forth. The Abercrombie boys kept looking at her. She had become, while Mint blinked, one of those untouchable concert demigods, enlightened, in control, the symphony conductor of the collective breathing of the crowd. Mint was jealous, had always been jealous, of people with passion.

And then, through the color and thrash, over the heads of petite trendy girls and through the momentary spaces between dancing kids, Mint recognized a face. It was there for one second, suspended, ghostly, for one long freeze-frame second. It was Claire Danes. Claire Danes, film star, actress, heroine of the 1990s *teen!* Star of "My So-Called Life," Juliet in Baz Luhrman's *Romeo and Juliet*, icon of a generation! Mint spun around, frantically searching for someone else who had seen what she had seen.

No one. Instinctively, she dropped her arm and dove into the crowd, kicked, burrowed awkwardly toward the space where Claire Danes was. The crowd didn't understand her urgency, and they flipped her off, muttered angrily. Mint couldn't explain it, but she knew she had to find Claire Danes. Claire Danes would know things, be able to tell her things. She was right over there, *so close,* just in the crowd, standing there, knowing.

But she couldn't find her. Mint was the last person to leave the Red Room that night, her dress drenched in other people's sweat, sort of beaten down and confused, an ache in her right arm. She lay awake in her house in the suburbs and felt an emptiness, or an *almost,* or perhaps a new sense of quest.

REVISED SCENE

A discordant drone of car horns assailed the rear of the car as Mint's mother drove the girls downtown to the show. She drove at 20 miles an hour not for safety, but because she enjoyed the closeness of people in a car. The girls sulked subtly, Lindsay in her lime green tank top and cuffed jeans, Mint in a yellow flowered halter dress cut too low, so she had to hold her shoulders back and her hands kept flying to her throat, wrists pressing the fabric up against her chest. Mint's mother bravely ignored the spike-jacketed punks and smoky-eyed daytime receptionists frowning against the fenders of their rusty Chryslers as she turned into the parking lot. She didn't say anything about drugs when the girls climbed out of the car in front of the Red Room steps. She could feel their shame like a release of heat as they slammed the doors shut and slipped away into the throng pushing toward the loaded darkness of the doorways. Mint's mother tried to listen to NPR on the way home, but she couldn't get her mind off that yellow halter dress, just hoping and hoping that it would stay up, and that the daringness of it would somehow make Mint happy.

Lindsay forged a path through the crowd inside, Mint close behind with one hand on her shoulder so she couldn't be lost. Mint was small but not slight—the kind of body that would be muscular if exercised. The yellow dress was striking against her fair skin in the light, but here in the dim crush, she looked washed out, mousy-haired and nervous. The first band was already playing, something loud and thrashy that made Mint think of animals and dirt. It was stirring up the boys, though. Mint wouldn't meet their eyes as she climbed through the jungle of bodies, slid across fleshy backs prickling with the first dew of concert sweat. She could feel the anticipation in taut shoulders, the trembling of the ones who would be dancing crazy before the night was over, inhibitions lost in the fray. Lindsay stopped in a little knot of guys in pop-punk band shirts and Abercrombie hats—older guys, maybe eighteen or nineteen—who pretended not to notice them. Mint kept her right arm across her chest. Lindsay leaned back to scream in her ear that it looked like she was saying the pledge of allegiance, but Mint couldn't hear over the music.

The second band came on and Mint didn't know them either. Lindsay was really into it, entranced and rocking back and forth. The Abercrombie boys kept looking at her. She had become, while Mint blinked, one of those untouchable concert demigods, enlightened, in control, the symphony conductor of the collective breathing of the crowd. Her hair, dark and barely wavy like the grain of cherry wood, fell in strands across her closed eyes, her high cheekbones. She had a small, squarish nose and lips like French women in advertisements. Mint was proud to be part of such beauty, like a pearl button on a mink coat.

Between songs, Lindsay was approached by a stocky, jittery guy with messy, dyed-black hair and a messenger bag plastered with the logos of more bands Mint had never heard of. He was really old, though, thought Mint, college-aged, and she watched him cock his head to the side and scratch his ear again and again while he talked. Lindsay was smiling and nodding—why for this guy?

Lindsay grabbed Mint's arm and yanked her closer just as the next song was starting. "THIS IS DAVE," she yelled. "DAVE IS A FILM INTERN." She nodded importantly. Dave smiled importantly. Lindsay held up two white slips he must have given her a moment ago.

"MINT!" Lindsay leaned in so close that Mint could feel her breath in her ear, heavy and cloying. "HE GAVE US PASSES. WE'RE GOING TO BE IN A MOVIE!" Mint glanced at Dave, startled. He grinned expectantly; he'd done his part, now he was in the clear. Slimy, thought Mint.

"WE ARE EXTRAS IN A BIG MOVIE! WITH CLAIRE DANES!" Lindsay pretend-grinned and turned back to Dave. Mint stood very, very still. A movie with Claire Danes? Claire Danes, her idol. Claire Danes, icon of a generation, star of "My So-Called Life," Juliet in Baz Luhrman's *Romeo and Juliet!* Dave wasn't so bad. Claire Danes! The rest of the concert passed in a daydream, in a room in Mint's brain where a switch had just flicked on. Something was going to *happen.*

She left the show with an ache in her right arm, too excited to care about her sweat-drenched dress, or to be embarrassed about climbing into her mother's blue Acura. Lindsay went with her, leaving Dave to curse and search through the crowd for whoever he'd come with. A pins-and-needles rain was just beginning to come down. The smokers pressed against the building under the shelter of the gutter watched the car crawl out of the parking lot and fade away into the city.

Commentary Sarah's revision is interesting both for what she took out and for what she put in.

Most obviously, she has taken out Claire Danes' appearance amid the concert crowd, and this seems right; in Sarah's original beginning, Mint's reaction at the moment of the actress's appearance in the original scene had seemed overstated and cryptic, and this change solves that problem for the most part. Also, a bit less noticeably, Sarah has struck a sentence from the end of third paragraph: "Mint was jealous, and had always been jealous, of people with passion." As the story developed and Mint's character grew clearer, this original observation was undercut. Mint now seems very much a person with passion, and her passion is very much at the heart of the story. Dropping this line seems a recognition of that fact.

In terms of what Sarah has put in here, most obviously she has given the reader a sharper physical picture of both Mint and Lindsay. Also, Sarah has decided to replace Mint's sudden sighting of Claire Danes in the concert crowd with Lindsay's meeting of a film intern who produces a pair of passes to the set of Claire Danes' movie as a way of getting into Lindsay's good graces. This interestingly solves several problems. First, it eliminates the red flag raised by the notion of a celebrity showing up in a very public setting where, presumably, she'd have little protection and would very quickly become the center of attention. It strains credibility to ask the reader to believe Claire Danes could just be "a face in the crowd," seen and then quickly lost to Mint's view. It's more likely that a celebrity in the midst of such a crowd would cause an immediate stir, transforming Mint's very private experience into an extremely and unpleasantly public one. It also makes it possible for Sarah to set up Mint's interest in Claire Danes a little more gradually, solving the problem mentioned in the critique of Sarah's beginning: that of the story seeming not to be taking the reader sufficiently into its confidence as regards Mint's feelings about the actress.

Concerns   While Sarah solves a number of technical problems with her revision, the problem remains of deepening the reader's understanding of Mint's feelings about Claire Danes—what she symbolizes, what answers Mint thinks she can provide to what urgent questions. Sarah has bought herself some time and has carved herself an easier path into the sort of characterization the story requires; now it remains for her to make sure the completed story accomplishes this work as she brings it together.

Alternative Writing Exercises

1. **Clean your story's windows.** For this exercise, you should choose one of the earlier exercises you've completed and go through it with a pen, circling every adjective, adverb and abstraction. When you've finished making your circles, do a tally. Now go back through and see whether there isn't some way you can expunge the abstractions entirely, and reduce the adjectives and adverbs by a half to two thirds, keeping only those which you believe are perfect for the job you're putting them to, and which aren't employed in a cliché or a stock phrase. *What you'll learn:* Story writing can usefully be compared to making a stained glass window. Good strong active verbs and vivid nouns can be said to be clear glass; adjectives and adverbs are at best translucent; and abstractions and clichés are opaque. If you were to assemble a stained glass window out of these types of glass, only the translucent and the clear varieties of glass would work; opaque glass keeps the light out—obviously not a desirable characteristic for a window.

2. **The cliché—a flaw or an opportunity?** Make an inventory of one of your scenes, this time searching for clichés, stock phrases and character types. Once you've found one (or two, or three, or four . . .), stop and meditate on it/them. Ask yourself whether there isn't something fresh or vital that's sealed inside that cliché, stock phrase and/or character type. Rewrite the scene so that it releases that unexpressed energy into the story. *What you'll learn:* The best that can be said of clichés is that, because they're familiar to nearly everyone, they get meaning across economically and quickly. The problem is, they're almost always so boring as to seem inert, and may even be offensive. Clichés are *reductive*, while good fiction is *expansive*. That said, it is also possible to say that clichés, stock phrases and

character types can be useful. Most often, they show up in first drafts where the writer is hurrying too much, or is having trouble really sinking into her material. It's useful to develop the habit of reading through your text when you're revising, looking for those places where you can break open the language or the character. Is there a way you can make "she was madder than a wet hen" into a depiction of a woman's anger that's really alive, and that helps us to understand her character and the very particular variety of her anger more deeply, adding energy to the scene and story you're writing?

3. **Q: Why did the writer rush the scene? A: To get to the other side . . .** Go through your exercises and reread them, looking for places where honesty compels you to admit that you haven't got the pacing quite right in a passage of dramatization. Revisit the writing of that scene now, and try to sink deeply into it. Rewrite the scene more fully, lingering especially in the telling details. *The point of this exercise:* One of the most common ways writers introduce flaws into their stories is by rushing through their scenes. This may be because they're having trouble getting in touch with the imperatives of character or situation, or it may be because they're so firmly focused on the *ends* the scene is working toward that they forget about fully fleshing out the *means*. Whatever the reason, it's something to fix, keeping in mind Aristotle's insistence on the importance of dramatized scene when he called tragedy an "imitation [of life] that works through [dramatized] action." If we are going to believe in the action a scene presents, it needs not just to be dramatized, but *sufficiently* dramatized.

4. **Are you a believer?** Ask a friend or a classmate—someone you feel you can depend upon to be honest—to read through a couple of your scenes. Ask this friend or classmate to answer three questions: 1) Do you believe in the characters? 2) Do you believe in what they do? 3) Do you believe in what they say? If your reader tells you he doesn't believe in a character, an action or a passage of dialogue, ask him to tell you why, and to be specific. *What you'll learn:* It can be difficult—and early in the process of drafting a story, nearly impossible—for us as writers to see clearly what's working and what's not working in the scenes we write. This is one of the reasons a well-run workshop and trustworthy critics can be so useful to us when we're trying to learn the ins and outs of story writing. It can be difficult to hear that what you've written has failed to come across, but keep in mind what Samuel Beckett said: "Ever tried. Ever failed. No matter. Try again. Fail again. Fail better." Good, compassionate critics are indispensable; find them, cultivate them, listen to them (however painful it might be at first, at least until you've grown a little scar tissue), and learn from them.

SHORT STORIES

❧ Not Even Angels Are Immortal ❧

Jeremy Blodgett

Charlie stood staring out of the second floor classroom's window onto the student parking lot below. School had just let out five minutes before and the lot was crawling with scores of eager students rushing out of the building and away from authority. Some jumped straight into their cars and drove away, others stood around in groups chatting and laughing while others sneaked cigarettes behind a van, out of the view of the parking lot monitor Charlie knew was standing in the doorway beneath the window. At the far end of the lot, a couple leaned against a car, making out.

"Charlie?"

Ms. Lonsdale had entered the room as Charlie watched the scene below; he turned around surprised and a bit embarrassed for having intruded into her room. The teacher noticed the faint hint of red in his cheeks as she set down the book of Gerard Manley Hopkins poems she had been carrying. She was an attractive woman in her late twenties, tall and slender with shoulder length, straight brown hair and bright penetrating blue eyes. Boys at the school would have liked her aside from the unforgivable fact that she was a good and dedicated teacher. She was a stickler for rules and didn't let anyone get away with anything. She dressed conservatively—long skirts and blouses—and wore no makeup. Ms. Lonsdale had two loves in her life: reading poetry and teaching poetry. That left little time for anything else.

"I came to turn in the homework for tomorrow. I'm going to be gone for a college visit."

"Well. You do realize that a college visit is an excused absence, so you have until Monday to hand it in?"

"Yes," Charlie crossed the room to the desk he'd left his backpack and rummaged through it for the right paper, "but I had a burst of inspiration, you could call it, last night, so I went ahead and wrote something. I think you might like it."

He found the paper and handed it to her. "Let me get my glasses and I'll give it a quick once over." She circled her desk, took her glasses out of the top drawer and slipped them on. If Charlie had been one to notice such things, he would have realized at that moment that Ms. Lonsdale's glasses fit her face better than any glasses have ever fit a face, and performed the impossible task of making her even more beautiful.

As she read the poem, she crossed back around the desk and sat on the front, "I'm impressed Charlie; this is quite good."

Charlie muttered, "Thanks."

"I'd like to ask you, though, if you don't mind, what inspired some of these lines. How about 'Heightened senses sense little/In a small world of false fronts'?"

Charlie looked down at his shoes. There was nothing interesting about his shoes. "It just sounded poetic, I think; that's all."

She looked at him for a moment, then down at the page again, "Can we talk as friends for a minute, not as teacher and student?"

Charlie looked up. He hoped his face looked adequately surprised to cover up his joy at her proposal. "I suppose so."

She set the paper down on the desk behind her, "What do you want to do with your life, Charlie?"

"Well, my parents want me to go to college then medical school so I can move back here and work with my dad until he retires and I can take over his practice."

Ms. Lonsdale shook her head slightly, "No Charlie, what do you want to do?" She paused. "Charlie, I've been reading and teaching poetry for a long time. High school students almost always write autobiographically, and if there's anything of you in this poem, in all of the poems you've written for my class, I can tell you don't want to be a doctor and you certainly don't want to move back here. There's restlessness in your poetry, and a question that you haven't been able to answer. Something inspires this poetry in you, something trapped inside looking for a release, and whether it be through poetry or another way, you need to let it out."

Charlie could not speak. He looked back at his shoes. He knew all of the things she had said before she had said them, but from her they became clear, they meant more. His poetry was about him and he didn't know what he wanted, but he knew he didn't want to be a doctor or to stay in some little, upstate suburb all his life.

After a few minutes of silence, Ms. Lonsdale spoke, "I'm not trying to tell you what path to take in life Charlie, I'm just telling you to find your own. Poetry is a beautiful art, but it can also be a means of self-reflection. Your poetry tells me you have a different calling than taking over your father's practice."

He looked up and began to open his mouth as if to speak—

"No. Now I'm going to be a teacher again." She smiled, "I've got some work to do so you had better go." "Thank you," he said, feeling equal parts gratitude for what she had said to him and for her not allowing him to respond. He grabbed his backpack and headed for the door.

"Oh Charlie," Ms. Lonsdale said before he was out of the room, "I want to hear about your college visit when you get back. Why don't you come by after school early next week and we can talk some more. Until then, think about what I said. Write it down if you have to, in iambic pentameter, then you can turn it in for the assignment Wednesday."

Charlie smiled and they both began to laugh.

"See you soon, Ms. Lonsdale."

Father Charles McLaughlin sat in the porch swing outside of the rectory. In front of the Victorian house in the middle of the vast city, children played hopscotch and rode bicycles on the sidewalk. It was a gorgeous early summer evening, a cool breeze blew through the trees and Fr. McLaughlin's hair, keeping the air and the man cool. The sun had dropped below the level of the buildings and trees in the distance, but there was still an hour or two of playtime before dark.

He had been stationed at the small St. Francis parish for nearly seven years, after a brief stint as an assistant priest in a larger parish just after he had graduated from seminary. The people of the parish liked Fr. McLaughlin and he liked his parish. The kids played in front of his house and were thrilled to have someone watching while they did tricks on their bikes or broke out new toys.

Fr. McLaughlin drank the last of his lemonade, stood up and went inside the house. He took the glass, now empty except for a couple small ice cubes, into the kitchen. He set about washing the dishes from dinner. Just as he got his hands wet, the telephone rang. He grabbed a towel and hurriedly dried his hands as he moved into the living room to answer the phone.

"Hello?"

"Hey, Charlie."

"Oh, hi Mike, I should have known it was you."

"What's that supposed to mean?"

"I had just started doing the dishes and you always call just when I'm starting something."

Father Mike Mullins worked at a parish across town. The two men had met a few years ago during a meeting of priests from the diocese. They were drawn together by their young age and instantly discovered their mutual love of baseball and the Yankees. Both had season tickets, and starting the first summer they knew each other they bought seats together.

"I'll make it up to you. Ditch the dishes and come out to the Yankees game with me tonight. I'll buy you a hot dog or something."

Fr. McLaughlin looked at his watch, "Oh, I didn't realize it was getting so late, the game starts in twenty minutes."

"Right, so you better get going."

"Ok, I'll be there in about half an hour, meet me outside the gate . . . and be ready to buy that hotdog!" Fr. McLaughlin could hear Fr. Mullins laughing as he hung up the phone. Fr. McLaughlin stepped over to the closet just inside the front door, and grabbed his lucky Yankees cap off the top shelf. He was just stepping out the door when the phone rang again. Looking at his watch, he reluctantly let go of the door and stepped over to answer the call.

"Hello?"

"Is this Fr. Charlie McLaughlin?" The female voice on the other end sounded tired, upset. "Yes. May I help you?"

"Yes, my name is Virginia Lonsdale, Eveline Lonsdale's sister. I understand you were one of her students?"

"Yes, that's right, years ago. Is something wrong?"

"I'm afraid so. Eveline has cancer."

"Is it serious?"

"Well, you know Eveline, she refused to take a day off from teaching to go see a doctor and now it's out of control. She doesn't have long." She let the words sink in. "She wanted to see you."

He hadn't seen Eveline in three years. They wrote each often, in long letters describing nearly every detail of their lives, but she never mentioned anything about feeling ill. "Where is she?"

"At St. Luke's, the doctors said there was no point taking her to a larger hospital."

"Ok, I'll have to borrow a car, but I'll be there as soon as I can."

"Oh, don't rush, they won't let you in to see her until tomorrow anyway. You might as well wait until then to make the drive."

. . .

Nearly an hour later, Fr. Mullins saw Fr. McLaughlin walking down the sidewalk to the front gate of Yankee stadium. He walked over to meet his friend, blatantly tapping his bare arm where a watch should have been.

"I've been waiting here for forty-five minutes. The game's already in the bottom of the fourth. Something happen?" Fr. McLaughlin was rarely late for anything.

"Yeah, you might say that," he wanted to sit down before they started talking, "let's get inside though."

"Sure."

They went in the stadium. Fr. Mullins made straight for a concession stand once they were inside. He bought a couple hot dogs and beers.

"As promised. Hope this might help you relax a bit."

The food, in fact, did make Fr. McLaughlin feel a bit better. The Yankees were just getting up to bat and the two found their seats.

They watched the Yankee side go out without a run. Between innings, as the pitcher warmed up, Fr. Mullins asked, "Do you want to talk about it?"

Fr. McLaughlin sighed. "An old teacher of mine, from high school, has terminal cancer. Her sister called me just as I was leaving. She—Eveline, the teacher—wants me to come visit tomorrow."

"Wow, Charlie, I'm sorry."

"She was more than just a teacher, Mike. I had a poetry class with her when I was a senior. I was a confused kid at the time. My parents wanted me to go to medical school, follow in my father's footsteps and all that, but I just didn't want to be like my parents: insincere, shallow, rude, fighting all the time. When I started writing poetry in Ms. Lonsdale's class, it hit on something deep inside me, a certain sympathy or desire, I suppose. It gave me some direction. Finally, I was able to tell Ms. Lonsdale about it, or, well, she kind of figured it out herself.

"Anyway, we started talking regularly, becoming friends you could say. She helped me find the conviction to go to college to study poetry, not medicine. My parents weren't happy, but I was. Without Ms. Lonsdale, I would probably be a doctor right now."

Fr. Mullins looked at him. "She seems like a very special person."

"Yes," he said, "she is."

"I hope you don't mind me asking, but there's one thing I don't understand. If you went to college to study poetry, how did you turn out as a priest?"

"I entered college with the intention of becoming a poet. I found, though, that as I learned more about my own poetry, it was full of a search for answers, usually spiritual ones. I had never paid much attention to religion before, but poetry led me in that direction. That's how I found my calling. I soon realized that writing wasn't enough, so I transferred to a seminary and I think you know the rest."

"Do you still write?"

"I haven't in years."

"I can't believe you've never told me this."

"They were kind of rough years for me. The priesthood agreed with me so much that I didn't often like to think back. Eveline and I wrote each other all the time, but only now that she's sick do I think about all she's done for me."

"You're going to see her, right? It'll be good for both of you."

"Well, I plan to . . . if I can find a car."

"Oh," Fr. Mullins drew out the word, "so you're asking for my car?"

He said suggestively. "If you're offering it, I suppose I'd accept."

"Just be sure to fill it with gas." He dropped the keys in Fr. McLaughlin's lap. "I'll take the bus home."

The crowd jumped to their feet as the Yankees hit a home run. The two priests joined in and for the rest of the game, having obtained a car and talked to someone, Fr. McLaughlin was able to half heartedly enjoy himself.

Fr. Charles McLaughlin stood looking out the hospital's second floor waiting room window. Below was the parking lot. He remembered the day nearly twenty years before when he had looked down on a parking lot while waiting to see Ms. Lonsdale. He watched the bodies of people below scurry to cars and leave. Today, no one stood about chatting or laughing, smoking or making out.

He had arrived at the hospital mid-morning. Eveline, however, was not able to see him until after lunch. He occupied himself with three month old copies of *Time* and *Newsweek,* occasionally chatting with other people waiting to see someone. A woman about his age had told him about her teenage son who had gotten into a car accident a month after getting his license; he had a broken collarbone and was still in the hospital for observation. The woman said her son would be fine, but made the point that he wouldn't be driving again any time soon.

"Was the accident his fault?"

"No, some jerk ran a red light, but I'm not going to let him back out there if I can help it."

Although he didn't agree with her reasoning, Fr. McLaughlin was sympathetic, "I hope he feels better soon."

Around lunchtime, Fr. McLaughlin hadn't found himself particularly hungry, but had felt he should probably eat something anyway. He had found the hospital cafeteria and grabbed a small bag of potato chips and an apple. He had eaten in the waiting room. He was looking out the window when the orderly approached him to say he could see Eveline.

"Fr. McLaughlin? You may go in now."

The information took a couple of seconds to process and by the time he had lifted himself from his thoughts enough to say "Thank you," the orderly was halfway down the hallway. Fr. McLaughlin followed quickly. The orderly stopped and pointed at a door near the end of the hallway on the right.

"You can go right in, she's feeling relatively well at the moment."

The room was spacious—housing two patients—with Eveline away from the door and a mystery patient behind a drawn curtain just inside the door. As Fr. McLaughlin walked over to the teacher's bed, he noticed the many assorted bouquets and arrangements of flowers in all colors and shapes surrounding her bed; the sweet perfume from the flowers made the sickly hospital smell disappear; a window behind her bed let in brilliant rays of sunlight that made the colors glow; a faint breeze came in through the window along with the sun and Fr. McLaughlin felt he had walked into a flower store or a beautiful garden, not a hospital room. Still, there in the center of the garden was Eveline's bed, where beneath a thin blanket lay the frail woman, radiant as ever, except for her eyes, once so vibrant and expressive in the past, now sunken and hollow, expressing only the occasional pain and recognition of her dire situation.

"Father McLaughlin?"

"Hello, Eveline. Please call me Charlie." She was the one person in the world he would still allow to call him Charlie. Mike called him that simply to spite him. That was how their relationship worked, built on a kind of sarcastic camaraderie. But Eveline was different; she was the one person Charlie had ever wanted to call him Charlie.

"Only if you call me Ms. Lonsdale." She smiled. Remarkably, she had retained her wry sense of humor through her illness. It was an important reason why she had managed to last so long. She was amazingly strong-willed.

"Very well then. So how are you, Ms. Lonsdale?"

"The food could be better, of course, but the service is pretty good. I don't have much to complain about, but I probably won't recommend this place to friends coming to town." They laughed, then Eveline coughed and the mood turned serious. "I want to thank you for coming."

"My pleasure, of course."

Charlie pulled a chair up to the bed and they talked non-stop for an hour about what books they'd read recently, news and happenings from their respective neighborhoods, baseball (although Eveline knew nothing about it, she tried as always), and about the incredible amount of flowers she had received, mostly from former students. Finally, a nurse came into the room and interrupted them. "Now Eveline, don't you think you should get some rest? You've had enough excitement for one afternoon."

"Ah, I see I should go," said Charlie.

"Just a moment, Lori, let my friend and me say our goodbyes."

"Ok, Eveline, I'll come back to check on you in about ten minutes."

Once the nurse had left, Eveline said, "Nice girl, but she could stand to be a little more strict at times."

"Good old Eveline," said Charlie.

"Hush now and give me my bag," said the teacher.

Charlie grabbed her bag from the table across the room and brought it to her. She reached in and pulled out a small rectangular bundle wrapped in newspaper and a tiny blue ribbon. "I've been meaning to give this to you for a long time. Don't open it here, wait until you are outside."

"I don't know what to say. You're not the one who's supposed to be giving gifts and I didn't bring you anything."

"Yes, you did. But if you must insist on giving me something else, I could use a blessing, Father."

Charlie was taken aback. Blessings were part of his job, his duty, but he felt so awkward with Eveline. He was still, however, compelled to honor her wish. He laid his hand on her forehead and said a brief blessing asking God to look over Eveline in her time of illness and asking for God's help in her recovery. Under his breath, inaudible to Eveline, he asked God to grant her a comfortable death, "In the name of the Father, of the Son, and of the Holy Spirit. Amen."

"Thank you Charlie," she coughed, "but I'm going to have to be a teacher now. I've got some things to do, so you better go." She attempted to smile but grimaced instead.

"When should I come back and see you again?"

"Not again Charlie. It was good seeing you, I'll write while I can."

"But—"

She interrupted, "Think of me from time to time, will you?" The nurse walked into the room, clearly meaning to get Fr. McLaughlin out of the room. He looked at the nurse before turning back to Eveline. "Goodbye."

"Goodbye, Father."

In Fr. Mullins' car in the parking lot of the hospital, Fr. McLaughlin looked at the gift Eveline had given him. He looked up to the second floor window where he stood earlier, wondering if someone was watching him now. Turning back to the gift on his lap, he carefully unwrapped the bundle. Inside he found a small leather bound book, hand sewn. He opened to a random page and read a few hand-written lines, the same lines he had once written for a class in high school. Charlie began to cry.

Fr McLaughlin knocked softly on the mahogany door. The grotesque brass knocker looked at him and warned him to go away. The door opened. His mother let out a short gasp.

"Why, Charles. You're the last person I expected to see. To what do we owe this honor?"

"May I come in, Louise?"

She moved away from the doorway and patronizingly waved an arm to the inside. "Our home is your home . . . or it was once."

He took the pointed comment in silence, he was in no mood to get in a fight with his mother now, not the first time he had seen her in six years, not mere hours after he had seen Eveline.

"Can I get you anything?" She asked sarcastically.

"Some tea would be nice." Fr. McLaughlin said absently, leaving Louise bound to her insincere effort at hospitality. She went into the kitchen.

Fr. McLaughlin looked around the living room. Nothing much had changed in the twenty years since he had lived here. They had bought a new TV a few years ago and it stuck out as a futuristic contraption in the otherwise antiquated room. All the furniture was the same. They had been content enough twenty years ago; they saw no need for unnecessary change. He sat on the sofa and picked up a copy of the *New York Times* from the coffee table. It had been folded, nearly completed crossword up. His father always did that to the paper; Charlie wondered where his father was.

Louise walked in from the kitchen, silently handing him the tea.

"Thank you," he replied.

Silence. Fr. McLaughlin studied the lamp on the stand beside the couch. Louise straightened the *TV Guides* on the coffee table. A tense minute passed.

"Bert!" Louise shrilly yelled. Fr. McLaughlin had never once missed that awful yell. "Bert! Come in here, we have a guest."

"Good God, Louise, I'm trying to finish these accounts." Fr. McLaughlin heard the muffled voice of his father from his study down the hall.

"Come on, then!"

Bert made his way into the living room, making plenty of noise in the process. He had always liked to make his movement through the house an event. He felt everyone should hear him coming. When he entered the living room he stopped and stood motionless for a moment.

"What are you doing here?" The question was simple, straightforward, uninviting.

Charlie looked at his father. He didn't know why he had come to his parents' house after seeing Eveline.

"I don't know. Eveline Lonsdale is in the hospital dying of cancer. I came to town to visit her and I ended up here."

"Well?"

"I guess I just want to talk."

"Then talk."

Fr. McLaughlin began getting frustrated, "Look at me, I'm a priest, I'm happy. Everyday people come to me with their troubles and I do my best to help them. People expect me to be able to solve their problems, but I can't even get along with my own parents. What kind of example is that?"

Bert chortled, "We didn't ask you to become a priest, did we? God no, you had to go ruin your life like that on your own." His father had never been a subtle man.

"I just want to sort things out between—"

His father cut him off, "You want to talk? OK, let's talk, but I'm not going to stand here while you whine about your life or your terrible parents, your sick teacher or your feelings." Things were beginning to get out of control.

"Maybe this was a bad idea." Fr. McLaughlin said as he began to stand.

"Damn straight it was."

Fr. McLaughlin got up from his chair. "Thank you for the tea, Louise." He looked at his father, nodded slightly and turned toward the door. "I can show myself out."

It was nearly ten p.m. before Fr. McLaughlin arrived back at the rectory. After the unfortunate experience with his parents, he had left town immediately. He was angry and frustrated, which translated into slow driving with the radio off and wandering thoughts.

Around seven, he had stopped at a little roadside diner to grab some food. By this time, his appetite had grown strong, so he ordered a large steak dinner. After a slice of coconut cream pie, while finishing his coffee, he pulled out the book Eveline had given him. With each poem he read, he was reminded more and more of the young man he had been and how much writing had always meant to him. The rest of the drive home, many of his thoughts came out in verse.

When he finally arrived back at the rectory, he parked Fr. Mullins' car in the garage, thinking he would return it tomorrow. Entering the house, he went straight upstairs to his study. He set Eveline's book on the desk, directly in front of where he sat, and picked up a pen. Inspiration had struck him on the way home and he began to write for the first time in twenty years.

By the time Charlie put down his pen, the sun had come up. Looking out the window of his study at the birds singing in the trees, he felt content. Turning back to the desk, he looked at the poem he had written, a long devotional poem of divine inspiration, dedicated to an angel named Eveline. Charlie folded the pages, put them in an envelope and addressed it to Eveline at St. Luke's Hospital. On the back of the envelope he wrote, *"To Eveline: A Gift."*

❧ Pretty Little Things ❧

Sarah Cornwell

Mint's mother drove Mint and Lindsay to the concert at twenty miles an hour, not for safety, but because she enjoyed the closeness of people in a car. The city nightlife was just kindling, those impossibly sleek young couples descending to the street to drink away the tension of the week. The girls sulked subtly in the back seat, Lindsay in her lime green tank top and cuffed jeans, Mint in a yellow flowered halter dress cut too low, so she had to hold her shoulders back and her hands kept flying to her throat, wrists pressing the fabric up against her chest. Mint's mother bravely ignored the spike-jacketed punks and smoky-eyed daytime receptionists frowning against the fenders of their rusty Chryslers as she turned into the parking lot. She didn't say anything about drugs when the girls climbed out of the car in front of the Red Room steps. She could feel their shame like a release of heat as they slammed the doors shut and slipped away into the throng pushing toward the loaded darkness of the doorways. Mint's mother tried to listen to NPR on the way home, but she couldn't get her mind off that yellow halter dress, just hoping and hoping that it would stay up, and that the daringness of it would somehow make Mint happy.

Lindsay forged a path through the crowd inside, Mint close behind with one hand on her shoulder so she couldn't be lost. Mint was small but not slight—the kind of body that would have been muscular if exercised. The yellow dress was striking against her fair skin in the light, but here in the dim crush, she looked washed out, mousy-haired and nervous. The first band was already playing, something loud and thrashy that made Mint think of animals and dirt. It was stirring up the boys, though. Mint wouldn't meet their eyes as she climbed through the jungle of bodies, slid across fleshy backs prickling with the first dew of concert-sweat. She could feel the anticipation in taut shoulders, the trembling of the ones who would be dancing crazy before the night was over, inhibitions lost in the fray. Lindsay stopped in a little knot of guys in pop-punk band shirts and Abercrombie hats—older guys, maybe eighteen or nineteen—who pretended not to notice them. Mint kept her right arm across her chest. Lindsay leaned back to scream in her ear that it looked like she was saying the pledge of allegiance, but Mint couldn't hear over the music.

The second band came on and Mint didn't know them either. Lindsay was really into it, entranced and rocking back and forth. The Abercrombie boys kept looking at her. She had become, while Mint blinked, one of those untouchable concert demigods, enlightened, in control, the symphony conductor of the collective breathing of the crowd. Her hair, dark and barely wavy like the grain of cherry wood, fell in strands across her closed eyes, her high cheekbones. She had a small, squarish nose and lips like French women in advertisements. Mint was proud to be part of such beauty, like a pearl button on a mink coat.

Between songs, a stocky, jittery guy with dyed black hair and a patch-plastered messenger bag sidled up to Lindsay. He might have been college-aged, and Mint watched him cock his head to the side and scratch his ear again and again while he talked to her. Lindsay was smiling and nodding—why for this guy?

Lindsay grabbed Mint's arm and yanked her closer just as the next song was starting. "THIS IS DAVE," she yelled. "DAVE IS A FILM INTERN." She nodded importantly. Dave smiled importantly. Lindsay held up two white slips he must have given her a moment ago.

"MINT!" Lindsay leaned in so close that Mint could feel her breath in her ear, heavy and cloying. "HE GAVE US PASSES. WE'RE GOING TO BE IN A MOVIE!" Mint glanced at Dave, startled. He grinned expectantly.

"WE ARE EXTRAS IN A BIG MOVIE! WITH CLAIRE DANES!" Lindsay pretend-grinned and turned back to Dave. Mint stood very, very still. A movie with Claire Danes? Claire Danes was her idol. Claire Danes, icon of a generation, star of *My So-Called Life*, Juliet in Baz Luhrman's *Romeo and Juliet!* Claire Danes! The rest of the concert passed in a daydream, in a room in Mint's brain where a switch had just flicked On. Something was going to *happen*.

She left the show with an ache in her right arm, too lost in thought to care about her sweat-drenched dress, or to be embarrassed about climbing into her mother's blue Acura outside the Red Room. Lindsay went with her, having refused to give Dave her phone number and left him to search through the crowd for whoever he'd come with. A pins-and-needles rain was just beginning to come down. The smokers pressed against the building under the shelter of the gutter watched the car crawl out of the parking lot and fade away into the city.

Lindsay, in the front seat, politely answered Mint's mother's questions about the concert, though the questions were obviously directed at Mint. The quiet in the car reverberated in Mint's skull, and when Lindsay turned the radio on, it sounded distant and unimportant. They coasted uptown, doors locked. Mint stared out the window at the dirty city speeding past. Bulky men in NFL jackets slouched outside of bars, women in skintight jeans and bustier tops leaned into the traffic. The people of the world seemed dingy and unkempt—sad, common people with skin imperfections and alcoholic spouses. They didn't even exist in the same world as Claire Danes.

Mint shut her eyes and ignored her mother's questions until they pulled up to their house, having dropped Lindsay off. She went straight to the kitchen for a glass of water, and her mother followed her in and sat down at the kitchen table.

"Please don't ignore me, honey. Amanda, I just want to know if you had a good time. Is that a crime? Amanda?"

Mint turned on the water violently. "Do you even *try* to remember my name?" She had thrown away the name Amanda almost six months ago, and every time her mother said it, she felt a shudder of childhood.

"Honey." Her mother's voice was self-consciously soft, pained. "Why are you distraught?"

Just hearing her mother use the word *distraught* made Mint squirm. She took her water and sat down at the far end of the table. "I'm not distraught, I'm thinking," she said, and smacked her glass down on a coaster unnecessarily. "Ok, I'm just . . ." She stopped and scrutinized her mother, deciding whether or not to talk. Her mother looked like she was holding her breath. She looked so damn *concerned*, as if there were something wrong with Mint that she wanted to wipe away with Bon Ami or

Windex. She looked like she thought she could understand, with her too-wide mouth and those puffs of gray-blond hair falling out of her ponytail.

Like a sitcom mom, she said, "Give me a chance."

Mint gave in. She kind of wanted to tell someone anyway. "This guy we met— Lindsay met—gave us passes to be extras in a movie with Claire Danes."

"Oh, how fun!" Her mother nodded eagerly and inclined her head, confused as to why this would cause her daughter *distress.*

"Claire Danes, you know, from *My So-Called Life?*" Mint thought of the star's face, the golden glow of celebrity that she radiated from red-carpet interviews, MTV guest-VJ appearances, starring roles. How could she explain the pressure of this op- portunity, her intense and stomach-wrenching desire to know how it was pulled off, how people managed to reach *perfection?* How could she explain the allure of maga- zine spreads, *Seventeen* interviews, compliments from Joan Rivers?

"But how can Lindsay and I do that?" Mint's question came out bulky and unan- swerable, but she watched her mother's face anyway, in case she could divine her daughter's thoughts with that motherly intuition you read about in books like *Little Women.* But the softening around her mother's mouth meant she didn't understand; she thought Mint was worried that Claire Danes would outshine her, or maybe that Lind- say would. *It was stupid to try to explain this to her,* she thought. It wasn't something she could put into words. All she knew was that there was too much quiet in her life, too much ugly and uncomfortable. Maybe this would be a chance to learn the secrets of stardom—how to glow, how to be at ease, how to be remembered. Of course her mother couldn't understand those things—a divorced, middle-aged office manager who refused to dye her hair or meet men. There were better things waiting for Mint. She left the water on the table and went upstairs to bed. When she woke up the next morning, she had the sense that she had dreamed a hundred dreams she would never remember.

Lindsay was keeping her pass under her pillow, but Mint worried that her own might get washed with her sheets, so she taped it onto her calendar over the third week of October. She slogged through days of high school distractedly, labeling her x and y axes, skipping seventh period to smoke on the fire escape in the art wing, holding her secret out of view like a firefly in cupped hands. Lindsay didn't tell people about it either—Mint was glad she understood that this was something that belonged to best friends. Mint could feel people start to notice her more and more—who's that girl who's always hanging out with Lindsay Minor this year? After school, Mint and Lind- say would walk the four city blocks to Mint's house, crushing crimson leaves beneath Steve Madden shoes. Sometimes Mint would rescue the prettiest ones to press.

Today the leaves escaped notice in the rush to get indoors—an unexpected cold front had blown in from the east during the school day. Mint and Lindsay crossed their arms and leaned into the wind. Mint giggled at their awkward hurry, backpacks smacking against their backs in the near-empty street, and they broke into a run. At the halfway point, Lindsay grabbed Mint's shoulder to slow down, but Mint only put on more speed, and the run silently became a race. A few old ladies waiting at the bus stop turned to watch them sprint by, unsmiling girls chased by invisible pursuers.

Mint reached her street first, and slowed to a walk when, around the corner, her mother came into view on a second story balcony, watering a row of potted plants.

Lindsay caught up, unphased. Mint's mother looked lumpy and oblivious, in a bright green sweater and jeans, waving at them with the watering can. Lindsay waved back, and then began to laugh uncontrollably at Mint's hair, blown straight back away from her face as if she were a shocked cartoon character. They took the elevator up to Mint's apartment and her mother ushered them inside, chatting brightly about how much she loved autumn, and something about stray cats, or the neighbor's cat.

They dropped their backpacks and dodged up a few steps to the TV room as they had done all week to watch taped episodes of My So-Called Life. Mint's mother called after them "Do you girls want a snack?"

"Yes," yelled Mint as she closed the door.

Breathless, Mint fed a tape into the VCR. Lindsay settled back against the brown-and-white striped futon in the middle of the room, opposite the television.

"Why is it always so bare in here?" Lindsay asked, surveying the plain white walls, the one framed picture of a sailboat, and the card table spread with the pieces of a barely begun puzzle.

"I don't know." Mint was fast-forwarding through the opening sequence of the episode. "I mean, yes I do. Mom won't let me tape things on the walls in here because it's supposed to be a guest bedroom some day. I don't know who she thinks is going to visit."

"Wouldn't she probably repaint it anyway? I mean, the paint is, like, cracked. Over there, and there." She pointed.

"Yeah, I think she just likes it boring or something. OK, ready." Mint pressed play and scrambled back to the futon.

There, on the screen, was Claire Danes, with that crimson hair, yearning for Jordan Catalano and delivering voice-over monologues all shivery with meaning. There she was, soft-faced and thoughtful and important. In this episode, the nerd, Brian, wrote a love letter to Claire Danes for Jordan to send her, when he was secretly in love with her too. Lindsay was leaning toward the screen with her elbows on her knees. She looked like she should have been taking notes. Mint watched her out of the corner of her eye. *Does she really care about Brian?* Mint wondered. *Does she have any idea what it's like for him, not to be sure about things?* She surprised herself by saying it out loud.

"Do you really care about Brian?"

Lindsay tore herself away from the screen to glance at Mint. "What do you mean?" There was a hint of danger in her tone, that edge that made people want to please her.

Mint tread carefully. "I just mean, because . . . you know that guy Dan? He's a lot like him. That guy who asked you out the first week of school?"

Lindsay's tone eased; she was comfortable with the subject. "Yeah, yeah, Dan. Yeah. I like Brian, but if he asked me out, like, in *real* life, I'd say no. I mean, would *you* date Brian?"

Mint didn't have to think. "No." Link yourself to a nerd like that and you'll never be elite. Mint watched Lindsay, so polished, her ticket out of invisibility.

Mint's mother knocked and brought in fruit and iced tea on a tray shaped like Noah's Ark. She lingered in the doorway a few seconds too long on the way out, trying to think of the right thing to say. Mint and Lindsay craned their necks back to see why she was still there, and they looked at each other for a moment, across an ocean of age and worry. "Enjoy . . ." said Mint's mother helplessly, and she left them alone.

.   .   .

It was 2 a.m., and the moon had just risen high enough or sunk low enough (Mint wasn't sure) to enter the square of the window at the head of her bed. Frustrated almost to tears by three and a half hours of wakefulness, Mint surveyed her room. There was something foreboding about the space right now, familiar objects made foreign by the cold moonlight. Her black corduroy armchair, shredded by some long-dead cat, hulked in the corner. The bookshelves that flanked the door opposite her bed sagged under the weight of former books—last week, Mint's mother had donated everything marked Young Adult to an elementary school. Her wooden bureau had grown a face in the moonlight, knot-eyes and a jutting bottom-drawer jaw. Mint looked away, embarrassed that she still saw monsters in the dark. The new posters gleamed in a minor key, as if the airbrushed stars—Leonardo DiCaprio, Gwen Stefani, Kirsten Dunst—were revolted by the grittiness of dark childhood things. Mint wanted so badly to sleep.

The door opened a crack, letting a sliver of light fall across Mint's folded hands like a cut-down tree. A tall, dark strip of her mother materialized in the crack as her eyes adjusted to the light. Mint squinted, trying to look asleep, but intrigued by the idea of watching her mother watch her. It should have made her mad, but it felt comforting tonight—someone looking in on her, making sure she was still there.

Her mother looked pathetic, standing in the doorway. Not pathetic-sad, but pathetic in the Greek tragedy sense of the word, English-class pathetic. Evoking pathos. Mint appraised her. *What a sad end*, she thought. To live out life as a divorcee, working late nights to afford vacations to colonial Williamsburg, vaccinations for the cat. The lines in her mother's face spoke to her of failure. She had looked beautiful in her wedding pictures, seventies-belle with long, blond feathered hair and two little girls holding the white silk train on her wedding dress. And from there, somehow, she had eroded into this frumpy middle-aged woman, spying on her daughter at 2 a.m. in furry slippers, with undereye circles like bruises. What did she have left? Mint realized her breathing had changed as the door opened wider and her mother padded over to her bed. She had given herself away.

"Mint," whispered her mother with a conscious tact that was so much worse than being called the wrong name. Mint didn't move. "Faker," said her mother. An involuntary smile twisted the corners of Mint's mouth. Mint's mother, surprised, seized the opportunity and slid into long-abandoned routine. "I know how to wake up sleeping girls . . ." she intoned, and bent down to kiss Mint's forehead gently. Then she leaned away as if expecting an explosion. Mint opened her eyes and her mother saw the same stale resentment there, but also a gratitude, a vulnerability—a silent admission that tenderness at night was allowed.

Mint's mother knelt by the bed, reckless at the opportunity to be heard. "Honey, I'm sorry I called you Amanda tonight. I'm sorry for all the times. It's just so *hard* for me to remember your new name. Why—"

"Mom!" Mint cut her off pleadingly. She was regretting her smile. The irrational fear flashed across her mind that someone could be watching, through a window or a concealed webcam. She propped herself up on her elbow and said weakly, staring at her hands, "Mom, don't. I'm fine."

Mint's mother had to get this out, just went on talking as if she had put too much work into this speech to cut it off early. "Why would you throw away the beautiful name your father and I chose for you? It's almost as if you've been acting a part since you changed it. You're—you're like a fortress. I'm not allowed inside, but sometimes you open a window and throw something out for me to study, to tuck into a pocket near my heart." Mint rolled onto her stomach, facing the dark other side of the room. "Mom," she protested tonelessly. She didn't want to acknowledge the guilt that rose like a lump in her throat when she heard her mother talk like this, earnest and pained and late-at-night.

Her mother touched her shoulder. "But you're still you, sweet girl." The old pet name hung in the air for a second, and Mint savored it secretly. Her mother stood up. "You can kick and scream, but you're still my Mandy. I don't know what's bothering you. I don't know why you won't talk to me anymore. But if you ever need anything, *ever*, I'm here." She stood a few moments longer, watching the rise and fall of Mint's back. Then, she closed the door behind her, and her slippers made scuffing noises as she walked down the hallway to her room. Mint turned onto her back and watched unspoken words escape from her forehead like steam.

At 9 a.m., Mint and Lindsay arrived at the filming site. Mint's mother handed them bagged lunches as they got out of the car, and they waited until she was out of sight to throw them away. They spoke to the guard and passed under the great stucco arch proclaiming, AMAZE-O-LAND! They knew the park had been reopened only for the filming, but it still felt strange to stand alone in the park's atrium. They stopped short to take it all in, to appreciate the sharp shivers of anticipation, or was it cold? They faced trinket shops, candy shops, old-fashioned photo shops not yet opened for the day, their window displays shining darkly. Beyond that, rides rose like giant metal skeletons from the trees and building tops. Mint blinked her eyes to regain depth perception, because it looked to her as she squinted into the distance that everything converged at one point; the epic rollercoasters, strange spherical vehicles, tubes, swings, inexplicable towers, and the Ferris wheel, all sprouting from the same square foot of cement. The paved walkway before them was clean and empty, like a yellow brick road leading them to adventure. It was an epic, an imaginary place. They started walking, and as they passed a fudge shop, a waft of chocolate scent hit them hard. Mint's acute sense of smell wouldn't let her enjoy it, though. She couldn't ignore the under-scents: the sourness of last night's hotdogs, dropped popcorn kernels, cotton candy tubes festering behind trashcans where the janitorial staff didn't care to reach.

Mint could feel her senses sharpen one by one as she drew nearer to the filming site at the base of the Ferris wheel. *This is it.* She thought. *This is it. I'm here.* Just around the next airbrushed shirt stand, there were camera crews and wardrobe mistresses. Claire Danes would be sitting in a director's chair with her name on the back, she thought. There would be two beautiful gay men dressed in black combing her hair. Mint glanced over at Lindsay, but she couldn't tell what she was thinking. Lindsay was like that: stoic and hip in a denim jacket, grey tube top, and grey GAP slacks. Mint looked down at her body and wished she had worn a dress. These capris made her ankles look fat, and her strappy sandals were making ugly red imprints on the top of her feet. She had on a yellow striped long-sleeved t-shirt, and she realized she was shivering.

They rounded the bend—the last bend—and they had arrived at the filming site. It was sparser than she had imagined it being, but still thrilling, still Hollywood. There were more ugly people than she had predicted, pimply tech guys in black t-shirts trotting back and forth with monstrous loops of wire hung on their shoulders, yelling things across the courtyard. The Ferris wheel was the center of the action. At its foot was a crowd of people whom Mint surmised to be extras, listening to a young man with spiky black hair and a clipboard. There weren't trailers, only tents. She couldn't tell which of the people milling around were important and which were just crew members. She looked furiously for Claire Danes, but she wasn't there. Had she arrived yet? What if she were sick, or dead?! Oh my God. Mint turned to Lindsay, but she was gone and it took a second to spot her twenty feet away, over by the Ferris wheel, signing the young man's clipboard. Mint took a deep breath and walked over.

The spiky-haired man looked her over curtly before handing her the clipboard. "Ok honey, there's a release to sign here, and then I need you and your friend riding the Ferris wheel, Ok? Just sit still and don't look at the camera. *Act normal.*" Mint took the clipboard and hunched over it, scrawling her name on the bottom line without reading the text.

Mint and Lindsay let themselves be ushered into a red car on the Ferris wheel, and hoisted into the air. The car was like a birdcage, with two benches facing each other and horizontal safety bars spaced six inches apart forming the upper half of the structure. They hung ten feet above the ground as the next extras were loaded in, then rose ten more. There they stopped. There was no one to ask what was going on, so they settled in for a wait, peering down at the miniature scurrying of Hollywood below them. Lindsay was picking at the old red paint on the car's safety bars, and she got a piece lodged underneath her fingernail.

"Damn it," she hissed, fussing with her hand. "That's hideous, it looks like my fingernails are bleeding! I guess if I just hold it in my lap . . ."

"Lindsay?" said Mint anxiously, "What if we get stuck up here? I mean, I'm sure they want the Ferris wheel turning for the movie, but what if Claire Danes is down there, and we're up here?"

Lindsay gave her a calculatedly scornful look. "Mint, goddamn it, what's your hangup? I mean, I'm a fan too, or whatever, but could you please look at the bigger picture?" She paused for just long enough to make Mint wonder what the "bigger picture" was. Her hair fell perfectly across the white of her neck as she leaned toward Mint. She was wearing berry lipstick and natural brown-toned eye makeup. She looked like a star should look the day she is Discovered. "We're in a *movie.* I could just die."

Yes, said Mint's inner monologue. *Please.*

At 10:20, the Ferris wheel started turning again. There was less movement on the ground—something was happening. In their rusty red car, Mint and Lindsay swayed past the highest point of the wheel, skybound and alone for one last moment before they began arcing downward. Mint felt that she was being inexorably drawn toward something; gravity dragged her down toward resolution. People below grew larger and larger, standing in clusters, clipboards clutched to their chests, watching some action unfold on the ground. The wheel groaned to a halt when Mint and Lindsay's car was just two cars up from the ground, exactly the height where they had waited on the way up. Mint stood up and pressed her head against the top of the safety bars to see what was going on just below them.

There, without warning, without a change in background music or an introductory voiceover, stood Claire Danes. Mint couldn't see her face from above, but she could tell it was her by the way people were fluttering around her, and by the part in her strawberry blonde-dyed hair, perfectly zig-zagged. She was standing still, and someone was adjusting a brown scarf around her neck, making it look unplanned. She was living, breathing in and out, just twenty feet away from Mint. They were probably recycling each other's carbon dioxide. *Look up*, thought Mint hard. *Just look up, now! Look up and see me here. Now. Now.*

Lindsay was standing now, too, breathless, and they watched as Claire Danes was carefully placed in a yellow car, two away from their own. Some tech people were working on affixing a giant camera to the outside of the car, and Mint wondered how they could be so calm in the face of flawlessness.

"Mint," said Lindsay, "stare much?" She laughed, but it was a conspiratorial laugh, because she was staring too. "It's so weird how movie stars are people, you know? They, like, brush their teeth and have doctor's appointments."

"Yeah," said Mint, but it didn't make any sense to her. As if Claire Danes had to brush her teeth. What a stupid idea. "Weird."

Lindsay was coming out of the initial stun and starting to get excited. "When they start filming, do you want to be talking to each other? Or fighting? Or what?" Mint tried to process this.

"I mean, because, we should *try* to act. Who knows, the director could notice us."

"Sure, uh, let's be talking," said Mint, hoping Lindsay would shut up so she could concentrate.

Claire Danes sat facing them in her accidentally mussed scarf and a jean jacket like Lindsay's. She wasn't speaking, and her eyes were closed. She glowed, ethereally pale and blond, glowed like a lit candle in a dark space. Mint tried to shake the surrealism that blurred the edges of her sight. Here she was, here was Claire Danes. This was Angela from *My So-Called Life*, this was a goddess, this was passion and beauty. This was how Mint could be, how she *knew* she was, beneath the awkwardness and inhibition. This was her secret self.

A handsome actor was ushered into the car next to Claire Danes, and they smiled at each other. The Ferris wheel creaked into motion, and somewhere, somebody yelled "Action!" Reality slid away and Mint was watching a movie, except on mute, because she couldn't hear what they were saying over the mechanical hum of the Ferris wheel. The man was talking, and then Claire Danes was talking, and laughing, and then they were near the top of the wheel, and looking out over the park, and then the man reached over and kissed her, and someone yelled "Cut!" They did this over and over, each time the wheel turned. Mint was fixated. She strained to catch the words, but the wind snatched each one away.

"You realize," Lindsay interrupted, forcing Mint into the present, "that there's no way we're in this shot? Why the hell did they have to put people in *every* car? The camera isn't even facing this way. It doesn't make any sense."

At that exact moment, while Lindsay was saying "sense," Mint and Claire Danes looked at each other. Straight at each other, without question. Beauty for beauty, secret for secret, they saw each other. Claire Danes began to open her mouth—she was going to say something! Mint strained forward, desperate for the secrets Claire Danes could tell her. It seemed like everyone was waiting, everyone was listening. Then, loudly, Claire Danes said—almost yelled, "Can I get down now?"

And then she looked away, and they got her down to her trailer and her next movie, whatever that might be. Everybody got down, and left, one by one, and there would never be another film shot at this location. Mint and Lindsay called their rides from a payphone and they waited on a bench outside the park gates, watching the crew pack up their vans and drive away. It was 1:00.

They sat in silence, because Mint could tell Lindsay would be snappish if she talked—she hadn't been discovered. Mint herself was surprised by how normal she felt. Her moment had come and gone, and here she was, on a bench. Her shoulder hurt from leaning against the safety bars in the Ferris wheel. Where was the punch, or the let-down? It struck her that nothing had happened. In the big picture, nothing had happened today at all. They were not in the shot. Claire Danes was still Claire Danes, her secrets kept. Glancing sideways at Lindsay, Mint felt vaguely sorry for her—such beauty wasted into droopy petulance. *Some day she will be discovered,* Mint thought, *and then she will rise away from all this and become an image on the screen, and I will only ever see her again behind glass.*

Lindsay stood up when her sister's jeep pulled into the parking lot. She called "See you," without turning around as she walked away. The door opened wide as she climbed up into the jeep, and Mint caught a glimpse of her sister, the picture of Lindsay, but bone-thin, her face a mask of makeup. Music blared as they drove away.

Mint's mother was ten minutes late. Mint thought she looked sleepy and surprised, as if she had just come out of a dark movie theater. She said, as Mint belted herself in, "I've got to do some errands on the way home—the post office, the market, you don't mind, do you? How was the taping?"

"It was great."

"And was the actress that you wanted to see there? Was she—" Mint's mother sighed, indulging in the memory of some thrill from her youth. "Exciting and beautiful?"

Mint studied her mother, since she was driving and couldn't look back. She was smiling in a way that Mint had never noticed before, a slight, wistful smile that vanished the wrinkles at the corners of her mouth and made her seem centered and far away. Mint wondered what the memory was that gave her mother this grace and gravity, or if she always looked this way when she smiled.

"Yes," answered Mint. "She was perfect. She was exciting and beautiful."

"Not like us." Mint's mother smiled boldly across the car and Mint felt vaguely annoyed—mothers aren't supposed to be ironic. They're supposed to tell you how beautiful you are, what a beautiful baby you were, how you never cried.

She slung her head back against the headrest. "Yeah. I guess without people like us, the exciting and beautiful ones wouldn't have a crowd to stand out from. I guess. I mean, it's funny. I was looking forward to this *so* much, and I don't feel any different. It's almost like it was a dream or something. Like I never saw her."

"Well, you didn't really see her, did you? Just whatever character she was playing." Mint's mother pulled into a parking spot in front of the post office and turned the car off.

"No, I saw her. I think she looked at me." Mint hardened. "But y'know, I'm not even in the shot. I guess it's because I'm not *exciting* or *beautiful*."

Her mother reached out, and Mint didn't shy away as she tucked a stray strand of hair back behind Mint's ear. "No, no, no, honey. I meant that she's not *exciting and beautiful* like us." She choked, looking for the right words. "That's no kind of beauty if it comes off at night, you know? We're the real thing. We're *real*." She got out of the car with unnecessary decisiveness, as if she had to leave as fast as she could so that Mint and *real* could sit in the car and stew. Through the windshield, Mint watched her recede toward the post office door.

There was a yellow Labrador tied to the leg of the big outgoing mailbox by the post office door, its leash wrapped around and around the mailbox. Its body heaved with the futile exertion of pulling in the wrong direction, the logical direction, away from the leash. Mint watched as her mother's gait slowed, as she appraised the dog, weighed the dangers, and knelt, offering it the back of her hand to sniff. Then she slid her fingers through its collar and led it in a circle around the mailbox. Mint's mother was wearing a long, red felt coat that swirled around her ankles as they circled, and circled again. A breeze picked up the orange and red leaves from the ground and danced them around her in spirals—red like lips, red like a heart.

When the leash was untangled, the dog stood, panting, watching Mint's mother and waiting for whatever would happen next. Mint's mother turned and waved at Mint. She looked flushed and happy, a little overweight but with the most beautiful tousled silvery-blond hair, the loveliest little expression of victory. She seemed almost movie-beautiful to Mint for a moment, like the older version of a main character—the old woman who appears at the beginning and end of a movie, and whose voiceovers you hear in every scene, telling the stories of her life. She looked like she didn't want to be anywhere else in the world than in front of the post office, standing next to a Labrador, playing the part of herself in her red coat. And Mint could feel it then, what *real* meant, could feel how life might change for her. It was a lightness that she knew wouldn't last the night, but it was also a promise that there would be chances, that there would be something waiting for her at the other end of uncertainty. She got out of the car and stood by the dog, as her mother picked up the mail, until its owner emerged from the post office to untie it and walk it home.

✎ REVELATION ✎

Flannery O'Connor

The doctor's waiting room, which was very small, was almost full when the Turpins entered and Mrs. Turpin, who was very large, made it look even smaller by her presence. She stood looming at the head of the magazine table set in the center of it, a living demonstration that the room was inadequate and ridiculous. Her little bright black eyes took in all the patients as she sized up the seating situation. There was one vacant chair and a place on the sofa occupied by a blond child in a dirty blue romper who should have been told to move over and make room for the lady. He was five or six, but Mrs. Turpin saw at once that no one was going to tell him to move over. He was slumped down in the seat, his arms idle at his sides and his eyes idle in his head; his nose ran unchecked.

Mrs. Turpin put a firm hand on Claud's shoulder and said in a voice that included anyone who wanted to listen, "Claud, you sit in that chair there," and gave him a push down into the vacant one. Claud was florid and bald and sturdy, somewhat shorter than Mrs. Turpin, but he sat down as if he were accustomed to doing what she told him to.

Mrs. Turpin remained standing. The only man in the room besides Claud was a lean stringy old fellow with a rusty hand spread out on each knee, whose eyes were closed as if he were asleep or dead or pretending to be so as not to get up and offer her his seat. Her gaze settled agreeably on a well-dressed gray-haired lady whose eyes met hers and whose expression said: if that child belonged to me, he would have some manners and move over—there's plenty of room there for you and him too.

Claud looked up with a sigh and made as if to rise.

Sit down," Mrs. Turpin said. "You know you're not supposed to stand on that leg. He has an ulcer on his leg," she explained.

Claud lifted his foot onto the magazine table and rolled his trouser leg up to reveal a purple swelling on a plump marble-white calf.

"My!" the pleasant lady said. "How did you do that?"

"A cow kicked him," Mrs. Turpin said.

"Goodness!" said the lady.

Claud rolled his trouser leg down.

"Maybe the little boy would move over," the lady suggested, but the child did not stir.

"Somebody will be leaving in a minute," Mrs. Turpin said She could not understand why a doctor—with as much money as they made charging five dollars a day to just stick their head in the hospital door and look at you—couldn't afford a decent-sized waiting room. This one was hardly bigger than a garage. The table was cluttered with limp-looking magazines and at one end of it there was a big green glass ash tray full of cigarette butts and cotton wads with little blood spots on them. If she had had anything to do with the running of the place, that would have been emptied every

217

so often. There were no chairs against the wall at the head of the room. It had a rectangular-shaped panel in it that permitted a view of the office where the nurse came and went and the secretary listened to the radio. A plastic fern in a gold pot sat in the opening and trailed its fronds down almost to the floor. The radio was softly playing gospel music.

Just then the inner door opened and a nurse with the highest stack of yellow hair Mrs. Turpin had ever seen put her face in the crack and called for the next patient. The woman sitting beside Claud grasped the two arms of her chair and hoisted herself up; she pulled her dress free from her legs and lumbered through the door where the nurse had disappeared.

Mrs. Turpin eased into the vacant chair, which held her tight as a corset. "I wish I could reduce," she said, and rolled her eyes and gave a comic sigh.

"Oh, *you* aren't fat," the stylish lady said.

"Ooooo I am too," Mrs. Turpin said. "Claud he eats all he wants to and never weighs over one hundred and seventy-five pounds, but me I just look at something good to eat and I gain some weight," and her stomach and shoulders shook with laughter. "You can eat all you want to, can't you, Claud?" she asked, turning to him.

Claud only grinned.

"Well, as long as you have such a good disposition," the stylish lady said, "I don't think it makes a bit of difference what size you are. You just can't beat a good disposition."

Next to her was a fat girl of eighteen or nineteen, scowling into a thick blue book which Mrs. Turpin saw was entitled *Human Development*. The girl raised her head and directed her scowl at Mrs. Turpin as if she did not like her looks. She appeared annoyed that anyone should speak while she tried to read. The poor girl's face was blue with acne and Mrs. Turpin thought how pitiful it was to have a face like that at that age. She gave the girl a friendly smile but the girl only scowled the harder. Mrs. Turpin herself was fat but she had always had good skin, and, though she was forty-seven years old, there was not a wrinkle in her face except around her eyes from laughing too much.

Next to the ugly girl was the child, still in exactly the same position, and next to him was a thin leathery old woman in a cotton print dress. She and Claud had three sacks of chicken feed in their pump house that was in the same print. She had seen from the first that the child belonged with the old woman. She could tell by the way they sat—kind of vacant and white-trashy, as if they would sit there until Doomsday if nobody called and told them to get up. And at right angles but next to the well-dressed pleasant lady was a lank-faced woman who was certainly the child's mother. She had on a yellow sweat shirt and wine-colored slacks, both gritty looking, and the rims of her lips were stained with snuff. Her dirty yellow hair was tied behind with a little piece of red paper ribbon. Worse than niggers any day, Mrs. Turpin thought.

The gospel hymn playing was, "When I looked up and He looked down," and Mrs. Turpin, who knew it, supplied the last line mentally, "And wona these days I know I'll we-eara crown."

Without appearing to, Mrs. Turpin always noticed people's feet. The well-dressed lady had on red and gray suede shoes to match her dress. Mrs. Turpin had on her good black patent leather pumps. The ugly girl had on Girl Scout shoes and heavy socks. The old woman had on tennis shoes and the white-trashy mother had on what appeared to be bedroom slippers, black straw with gold braid threaded through them—exactly what you would have expected her to have on.

Sometimes at night when she couldn't go to sleep, Mrs. Turpin would occupy herself with the question of who she would have chosen to be if she couldn't have been herself. If Jesus had said to her before he made her, "There's only two places available for you. You can either be a nigger or white-trash," what would she have said? "Please, Jesus, please," she would have said, "just let me wait until there's another place available," and he would have said, "No, you have to go right now and I have only those two places so make up your mind." She would have wiggled and squirmed and begged and pleaded but it would have been no use and finally she would have said, "All right, make me a nigger then—but that don't mean a trashy one." And he would have made her a neat clean respectable Negro woman, herself but black.

Next to the child's mother was a red-headed youngish woman, reading one of the magazines and working a piece of chewing gum, hell for leather, as Claud would say. Mrs. Turpin could not see the woman's feet. She was not white-trash, just common. Sometimes Mrs. Turpin occupied herself at night naming the classes of people. On the bottom of the heap were most colored people, not the kind she would have been if she had been one, but most of them; then next to them—not above, just away from—were the white-trash; then above them were the home-owners, and above them the home-and-land owners, to which she and Claud belonged. Above she and Claud were people with a lot of money and much bigger houses and much more land. But here the complexity of it would begin to bear in on her, for some of the people with a lot of money were common and ought to be below she and Claud and some of the people who had good blood had lost their money and had to rent and then there were colored people who owned their homes and land as well. There was a colored dentist in town who had two red Lincolns and a swimming pool and a farm with registered white-face cattle on it. Usually by the time she had fallen asleep all the classes of people were moiling and roiling around in her head, and she would dream they were all crammed in together in a box car, being ridden off to be put in a gas oven.

"That's a beautiful clock," she said and nodded to her right. It was a big wall clock, the face encased in a brass sunburst.

"Yes, it's very pretty," the stylish lady said agreeably. "And right on the dot too," she added, glancing at her watch.

The ugly girl beside her cast an eye upward at the clock, smirked, then looked directly at Mrs. Turpin and smirked again. Then she returned her eyes to her book. She was obviously the lady's daughter because, although they didn't look anything alike as to disposition, they both had the same shape of face and the same blue eyes. On the lady they sparkled pleasantly but in the girl's seared face they appeared alternately to smolder and to blaze.

What if Jesus had said, "All right, you can be white-trash or a nigger or ugly"!

Mrs. Turpin felt an awful pity for the girl, though she thought it was one thing to be ugly and another to act ugly.

The woman with the snuff-stained lips turned around in her chair and looked up at the clock. Then she turned back and appeared to look a little to the side of Mrs.

Turpin. There was a cast in one of her eyes. "You want to know wher you can get you one of themther clocks?" she asked in a loud voice.

"No, I already have a nice clock," Mrs. Turpin said. Once somebody like her got a leg in the conversation, she would be all over it.

"You can get you one with green stamps," the woman said. "That's most likely wher he got hisn. Save you up enough, you can get you most anythang. I got me some joo'ry."

Ought to have got you a wash rag and some soap, Mrs. Turpin thought.

"I get contour sheets with mine," the pleasant lady said.

The daughter slammed her book shut. She looked straight in front of her, directly through Mrs. Turpin and on through the yellow curtain and the plate glass window which made the wall behind her. The girl's eyes seemed lit all of a sudden with a peculiar light, an unnatural light like night road signs give. Mrs. Turpin turned her head to see if there was anything going on outside that she should see, but she could not see anything. Figures passing cast only a pale shadow through the curtain. There was no reason the girl should single her out for her ugly looks.

"Miss Finley," the nurse said, cracking the door. The gum-chewing woman got up and passed in front of her and Claud and went into the office. She had on red high-heeled shoes.

Directly across the table, the ugly girl's eyes were fixed on Mrs. Turpin as if she had some very special reason for disliking her.

"This is wonderful weather, isn't it?" the girl's mother said.

"It's good weather for cotton if you can get the niggers to pick it," Mrs. Turpin said, "but niggers don't want to pick cotton any more. You can't get the white folks to pick it and now you can't get the niggers—because they got to be right up there with the white folks."

"They gonna try anyways," the white-trash woman said, leaning forward.

"Do you have one of the cotton-picking machines?" the pleasant lady asked.

"No," Mrs. Turpin said, "they leave half the cotton in the field. We don't have much cotton anyway. If you want to make it farming now, you have to have a little of everything. We got a couple of acres of cotton and a few hogs and chickens and just enough white-face that Claud can look after them himself."

"One thang I don't want," the white-trash woman said, wiping her mouth with the back of her hand. "Hogs. Nasty stinking things, a-gruntin and a-rootin all over the place."

Mrs. Turpin gave her the merest edge of her attention. "Our hogs are not dirty and they don't stink," she said. "They're cleaner than some children I've seen. Their feet never touch the ground. We have a pig-parlor—that's where you raise them on concrete," she explained to the pleasant lady, "and Claud scoots them down with the hose every afternoon and washes off the floor." Cleaner by far than that child right there, she thought. Poor nasty little thing. He had not moved except to put the thumb of his dirty hand into his mouth.

The woman turned her face away from Mrs. Turpin. "I know I wouldn't scoot down no hog with no hose," she said to the wall.

You wouldn't have no hog to scoot down, Mrs. Turpin said to herself.

"A-gruntin and a-rootin and a-groanin," the woman muttered.

"We got a little of everything," Mrs. Turpin said to the pleasant lady. "It's no use in having more than you can handle yourself with help like it is. We found enough nig-gers to pick our cotton this year but Claud he has to go after them and take them home again in the evening. They can't walk that half a mile. No they can't. I tell you," she said and laughed merrily, "I sure am tired of buttering up niggers, but you got to love em if you want em to work for you. When they come in the morning, I run out and I say, 'Hi yawl this morning?' and when Claud drives them off to the field I just wave to beat the band and they just wave back." And she waved her hand rapidly to illustrate.

"Like you read out of the same book," the lady said, showing she understood perfectly.

"Child, yes," Mrs. Turpin said. "And when they come in from the field, I run out with a bucket of icewater. That's the way it's going to be from now on," she said. "You may as well face it."

"One thang I know," the white-trash woman said. "Two thangs I ain't going to do: love no niggers or scoot down no hog with no hose." And she let out a bark of contempt.

The look that Mrs. Turpin and the pleasant lady exchanged indicated they both understood that you had to *have* certain things before you could *know* certain things. But every time Mrs. Turpin exchanged a look with the lady, she was aware that the ugly girl's peculiar eyes were still on her, and she had trouble bringing her attention back to the conversation.

"When you got something," she said, "you got to look after it." And when you ain't got a thing but breath and britches, she added to herself, you can afford to come to town every morning and just sit on the Court House coping and spit.

A grotesque revolving shadow passed across the curtain behind her and was thrown palely on the opposite wall. Then a bicycle clattered down against the out-side of the building. The door opened and a colored boy glided in with a tray from the drugstore. It had two large red and white paper cups on it with tops on them. He was a tall, very black boy in discolored white pants and a green nylon shirt. He was chewing gum slowly, as if to music. He set the tray down in the office opening next to the fern and stuck his head through to look for the secretary. She was not in there. He rested his arms on the ledge and waited, his narrow bottom stuck out, swaying slowly to the left and right. He raised a hand over his head and scratched the base of his skull.

"You see that button there, boy?" Mrs. Turpin said. "You can punch that and she'll come. She's probably in the back somewhere."

"Is thas right?" the boy said agreeably, as if he had never seen the button before. He leaned to the right and put his finger on it. "She sometime out," he said and twisted around to face his audience, his elbows behind him on the counter. The nurse appeared and he twisted back again. She handed him a dollar and he rooted in his pocket and made the change and counted it out to her. She gave him fifteen cents for a tip and he went out with the empty tray. The heavy door swung to slowly and closed at length with the sound of suction. For a moment no one spoke.

"They ought to send all them niggers back to Africa," the white-trash woman said. "That's wher they come from in the first place."

"Oh, I couldn't do without my good colored friends," the pleasant lady said.

"There's a heap of things worse than a nigger," Mrs. Turpin agreed. "It's all kinds of them just like it's all kinds of us."

"Yes, and it takes all kinds to make the world go round," the lady said in her musical voice.

As she said it, the raw-complexioned girl snapped her teeth together. Her lower lip turned downwards and inside out, revealing the pale pink inside of her mouth. After a second it rolled back up. It was the ugliest face Mrs. Turpin had ever seen anyone make and for a moment she was certain that the girl had made it at her. She was looking at her as if she had known and disliked her all her life—all of Mrs. Turpin's life, it seemed too, not just all the girl's life. Why, girl, I don't even know you, Mrs. Turpin said silently.

She forced her attention back to the discussion. "It wouldn't be practical to send them back to Africa," she said. "They wouldn't want to go. They got it too good here."

"Wouldn't be what they wanted—if I had anythang to do with it," the woman said.

"It wouldn't be a way in the world you could get all the niggers back over there," Mrs. Turpin said. "They'd be hiding out and lying down and turning sick on you and wailing and hollering and raring and pitching. It wouldn't be a way in the world to get them over there."

"They got over here," the trashy woman said. "Get back like they got over."

"It wasn't so many of them then," Mrs. Turpin explained.

The woman looked at Mrs. Turpin as if here was an idiot indeed but Mrs. Turpin was not bothered by the look, considering where it came from.

"Nooo," she said, "they're going to stay here where they can go to New York and marry white folks and improve their color. That's what they all want to do, every one of them, improve their color."

"You know what comes of that, don't you?" Claud asked.

"No, Claud, what?" Mrs. Turpin said.

Claud's eyes twinkled. "White-faced niggers," he said with never a smile.

Everybody in the office laughed except the white-trash and the ugly girl. The girl gripped the book in her lap with white fingers. The trashy woman looked around her from face to face as if she thought they were all idiots. The old woman in the feed sack dress continued to gaze expressionless across the floor at the high-top shoes of the man opposite her, the one who had been pretending to be asleep when the Turpins came in. He was laughing heartily, his hands still spread out on his knees. The child had fallen to the side and was lying now almost face down in the old woman's lap.

While they recovered from their laughter, the nasal chorus on the radio kept the room from silence.

"You go to blank blank
And I'll go to mine
But we'll all blank along
To-geth-ther,

And all along the blank
We'll hep eachother out
Smile-ling in any kind of
Weath-ther!"

Mrs. Turpin didn't catch every word but she caught enough to agree with the spirit of the song and it turned her thoughts sober. To help anybody out that needed it was her philosophy of life. She never spared herself when she found somebody in need, whether they were white or black, trash or decent. And of all she had to be thankful for, she was most thankful that this was so. If Jesus had said, "You can be high society and have all the money you want and be thin and svelte-like, but you can't be a good woman with it," she would have had to say, "Well don't make me that then. Make me a good woman and it don't matter what else, how fat or how ugly or how poor!" Her heart rose. He had not made her a nigger or white-trash or ugly! He had made her herself and given her a little of everything. Jesus, thank you! she said. Thank you thank you thank you! Whenever she counted her blessings she felt as buoyant as if she weighed one hundred and twenty-five pounds instead of one hundred and eighty.

"What's wrong with your little boy?" the pleasant lady asked the white-trashy woman.

"He has a ulcer," the woman said proudly. "He ain't give me a minute's peace since he was born. Him and her are just alike," she said, nodding at the old woman, who was running her leathery fingers through the child's pale hair. "Look like I can't get nothing down them two but Co' Cola and candy."

That's all you try to get down em, Mrs. Turpin said to herself. Too lazy to light the fire. There was nothing you could tell her about people like them that she didn't know already. And it was not just that they didn't have anything. Because if you gave them everything, in two weeks it would all be broken or filthy or they would have chopped it up for lightwood. She knew all this from her own experience. Help them you must, but help them you couldn't.

All at once the ugly girl turned her lips inside out again. Her eyes fixed like two drills on Mrs. Turpin. This time there was no mistaking that there was something ur-gent behind them.

Girl, Mrs. Turpin exclaimed silently, I haven't done a thing to you! The girl might be confusing her with somebody else. There was no need to sit by and let herself be intimidated. "You must be in college," she said boldly, looking directly at the girl. "I see you reading a book there."

The girl continued to stare and pointedly did not answer.

Her mother blushed at this rudeness. "The lady asked you a question, Mary Grace," she said under her breath.

"I have ears," Mary Grace said.

The poor mother blushed again. "Mary Grace goes to Wellesley College," she ex-plained. She twisted one of the buttons on her dress. "In Massachusetts," she added with a grimace. "And in the summer she just keeps right on studying. Just reads all the time, a real book worm. She's done real well at Wellesley; she's taking English and Math and History and Psychology and Social Studies," she rattled on, "and I think it's too much. I think she ought to get out and have fun."

The girl looked as if she would like to hurl them all through the plate glass window.

"Way up north," Mrs. Turpin murmured and thought, well, it hasn't done much for her manners.

"I'd almost rather to have him sick," the white-trash woman said, wrenching the attention back to herself. "He's so mean when he ain't. Look like some children just take natural to meanness. It's some gets bad when they get sick but he was the opposite. Took sick and turned good. He don't give me no trouble now. It's me waitin to see the doctor," she said.

If I was going to send anybody back to Africa, Mrs. Turpin thought, it would be your kind, woman. "Yes, indeed," she said aloud, but looking up at the ceiling, "it's a heap of things worse than a nigger." And dirtier than a hog, she added to herself.

"I think people with bad dispositions are more to be pitied than anyone on earth," the pleasant lady said in a voice that was decidedly thin.

"I thank the Lord he has blessed me with a good one," Mrs. Turpin said. "The day has never dawned that I couldn't find something to laugh at."

"Not since she married me anyways," Claud said with a comical straight face.

Everybody laughed except the girl and the white-trash.

Mrs. Turpin's stomach shook. "He's such a caution," she said, "that I can't help but laugh at him."

The girl made a loud ugly noise through her teeth.

Her mother's mouth grew thin and tight. "I think the worst thing in the world," she said, "is an ungrateful person. To have everything and not appreciate it. I know a girl," she said, "who has parents who would give her anything, a little brother who loves her dearly, who is getting a good education, who wears the best clothes, but who can never say a kind word to anyone, who never smiles, who just criticizes and complains all day long."

"Is she too old to paddle?" Claud asked.

The girl's face was almost purple.

"Yes," the lady said, "I'm afraid there's nothing to do but leave her to her folly. Some day she'll wake up and it'll be too late."

"It never hurt anyone to smile," Mrs. Turpin said. "It just makes you feel better all over."

"Of course," the lady said sadly, "but there are just some people you can't tell anything to. They can't take criticism."

"If it's one thing I am," Mrs. Turpin said with feeling, "it's grateful. When I think who all I could have been besides myself and what all I got, a little of everything, and a good disposition besides, I just feel like shouting, 'Thank you, Jesus, for making everything the way it is!' It could have been different!" For one thing, somebody else could have got Claud. At the thought of this, she was flooded with gratitude and a terrible pang of joy ran through her. "Oh thank you, Jesus, Jesus, thank you!" she cried aloud.

The book struck her directly over her left eye. It struck almost at the same instant that she realized the girl was about to hurl it. Before she could utter a sound, the raw face came crashing across the table toward her, howling. The girl's fingers sank like clamps into the soft flesh of her neck. She heard the mother cry out and Claud shout,

"Whoa!" There was an instant when she was certain that she was about to be in an earthquake.

All at once her vision narrowed and she saw everything as if it were happening in a small room far away, or as if she were looking at it through the wrong end of a telescope. Claud's face crumpled and fell out of sight. The nurse ran in, then out, then in again. Then the gangling figure of the doctor rushed out of the inner door. Magazines flew this way and that as the table turned over. The girl fell with a thud and Mrs. Turpin's vision suddenly reversed itself and she saw everything large instead of small. The eyes of the white-trashy woman were staring hugely at the floor. There the girl, held down on one side by the nurse and on the other by her mother, was wrenching and turning in their grasp. The doctor was kneeling astride her, trying to hold her arm down. He managed after a second to sink a long needle into it.

Mrs. Turpin felt entirely hollow except for her heart which swung from side to side as if it were agitated in a great empty drum of flesh.

"Somebody that's not busy call for the ambulance," the doctor said in the off-hand voice young doctors adopt for terrible occasions.

Mrs. Turpin could not have moved a finger. The old man who had been sitting next to her skipped nimbly into the office and made the call, for the secretary still seemed to be gone.

"Claud!" Mrs. Turpin called.

He was not in his chair. She knew she must jump up and find him but she felt like some one trying to catch a train in a dream, when everything moves in slow motion and the faster you try to run the slower you go.

"Here I am," a suffocated voice, very unlike Claud's, said.

He was doubled up in the corner on the floor, pale as paper, holding his leg. She wanted to get up and go to him but she could not move. Instead, her gaze was drawn slowly downward to the churning face on the floor, which she could see over the doctor's shoulder.

The girl's eyes stopped rolling and focused on her. They seemed a much lighter blue than before, as if a door that had been tightly closed behind them was now open to admit light and air.

Mrs. Turpin's head cleared and her power of motion returned. She leaned forward until she was looking directly into the fierce brilliant eyes. There was no doubt in her mind that the girl did know her, knew her in some intense and personal way, beyond time and place and condition. "What you got to say to me?" she asked hoarsely and held her breath, waiting, as for a revelation.

The girl raised her head. Her gaze locked with Mrs. Turpin's. "Go back to hell where you came from, you old wart hog," she whispered. Her voice was low but clear. Her eyes burned for a moment as if she saw with pleasure that her message had struck its target.

Mrs. Turpin sank back in her chair.

After a moment the girl's eyes closed and she turned her head wearily to the side.

The doctor rose and handed the nurse the empty syringe. He leaned over and put both hands for a moment on the mother's shoulders, which were shaking. She was sitting on the floor, her lips pressed together, holding Mary Grace's hand in her lap. The girl's fingers were gripped like a baby's around her thumb. "Go on to the hospital," he said. "I'll call and make the arrangements."

"Now let's see that neck," he said in a jovial voice to Mrs. Turpin. He began to inspect her neck with his first two fingers. Two little moon-shaped lines like pink fish bones were indented over her windpipe. There was the beginning of an angry red swelling above her eye. His fingers passed over this also.

"Lea' me be," she said thickly and shook him off. "See about Claud. She kicked him."

"I'll see about him in a minute," he said and felt her pulse. He was a thin gray-haired man, given to pleasantries. "Go home and have yourself a vacation the rest of the day," he said and patted her on the shoulder.

Quit your pattin me, Mrs. Turpin growled to herself.

"And put an ice pack over that eye," he said. Then he went and squatted down beside Claud and looked at his leg. After a moment he pulled him up and Claud limped after him into the office.

Until the ambulance came, the only sounds in the room were the tremulous moans of the girl's mother, who continued to sit on the floor. The white-trash woman did not take her eyes off the girl. Mrs. Turpin looked straight ahead at nothing. Presently the ambulance drew up, a long dark shadow, behind the curtain. The attendants came in and set the stretcher down beside the girl and lifted her expertly onto it and carried her out. The nurse helped the mother gather up her things. The shadow of the ambulance moved silently away and the nurse came back in the office.

"That ther girl is going to be a lunatic, ain't she?" the white-trash woman asked the nurse, but the nurse kept on to the back and never answered her.

"Yes, she's going to be a lunatic," the white-trash woman said to the rest of them.

"Po' critter," the old woman murmured. The child's face was still in her lap. His eyes looked idly out over her knees. He had not moved during the disturbance except to draw one leg up under him.

"I thank Gawd," the white-trash woman said fervently, "I ain't a lunatic."

Claud came limping out and the Turpins went home.

As their pick-up truck turned into their own dirt road and made the crest of the hill, Mrs. Turpin gripped the window ledge and looked out suspiciously. The land sloped gracefully down through a field dotted with lavender weeds and at the start of the rise their small yellow frame house, with its little flower beds spread out around it like a fancy apron, sat primly in its accustomed place between two giant hickory trees. She would not have been startled to see a burnt wound between two blackened chimneys.

Neither of them felt like eating so they put on their house clothes and lowered the shade in the bedroom and lay down, Claud with his leg on a pillow and herself with a damp washcloth over her eye. The instant she was flat on her back, the image of a razor-backed hog with warts on its face and horns coming out behind its ears snorted into her head. She moaned, a low quiet moan.

"I am not," she said tearfully, "a wart hog. From hell." But the denial had no force. The girl's eyes and her words, even the tone of her voice, low but clear, directed only to her, brooked no repudiation. She had been singled out for the message, though there was trash in the room to whom it might justly have been applied. The full force of this fact struck her only now. There was a woman there who was neglecting her own child but she had been overlooked. The message had been given to Ruby

Turpin, a respectable, hard-working, church-going woman. The tears dried. Her eyes began to burn instead with wrath.

She rose on her elbow and the washcloth fell into her hand. Claud was lying on his back, snoring. She wanted to tell him what the girl had said. At the same time, she did not wish to put the image of herself as a wart hog from hell into his mind.

"Hey, Claud," she muttered and pushed his shoulder.

Claud opened one pale baby blue eye.

She looked into it warily. He did not think about anything. He just went his way.

"Wha, whasit?" he said and closed the eye again.

"Nothing," she said. "Does your leg pain you?"

"Hurts like hell," Claud said.

"It'll quit terreckly," she said and lay back down. In a moment Claud was snoring again. For the rest of the afternoon they lay there. Claud slept. She scowled at the ceiling. Occasionally she raised her fist and made a small stabbing motion over her chest as if she was defending her innocence to invisible guests who were like the comforters of Job, reasonable-seeming but wrong.

About five-thirty Claud stirred. "Got to go after those niggers," he sighed, not moving.

She was looking straight up as if there were unintelligible handwriting on the ceiling. The protuberance over her eye had turned a greenish-blue. "Listen here," she said.

"What?"

"Kiss me."

Claud leaned over and kissed her loudly on the mouth. He pinched her side and their hands interlocked. Her expression of ferocious concentration did not change. Claud got up, groaning and growling, and limped off. She continued to study the ceiling.

She did not get up until she heard the pick-up truck coming back with the Negroes. Then she rose and thrust her feet in her brown oxfords, which she did not bother to lace, and stumped out onto the back porch and got her red plastic bucket. She emptied a tray of ice cubes into it and filled it half full of water and went out into the back yard. Every afternoon after Claud brought the hands in, one of the boys helped him put out hay and the rest waited in the back of the truck until he was ready to take them home. The truck was parked in the shade under one of the hickory trees.

"Hi yawl this evening?" Mrs Turpin asked grimly, appearing with the bucket and the dipper. There were three women and a boy in the truck.

"Us doin nicely," the oldest woman said. "Hi you doin?" and her gaze stuck immediately on the dark lump on Mrs. Turpin's forehead. "You done fell down, ain't you?" she asked in a solicitous voice. The old woman was dark and almost toothless. She had on an old felt hat of Claud's set back on her head. The other two women were younger and lighter and they both had new bright green sun hats. One of them had hers on her head; the other had taken hers off and the boy was grinning beneath it.

Mrs. Turpin set the bucket down on the floor of the truck. "Yawl hep yourselves," she said. She looked around to make sure Claud had gone. "No, I didn't fall down," she said, folding her arms. "It was something worse than that."

"Ain't nothing bad happen to you!" the old woman said. She said it as if they all knew that Mrs. Turpin was protected in some special way by Divine Providence. "You just had you a little fall."

"We were in town at the doctor's office for where the cow kicked Mr. Turpin," Mrs. Turpin said in a flat tone that indicated they could leave off their foolishness. "And there was this girl there. A big fat girl with her face all broke out. I could look at that girl and tell she was peculiar but I couldn't tell how. And me and her mama was just talking and going along and all of a sudden WHAM! She throws this big book she was reading at me and . . ."

"Naw!" the old woman cried out.

"And then she jumps over the table and commences to choke me."

"Naw!" they all exclaimed, "naw!"

"Hi come she do that?" the old woman asked. "What ail her?"

Mrs. Turpin only glared in front of her.

"Somethin ail her," the old woman said.

"They carried her off in an ambulance," Mrs. Turpin continued, "but before she went she was rolling on the floor and they were trying to hold her down to give her a shot and she said something to me." She paused. "You know what she said to me?"

"What she say?" they asked.

"She said," Mrs. Turpin began, and stopped, her face very dark and heavy. The sun was getting whiter and whiter, blanching the sky overhead so that the leaves of the hickory tree were black in the face of it. She could not bring forth the words. "Something real ugly," she muttered.

"She sho shouldn't said nothin ugly to you," the old woman said. "You so sweet. You the sweetest lady I know."

"She pretty too," the one with the hat on said.

"And stout," the other one said. "I never knowed no sweeter white lady."

"That's the truth befo' Jesus," the old woman said. "Amen! You des as sweet and pretty as you can be."

Mrs. Turpin knew exactly how much Negro flattery was worth and it added to her rage. "She said," she began again and finished this time with a fierce rush of breath, "that I was an old wart hog from hell."

There was an astounded silence.

"Where she at?" the youngest woman cried in a piercing voice.

"Lemme see her. I'll kill her!"

"I'll kill her with you!" the other one cried.

"She b'long in the sylum," the old woman said emphatically. "You the sweetest white lady I know."

"She pretty too," the other two said. "Stout as she can be and sweet. Jesus satisfied with her!"

"Deed he is," the old woman declared.

Idiots! Mrs. Turpin growled to herself. You could never say anything intelligent to a nigger. You could talk at them but not with them. "Yawl ain't drunk your water," she said shortly. "Leave the bucket in the truck when you're finished with it. I got more to do than just stand around and pass the time of day," and she moved off and into the house.

She stood for a moment in the middle of the kitchen. The dark protuberance over her eye looked like a miniature tornado cloud which might any moment sweep across the horizon of her brow. Her lower lip protruded dangerously. She squared her massive shoulders. Then she marched into the front of the house and out the side door and started down the road to the pig parlor. She had the look of a woman going single-handed, weaponless, into battle.

The sun was a deep yellow now like a harvest moon and was riding westward very fast over the far tree line as if it meant to reach the hogs before she did. The road was rutted and she kicked several good-sized stones out of her path as she strode along. The pig parlor was on a little knoll at the end of a lane that ran off from the side of the barn. It was a square of concrete as large as a small room, with a board fence about four feet high around it. The concrete floor sloped slightly so that the hog wash could drain off into a trench where it was carried to the field for fertilizer. Claud was standing on the outside, on the edge of the concrete, hanging onto the top board, hosing down the floor inside. The hose was connected to the faucet of a water trough nearby.

Mrs. Turpin climbed up beside him and glowered down at the hogs inside. There were seven long-snouted bristly shoats in it—tan with liver-colored spots—and an old sow a few weeks off from farrowing. She was lying on her side grunting. The shoats were running about shaking themselves like idiot children, their little slit pig eyes searching the floor for anything left. She had read that pigs were the most intelligent animal. She doubted it. They were supposed to be smarter than dogs. There had even been a pig astronaut. He had performed his assignment perfectly but died of a heart attack afterwards because they left him in his electric suit, sitting upright throughout his examination when naturally a hog should be on all fours.

A-gruntin and a-rootin and a-groanin.

"Gimme that hose," she said, yanking it away from Claud. "Go on and carry them niggers home and then get off that leg."

"You look like you might have swallowed a mad dog," Claud observed, but he got down and limped off. He paid no attention to her humors.

Until he was out of earshot, Mrs. Turpin stood on the side of the pen, holding the hose and pointing the stream of water at the hind quarters of any shoat that looked as if it might try to lie down. When he had had time to get over the hill, she turned her head slightly and her wrathful eyes scanned the path. He was nowhere in sight. She turned back again and seemed to gather herself up. Her shoulders rose and she drew in her breath.

"What do you send me a message like that for?" she said in a low fierce voice, barely above a whisper but with the force of a shout in its concentrated fury. "How am I a hog and me both? How am I saved and from hell too?" Her free fist was knotted and with the other she gripped the hose, blindly pointing the stream of water in and out of the eye of the old sow whose outraged squeal she did not hear.

The pig parlor commanded a view of the back pasture where their twenty beef cows were gathered around the hay-bales Claud and the boy had put out. The freshly cut pasture sloped down to the highway. Across it was their cotton field and beyond that a dark green dusty wood which they owned as well. The sun was behind the wood, very red, looking over the paling of trees like a farmer inspecting his own hogs.

"Why me?" she rumbled. "It's no trash around here, black or white, that I haven't given to. And break my back to the bone every day working. And do for the church."

She appeared to be the right size woman to command the arena before her. "How am I a hog?" she demanded. "Exactly how am I like them?" and she jabbed the stream of water at the shoats. "There was plenty of trash there. It didn't have to be me.

"If you like trash better, go get yourself some trash then," she railed. "You could have made me trash. Or a nigger. If trash is what you wanted why didn't you make me trash?" She shook her fist with the hose in it and a watery snake appeared momentarily in the air. "I could quit working and take it easy and be filthy," she growled. "Lounge about the sidewalks all day drinking root beer. Dip snuff and spit in every puddle and have it all over my face. I could be nasty.

"Or you could have made me a nigger. It's too late for me to be a nigger," she said with deep sarcasm, "but I could act like one. Lay down in the middle of the road and stop traffic. Roll on the ground."

In the deepening light everything was taking on a mysterious hue. The pasture was growing a peculiar glassy green and the streak of highway had turned lavender. She braced herself for a final assault and this time her voice rolled out over the pasture. "Go on," she yelled, "call me a hog! Call me a hog again. From hell. Call me a wart hog from hell. Put that bottom rail on top. There'll still be a top and bottom!"

A garbled echo returned to her.

A final surge of fury shook her and she roared, "Who do you think you are?"

The color of everything, field and crimson sky, burned for a moment with a transparent intensity. The question carried over the pasture and across the highway and the cotton field and returned to her clearly like an answer from beyond the wood.

She opened her mouth but no sound came out of it.

A tiny truck, Claud's, appeared on the highway, heading rapidly out of sight. Its gears scraped thinly. It looked like a child's toy. At any moment a bigger truck might smash into it and scatter Claud's and the niggers' brains all over the road.

Mrs. Turpin stood there, her gaze fixed on the highway, all her muscles rigid, until in five or six minutes the truck reappeared, returning. She waited until it had had time to turn into their own road. Then like a monumental statue coming to life, she bent her head slowly and gazed, as if through the very heart of mystery, down into the pig parlor at the hogs. They had settled all in one corner around the old sow who was grunting softly. A red glow suffused them. They appeared to pant with a secret life.

Until the sun slipped finally behind the tree line, Mrs. Turpin remained there with her gaze bent to them as if she were absorbing some abysmal life-giving knowledge. At last she lifted her head. There was only a purple streak in the sky, cutting through a field of crimson and leading, like an extension of the highway, into the descending dusk. She raised her hands from the side of the pen in a gesture hieratic and profound. A visionary light settled in her eyes. She saw the streak as a vast swinging bridge extending upward from the earth through a field of living fire. Upon it a vast horde of souls were rumbling toward heaven. There were whole companies of white-trash, clean for the first time in their lives, and bands of black niggers in white robes, and battalions of freaks and lunatics shouting and clapping and leaping like frogs. And bringing up the end of the procession was a tribe of people whom she recognized at once as those who, like herself and Claud, had always had a little of everything and the God-given wit to use it right. She leaned forward to observe them closer. They were marching behind the others with great dignity, accountable as they had always been for good order and common sense and respectable behavior. They alone were on key. Yet she could see by their shocked and altered faces that even their virtues were being burned away. She lowered her hands and gripped the rail of the hog pen, her eyes small but fixed unblinkingly on what lay ahead. In a moment the vision faded but she remained where she was, immobile.

At length she got down and turned off the faucet and made her slow way on the darkening path to the house. In the woods around her the invisible cricket choruses had struck up, but what she heard were the voices of the souls climbing upward into the starry field and shouting hallelujah.

✀ A Man of Few Words ✀

Judith Claire Mitchell

Only minutes after he died at age seventy-eight Ike Grossbart had come to understand he could enjoy, one more time, a pleasure from his life. It was up to him to choose which pleasure that would be. Ike was surprised and grateful. He had been expecting earthworms and dirt. Instead—or at least, first—here was a squirt of whipped cream to top off his time on earth.

He mulled over the various joys and delights he had known. He did not want to choose precipitously. But deciding was difficult, and made even more so by a conversation he'd had only hours before and could not shake from his head.

"Ike, remember the knishes they had at Zalman's in Flatbush?" his brother-in-law had asked. "Wouldn't you love one of those now?"

"One of those now would kill me," Ike had said. His voice was near gone. He'd never imagined he'd use up his voice over the course of his life as if it were ink in a pen. Thank goodness he'd been a man of few words. "All that salt and fat," he managed to rasp. "Anyway, the best knishes were from Dubin's."

"Dubin's?" Ike's daughter asked. "Was I ever there?"

His wife had looked up from her crossword puzzle. She was sitting in the recliner the orderlies had dragged in so she could spend nights in the hospital room. "What are you saying?" she said. "Are you saying the best knishes weren't from Yonah Shlissel's?"

Yonah Shlissel's. Of course. The two men murmured the name out loud, and sighed as if recalling the most beautiful woman they'd ever laid eyes on. It was a sigh of fond remembrance but also of regret. The beautiful woman was long gone, and Ike and his brother-in-law so old they had to be reminded she'd existed at all.

"What made that place so good?" Ike's daughter asked.

"I heard Yonah had a secret ingredient," his wife said. "Once I heard oil imported from the old country. Another time I heard potatoes from some farm out in Jersey."

"Nah, it was water they pumped in special," the brother-in-law said. He was the kind of man who had to let people know he was smarter than they were. Ike had never understood how his sister endured this man's blather. Nevertheless, she had, and so, though his sister was gone, the man remained family.

Ike had shrugged. "All I know is my wife is as usual right. No one matched Yonah Shlissel's potato knishes."

It was a few hours later—the brother-in-law gone home, the daughter in the cafeteria having a late-night snack, the Grossbarts asleep—that death came for Ike. *Yitzchak ben Moshe*, death sang like a rabbi honoring a congregant by calling him to the pulpit to bless the Torah. Ike left the hospital room quietly, obediently. He was thankful he hadn't been asked to say good-bye to his wife; he could not imagine anything more difficult.

Now he wishes he could ask her advice. She'd been the wise one, the expert on emotions and pleasure and pain. "Life is so full of heartache and loss," she used to say to the kids. "Whenever the chance for happiness comes along, I want you to fill both hands."

Ike's hands are empty. It's not that there's a dearth of pleasures to choose from. He just doesn't know which one to pick. He considers weddings, his own, his son's. He considers Bar Mitzvahs, his own, his son's. Birthday parties, even days with the family at the beach. But knishes keep pushing these memories out of his head.

You are spending far too much energy chasing knishes away, he scolds himself. Don't be so frivolous. Food has always meant far too much to you.

Although he was gaunt when he died, he had the clogged arteries and overburdened heart of a fat man. He had always loved to eat. From growing up poor, he supposed. Columns of gingersnaps, spoonfuls of peanut butter, and the skins of barbecued chickens, which he'd pull off the birds and roll in his fingers as if he were rolling a cigarette and then noisily slurp down the way the kids sucked spaghetti.

Jewish food, the food his mother used to make, was his weakness. He once encountered an anti-Semite who called Jews not kikes or sheenies but bagels. You goddam Jew-bagel, he'd say. Ike had found it hard to take offense. After his second heart attack, only days before, he'd offered the floor nurse five dollars to sneak a bagel to him. I'm at death's door, he thought when she refused, what can it matter? Finally, when neither the nurse nor his wife was looking, his daughter brought him a jumbo deluxe from Weinstein's, the crusts sticky with brown onions and the soft-toasted middle smeared with at least an inch of cream cheese. The two of them had shared it. It had been a foolish thing to do. His daughter was already fat enough and just look where it had gotten him. Still, that had been a nice moment, maybe as nice as any.

Can a dead man blush? Apparently, yes. Shame on you, he thinks. He will not go out a glutton, a pig. He'll select a meaningful moment of his life to enjoy again, a memory sweet enough to sustain him through eternity. If now is not the time for meaningful memories, then someone should tell him when is.

Yet as he reflects and ponders he realizes his difficulty in choosing is compounded by the number of precious memories that sustain him already. He has not made love to his wife in fifteen years, for instance, but now, when he thinks of her, he feels sated and sleepy as if they last lay together moments ago. He can taste her mouth, feel her soft, round belly and the breasts that, as if he had been granted a wish by a genie, had grown larger with each of the children she gave him. To seek even one more time with his wife strikes him as greedy and, in a way, superfluous. She is with him still. Leave well enough alone, he thinks.

He considers, too, reliving the day his youngest was born—the boy, a son. As the baby came into the world, Ike had paced in the waiting room down the hall. He smoked a few packs of Luckies, ate three or four Hershey bars. It was what men did in those days. He was glad for it. He had no interest in participating in birth the way fathers had to now—catching the baby, cutting the cord, seeing one's beloved wife open and as red as the meat of a plum. But to go back once again to the waiting room, that might be nice. To hear once again *Mr. Grossbart, it's a boy.*

Yet just thinking about his son's birth causes the same explosion of pride beneath his ribs that he experienced forty-one years ago. An explosion he had not felt when his daughter had been born seven years prior. An explosion, he now realizes, not all that different from a minor heart attack. *Mr. Grossbart, it's a boy,* and his heart twisted like a wrung dishrag. He felt fear and pain; he felt small and inadequate—mortal. It was as if his body, aware that his head and his tongue were too stunned to thank God in words, began to express his awe and gratitude through trembling and aching and terror. And then, as if God heard and responded to his body's prayer—for that's what it had been, a prayer spoken by flesh and bones—Ike's heart had been soothed. Comfort and hope and optimism had rested on his shoulder like a reassuring hand.

It was the most powerful moment of his life. Perhaps for that reason he does not want to live it again. If his son could overhear these thoughts, Ike knows, he would feel only rejection. He would resent Ike's decision to choose a different moment to return to. He would not understand the love in this decision.

Other good days—the birth of his chubby, uncomplicated daughter, the day Hitler got his, the morning in the middle of the Depression when Ike found a twenty on a subway platform—none of those other good days have faded for him, either.

He is getting nervous now. What if there is only so much time in which to choose? Maybe a buzzer will go off soon. An egg timer might ring. He racks his brain. It's still full of knishes. Perhaps, he thinks, there's a reason for this.

So at last he decides, why not? Why not choose a Yonah Shlissel knish? That overstuffed pillow, yellow as gold, salty as sea air. Why not choose to relive the simplest pleasure of all? He'll have a knish, but before he does, he'll bow his head, recite the proper blessing so God will know he is thankful for even small pleasures. And then he will call it a day.

The Lower East Side has been given over to colored people. West Africans and Haitians and Jamaicans, dark-skinned Cubans. The buildings shake from drumming and radios and languages. The sidewalk is broken, and the street with its potholes resembles the soles of a poor man's shoes.

When Ike was a boy, the air here smelled of garlic pickles and sauerkraut. Now the air reeks from fumes expelled by idling delivery trucks and city buses. When Ike was a boy, the stores here sold felt derbies and fresh fish and used books. Now they sell knock-off designer sneakers, vinyl leather jackets, and T-shirts with dirty sayings across the front.

This is why he has avoided the area for decades. He feels discouraged now that he's here, a little downhearted as he keeps walking east. He thinks about the other, better choices he could have made—even the day Kennedy squeaked by Nixon might have been better, even the first time he watched TV he felt more excitement. How about his first car, the gray Plymouth, that boat.

Then suddenly, his feet stop short. If he'd been the Plymouth, his brakes would have squealed.

"*Kineahora,*" he whispers.

He is standing in front of Yonah Shlissel's. It's there—here—right where he left it, right where it ought to no longer be.

His no-good heart pounds. He hesitates. In his head, he counts to three, and on three he pulls open the dark heavy door. He steps tentatively into a vestibule with a wooden slat bench used not for sitting but for piling. Even now it's covered with stacks of Jewish newspapers and political pamphlets. He takes a breath. With a trembling hand, he turns the mock crystal knob of the next heavy door. He steps inside. It's the same. It's Yonah's.

If earlier that day his wife had challenged him to describe Yonah Shlissel's, Ike would have replied that he couldn't remember what he'd had that morning for break-fast, much less the interior of a restaurant he last saw fifty years ago. But seeing it now, he knows every detail is one hundred percent correct. The wooden floors, scuffed and warped. The round wooden tables, each with a waiter's pad shoved be-neath one leg to quiet its rocking. He remembers that—yes—there were no windows, yes, the place was dimly lit, yes, the waiters ran about in clean white aprons and con-fided the customers' orders to Yonah in the kitchen as if they were passing along gov-ernment secrets.

Is it an illusion? A gag? Ike knows hair continues to grow after death, but do dreams continue to spin? He reaches for one of the mints in the bowl by the cash reg-ister and chews it cautiously. It's stale. It tastes more like soap than mint. It's the same as ever. The mints, at least, are real.

And now here comes the frowzy, fat hostess in her polka-dot dress. She wears a brown wig meaning she is married, this battle-ax, maybe to Yonah himself. In those days the married women covered their hair when they went out in public. He'd nearly forgotten, but now he remembers and remembers, also, his mother's wig. He remem-bers it suddenly, fondly, and then with tears that shine but don't fall. His mother's wig also was brown, always askew, and so cheap he could see the stitches holding the strands to its net crown.

"Party of, what, only one?" The fat woman is annoyed. Ike remembers this woman now as clearly as he remembers the wobbly tables and soapy mints. When he was a child she frightened him. Now he is a seventy-eight-year-old dead man and she still gives him the heebie-jeebies.

Why is she so aggravated with him? Did his wish to return here disturb her own rest? Had she been forced to rouse herself, stretch her bare bones, tunnel up through six feet of beetles and ruin, all the while bobby-pinning that wig to her head, just so she could get to Yonah's in time to seat him, this negligible party of one?

"Poppa, why are they so grouchy here?"

"Did we come to make friends or have lunch?"

Yes, Ike thinks. Yes, he is only one. Yes, he's alone. We come in alone, go out the same way. God knows he wishes that wasn't how it worked. God knows already he misses his wife, wishes she were at his side. Or no, he doesn't wish that. That would be wishing her dead. He wishes he knew what one had the right to wish for under these circumstances. He might have wished not to go back into his life but forward into his death where his loved ones who'd left him might be waiting.

He says nothing, of course. He is too shy to speak, too tongue-tied. And what would be the point of philosophizing with Mrs. Shlissel? The woman has been dead at least half a century. To her nothing he could say about death would be news. To him everything about death—even the fact of it—is a revelation. It came as a shock. Of course all the time he knew. All his life he knew everyone gets old, sick, dies. It wasn't exactly top secret. But somehow all along he figured nobody really meant *him*. Not him, not little Yitzchak Grossbart. But of course, that's just who they meant. The proof was in the pudding. Here was little Yitzchak Grossbart standing in a building demolished during the Korean conflict, talking away in his head to a fat dead lady.

She does not even look at him. She waddles to an empty table near the counter intending for him to follow. As he does he thinks that today a woman with such a rump would never wear that skinny cloth belt nor those big white polka dots. His daughter always wore big shirts that skimmed her tush, covered the thighs, and always they were black. "Am I ever going to see you in anything but mourning rags?" he'd once heard his wife ask. A similar comment would have hurt his son's feelings, but his daughter had laughed and said she liked to be comfortable and that black didn't show dirt. Maybe he should have said something then. He didn't mind a girl with a fanny on her. But it had not seemed proper. It had not seemed like something a father should say.

A waiter comes, places a wooden bowl filled with slices of bread—seeded rye, black pumpernickel, braided challah—onto the table. "You need time?" the waiter asks. Ike nods. He needs time.

He cranes his neck so he can see the long cases beneath the counter. A wall of food under glass. Kishke, kasha, kugel. Herring. Greek olives, black and wrinkled like the skin on the hands of the old man sweeping the floors. Lox as pink as flamingo, gefilte fish pocked and slimy, and rows of white fish still sheathed in their gold scales, their dead eyes like opals. And, then, in another case, meat. The salami and franks, the corned beef and pastrami, the tongue. Agents of death all looking as benign as a schoolboy twiddling his thumbs.

The knishes have an entire compartment to themselves not in respect of any dietary law, but rather the same way royalty is given a private box in the concert hall.

Ike sighs. He truly is at Yonah Shlissel's again. It's a miracle and a blessing. It was, he thinks, a pretty good choice. It reminds him of his boyhood, his father, even of something his daughter had said when she'd split that bagel with him. She'd been violating not only the rules of his diet that day, but the rules of her own as well. She was perpetually starving herself, that one, never with any discernible results. She'd inherited his appetite and God knows whose metabolism.

"I'm so bad," she had said, but it was clearly a fine moment for her, maybe the moment she'd return to someday. She'd rolled her eyes and licked her fingers. "Oh, God," she'd said. "I've died and gone to heaven."

His time is up; the waiter is back, tapping pencil against pad. "I haven't got all day, mister," he says. "You want to order before it's tomorrow?"

Ike remembers the waiter now, too. Abrupt and arrogant. A Shlissel for sure. Always acting like there's somewhere more important he has to rush off to.

"Pardon me," Ike says. "One potato knish."

The waiter scurries off. Ike looks around at the other customers. Are they props, are they real men, or are they his comrades, other dead Jews who have chosen Yonah's? They are mostly old men, he sees. Many of them are reading the *Forward*. The newspapers smudge their fingers and conceal their faces. It's from seeing their hands that Ike knows the men are old. Brown spots stain old hands the way rust stains old cars.

When they were youngsters, he and his sister had called such hands old lady hands. Old lady hands, as if a man's hands never withered, never wrinkled, never became bent and blue with veins. After a bath, he and his sister would show their wrinkled, pruney fingers to each other. His sister's singsong taunt: *Yitzchak's got old lady hands.*

He'd held her old lady hands when she died. She'd passed a decade ago, beaten by the same ailment that got him years later . . . minutes earlier. A heart whose muscles sagged from working too hard for so many years until it could no longer beat, and slowly came to a stop. It was how hearts were designed, like old-fashioned windup toys.

He had held her hands and thought about singing her song back to her: *Look now who's got old lady hands.* Not as a taunt, of course. More like a lullaby. He hoped she'd remember the time they were so young they could bathe naked together, laugh at old age. *Wisenheimer*, she'd maybe have whispered. *Ishkabibble.* These were the worst things she'd ever called him. Much nicer than asshole, which is what his son used to call his daughter when she teased him too hard.

Ike had not sung to his sister. Something had stopped him. He'd worried she might not have remembered. It would have been terrible had she taken it wrong. So he'd kept quiet. What does one say at such moments? Is anyone so wise they know? Certainly not Ike, not someone like Ike. As his sister passed on, he squeezed her hands and thought, She looks so much like Mama. This had comforted him. Anyone in heaven who took one look at his sister would know just who to direct her to.

Again there are tears in his eyes. He is able to blink them away. He tells himself to stop. You are squandering your moment, he thinks. It's supposed to be a moment of pleasure.

So he focuses on the task at hand. He prepares for the meal to come. He gets up, goes to the sink in the corner of the restaurant, washes his hands. In his own home he and his wife were never so observant, but here it seems fitting. He returns to his table and tears a piece of challah. He considers his life. He'd lived it as right as he knew how. He loved his wife, had a daughter who was good-natured and smart, had a beloved son he could name after his father. He had grief and loss; he had modest pleasures and joys. He never would have asked for more but now he has been given more, just a little bit more. He recites the blessing for bread.

Twice a year his father took him to Delancey Street to buy a new suit. Once in the fall for Rosh Hashanah; again in the spring for Pesach. And then after, as a reward for not bellyaching during the fitting, his father would take him to Yonah Shlissel's. Just the two of them, father and son, twice a year. Just the men in the family.

Like the old men here now, his father hid behind a newspaper. Ike, six or seven, pretended the paper was a shield that made persons on either side of it invisible and invincible.

Six or seven, he ate his knish with his fingers. He peeled the thin crust apart and then, like the boy in the nursery rhyme, he stuck in his thumb. But he did not pull out a plum. He merely pulled out that same thumb coated with hot mashed potato. Nor did he say, What a good boy am I! He knew this was not something a good boy would do. He would not have done this in front of his mother. But his father, absorbed, never noticed.

His table manners were never what they should have been. He was the child of immigrants, unschooled and unsophisticated. If he'd grown up during his son's era instead of his own, he'd have blamed this shortcoming on his father. *I'd stick my thumb into a knish and you wouldn't say boo; how was I supposed to learn better? No wonder I was never asked to join a fancy men's eating club.*

No one cares about table manners at Yonah Shlissel's. Everyone here slurps, sighs, grunts, belches. We are descendants of peasants, Ike thinks not without pride. Children of immigrants, adventurers, survivors. And this our reward for feeling no shame. This place of our people. This wonderful repast. Manna from Yonah's. Something his children have never tasted, will never taste.

His daughter would have loved it here, he thinks. She would have run about, pressing her nose to the glass cases. *What's that? What's that? Let's try some of this.* He never brought her here, though he remembers one time taking her to that same children's clothing shop. His son was an infant with the croup, the Holy Days were around the corner, and the girl needed a new dress. Ike remembers sitting in a chair feeling useless and bored while his daughter emerged from the dressing room in one matronly purple dress after another, baby fat distorting the lines of each one, her head lowered—sulking only emphasized the double chins—and the saleslady shaking her head. "She has a bit of a belly, doesn't she?" the woman had said, and Ike had shrugged.

By the time his son was old enough both the clothing shop and Yonah Shlissel's were gone. It didn't matter. His son would have despised Delancey Street. His son despised his own heritage. It was too bad, then, that it had been his son who inherited Ike's face, the same face Ike had inherited from his own father. The huge ears that winged from the head and had been ridiculed even during Gable's heyday. The narrow horned beak rising between bushy brows, bestowing a cross-eyed and angry appearance. Those three faces repeated generation to generation had proclaimed, probably too loudly, their lineage. Those faces had gotten each of them beaten up, one time or another, by tough Catholic boys in prim navy blue uniforms.

Still, it had never occurred to Ike to try to change his face. He'd never really tried to change much about himself. When he married his wife he had warned her. He was not a plant who, with water and sunlight, would bloom and grow into a flowering thing of beauty. He was a homely, hard-working, straightforward man who felt silly saying honey bunch or sweetie pie. He called his wife *fleegle*—Yiddish for chicken wing.

His son believed in change. His son changed his name from Grossbart to Garner. Then he changed his religion. "So what should we call him now?" Ike had asked his wife, "Mahatma Garner?" His son had changed even his face. His son had his ears pasted back. He had his nose shaved and trimmed as if it were a mustache rather than hard bone and cartilage.

The boy had shown up at their house one Sunday modeling the new face, preening like a woman in a hat. Ike had said nothing. He left the kitchen, shut the bedroom door with more noise than required. "It's my money," the boy hollered after him, "and my face."

Ike lay on his bed, turned on a ball game with the remote. He closed his eyes.

He didn't object to the way his son spent his money. But the rest of what his son had hollered up at him . . . how could the boy think his face belonged to him only? When his son studied his new reflection, whose child did he see?

When his wife joined him in bed that night, Ike said, "You know, *fleegle*, some-times, I catch a glimpse of myself in a mirror when I don't expect to, and I think, 'Hey, that guy looks like a member of my family.' I like that. I take pleasure in being from this family." A veritable speech, an outburst.

His wife had said, "And why are you telling this to me?"

"There's a point in telling him?" Ike never mentioned it again. He said nothing about it even though it hurt to look at that face. Revised, his son looked not like a Grossbart, not like a Garner, not like a Jew or the Hindu he claimed to be, but like an owl with a big round head, angry yellow brown eyes and, lost in the middle, a tiny snipped beak.

And yet, in the end, it was the boy who refused to look at Ike. During those terrible months after the boy's marriage ended and he'd moved back home, he refused to sit at the same table with Ike.

It was his table manners the boy objected to. "It's disgusting," Ike heard his son say. "He just sits there and shovels it in. No wonder he can't make conversation, with his mouth stuffed like that. It makes me sick. I'll eat in my room."

Like a servant, Ike's wife carried the boy's plate—the boy; the boy was thirty-six—up to his old bedroom, where once again he was living, holed up like a hermit, the room a mess as it had been when he truly was a boy, all his clothes on the floor, dirty Kleenexes and rotted banana peels overflowing the trash basket, and the mattress he slept on bare, not a sheet, not even a pad, and yet this was where he wanted to be. Sometimes he did not come out for days, at least not while Ike was awake.

Sometimes the creak of floorboards, the snap of a light switch woke Ike before sunrise. He lay in bed and told himself that another father would get out of bed and go downstairs. Another father would pull up a chair, pour two strong drinks, get the kid to open up. *Talk to me, son, tell me what's wrong.* But after that, what does one say at such a time? Besides, as the father of this boy, Ike knew getting up and going down-stairs would be futile. There was nothing anyone could say to this boy. Not even Ike's wife knew what to say. She'd say, "You want at least a mattress pad, honey?" and the kid would look at her like she'd accused him of child murder.

Ike had been grateful for whatever snippets of time his father had managed to give him. At Yonah Shlissel's, Ike sucked potato off his thumb. He blew air through his straw turning his glass of celery tonic into a bubbling caldron. His father said noth-ing. Ike balanced on two legs of his chair and worked up some jokes, the funniest being a variation of an old one that, to set the stage, he now told his father. "Hey, Poppa." A grunt. "Poppa, what's black and white and red all over?" "What?" his father asked, still hidden behind the newspaper shield. Ike gave the answer. He gave it loud so his voice would penetrate newsprint and Yiddish. "A newspaper." "Mmm-hmmm," his father said. "Hey, Poppa." His father grunted. "Hey, Poppa. Over all red and white and black is what?" A second grunt. "The Jewish newspaper," Ike said. "Get it? On account of you read it backwards."

"Very good," his father said. "Be quiet. Eat your knish."

Whenever Ike felt sad because his father was not conversing with him, was not asking about school or laughing at Ike's jokes or telling a few of his own, then Ike would think the following: *the two men shared a companionable silence.*

From what radio show or dime novel he had gotten that phrase, he had no idea.

But it made him feel better to think it. It was the way men behaved together. Not like his sister and mother who babbled endlessly, clucking chickens. Not like women. Men shared companionable silences.

But the silence he shared with his son had not been so companionable, and he thinks now of his grown son returned to the narrow bed of childhood, where he keened like a lost goat, cried to Ike's wife what a terrible father Ike had been. Distant, his son wailed. Withholding.

Like a drill his son's voice bored through the walls of the house Ike had worked his whole life to pay off. Like a jackhammer, the voice of his son—his heir, his devisee— shattered walls into splintery fragments. It made Ike hate the house. It made him see it as flimsy and cheap. "He never played catch with me," Ike's son wept. Crash, a wrecking ball knocking down plaster. "He never took me fishing." Boom, a sledge-hammer punching holes in the framing. "He never talked to me about women. How was I supposed to know what to do when Dinah got so unhappy?" Thirty-six and bleating like a goat. "Never once did he say he loved me."

"He's angry?" Ike asked when his wife came to bed.

"At the world," she said. "Don't take it personal."

"Did your parents ever say they loved you, *fleegle*?"

"I'd have dropped dead twice from shock, *fleegle*." She hesitated. "But since he wants to hear it, what could it hurt?"

He couldn't sleep. Had his own father ever tossed him a ball, ever taken him fishing? And he could only thank God his father had never talked to him about women. It would have been excruciating for both of them. His son had seen too many TV fathers on the TV sets Ike had bought through the years, the black-and-white consoles, the big-screen colors, the miniatures you could hold in your hand as you lay on your naked mattress and bleated like a goat. Fathers in ties spouting philosophy whispered into their pasted ears by a team of professional writers.

Nobody fed Ike dialogue. Growing up nobody fed him delusions. His father had been too busy working double shifts in a factory to be a television father. A teacher in Poland, in Brooklyn Ike's father worked in a dye factory. He came home late and exhausted and his fingernails were tinted blue as the summer sky.

Ike got out of bed. He knocked on his son's bedroom door. No response. He went in anyway. "You really don't know I love you?" he asked. "I know I'm not the father you wanted, but you have to at least know I love you. You have to know that. You're my only son."

"How does a person know what he's never been told?" his son had said. His unfamiliar face was pressed into a bare pillow with a small tear in the side. Little white feathers floated from it, lighthearted and comical.

By the color of fingernails, Ike wanted to say. But he did what he had come to do. "I love you," he said.

"Too little too late," said his son.

The next time Ike saw his daughter, he felt obliged to ask her if she knew he loved her. She shivered and said, "Oh, Pop, please don't." She brought up the time he'd taken her to Delancey for that dress. "Remember how that heinous saleslady kept harping about how fat I was?" she said. She reddened a little. Ike was not sure if she was embarrassed or angry on behalf of the chubby little girl modeling purple. "And I was so miserable," she said, "until finally you jumped up and picked out that beautiful ivory smock with the shirred bodice and scalloped hem? And I remember thinking, My father knows how to make me look pretty. My father knows what I look like. No one else in this world saw me the way you did. That's how you told me you loved me."

Ike tried to remember the day. He remembered the chair he sat in, he remembered checking the clock on the wall, he remembered the ball game he wanted to get home for, to watch on TV.

"It was such a special moment for me," his daughter said, still red-faced, a girlish blush. "Really, the best. I have that dress still. Can you believe it? In a box in an attic, the way some women preserve their wedding gowns." She was looking at him smiling, expecting something.

"Still, I hope someday you get married," Ike said.

It was a nice speech she made. Maybe she'd make the same speech over his grave. Later that same day his memory finally dredged up the dress. He'd been impatient. He wanted to get home to that ball game, to his new baby boy. The ivory dress was the only one left on the rack she hadn't already tried on and rejected.

At last. The waiter has placed the knish before him. It sits on a pristine white plate. It glistens with oil. Ike pierces the center with the tines of his fork. From the pricks in its belly come perfume and heat.

He cuts off a piece with the side of his fork, carries it up to his lips. It is steaming. It is too hot to eat. He blows on it. His breath is not yet chill enough to cool it.

He could have brought the girl here. The day they picked out the dress, Yonah Shlissel's had still been standing. They could have walked here, her dimpled hand in his, and he could have bought her one of these potato dumplings, could have called her potato dumpling, a little joke between the two of them. He could have told her jokes.

It had never crossed his mind. Yonah Shlissel's had been for the men in the family. It had not crossed his mind. There was a ball game on TV he wanted to watch. He was waiting to take the boy. By the time the boy was old enough, Yonah Shlissel's was gone.

The boy would have hated it anyway. Even had he brought the boy here, the boy never would have returned on his own, certainly would not be here now.

Ike blows again on the knish. He thinks, I had a boy who heard nothing in silence that was rich with meaning, and a girl who heard everything in silence that was nothing but silence. Which child was more foolish?

Which child, he wonders, was he? He remembers visiting his own father weeks before the old man's death. His daughter, a teenager then, had come along. His father, who lived in a not-so-hot neighborhood, had complained he couldn't sleep. "It's the blue-ers," he grumbled, "up all night playing their radios."

"What's that, a blue-er?" Ike's daughter had asked.

"Well, you can't call them shvartzers anymore," his father said. "They know what it means."

The girl had smiled. "We'll buy you earplugs," she'd said. "You can't stop people from playing music. You know what God says. Make a joyful noise unto the Lord."

"He says, too, 'Be silent and know that I'm God.'"

Ike had considered engraving those words on his father's headstone. He is certain the pleasure his father chose to reclaim had been silence. Perhaps the late hour when the kids on the street finally turned off their music. That moment of peace before sleep comes. Ike knows at least this much—his father had not returned here to the site of their twice-yearly father and son lunches. He has already scanned the room for blue fingernails, hoping, finding none.

In the reverent quiet of Yonah Shlissel's, Ike puts down his fork. It chimes when it touches the wooden table. The waiter looks up, comes over as if summoned. "Something wrong with your knish, mister?"

Ike gestures for the waiter to lean closer. "I think I made the wrong choice," Ike whispers.

The waiter clearly has never before heard such a thing. He frowns. "You can never go wrong with a Yonah Shlissel potato knish," he tells Ike.

"I completely agree, but I think maybe still I want something else."

"What do you mean something else? You already ordered."

Ike wishes again he knew the rules of wishing. Who makes the rules? Is there someone he can talk to? What is the point—this is what he wants to know—what point is there in experiencing again a joy from a life now complete? Better, one should be able to return and rectify an error. One should be allowed to meet with departed loved ones, brainstorm, figure out how to improve things for the grandchildren. Better yet, one should be able to hover over loved ones still living and guide them a little.

If he could do that, he'd return to his son, steer him toward simple pleasures. He is concerned that the boy will have no pleasurable moment to return to someday.

Not true, Ike thinks. He remembers his son as a child—baseball games, roller skates, Schwinns, picnics. Pleasure after pleasure. Sitting in sunlight. If Ike had made a mistake, it was not his failure to shout his love. It was his failure to teach the boy how to say "Boy, oh boy, that sun feels good on the back, doesn't it?"

Now a short man, a bald-headed man in a stained apron is walking Ike's way. He is muscular and sweaty, a man with glittering eyes and a scowl, someone who, despite his scant height, Ike would not wish to anger or fight.

"I hear you don't like my food," the man says.

Yonah Shlissel, Ike thinks. He has never laid eyes on Yonah Shlissel before. He is in awe. It's like meeting a celebrity—Joe DiMaggio striding up to your table. At the same time, there's a part of him wanting to laugh. He is picturing the Shlissel family, this stunted chef, the fat woman in polka dots, the crotchety waiter.

"It's not that I don't like your food," Ike says. "God knows it's not that. It's just that I was thinking I need to be somewhere else."

"What, you got an appointment with Roosevelt to bring world peace?"

Ike shrugs, tries to smile as if he and Yonah were pals, joking.

"You got a cure for the common cold maybe? You have to run and share it with all of mankind?"

"You're the one with the cure for the common cold," Ike says. He means to be ingratiating, disarming. "Your matzo ball soup, right?"

It works. Yonah softens. "So, just to make conversation, where do you think you should be instead of my place?"

"There's this kid's clothing store around here," Ike says. "Somewhere near here. My daughter is trying on dresses. Or will be. Or might be. I don't know. I got to go there in case. I need to hand her an ivory smock."

"She can't pick out a smock herself?"

"She's a kid. She needs me to find it for her. She doesn't have the sense of herself that I do. You know what I mean."

Yonah shakes his head. "I'm not one for fashion. I'm a cook, plain and simple." He is considering. Then he says, "You'd rather hand a kid a dress than eat my food?"

"I want to see the look on her face," Ike says. "I want to say how pretty she looks."

At that Yonah laughs. It is not an especially pleasant laugh.

"All right, all right," Ike says. "You're right. It would never come out of this mouth. I've never been Mr. Smooth. But I want at least to look at her like . . ."

He wants to look at her with love this time. He doesn't want his daughter to end up the foolish one. But Yonah's laughter has made Ike self-conscious. He can't think. Words stop coming into his head. He can't form the thought. Just sits there and feels it and doesn't know how to say it.

Yonah sighs. "The customer," he says, "is not always right." He takes the white plate back to the kitchen.

Ike sits very still, not sure what to do next, aware that now he has nothing.

Then the waiter returns with two packages—white butcher paper, a bit oily, tied with red-and-white string, the kind of string that came wrapped around the box when Ike's wife brought bakery cake as a present for friends.

"From Mister Shlissel," the waiter says. He sounds crabby and put-upon. "Potato knish to go. He says you should give one to your daughter, she should know how good they are."

The waiter holds the packages out to Ike. Ike takes one in each hand.

Out on Delancey Ike walks past stores and loitering youth. He doesn't remember the name of the dress shop. Pinsky's, he thinks. Maybe Pincus's. He's not sure if he will find it or when or where. He has no idea what time it is, whether he sat in Yonah's for minutes or decades. He doesn't know what else to do now but walk. It's a nice enough day. The smell of the gift-wrapped knishes he carries is stronger than the bus fumes. The smell of good simple food envelops him. The promise of tasting it sometime soon gives him the strength to go on forever.

✄ BULLET IN THE BRAIN ✄

Tobias Wolff

Anders couldn't get to the bank until just before it closed, so of course the line was endless and he got stuck behind two women whose loud, stupid conversation put him in a murderous temper. He was never in the best of tempers anyway, Anders—a book critic known for the weary, elegant savagery with which he dispatched almost everything he reviewed.

With the line still doubled around the rope, one of the tellers stuck a "POSITION CLOSED" sign in her window and walked to the back of the bank, where she leaned against a desk and began to pass the time with a man shuffling papers. The women in front of Anders broke off their conversation and watched the teller with hatred. "Oh, that's nice," one of them said. She turned to Anders and added, confident of his accord, "One of those little human touches that keep us coming back for more."

Anders had conceived his own towering hatred of the teller, but he immediately turned it on the presumptuous crybaby in front of him. "Damned unfair," he said. "Tragic, really. If they're not chopping off the wrong leg, or bombing your ancestral village, they're closing their positions."

She stood her ground. "I didn't say it was tragic," she said. "I just think it's a pretty lousy way to treat your customers."

"Unforgivable," Anders said. "Heaven will take note."

She sucked in her cheeks but stared past him and said nothing. Anders saw that the other woman, her friend, was looking in the same direction. And then the tellers stopped what they were doing, and the customers slowly turned, and silence came over the bank. Two men wearing black ski masks and blue business suits were standing to the side of the door. One of them had a pistol pressed against the guard's neck. The guard's eyes were closed, and his lips were moving. The other man had a sawed-off shotgun. "Keep your big mouth shut!" the man with the pistol said, though no one had spoken a word. "One of you tellers hits the alarm, you're all dead meat. Got it?"

The tellers nodded.

"Oh, bravo," Anders said. *"Dead meat."* He turned to the woman in front of him. "Great script, eh? The stern, brass knuckled poetry of the dangerous classes."

She looked at him with drowning eyes.

The man with the shotgun pushed the guard to his knees. He handed the shotgun to his partner and yanked the guard's wrists up behind his back and locked them together with a pair of handcuffs. He toppled him onto the floor with a kick between the shoulder blades. Then he took his shotgun back and went over to the security gate at the end of the counter. He was short and heavy and moved with peculiar slowness, even torpor. "Buzz him in," his partner said. The man with the shotgun opened the gate and sauntered along the line of tellers, handing each of them a Hefty bag. When he came to the empty position he looked over at the man with the pistol, who said, "Whose slot is that?"

Anders watched the teller. She put her hand to her throat and turned to the man she'd been talking to. He nodded. "Mine," she said.

"Then get your ugly ass in gear and fill that bag."

"There you go," Anders said to the woman in front of him. "Justice is done."

"Hey! Bright boy! Did I tell you to talk?"

"No," Anders said.

"Then shut your trap."

"Did you hear that?" Anders said. "'Bright boy.' Right out of 'The Killers.'"

"Please be quiet," the woman said.

"Hey, you deaf or what?" The man with the pistol walked over to Anders. He poked the weapon into Anders' gut. "You think I'm playing games?"

"No," Anders said, but the barrel tickled like a stiff finger and he had to fight back the titters. He did this by making himself stare into the man's eyes, which were clearly visible behind the holes in the mask: pale blue and rawly red-rimmed. The man's left eyelid kept twitching. He breathed out a piercing, ammoniac smell that shocked Anders more than anything that had happened, and he was beginning to develop a sense of unease when the man prodded him again with the pistol.

"You like me, bright boy?" he said. "You want to suck my dick?"

"No," Anders said.

"Then stop looking at me."

Anders fixed his gaze on the man's shiny wing-tip shoes.

"Not down there. Up there." He stuck the pistol under Anders' chin and pushed it upward until Anders was looking at the ceiling.

Anders had never paid much attention to that part of the bank, a pompous old building with marble floors and counters and pillars, and gilt scrollwork over the tellers' cages. The domed ceiling had been decorated with mythological figures whose fleshy, toga-draped ugliness Anders had taken in at a glance many years earlier and afterward declined to notice. Now he had no choice but to scrutinize the painter's work. It was even worse than he remembered, and all of it executed with the utmost gravity. The artist had a few tricks up his sleeve and used them again and again—a certain rosy blush on the underside of the clouds, a coy backward glance on the faces of the cupids and fauns. The ceiling was crowded with various dramas, but the one that caught Anders' eye was Zeus and Europa—portrayed, in this rendition, as a bull ogling a cow from behind a haystack. To make the cow sexy, the painter had canted her hips suggestively and given her long, droopy eyelashes through which she gazed back at the bull with sultry welcome. The bull wore a smirk and his eyebrows were arched. If there'd been a bubble coming out of his mouth, it would have said, "Hubba hubba."

"What's so funny, bright boy?"

"Nothing."

"You think I'm comical? You think I'm some kind of clown?"

"No."

"You think you can fuck with me?"

"No."

"Fuck with me again, you're history. *Capiche?*"

Anders burst out laughing. He covered his mouth with both hands and said, "I'm sorry, I'm sorry," then snorted helplessly through his fingers and said, "*Capiche*—oh, God, *capiche*," and at that the man with the pistol raised the pistol and shot Anders right in the head.

The bullet smashed Anders' skull and ploughed through his brain and exited behind his right ear, scattering shards of bone into the cerebral cortex, the corpus callosum, back toward the basal ganglia, and down into the thalamus. But before all this occurred, the first appearance of the bullet in the cerebrum set off a crackling chain of ion transports and neuro-transmissions. Because of their peculiar origin these traced a peculiar pattern, flukishly calling to life a summer afternoon some forty years past, and long since lost to memory. After striking the cranium the bullet was moving at 900 feet per second, a pathetically sluggish, glacial pace compared to the synaptic lightning that flashed around it. Once in the brain, that is, the bullet came under the mediation of brain time, which gave Anders plenty of leisure to contemplate the scene that, in a phrase he would have abhorred, "passed before his eyes."

It is worth noting what Anders did not remember, given what he did remember. He did not remember his first lover, Sherry, or what he had most madly loved about her, before it came to irritate him—her unembarrassed carnality, and especially the cordial way she had with his unit, which she called Mr. Mole, as in, "Uh-oh, looks like Mr. Mole wants to play!" and, "Let's hide Mr. Mole!" Anders did not remember his wife, whom he had also loved before she exhausted him with her predictability, or his daughter, now a sullen professor of economics at Dartmouth. He did not remember standing just outside his daughter's door as she lectured her bear about his naughtiness and described the truly appalling punishments Paws would receive unless he changed his ways. He did not remember a single line of the hundreds of poems he had committed to memory in his youth so that he could give himself the shivers at will—not "Silent, upon a peak in Darien," or "My God, I heard this day," or "All my pretty ones? Did you say all? O hell-kite! All?" None of these did he remember; not one. Anders did not remember his dying mother saying of his father, "I should have stabbed him in his sleep."

He did not remember Professor Josephs telling his class how Athenian prisoners in Sicily had been released if they could recite Aeschylus, and then reciting Aeschylus himself, right there, in the Greek. Anders did not remember how his eyes had burned at those sounds. He did not remember the surprise of seeing a college classmate's name on the jacket of a novel not long after they graduated, or the respect he had felt after reading the book. He did not remember the pleasure of giving respect.

Nor did Anders remember seeing a woman leap to her death from the building opposite his own just days after his daughter was born. He did not remember shouting, "Lord have mercy!" He did not remember deliberately crashing his father's car into a tree, or having his ribs kicked in by three policemen at an anti-war rally, or waking himself up with laughter. He did not remember when he began to regard the heap of books on his desk with boredom and dread, or when he grew angry at writers for writing them. He did not remember when everything began to remind him of something else.

This is what he remembered. Heat. A baseball field. Yellow grass, the whirr of insects, himself leaning against a tree as the boys of the neighborhood gather for a pickup game. He looks on as the others argue the relative genius of Mantle and Mays.

They have been worrying this subject all summer, and it has become tedious to An-ders: an oppression, like the heat.

Then the last two boys arrive, Coyle and a cousin of his from Mississippi. Anders has never met Coyle's cousin before and will never see him again. He says hi with the rest but takes no further notice of him until they've chosen sides and someone asks the cousin what position he wants to play. "Shortstop," the boy says. "Short's the best position they is." Anders turns and looks at him. He wants to hear Coyle's cousin re-peat what he's just said, but he knows better than to ask. The others will think he's being a jerk, ragging the kid for his grammar. But that isn't it, not at all—it's that An-ders is strangely roused, elated, by those final two words, their pure unexpectedness and their music. He takes the field in a trance, repeating them to himself.

The bullet is already in the brain; it won't be outrun for ever, or charmed to a halt. In the end it will do its work and leave the troubled skull behind, dragging its comet's tail of memory and hope and talent and love into the marble hall of commerce. That can't be helped. But for now Anders can still make time. Time for the shadows to lengthen on the grass, time for the tethered dog to bark at the flying ball, time for the boy in right field to smack his sweat-blackened mitt and softly chant, *They is, they is, they is.*

✂ THE ALEPH ✂

Jorge Luis Borges

Translated by Anthony Kerrigan

O God, I could be bounded in a nutshell and count myself a King of infinite space.
—HAMLET, II, 2

But they will teach us that Eternity is the Standing still of the Present Time, a Nunc-stans (as the Schools call it); which neither they, nor any else understand, no more than they would a Hic-stans for an Infinite greatness of Place.
—LEVIATHAN, IV, 46

On the incandescent February morning Beatriz Viterbo died, after a death agony so imperious it did not for a moment descend into sentimentalism or fear, I noticed that the iron billboards in the Plaza Constitución bore new advertisements for some brand or other of Virginia tobacco; I was saddened by this fact, for it made me realize that the incessant and vast universe was already moving away from her and that this change was the first in an infinite series. The universe would change but I would not, I thought with melancholy vanity; I knew that sometimes my vain devotion had exasperated her; now that she was dead, I could consecrate myself to her memory, without hope but also without humiliation. I thought of how the thirtieth of April was her birthday; to visit her house in Calle Garay on that day and pay my respects to her father and Carlos Argentino Daneri, her first cousin, would be an act of courtesy, irreproachable and perhaps even unavoidable. I would wait, once again, in the twilight of the overladen entrance hall; I would study, one more time, the particulars of her numerous portraits: Beatriz Viterbo in profile, in color; Beatriz wearing a mask, during the Carnival of 1921; Beatriz at her First Communion; Beatriz on the day of her wedding to Roberto Alessandri; Beatriz a little while after the divorce, at a dinner in the Club Hípico; Beatriz with Delia San Marco Porcel and Carlos Argentino; Beatriz with the Pekingese which had been a present from Villegas Haedo; Beatriz from the front and in a three-quarter view, smiling, her hand under her chin. . . . I would not be obliged, as on other occasions, to justify my presence with moderate-priced offerings of books, with books whose pages, finally, I learned to cut beforehand, so as to avoid finding, months later, that they were still uncut.

Beatriz Viterbo died in 1929. From that time on, I never let a thirtieth of April go by without a visit to her house. I used to arrive there around seven-fifteen and stay about twenty-five minutes. Every year I came a little later and stayed a little longer. In 1933 a torrential rain worked to my advantage: they were forced to invite me to dine. I did not fail to avail myself of this advantageous precedent. In 1934, I appeared, just after eight, with a honey nutcake from Santa Fe. With the greatest naturalness, I remained for supper. And thus, on these melancholy and vainly erotic anniversaries, Carlos Argentino Daneri began gradually to confide in me.

Beatriz was tall, fragile, lightly leaning forward: there was in her walk (if the oxymoron is acceptable) a kind of gracious torpor, the beginnings of an ecstasy. Carlos Argentino is rosy, important, gray-haired, fine-featured. He holds some subordinate position or other in an illegible library in the south side suburbs. He is authoritarian, but also ineffective. Until very recently, he took advantage of nights and holidays to avoid going out of his house. At a remove of two generations, the Italian s and the copious gesticulation of the Italians survive in him. His mental activity is continuous, impassioned, versatile, and altogether insignificant. He abounds in useless analogies and fruitless scruples. He possesses (as did Beatriz) long, lovely, tapering hands. For several months he was obsessed with Paul Fort, less with his ballads than with the idea of irreproachable glory. "He is the Prince of the poets of France," he would repeat fatuously. "You will set yourself against him in vain; no, not even your most poisoned barb will reach him."

The thirtieth of April, 1941, I allowed myself to add to the gift of honey nutcake a bottle of Argentine cognac. Carlos Argentino tasted it, judged it "interesting," and, after a few glasses, launched on a vindication of modern man.

"I evoke him," he said with rather inexplicable animation, "in his studio laboratory, in the city's watchtowers, so to say, supplied with telephones, telegraphs, phonographs, radiotelephone apparatus, cinematographic equipment, magic lanterns, glossaries, timetables, compendiums, bulletins. . . ."

He remarked that for a man of such faculties the act of travel was useless. Our twentieth century had transformed the fable of Mohammed and the mountain: the mountains, now, converged upon the modern Mohammed.

His ideas seemed so inept to me, their exposition so pompous and so vast, that I immediately related them to literature: I asked him why he did not write them down. Foreseeably he replied that he had already done so: these concepts, and others no less novel, figured in the Augural Canto, or more simply, the Prologue Canto, of a poem on which he had been working for many years, without publicity, without any deafening to-do, putting his entire reliance on those two props known as work and solitude. First, he opened the floodgates of the imagination; then he made use of a sharp file. The poem was titled *The Earth*; it consisted of a description of the planet, wherein, naturally, there was no lack of picturesque digression and elegant apostrophe.

I begged him to read me a passage, even though brief. He opened a drawer in his desk, took out a tall bundle of pages from a pad, each sheet stamped with the letterhead of the Juan Crisóstomo Lafinur Library, and, with sonorous satisfaction, read out:

> *I have seen, like the Greek, the cities of men and their fame,*
> *Their labor, days of various light, hunger's shame;*
> *I correct no event, falsify no name,*
> *But the voyage I narrate is . . .* autour de ma chambre.

"By all lights an interesting strophe," he opined. "The first line wins the applause of the professor, the academician, the Hellenist, if not of superficial pedants, who form, these last, a considerable sector of public opinion. The second passes from Homer to Hesiod (the entire verse an implicit homage, writ on the façade of the resplendent building, to the father of didactic poetry), not without rejuvenating a procedure whose lineage goes back to Scripture, that of enumeration, congeries of conglomeration. The third line—Baroquism? Decadentism? Purified and fanatical cult of form?—is composed of two twin hemistichs. The fourth, frankly bilingual, assures me the unconditional support of every spirit sensitive to the gay lure of graceful play. I say nothing of the rare rhyme, nor of the learning which permits me—without any pedantry!—to accumulate, in four lines, three erudite allusions encompassing thirty centuries of compressed literature: first to the *Odyssey*, second to *Works and Days*, third to the immortal bagatelle proffered us through the idling of the Savoyard's pen. . . . Once more I have understood that modern art requires the balsam of laughter, the *scherzo*. Decidedly, Goldoni has the floor!"

He read me many another stanza, each of which obtained his approbation and profuse commentary, too. There was nothing memorable in any of them. I did not even judge them very much worse than the first one. There had been a collaboration, in his writing, between application, resignation, and chance; the virtues which Daneri attributed to them were posterior. I realized that the poet's labor lay not with the poetry, but with the invention of reasons to make the poetry admirable; naturally, this ulterior and subsequent labor modified the work for him, but not for others. Daneri's oral style was extravagant; his metric heaviness hindered his transmitting that extravagance, except in a very few instances, to the poem.*

Only once in my life have I had occasion to examine the fifteen thousand dodecasyllabic verses of the *Poly-Olbion*, that topographic epic poem in which Michael Drayton recorded the flora, fauna, hydrography, orography, military and monastic history of England; I am sure that this considerable, but limited, production is less tedious than the vast congeneric enterprise of Carlos Argentino. The latter proposed to put into verse the entire face of the planet; in 1941, he had already dispatched several hectares of the State of Queensland, in addition to one kilometer of the course of the River Ob, a gasometer north of Veracruz, the main business houses in the parish of La Concepción, the villa owned by Mariana Cambaceres de Alvear on Eleventh of September street, in Belgrano, and an establishment devoted to Turkish baths not far from the famous Brighton Aquarium. He read me from his poem certain laborious passages concerning the Australian zone; these large and formless alexandrines lacked the relative agitation of the Preface. I copy one stanza:

> *Know ye. To the right hand of the routinary post*
> *(Coming, of course, from the North-northwest)*

---

*I recall, nevertheless, the following lines from a satire in which he harshly fustigated bad poets:

> *This one gives his poem bellicose armorings*
> *Of erudition; that one puts in pomp and jubilee.*
> *Both in vain beat their ridiculous wings . . .*
> *Forgetting, the wretches, the factor BEAUTY!*

Only the fear of creating for himself an army of implacable and powerful foes dissuaded him (he told me) from fearlessly publishing this poem.

One wearies out a skeleton—Color? White-celeste—
Which gives the sheep run an ossuary cast.

"Two audacious strokes," he cried out in exultation, "redeemed, I can hear you muttering, by success! I admit it, I admit it. One, the epithet *routinary*, which accurately proclaims, *en passant*, the inevitable tedium inherent in pastoral and farming chores, a tedium which neither georgic poetry nor our already laureled *Don Segundo* ever ventured to denounce in this way, in red-hot heat. The other, the energetic prosaicism of *one wearies out a skeleton*, a phrase which the prudish will want to excommunicate in horror, but which the critic with virile taste will appreciate more than his life. For the rest, the entire line is of high carat, the highest. The second hemistich engages the reader in the most animated converse; it anticipates his lively curiosity, places a question in his mouth and answers it . . . instantly. And what do you tell me of that find of mine: *white-celeste?* This picturesque neologism insinuates the sky, which is a very important factor in the Australian landscape. Without this evocation, the colors of the sketch would be much too somber, and the reader would find himself compelled to close the book, wounded in the innermost part of his soul by a black and incurable melancholy."

Toward midnight, I took my leave.

Two Sundays later, Daneri called me on the telephone, for the first time in his life, I believe. He proposed that we meet at four o'clock, "to drink a glass of milk together, in the salon-bar next door, which the progressivism of Zunino and of Zungri—the proprietors of my house, you will recall—is causing to be inaugurated on the corner. Truly, a confectionery shop you will be interested in knowing about." I accepted, with more resignation than enthusiasm. There was no difficulty in finding a table; the "salon-bar," inexorably modern, was just slightly less atrocious than what I had foreseen; at the neighboring tables an excited public mentioned the sums which Zunino and Zungri had invested without batting an eye. Carlos Argentino feigned astonishment over some wonder or other in the lighting installations (which he doubtless already knew about), and he said to me, with a certain severity:

"You'll have to admit, no matter how grudgingly, that these premises vie successfully with the most renowned of Flores."

Then, he reread me four or five pages of his poem. He had made corrections in accordance with a depraved principle of verbal ostentation: where he had formerly written *azurish*, he now put *azuritic, azuritish,* and even *azury*. The word *lacteous* proved not ugly enough for him; in the course of an impetuous description of a wool washer, he preferred *lactary, lactinous, lactescent, lactiferous.* . . . He bitterly reviled the critics; later, in a more benign spirit, he compared them to persons "who dispose of no precious metals, nor steam presses, nor rolling presses, nor sulphuric acids for minting treasures, but who can *indicate* to *others* the *site* of a treasure." Next he censured *prologomania* "which the Prince of Talents, in the graceful prefacing of his *Don Quixote*, already ridiculed." He nevertheless admitted to me now that by way of frontispiece to the new work a showy prologue, an accolade signed by the feather pen of a bird of prey, of a man of weight, would be most convenient. He added that he planned to bring out the initial cantos of his poems. I understood, then, the singular telephonic invitation; the man was going to ask me to preface his pedantic farrago.

My fears proved unfounded: Carlos Argentino observed, with rancorous admiration, that he did not misuse the epithet in denominating as *solid* the prestige achieved in all circles by Álvaro Melián Lafinur, man of letters, who would, if I insisted on it, delightfully prologue the poem. So as to avoid the most unpardonable of failures, I was to make myself spokesman for two undeniable merits: formal perfection and scientific rigor, "inasmuch as this vast garden of tropes, figures of speech, and elegance, allows no single detail which does not confirm the severe truth." He added that Beatriz had always enjoyed herself with Álvaro.

I assented, assented profusely. For greater conviction, I promised to speak to Álvaro on Thursday, rather than wait until the following Monday: we could meet at the small supper that usually climaxes every reunion of the Writers' Club. (There are no such suppers, but it is an irrefutable fact that the reunions do take place on Thursdays, a point which Carlos Argentino Daneri would find confirmed in the daily newspapers, and which lent a certain reality to the phrase.) Adopting an air halfway between divinatory and sagacious, I told him that before taking up the question of a prologue, I would delineate the curious plan of the book. We took our leave of each other. As I turned the corner into Calle Bernardo de Irigoyen, I impartially considered the alternatives before me: a) I could talk to Álvaro and tell him how that cousin of Beatriz' (this explicatory euphemism would allow me to say her name) had elaborated a poem which seemed to dilate to infinity the possibilities of cacophony and chaos; b) I could fail to speak to Álvaro altogether. I foresaw, lucidly, that my indolence would choose b.

From early Friday morning the telephone began to disquiet me. It made me indignant to think that this instrument, which in other days had produced the irrecoverable voice of Beatriz, could lower itself to being a receptacle for the useless and perhaps even choleric complaints of that deceived man Carlos Argentino Daneri. Luckily, nothing awful occurred—except the inevitable animosity inspired by that man, who had imposed on me a delicate mission and would later forget me altogether.

The telephone lost its terrors; but then toward the end of October, Carlos Argentino called me again. He was terribly agitated; at first I could not identify the voice. Sadly and yet wrathfully he stammered that the now uncurbed Zunino and Zungri, under the pretext of enlarging their outrageous confectionery, were going to demolish his house.

"The house of my fathers! My house, the inveterate house of the Calle Garay!" he went on repeating, perhaps forgetting his grief in the melody.

It was not difficult for me to share his grief. Once past forty, every change is a detestable symbol of the passage of time. Besides, at stake was a house that, for me, infinitely alluded to Beatriz. I wanted to bring out this most delicate point; my interlocutor did not hear me. He said that if Zunino and Zungri persisted in their absurd proposal, Doctor Zunni, his lawyer, would enter an action *ipso facto* for damages and would oblige them to pay one hundred thousand *pesos nacionales* in compensation.

I was impressed to hear the name of Zunni: his practice, out of his office at the corner of Caseros and Tacuarí, was of a proverbial and solemn reliability. I asked if

Zunni had already taken charge of the matter. Daneri said he would speak to him that very afternoon. He hesitated, and then, in that level, impersonal voice to which we all have recourse for confiding something very intimate, he told me that in order to finish the poem the house was indispensable to him, for in one of the cellar corners there was an Aleph. He indicated that an Aleph is one of the points in space containing all points.

"It's in the dining-room cellar," he explained, his diction grown hasty from anxiety. "It's mine, it's mine; I discovered it in childhood, before I was of school age. The cellar stair is steep, and my aunt and uncle had forbidden me to go down it. But someone said that there was a world in the cellar. They were referring, I found out later, to a trunk, but I understood there was a world there. I descended secretly, went rolling down the forbidden stairs, fell off. When I opened my eyes I saw the Aleph."

"The Aleph?" I echoed.

"Yes, the place where, without any possible confusion, all the places in the world are found, seen from every angle. I revealed my discovery to no one, and I returned there. The child could not understand that this privilege was proffered him so that the man might chisel out the poem! Zunino and Zungri will not dislodge me, no, a thousand times no. With the code of laws in hand, Doctor Zunni will prove that my Aleph is *inalienable*."

I attempted to reason with him.

"But, isn't the cellar very dark?"

"Really, truth does not penetrate a rebellious understanding. If all the places on earth are in the Aleph, the Aleph must also contain all the illuminations, all the lights, all the sources of light."

"I will go and see it at once."

I hung up, before he could issue a prohibition. The knowledge of one fact is enough to allow one to perceive at once a whole series of confirming traits, previously unsuspected. I was astonished not to have understood until that moment that Carlos Argentino was a madman. All the Viterbos, for that matter . . . Beatriz (I often say so myself) was a woman, a girl, of an almost implacable clairvoyance, but there was about her a negligence, a distraction, a disdain, a real cruelty, which perhaps called for a pathological explanation. The madness of Carlos Argentino filled me with malicious felicity; in our innermost beings, we had always detested each other.

In Calle Garay, the serving woman asked me if I would be kind enough to wait. The child was, as always, in the cellar, developing photographs. Next to the flower vase without a single flower in it, atop the useless piano, there smiled (more timeless than anachronic) the great portrait of Beatriz, in dull colors. No one could see us; in an access of tender despair I went up close and told her:

"Beatriz, Beatriz Elena, Beatriz Elena Viterbo, beloved Beatriz, Beatriz lost forever, it's me, Borges."

A little later Carlos came in. He spoke with a certain dryness. I understood that he was incapable of thinking of anything but the loss of the Aleph.

"A glass of the pseudo-cognac," he ordered, "and then you can duck into the cellar. As you already know, the dorsal decubitus is imperative. And so are darkness, immobility, and a certain ocular accommodation. You lie down on the tile floor and fix your eyes on the nineteenth step of the pertinent stairs. I leave, lower the trap door, and you're alone. Quite likely—it should be easy!—some rodent will scare you! In a few minutes you will see the Aleph. The microcosm of alchemists and cabalists, our proverbial concrete friend, the *multum in parvo!*"

Once we were in the dining room he added:

"Of course if you don't see it, your incapacity in no way invalidates my testimony. . . . Now, down with you. Very shortly you will be able to engage in a dialogue with *all* of the images of Beatriz."

I rapidly descended, tired of his insubstantial words. The cellar, barely wider than the stairs, had much of a well about it. I gazed about in search of the trunk of which Carlos Argentino had spoken. Some cases with bottles in them and some canvas bags cluttered one corner. Carlos picked up one of the bags, folded it in half and placed it exactly in a precise spot.

"A humble pillow," he explained, "but if I raise it one centimeter, you won't see a thing, and you'll be left abashed and ashamed. Stretch your bulk out on the floor and count off nineteen steps."

I complied with his ridiculous requisites; and at last he went away. Carefully he closed the trap door; the darkness, despite a crevice which I discovered later, seemed total. And suddenly I realized the danger I ran: I had allowed myself to be buried by a madman, after having drunk some poison! Behind the transparent bravado of Carlos was the intimate terror that I would not see the prodigy; to defend his delirium, to avoid knowing that he was mad, Carlos *had to kill me.* A confused malaise swept over me; I attempted to attribute it to my rigid posture rather than to the operation of a narcotic. I closed my eyes; opened them. Then I saw the Aleph.

I arrive, now, at the ineffable center of my story. And here begins my despair as a writer. All language is an alphabet of symbols whose use presupposes a past shared by all the other interlocutors. How, then, transmit to others the infinite Aleph, which my fearful mind scarcely encompasses? The mystics, in similar situations, are lavish with emblems: to signify the divinity, a Persian speaks of a bird that in some way is all birds; Alanus de Insulis speaks of a sphere whose center is everywhere and whose circumference is nowhere; Ezekiel, of an angel with four faces who looks simultaneously to the Orient and the Occident, to the North and the South. (Not vainly do I recall these inconceivable analogies; they bear some relation to the Aleph.) Perhaps the gods would not be against my finding an equivalent image, but then this report would be contaminated with literature, with falsehood. For the rest, the central problem is unsolvable: the enumeration, even if only partial, of an infinite complex. In that gigantic instant I saw millions of delightful and atrocious acts; none astonished me more than the fact that all of them together occupied the same point, without superposition and without transparency. What my eyes saw was simultaneous: what I shall transcribe is successive, because language is successive. Nevertheless, I shall cull something of it all.

In the lower part of the step, toward the right, I saw a small iridescent sphere, of almost intolerable brilliance. At first I thought it rotary; then I understood that this movement was an illusion produced by the vertiginous sights it enclosed. The

Aleph's diameter must have been about two or three centimeters, but Cosmic Space was in it, without diminution of size. Each object (the mirror's glass, for instance) was infinite objects, for I clearly saw it from all points in the universe. I saw the heavy-laden sea; I saw the dawn and the dusk; I saw the multitudes of America; I saw a silver-plated cobweb at the center of a black pyramid; I saw a tattered labyrinth (it was London); I saw interminable eyes nearby looking at me as if in a mirror; I saw all the mirrors in the planet and none reflected me; in an inner patio in the Calle Soler I saw the same paving tile I had seen thirty years before in the entranceway to a house in the town of Fray Bentos; I saw clusters of grapes, snow, tobacco, veins of metal, steam; I saw convex equatorial deserts and every grain of sand in them; I saw a woman at Inverness whom I shall not forget: I saw her violent switch of hair, her proud body, the cancer in her breast; I saw a circle of dry land on a sidewalk where formerly there had been a tree; I saw a villa in Adrogué; I saw a copy of the first English version of Pliny, by Philemon Holland, and saw simultaneously every letter on every page (as a boy I used to marvel that the letters in a closed book did not get mixed up and lost in the course of a night); I saw night and day contemporaneously; I saw a sunset in Querétaro which seemed to reflect the color of a rose in Bengal; I saw my bedroom with nobody in it; I saw in a study in Alkmaar a terraqueous globe between two mirrors which multiplied it without end; I saw horses with swirling manes on a beach by the Caspian Sea at dawn; I saw the delicate bone structure of a hand; I saw the survivors of a battle sending out post cards; I saw a deck of Spanish playing cards in a shopwindow in Mirzapur; I saw the oblique shadows of some ferns on the floor of a hothouse; I saw tigers, emboli, bison, ground swells, and armies; I saw all the ants on earth; I saw a Persian astrolabe; in a desk drawer I saw (the writing made me tremble) obscene, incredible, precise letters, which Beatriz had written Carlos Argentino; I saw an adored monument in La Chacarita cemetery; I saw the atrocious relic of what deliciously had been Beatriz Viterbo; I saw the circulation of my obscure blood; I saw the gearing of love and the modifications of death; I saw the Aleph from all points; I saw the earth in the Aleph and in the earth the Aleph once more and the earth in the Aleph; I saw my face and my viscera; I saw your face and felt vertigo and cried because my eyes had seen that conjectural and secret object whose name men usurp but which no man has gazed on: the inconceivable universe.

I felt infinite veneration, infinite compassion.

"You must be good and dizzy from peering into things that don't concern you," cried a hateful, jovial voice. "Even if you rack your brains, you won't be able to pay me back in a century for this revelation. What a formidable observatory, eh, Borges!"

Carlos Argentino's feet occupied the highest step. In the half-light I managed to get up and to stammer:

"Formidable, yes, formidable."

The indifference in the sound of my voice surprised me. Anxiously Carlos Argentino insisted:

"You saw it all, in colors?"

It was at that instant that I conceived my revenge. Benevolently, with obvious pity, nervous, evasive, I thanked Carlos Argentino for the hospitality of his cellar and urged him to take advantage of the demolition of his house to get far away from the pernicious capital, which is easy on no one, believe me, on no one! I refused, with suave energy, to discuss the Aleph; I embraced him on leaving, and repeated that the country and its quiet are two grand doctors.

In the street, on the Constitución stairs, in the subway, all the faces struck me as familiar. I feared that not a single thing was left to cause me surprise; I was afraid I would never be quit of the impression that I had "returned." Happily, at the end of a few nights of insomnia, forgetfulness worked in me again.

P.S. MARCH 1, 1943

Six months after the demolition of the building in Calle Garay, Procusto Publishers did not take fright at the length of Argentino's considerable poem and launched upon the reading public a selection of "Argentino Extracts." It is almost needless to repeat what happened: Carlos Argentino Daneri received Second Prize, of the National Prizes for Literature.* First Prize was awarded to Doctor Aita; Third, to Doctor Mario Bonfanti; incredibly, my book *The Cards of the Cardsharp* did not get a single vote. Once again incomprehension and envy won the day! For a long time now I have not been able to see Daneri; the daily press says he will soon give us another volume. His fortunate pen (no longer benumbed by the Aleph) has been consecrated to versifying the epitomes of Doctor Acevedo Diaz.

I would like to add two further observations: one, on the nature of the Aleph; the other, on its name. As is well known, the latter is the name of the first letter of the alphabet of the sacred language. Its application to the cycle of my story does not appear mere chance. For the cabala, this letter signifies the En-Sof, the limitless and pure divinity; it has also been said that it has the form of a man who points out heaven and earth, to indicate that the inferior world is the mirror and map of the superior; for the *Mengenlehre*, it is the symbol of transfinite numbers, in which the whole is no greater than any of its parts. I wanted to know: Had Carlos Argentino chosen this name, or had he read it, *applied to another point where all points converge*, in some one of the innumerable texts revealed to him by the Aleph in his house? Incredible as it may seem, I believe there is (or was) another Aleph; I believe that the Aleph in the Calle Garay was a false Aleph.

Here are my reasons. Toward 1867, Captain Burton held the office of British Consul in Brazil. In July, 1942, Pedro Henríquez Ureña discovered, in a library at Santos, a manuscript by Burton dealing with the mirror which the Orient attributes to Iskandar Zu al-Karnayn, or Alexander Bicornis of Macedonia. In its glass the entire world was reflected. Burton mentions other artifices of like kind: the septuple goblet of Kai Josru; the mirror which Tarik Benzeyad found in a tower (*The Thousand and One Nights*, 272); the mirror which Lucian of Samosata was able to examine on the moon (*True History*, 1, 26); the diaphanous spear which the first book of Capella's *Satyricon* attributes to Jupiter; the universal mirror of Merlin, "round and hollow . . . and seemed a world of glas" (*The Faerie Queene*, III, 2, 19). And he adds these curious

---

*"I received your pained congratulations," he wrote me. "You huff and puff with envy, my lamentable friend, but you must confess—though you choke!—that this time I was able to crown my bonnet with the reddest of feathers, to put in my turban the *caliph* of rubies."

words: "But the former (besides the defect of not existing) are mere instruments of optics. The Faithful who attend the Mosque of Amr, in Cairo, know very well that the universe is in the interior of one of the stone columns surrounding the central courtyard. . . . No one, of course, can see it, but those who put their ears to the surface claim to hear, within a short time, its workaday rumor. . . . The mosque dates from the seventh century; the columns come from other, pre-Islamic, temples, for as ibn-Khaldûn has written: '*In republics founded by nomads, the assistance of foreigners is indispensable in all that concerns masonry.*'"

Does that Aleph exist in the innermost recess of a stone? Did I see it when I saw all things, and have I forgotten it? Our minds are porous with forgetfulness; I myself am falsifying and losing, through the tragic erosion of the years, the features of Beatriz.

❧ The Traveler ❧

Wallace Stegner

He was rolling in the first early dark down a snowy road, his headlights pinched between dark walls of trees, when the engine coughed, recovered, coughed again, and died. Down a slight hill he coasted in compression, working the choke, but at the bottom he had to pull over against the three-foot wall of plowed snow. Snow creaked under the tires as the car eased to a stop. The heater fan unwound with a final tinny sigh.

Here in its middle age this hitherto dependable mechanism had betrayed him, but he refused to admit immediately that he was betrayed. Some speck of dirt or bubble of water in the gas line, some momentary short circuit, some splash of snow on distributor points or plug connections—something that would cure itself before long. But turning off the lights and pressing on the starter brought no result; he held the choke out for several seconds, and got only the hopeful stink of gasoline; he waited and let the flooded carburetor rest and tried again, and nothing. Eventually he opened the door and stepped out onto the packed snow of the road.

It was so cold that his first breath turned to iron in his throat, the hairs in his nostrils webbed into instant ice, his eyes stung and watered. In the faint starlight and the bluish luminescence of the snow everything beyond a few yards away swam deceptive and without depth, glimmering with things half seen or imagined. Beside the dead car he stood with his head bent, listening, and there was not a sound. Everything on the planet might have died in the cold.

Indecisively seeking help, he walked to the top of the next rise, but the faintly darker furrow of the road blurred and disappeared in the murk, the shadows pressed inward, there was no sign of a light. Back at the car he made the efforts that the morality of self-reliance demanded: trying to see by the backward diffusion of the headlamps, he groped over the motor, feeling for broken wires or loose connections, until he had satisfied himself that he was helpless. He had known all along that he was.

His hands were already stung with cold, and around his ankles between low shoes and trouser cuffs he felt the chill like leg irons. When he had last stopped, twenty miles back, it had been below zero. It could be ten or fifteen below now. So what did he do, stranded in mid-journey fifty miles or more from his destination? He could hardly go in for help, leaving the sample cases, because the right rear door didn't lock properly. A little jiggling swung it open. And all those drugs, some of them designed to cure anything—wonder drugs, sulfas, streptomycin, Aureomycin, penicillin, pills and anti-toxins and unguents—represented not only a value but a danger. They should not be left around loose. Someone might think they really would cure anything.

Not quite everything, he told the blue darkness. Not a fouled-up distributor or a cranky coil box. Absurdly, there came into his mind a fragment of an ancient hymn to mechanical transport:

If she runs out of dope, just fill her up with soap
And the little Ford will ramble right along.

He saw himself pouring a bottle of penicillin into the gas tank and driving off with the exhaust blowing happy smoke rings. A mock-heroic montage of scientific discovery unreeled itself—white-coated scientists peering into microscopes, adjusting gauges, pipetting precious liquids, weighing grains of powder on minuscule scales. Messenger boys sped with telegrams to the desks of busy executives. A group of observers stood beside an assembly line while the first tests were made. They broke a car's axle with sledges, gave it a drink of the wonder compound, and drove it off. They demolished the carburetor and cured it with one application. They yanked loose all the wires and watched the same magic set the motor purring.

But here he stood in light overcoat and thin leather gloves, without overshoes, and his car all but blocked the road, and the door could not be locked, and there was not a possibility that he could carry the heavy cases with him to the next farm or village. He switched on the headlights again and studied the roadside they revealed, and saw a rail fence, with cedars and spruces behind it. When more complex gadgets and more complex cures failed, there was always the lucifer match.

Ten minutes later he was sitting with the auto robe over his head and shoulders and his back against the plowed snowbank, digging the half-melted snow from inside his shoes and gloating over the growing light and warmth of the fire. He had a supply of fence rails good for an hour. In that time, someone would come along and he could get a push or two. In this country, in winter, no one ever passed up a stranded motorist.

In the stillness the flames went straight upward; the heat was wonderfully pleasant on icy hands and numb ankles and stiffened face. He looked across the road, stained by horses, broken by wheel and runner tracks, and saw how the roadside acquired definition and sharp angles and shadows in the firelight. He saw too how he would look to anyone coming along: like a calendar picture.

But no one came along. Fifteen minutes stretched into a half hour, he had only two broken pieces of rail left, the fire sizzled, half floating in the puddle of its melting. Restlessly he rose with the blanket around him and walked back up the road a hundred steps. Eastward, above jagged trees, he saw the sky where it lightened to moonrise, but here there was still only the blue glimmer of starlight on the snow. Something long buried and forgotten tugged in him, and a shiver not entirely from cold prickled his whole body with gooseflesh. There had been times in his childhood when he had walked home alone and been temporarily lost in nights like this. In many years he could not remember being out alone under such a sky. He felt spooked, his feet were chilled lumps, his nose leaked. Down the hill, car and snow swam deceptively together; the red wink of the fire seemed inexpressibly far off.

Abruptly he did not want to wait in that lonely snow-banked ditch any longer. The sample cases could look after themselves, any motorist who passed could take his own chances. He would walk ahead to the nearest help, and if he found himself getting too cold on the way, he could always build another fire. The thought of action cheered him; he admitted to himself that he was all but terrified at the silence and the iron cold.

Closing the car doors, he dropped his key case, and panic stopped his pulse as he bent and frantically, with bare hand, brushed away the snow until he found it. The powdery snow ached and burned at his fingertips. He held them a last moment to the fire, and then, bundled like a squaw, with the blanket held across nose and mouth to ease the harshness of the cold in his lungs, he started up the road that looked as smooth as a tablecloth, but was deceptively rough and broken. He thought of what he had had every right to expect for this evening. By now, eight o'clock or so, he should have had a smoking supper, the luxury of a hot bath, the pleasure of a brandy in a comradely bar. By now he should be in pajamas making out sales reports by the bedlight, in a room where steam knocked comfortingly in the radiators and the help of a hundred hands was available to him at a word into the telephone. For all of this to be torn away suddenly, for him to be stumbling up a deserted road in danger of freezing to death, just because some simple mechanical part that had functioned for thirty thousand miles refused to function any longer, this was outrage, and he hated it. He thought of garage men and service station attendants he could blame. Ignoring the evidence of the flooded carburetor, he brooded about watered gas that could make ice in the gas line. A man was dependent on too many people; he was at everybody's mercy.

And then, on top of the second long rise, he met the moon.

Instantly the character of the night changed. The uncertain starlight was replaced at a step by an even flood of blue-white radiance. He looked across a snow meadow and saw how a rail fence had every stake and rider doubled in solid shadow, and how the edge of woods beyond was blackest India ink. The road ahead was drawn with a ruler, one bank smoothed by the flood of light, the other deeply shadowed. As he looked into the eye of the moon he saw the air shiver and glint with falling particles of frost.

In this White Christmas night, this Good King Wenceslas night, he went warily, not to be caught in sentimentality, and to an invisible audience he deprecated it profanely as a night in which no one would believe. Yet here it was, and he in it. With the coming of the moon the night even seemed to warm; he found that he could drop the blanket from across his face and drink the still air.

Along the roadside as he passed the meadow and entered woods again the moon showed him things. In moonlit openings he saw the snow stitched with tiny perfect tracks, mouse or weasel or the three-toed crowding tracks of partridge. These too, an indigenous part of the night, came back to him as things once known and long forgotten. In his boyhood he had trapped and hunted the animals that made such tracks as these; it was as if his mind were a snowfield where the marks of their secret little feet had been printed long ago. With a queer tightening of the throat, with an odd pride, he read the trail of a fox that had wallowed through the soft snow from the woods, angling into the packed road and along it for a little way and out again, still angling, across the plowed bank, and then left a purposeful trail of cleanly punched tracks, the hind feet in line with the front, across the clean snow and into the opposite woods, from shadow across moonlight and into shadow again.

Turning with the road, he passed through the stretch of woods and came into the open to see the moon-white, shadow-black buildings of a farm, and the weak bloom of light in a window.

His feet whined on the snow, dry as metal powder, as he turned in the loop of drive the county plow had cleared. But as he approached the house doubt touched him. In spite of the light, the place looked unused, somehow. No dog welcomed him. The sound of his feet in the snow was alien, the hammer of his knuckles on the door an intrusion. Looking upward for some trace of telephone wires, he saw none, and he could not tell whether the quivering of the air that he thought he saw above the chimney was heat or smoke or the phantasmal falling frost.

"Hello?" he said, and knocked again. "Anybody home?" No sound answered him. He saw the moon glint on the great icicles along the eaves. His numb hand ached with the pain of knocking; he pounded with the soft edge of his fist.

Answer finally came, not from the door before which he stood, but from the barn, down at the end of a staggered string of attached sheds. A door creaked open against a snowbank and a figure with a lantern appeared, stood for a moment, and came running. The traveler wondered at the way it came, lurching and stumbling in the uneven snow, until it arrived at the porch and he saw that it was a boy of eleven or twelve. The boy set his lantern on the porch; between the upturned collar of his mackinaw and the down-pulled stocking cap his face was a pinched whiteness, his eyes enormous. He stared at the traveler until the traveler became aware of the blanket he still held over head and shoulders, and began to laugh.

"My car stopped on me, a mile or so up the road," he said. "I was just hunting a telephone or some place where I could get help."

The boy swallowed, wiped the back of his mitt across his nose. "Grandpa's sick!" he blurted, and opened the door. Warmth rushed in their faces, cold rushed in at their backs, warm and cold mingled in an eddy of air as the door closed. The traveler saw a cot bed pulled close to the kitchen range, and on the cot an old man covered with a quilt, who breathed heavily and whose closed eyes did not open when the two came near. The gray-whiskered cheeks were sunken, the mouth open to expose toothless gums in a parody look of ancient mischief.

"He must've had a shock," the boy said. "I came in from chores and he was on the floor." He stared at the mummy under the quilt, and he swallowed.

"Has he come to at all?"

"No."

"Only the two of you live here?"

"Yes."

"No telephone?"

"No."

"How long ago did you find him?"

"Chore time. About six."

"Why didn't you go for help?"

The boy looked down, ashamed. "It's near two miles. I was afraid he'd . . ."

"But you left him. You were out in the barn."

"I was hitching up to go," the boy said. "I'd made up my mind."

The traveler backed away from the stove, his face smarting with the heat, his fingers and feet beginning to ache. He looked at the old man and knew that here, as at the car, he was helpless. The boy's thin anxious face told him how thoroughly his own emergency had been swallowed up in this other one. He had been altered from a man in need of help to one who must give it. Salesman of wonder cures, he must now produce something to calm this over-worried boy, restore a dying man. Rebelliously, victimized by circumstances, he said, "Where were you going for help?"

"The Hill place. They've got a phone."

"How far are they from a town?"

"About five miles."

"Doctor there?"

"Yes."

"If I took your horse and—what is it, sleigh?—could someone at the Hills' bring them back, do you think?"

"Cutter. One of the Hill boys could, I should say."

"Or would you rather go, while I look after your grandpa?"

"He don't know you," the boy said directly. "If he should wake up he might . . . wonder . . . it might . . ."

The traveler grudgingly gave up the prospect of staying in the warm kitchen while the boy did the work. And he granted that it was extraordinarily sensitive of the boy to know how it might disturb a man to wake from sickness in his own house and stare into the face of an utter stranger. "Yes," he said. "Well, I could call the doctor from the Hills'. Two miles, did you say?"

"About." The boy had pulled the stocking cap off so that his hair stood on end above his white forehead. He had odd eyes, very large and dark and intelligent, with an expectancy in them.

The traveler, watching him with interest, said, "How long have you lived with your grandfather?"

"Two years."

"Parents living?"

"No, sir, that's why."

"Go to school?"

He got a queer sidling look. "Have to till you're sixteen."

"Is that the only reason you go?"

What he was trying to force out of the boy came out indirectly, with a shrugging of the shoulders. "Grandpa would take me out if he could."

"Would you be glad?"

"No, sir," the boy said, but would not look at him. "I like school."

The traveler consciously corked his flow of questions. Once he himself had been an orphan living with his grandparents on a back farm; he wondered if this boy went as he had gone, knocking in imagination at all of life's closed doors.

The old man's harsh breathing filled the overwarm room. "Well," the traveler said, "maybe you'd better go finish hitching up. It's been thirty years since I harnessed a horse. I'll keep an eye on your grandpa."

Pulling the stocking cap over his disheveled hair, the boy slid out of the door. The traveler unbuttoned his overcoat and sat down beside the old man, felt the spurting weak pulse, raised one eyelid with his thumb and looked without comprehension at the uprolled eye. He knew it was like feeling over a chilling motor for loose wires, and after two or three abortive motions he gave it up and sat contemplating the gray, sunken face, the unfamiliar face of an old man who would die, and thinking that the face was the only unfamiliar thing about the whole night. The kitchen smells, coffee and peanut butter and the moldy, barky smell of wood from the woodbox, and the smell of the hot range and of paint baking in the heat, those were as familiar as light or dark. The spectacular night outside, the snowfields and the moon and the mysterious woods, the tracks venturing out across the snow from the protective eaves of firs and skunk spruce, the speculative, imagining expression of the boy's eyes, were just as familiar. He sat bemused, touching some brink as a man will walk along a cutbank trying to knock loose the crumbling overhang with an outstretched foot. The ways a man fitted in with himself and with other human beings were curious and complex.

And when he heard the jingle and creak outside, and buttoned himself into the overcoat again and wrapped his shoulders in the blanket and stepped out into the yard, there was a moment when the boy passed him the lines and they stood facing each other in the broken snow.

It was a moment like farewell, like a poignant parting. Touched by his pressing sense of familiarity and by a sort of compassion, the traveler reached out and laid his hand on the boy's shoulder. "Don't worry," he said. "I'll have someone back here right away. Your grandfather will be all right. Just keep him warm and don't worry."

He climbed into the cutter and pulled over his lap the balding buffalo robe he found there; the scallop of its felt edges was like a key that fitted a door. The horses breathed jets of steam in the moonlight, restlessly moving, jingling their harness bells, as the moment lengthened itself. The traveler saw how the boy, now that his anxiety was somewhat quieted, now that he had been able to unload part of his burden, watched him with a thousand questions in his face, and he remembered how he himself, thirty years ago, had searched the faces of passing strangers for something he could not name, how he had listened to their steps and seen their shadows lengthen ahead of them down roads that led to unimaginable places, and how he had ached with the desire to know them, who they were. But none of them had looked back at him as he tried now to look at this boy.

He was glad that no names had been spoken and no personal histories exchanged to obscure this meeting, for sitting in the sleigh above the boy's white upturned serious face, he felt that some profound contact had unintentionally, almost casually, been made.

For half a breath he was utterly bewitched, frozen at the heart of some icy dream. Abruptly he slapped the reins across the backs of the horses; the cutter jerked and then slid smoothly out towards the road. The traveler looked back once, to fix forever the picture of himself standing silently watching himself go. As he slid into the road the horses broke into a trot. The icy flow of air locked his throat and made him let go the reins with one hand to pull the hairy, wool-smelling edge of the blanket all but shut across his face.

Along a road he had never driven he went swiftly towards an unknown farm and an unknown town, to distribute according to some wise law part of the burden of the boy's emergency and his own; but he bore in his mind, bright as moonlight over snow, a vivid wonder, almost an awe. For from the most chronic and incurable of ills, identity, he had looked outward and for one unmistakable instant recognized himself.

✤ THESE HANDS ✤

Kevin Brockmeier

The protagonist of this story is named Lewis Winters. He is also its narrator, and he is also me. Lewis is thirty-four years old. His house is small and tidy and sparsely furnished, and the mirrors there return the image of a man inside of whom he is nowhere visible, a face within which he doesn't seem to belong: there is the turn of his lip, the knit of his brow, and his own familiar gaze: there is the promise of him, but where is he? Lewis longs for something not ugly, false, or confused. He chases the yellow-green bulbs of fireflies and cups them between his palms. He watches copter-seeds whirl from the limbs of great trees. He believes in the bare possibility of grace, in kindness and the memory of kindness, and in the fierce and sudden beauty of color. He sometimes believes that this is enough. On quiet evenings, Lewis drives past houses and tall buildings into the flat yellow grasslands that embrace the city. The black road tapers to a point, and the fields sway in the wind, and the sight of the sun dropping red past the hood of his car fills him with sadness and wonder. Lewis lives alone. He sleeps poorly. He writes fairy tales. This is not one of them.

The lover, now absent, of the protagonist of this story is named Caroline Mitchell. In the picture framed on his desk, she stands gazing into the arms of a small tree, a mittened hand at her eyes, lit by the afternoon sun as if through a screen of water. She looks puzzled and eager, as if the wind had rustled her name through the branches; in a moment, a leaf will tumble onto her forehead. Caroline is watchful and sincere, shy yet earnest. She seldom speaks, and when she does her lips scarcely part, so that sometimes Lewis must listen closely to distinguish her voice from the cycling of her breath. Her eyes are a miracle—a startled blue with frail green spokes bound by a ring of black—and he is certain that if he could draw his reflection from them, he would discover there a face neither foreign or lost. Caroline sleeps face down, her knees curled to her chest: she sleeps often and with no sheets or blankets. Her hair is brown, her skin pale. Her smile is vibrant but brief, like a bubble that lasts only as long as the air is still. She is eighteen months old.

A few questions deserve answer, perhaps, before I continue. So then: The walls behind which I'm writing are the walls of my home—the only thing padded is the furniture, the only thing barred the wallpaper. Caroline is both alive and (I imagine—I haven't seen her now in many days) well. And I haven't read Nabokov—not ever, not once.

All this said, it's time we met, my love and I.

It was a hopeful day of early summer, and a slight, fresh breeze tangled through the air. The morning sun shone from telephone wires and the windshields of resting cars, and high clouds unfolded like the tails of galloping horses. Lewis stood before a handsome dark-brick house, flattening his shirt into his pants. The house seemed to conceal its true dimensions behind the planes and angles of its front wall. An apron of hedges stretched beneath its broad lower windows, and a flagstone walk, edged with black soil, elbowed from the driveway to the entrance. He stepped to the front porch and pressed the doorbell.

"Just a minute," called a faint voice.

Lewis turned to look along the street, resting his hand against a wooden pillar. A chain of lawns glittered with dew beneath the blue sky—those nearby green and bristling, those in the distance merely panes of white light. A blackbird lighted on the stiffened flag of a mailbox. From inside the house came the sound of a door wheeling on faulty hinges, a series of quick muffled footsteps, and then an abrupt reedy squeak. *Hello,* thought Lewis: *Hello, I spoke to you on the telephone.* The front door drew inward, stopped short on its chain, and shut. He heard the low mutter of a voice, like residual water draining through a straw. Then the door opened to reveal a woman in a billowy cotton bathrobe, the corner of its hem dark with water. A lock of black hair swept across her cheek from under the dome of a towel. In her hand she carried a yellow toy duck. "Yes?" she said.

"Hello," said Lewis. "I spoke to you on the telephone." The woman gave him a quizzical stare. "The nanny position? You asked me to stop by this morning for an interview." When she cocked an eyebrow, he withdrew a step, motioning toward his car. "If I'm early, I can—."

"Oh!" realized the woman. "Oh, yes." She smiled, tucking a few damp hairs behind the rim of her ear. "The interview. I'm sorry. Come in." Lewis followed her past a small brown table and a rising chain of wooden banisters into the living room. A rainbow of fat plastic rings littered the silver-gray carpet, and a grandfather clock ticked against the far wall. She sank onto the sofa, crossing her legs. "Now," she said, beckoning him to sit beside her. "I'm Lisa. Lisa Mitchell. And you are . . . ?"

"Lewis Winters." He took a seat. "We spoke earlier."

"Lewis . . . ?" Lisa Mitchell gazed into the whir of the ceiling fan, then gave a swift decisive nod. "Aaah!" she lilted, a smile softening her face. "You'll have to excuse me. It's been a hectic morning. When we talked on the phone, I assumed you were a woman. Lois, I thought you said. Lois Winters. We haven't had too many male applicants." Her hand fluttered about dismissively as she spoke, and the orange bill of the rubber duck bobbed past her cheek "This would seem to explain the deep voice, though, wouldn't it?" She smoothed the sash of her bathrobe down her thigh. "So, tell me about your last job. What did you do?"

"I'm a storyteller," said Lewis.

"Pardon?"

"I wrote—write—fairy tales."

"Oh!" said Lisa. "That's good. Thomas—that's my husband, Thomas—." She patted a yawn from her lips. "Excuse me. Thomas will like that. And have you looked after children before?"

"No," Lewis answered. "No, not professionally. But I've worked with *groups* of children. I've read stories in nursery schools and libraries." His hands, which had been clasped, drew apart. "I'm comfortable with children, and I think I understand them."

"When would you be free to start?" asked Lisa.

"Tomorrow," said Lewis. "Today."

"Do you live nearby?"

"Not far. Fifteen minutes."

"Would evenings be a problem?"

"Not at all."

"Do you have a list of references?" At this Lisa closed her grip on the yellow duck, and it emitted a querulous little peep. She gave a start, then laughed, touching her free hand to her chest. She held the duck to her face as it bloomed with air. "Have I had him all this time?" she asked, thumbing its bill.

Somewhere in the heart of the house, a child began to wail. The air seemed to grow thick with discomfort as they listened. "*Someone's* cranky," said Lisa. She handed Lewis the duck as she stood. "Excuse me," she said. She hurried past a floor lamp and the broad green face of a television, then slipped away around the corner.

The grandfather clock chimed the hour as Lewis waited, its brass tail pendulating behind a tall glass door. He scratched a ring of grit from the dimple of the sofa cushion. He inspected the toy duck—its popeyes and the upsweep of its tail, the pock in the center of its flat yellow belly—then waddled it along the seam of a throw pillow. *Quack*, he thought. *Quack quack*. Lewis pressed its navel to the back of his hand, squeezing, and it constricted with a squeak; when he released it, it puckered and gripped him. He heard Lisa's voice in an adjacent room, all but indistinct above a siren-roll of weeping. "Now, now," she was saying. "Now, now." Lewis removed the duck.

When Lisa returned, a small child was gathered to her shoulder. She was wrapped in fluffy red pajamas with vinyl pads at the feet, and her slender neck rose from the wreath of a wilted collar. "Shhh," Lisa whispered, gently patting her daughter's back. "Shhh."

Lisa's hair fell unbound past her forehead, its long wet strands twisted like roads on a map. Her daughter clutched the damp towel in her hands, nuzzling it as if it were a comfort blanket. "Little Miss Grump," chirped Lisa, standing at the sofa. "Aren't you, sweetie?" Caroline fidgeted and whimpered, then began to wail again.

Lisa frowned, joggling her in the crook of her arm.

"Well," she said, "let's see how the two of you get along. Caroline—." With a thrust and a sigh, she presented her daughter, straightening her arms as if engaged in a push-up. "This is Lewis. Lewis . . ." And she was thrashing in my hands, muscling away from me, the weight of her like something lost and suddenly remembered: a comfort and a promise, a slack sail bellying with wind.

Her voice split the air as she twitched from side to side. Padding rustled at her waist.

"Oh, dear," said Lisa. "Maybe we'd better. . . ."

But Lewis wasn't listening; instead, he drew a long heavy breath. If he could pretend himself into tears, he thought, perhaps he could calm her. For a moment as sharp as a little notched hook, he whimpered and circled toward Caroline, holding her gaze. Then, shuddering, he burst into tears. His eyes sealed fast and his lips flared wide. With a sound like the snap and rush of a struck match, his ears opened and filled with air. Barbs of flickering blue light hovered behind his eyes. He could hear the world outside growing silent and still as he wept.

When he looked out at her, Caroline was no longer crying. She blinked out at him from wide bewildered eyes, her bottom lip folding in hesitation. Then she handed him the damp towel.

It was a gesture of sympathy—meant, Lewis knew, to reassure him—and as he draped the towel over his shoulder, a broad grin creased his face.

Lisa shook her head, laughing. "Look," she said, "Thomas and I have plans for this evening, and we still haven't found a baby-sitter. So if you could come by around six—?"

Caroline heard the sound of laughter and immediately brightened, smiling and tucking her chin to her chest. Lewis brushed a finger across her cheek. "Of course," he said.

"Good." Lisa lifted her daughter from his arms. "We'll see how you do, and if all goes well. . . ."

All did. When Lisa and Thomas Mitchell returned late that night—his keys and loose change jingling in his pocket, her perfume winging past him as she walked into the living room—Caroline was asleep in his lap. A pacifier dangled from her mouth. The television mumbled in the comer. Lewis started work the next morning.

As a matter of simple aesthetics, the ideal human form is that of the small child. We lose all sense of grace as we mature, all sense of balance and all sense of restraint. Tufts of wiry hair sprout like moss in our hollows; our cheekbones edge to an angle and our noses stiffen with cartilage; we buckle and curve, widen and purse, like a vinyl record left too long in the sun. The journey into our fewscore years is a journey beyond that which saw us complete. Many is the time I have wished that Caroline and I might have made this journey together. If I could, I would work my way backward, paring away the years. I would reel my life around the wheel of this longing like so much loose wire. I would heave myself past adolescence and boyhood, past infancy and birth—into the first thin parcel of my flesh and the frail white trellis of my bones. I would be a massing of tissue, a clutch of cells, and I'd meet with her on the other side. If I could, I would begin again—but nothing I've found will allow it. We survive into another and more awkward age than our own.

Caroline was sitting in a saddle-chair, its blue plastic tray freckled with oatmeal. She lifted a bright wedge of peach to her lips, and its syrup wept in loose strings from her fist to her bib. Lewis held the back of a polished silver spoon before her like a mirror. "Who's that?" he said. "Who's inside that spoon? Who's that in there?" Caroline gazed into its dome as she chewed her peach. "Cah-line," she said.

Lewis reversed the spoon, and her reflection toppled over into its bowl. "Oh my goodness!" he said. His voice went weak with astonishment. "Caroline is standing on her head!" Caroline prodded the spoon, then taking it by the handle, her hand on his, steered it into her mouth. When she released it, Lewis peered inside. "Hey!" he said. His face grew stern. "Where did you put Caroline?"

She patted her stomach, smiling, and Lewis gasped. "You *ate* Caroline!"

Caroline nodded. Her eyes, as she laughed, were as sharp and rich as light edging under a door.

The upstairs shower disengaged with a discrete shudder, and Lewis heard water suddenly gurgling through the throat of the kitchen sink. Mr. Mitchell dashed into the kitchen swinging a brown leather briefcase. He straightened his hat and drank a glass of orange juice. He skinned an apple with a paring knife. Its cortex spiraled cleanly away from the flesh and, when he left for work, it remained on the counter like a little green basket. "Six o'clock," said Mrs. Mitchell, plucking an umbrella from around a doorknob. "Seven at the outside. Think you can make it till then?" She kissed her daughter on the cheek, then waggled her earlobe with a fingertip. "Now you be a good girl, okay?" she said. She tucked a sheaf of papers into her purse and nodded good-bye, extending her umbrella as she stepped into the morning.

That day, as a gentle rain dotted the windows, Lewis swept the kitchen and vacuumed the carpets. He dusted the roofs of dormant appliances—the oven and the toaster, the pale, serene computer. He polished the bathroom faucets to a cool silver. When Caroline knocked a pair of ladybug magnets from the refrigerator, he showed her how to nudge them across a tabletop, one with the force of the other, by pressing them pole to common pole. "You see," he said, "there's something there. It looks like nothing, but you can feel it." In the living room, they watched a sequence of animated cartoons—nimble, symphonic, awash with color. Caroline sat at the base of the television, smoothing fields of static from its screen with her palm. They read a flap-book with an inset bunny. They assembled puzzles onto sheets of corkboard. They constructed a fortress with the cushions of the sofa; when bombed with an unabridged dictionary, it collapsed like the huskwood of an old fire.

That afternoon, the sky cleared to a proud, empty blue, and Lewis walked with Caroline to the park. The children there were pitching stones into a seething brown creek, fat with new rain, and the birds that wheeled above them looked like tiny parabolic M's and W's. The wind smelled of pine and wet asphalt.

Lewis strapped Caroline into the bucket of a high swing. He discovered a derelict kickball between two rocking horses and, standing before her, tossed it into the tip of her swing, striking her knee, her toe, her shin. "Do it 'gain," she said as the force of her momentum shot the ball past his shoulder, or sent it soaring like a loose balloon into the sky. It disappeared, finally, into a nest of brambles. Pushing Caroline from behind, Lewis watched her arc away from him and back, pausing before her return like a roller-toy he'd once concocted from a coffee can and a rubber band. She weighed so little, and he knew that—if he chose—he could propel her around the axle of the swing set, that with a single robust shove she would spin like a second hand from twelve to twelve to twelve. Instead, he let her swing to a stop, her arms falling limp from the chains as she slowed. A foam sandal dangled uncertainly from her big toe. Her head lolled onto her chest. She was, suddenly, asleep. As Lewis lifted her from the harness, she relaxed into a broad yawn, the tip of her tongue settling gently between her teeth. He carried her home.

After he had put her to bed, Lewis drew the curtains against the afternoon sun and pulled a small yellow table to her side. He sat watching her for a moment. Her breath sighed over her pillowcase, the turn of fabric nearest her lips flitting slightly with each exhalation. She reached for a stuffed bear, cradling it to her heart, and her eyes began to jog behind their lids. Gingerly, Lewis pressed a finger to one of them—he could feel it twitching at his touch like a chick rolling over in its egg. What could she be dreaming, he wondered, and would she remember when she woke? How could something so close be so hidden? And how was it that in the light of such a question we could each of us hold out hope—search eyes as dark as winter for the flicker of intimacy, dream of seizing one another in a fit of recognition? As he walked silently from her bedroom, Lewis lifted from the toyshelf a red plastic See 'n Say, its face wreathed with calling animals. In the hallway, he trained its index on the picture of a lion, depressing the lever cocked at its frame. *This*, said the machine, *is a robin*, and it whittered a little aria. When he turned the dial to a picture of a lamb on a tussock of grass, it said the same thing. Dog and pony, monkey and elephant: *robin—twit twit whistle*. Lewis set the toy against a wall, listening to the cough of a receding car. He passed through the dining room and climbed the back stairway, wandered the deep and inviolate landscape of the house solemn with the thought of faulty lessons, and of how often we are shaped in this way.

An old story tells of a man who grew so fond of the sky—of the clouds like hills and the shadows of hills, of the birds like notes of music and the stars like distant blessings—that he made of his heart a kite and sailed it into the firmament. There he felt the high mechanical tug of the air. The sunlight rushed through him, and the sharp blue wind, and the world seemed a far and a learnable thing. His gaze (the story continues) he tethered like a long string to his heart—and never looking down, lest he pull himself to earth, he wandered the world ever after in search of his feet.

Talking about love, I suspect, is much like this story. What is it, then, that insists that we make the attempt? The hope of some new vision? The drive for words and order? We've been handed a map whose roads lead to a place we understand: *Now*, says a voice, *disentangle them*. And though we fear that we will lose our way, still, there is this wish to try. Perhaps, though, if we allow our perceptions of love to brighten and fade as they will, allow it even if they glow no longer than a spark launched from a fire, perhaps we will not pull our heart from its course: surely this is possible.

My love, then, for Caroline is what slows me into sleep at night. It is a system of faith inhabiting some part of me that's deeper than I've traveled The thought of her fills me with comfort and balance, like heat spilling from the floor register of an old building. Her existence at this moment, alongside me in time—unhesitating and sure—all of this, the *now* of her, is what stirs through me when I fail. My love for Caroline is the lens through which I see the world, and the world through that lens is a place whose existence addresses the fact of my own.

Caroline chews crayons—red like a firetruck, green like a river, silver like the light from passing airplanes—and there's something in my love for her that speaks this same urge: I want to receive the world inside me. My love for Caroline is the wish that we might spend our lives together: marry in a hail of rice, watch the childhood of our children disappear, and think to ourselves someday: when this person is gone, no one in all the world will remember the things I remember.

Salient point is an early and sadly obsolete term for the heart as it first appears in the embryo: I fell upon it in a book of classical obstetrics with a sense of celebration. The heart, I believe, is that point where we merge with the universe. It is salient as a jet of water is salient—leaping continually upward—and salient as an angle is salient—its vertex projecting into this world, its limbs fanning out behind the frame of another. What I love of Caroline is that space of her at rest behind the heart—true and immanent, hidden and vast, the arc that this angle subtends.

I would like to cobble such few sentences into a tower, placing them in the world, so that I might absorb what I can of these things in a glance. But when we say *I love you*, we say it not to shape the world. We say it because there's a wind singing through us that knows it to be true and because even when we speak them without shrewdness or understanding—it is good, we know, to say these things.

The dishwasher thrummed in the kitchen, and the thermostat ticked in the hallway, and the tumble-drier called from the basement like a tittuping horse. Caroline lay on the silver-gray carpet, winking each eye in turn as she scrutinized her thumb. Her hair was drawn through the teeth of a barrette, and the chest of her shirt was pulled taut beneath one arm. Lewis could see her heartbeat welling through the gate of her ribs. It called up in him the memory of a time when, as a schoolboy, his teacher had allowed him to hold the battery lamp during a power failure. He had lain on the floor, balancing the lamp atop his chest, and everywhere in the slate-black schoolroom the light had pulsed with his heart. Like a shaken belief or a damaged affection, the life within such a moment could seem all but irreclaimable.

The seconds swayed past in the bob-weight of the grandfather clock.

"Come here," said Lewis, beckoning to Caroline, and when she'd settled into his lap, he told her this story: In a town between a forest and the sea there lived a clever and gracious little girl. She liked to play with spoons and old buttons, to swat lumpbugs and jump over things, and her name was Caroline.

("I don' like *spoons*," said Caroline. *Spoons?* said Lewis. *Did I say spoons? I meant goons.* Caroline giggled and shook her head. "No-o." *Prunes?* "Nuh-uh." *Baboons?* Caroline paused to consider this, her finger paddling lazily against her shirt collar. "Okay.")

So then: Caroline, who played with buttons and baboons, had all the hours from sun to moon to wander the city as she wished, scratching burrs from her socks or thumping dandelion heads. The grownups offered her but one caution: if ever the sky should threaten rain, the clouds begin to grumble or the wind blow suddenly colder, she must hurry indoors. The grownups had good reason to extend such a warning, for the town in which they lived was made entirely of soap. It had been whittled and sliced from the Great Soap Mountains. There were soaphouses and soapscrapers, chains of soap lampposts above wide soap roadways, and in the town center, on a pedestal of marbled soap, a rendering of a soapminer, his long proud shovel at his side. Sometimes, when the dark sky ruptured and the rains came daggering across the land, those of the town who had not taken shelter—the tired and the lost, the poky and the dreamy—would vanish, never to return. "Washed clean away," old-timers would declare, nodding sagely.

One day, Caroline was gathering soapberries from a glade at the lip of the forest. Great somber clouds, their bellies black with rain, had been weltering in from the ocean for hours, but she paid them no mind: she had raced the rain before, and she could do it again. When a cloud discharged a hollow growl, she thought it was her stomach, hungry for soapberries—and so ate a few. When the wind began to swell and chill, she simply zippered her jacket. She bent to place a berry in her small blue hat, and felt her skin pimpling at the nape of the neck, and when she stood again, the rain was upon her.

Caroline fled from the forest. She arrowed past haystacks and canting trees, past empty pavilions and blinking red stoplights. A porchgate wheeled on its hinges and slammed against a ventilation tank. A lamplight burst in a spray of orange sparks. Almost, thought Caroline, as her house, then her door, then the glowspeck of her doorbell came into view. And at just that moment, as she blasted past the bakery to her own front walk, a tremendous drift of soapsuds took hold of her from behind, whipping her up and toward the ocean.

When Caroline awoke, the sunlight was lamping over her weary body. Her skin was sticky with old soap. Thin whorls of air iridesced all around her. She shook her head, unfolded in a yawn, and watched a bluebird flap through a small round cloud beneath her left elbow. That was when she realized: she was bobbing through the sky inside a bubble! She tried to climb the inside membrane of the vessel, but it rolled her onto her nose. She prodded its septum with her finger and it stretched and recoiled, releasing a few airy driblets of soap that popped when she blew on them. *Bubble, indeed,* she thought—indignant, arms akimbo. Caroline (though a clever and a gracious little girl) could not think of a single solution to her dilemma—for if her craft were to erupt she would surely fall to earth, and if she fell to earth she would shatter like a snowball—so she settled into the bay of her bubble, watching the sky and munching the soapberries from her small blue hat.

There is little to see from so high in the air: clouds and stars and errant birds; the fields and the hills, the rivers and highways, as small and distinct as the creases in your palm. There is a time as the morning brightens when the lakes and rivers, catching the first light, will go silvering through the quiet black land. And in the evening, when the sun drops, a flawless horizon will prism its last flare into a haze of seven colors. Once, Caroline watched a man's heart sail by like a kite, once a golden satellite swerving past the moon. Preoccupied birds sometimes flew straight toward her—their wings stiff and open, their beaks like drawn swords—yawing away before they struck her bubble. On a chilly afternoon, an airplane passed so close that she counted nineteen passengers gaping at her through its windows, their colorless faces like a series of stills on a film strip. And on a delicate, breezy morning, as she stared through a veining of clouds at the land, Caroline noticed that the twists of color had faded from the walls of her bubble. Then, abruptly, it burst.

Caroline found herself plummeting like a buzzbomb from the sky, the squares of far houses growing larger and larger. Her hair strained upward against the fall, tugging at her scalp. Her cheeks beat like pennants in the wind. She shut her eyes. As for what became of her, no one is certain—or rather there are many tales, and many tellers, each as certain as the last. Some say she spun into the arms of a startled baboon, who raised her in the forest on coconuts and turnip roots. Some say she dropped onto the Caroline Islands, striking the beach in a spasm of sand, and so impressed the islanders with the enthusiasm of her arrival that with a mighty shout they proclaimed her Minister of Commerce. And some say she landed in this very house—on this very couch, in this very room—where I told her this story and put her to bed.

. . .

The human voice is an extraordinary thing: an alliance of will and breath that, without even the fastening of hands can forge for us a home in other people. Air is sent trembling through the frame of the mouth, and we find ourselves admitted to some far, unlikely country: this must, I think, be regarded as nothing short of wondrous. The first voice I remember hearing belonged, perhaps, to a stranger or a lost relation, for I cannot place it within my family: it sounded like a wooden spool rolling on a wooden floor. My father had a voice like cement revolving in a drum, my mother like the whirring of many small wings. My own, I've been told, resembles the rustling of snow against a windowpane. What must the mother's voice—beneath the whisper of her lungs, beneath the little detonations of her heartbeat—sound like to the child in the womb? A noise without design or implication—as heedless as growth, as mechanical as thunder? Or the echo of some nascent word come quaking through the body? Is it the first intimation of another life cradling our own, a sign that suggests that this place is a someone? Or do children—arriving from some other, more insistent landscape—need such testimony? If the human voice itself does not evince a living soul, then that voice raised in song surely must.

Things go right, things go wrong / hearts may break but not for long /you will grow up proud and strong/sleepy little baby.

Of all the forms of voice and communion, a song is perhaps the least mediated by the intellect. It ropes its way through the tangle of our cautions, joining singer to listener like a vine between two trees. I once knew a man whose heart percussed in step with the music that he heard; he would not listen to drums played in hurried or irregular cadence; he left concerts and dances and parties, winced at passing cars, and telephoned his neighbors when they played their stereos too loudly—in the fear that with each unsteady beat he might malfunction. Song is an exchange exactly that immediate and physiological. It attests to the life of the singer through our skin and through our muscles, through the wind in our lungs and the fact of our own beating heart. The evidence of other spirits becomes that of our own body. Speech is sound shaped into meaning through words, inflection, and modulation. Music is sound shaped into meaning through melody, rhythm, and pitch. A song arises at the point where these two forces collide. But such an encounter can occur in more than one place. Where, then, is song most actual and rich—in the singer or in the audience?

Dream pretty dreams / touch beautiful things /let all the skies surround you /swim with the swans /and believe that upon /some glorious dawn love will find you.

A successful song comes to sing itself inside the listener. It is cellular and seismic, a wave coalescing in the mind and in the flesh. There is a message outside, and a message inside, and those messages are the same, like the pat and thud of two heartbeats, one within you, one surrounding. The message of the lullaby is that it's okay to dim the eyes for a time, to lose sight of yourself as you sleep and as you grow: if you drift—it says—you'll drift ashore: if you fall, you will fall into place.

And if you see some old fool / who looks like a friend / tell him good night old man / my friend.

Lewis stood with a washcloth before Caroline's highchair, its tray white with milk from a capsized tumbler. A streetlamp switched on outside the kitchen window, and as he turned to look, another did the same. The sun had left channels of pink and violet across the sky in which a few wavering stars were emerging. He could hear the rush of commuter traffic behind the dry autumn clicking of leaves—motor horns calling forlornly, a siren howling in the distance. The highchair stood like a harvest crab on its thin silver stilts. Lewis sopped the milk up from its tray and brushed the crumbs from its seat, rinsing his washcloth at the gurgling sink. All around the city—he thought, staring into the twilight—streetlamps were brightening one by one, generating warm electric purrs and rings of white light. From far above, as they blinked slowly on and off, they would look like rainwater striking the lid of a puddle.

In the living room, Caroline sat at the foot of the television, several inches from the screen, watching a small cartoon Martian chuckle perniciously as he fashioned an enormous ray gun. Lewis knelt beside her and, just for a moment, saw the black egg of the Martian's face shift beneath his gleaming helmet—but then his eyes began to tingle, and his perception flattened, and it was only a red-green-blueness of phosphorescent specks and the blade of his own nose. He flurried his hand through Caroline's hair, then pinched a dot of cookie from her cheek. "Sweetie," he said to her, standing. When his knees cracked, she started.

A set of cardboard blocks—red and blue and thick as breadloaves—were clustered before a reclining chair. They looked like something utterly defeated, a grove of pollard trees or the frame of a collapsed temple. Earlier in the day, Lewis had played a game with Caroline in which he stacked them two on two to the ceiling and she charged them, arms swinging, until they toppled to the carpet. Each time she rushed them, she would rumble like a speeding truck. Each time they fell she would laugh with excitement, bobbing up and down in a stiff little dance. She rarely tired of this game. As often as not, actually, she descended upon the structure in a sort of ambush before it was complete: Lewis would stoop to collect another block, hear the drum of running feet, and down they would go. Now, as she peered at the television, he stacked the blocks into two narrow columns, each its own color, and bridged them carefully at the peak; satisfied, he lapsed onto the sofa.

Propping his glasses against his forehead, he yawned and pressed his palms to his eyes. Grains of light sailed through the darkness, like snow surprised by a headlamp, and when he looked out at the world again, Caroline had made her way to his side. She flickered her hands and burbled a few quick syllables, her arms swaying above her like the runners of a sea plant: in her language of blurt and gesture, this meant *carry me,* or *hold me,* or *pick me up*—and swinging into her, Lewis did just that. She stood in his lap, balancing with one smooth-socked foot on either thigh, and reached for his forehead. "'lasses," she said. Lewis removed his glasses, handing them to her, and answered, "That's right." An ice-white bloom of television flashed from each lens as Caroline turned them around in her palms. When she pressed them to her face, the stems floated inches from her ears; then they slipped past her nose and hitched around her shoulders, hanging there like a necklace or a bow-tie. Lewis felt himself smiling as he retrieved them He polished them on the tail of his shirt and returned them to their rightful perch.

He looked up to find Caroline losing her balance, foundering toward him. Her foot slid off his leg onto the sofa and her arms lurched up from her side. "Whoa," he said, catching her. "You okay?" She tottered back onto his lap, her head pressing against his cheek. He could feel the dry warmth of her skin, the arching of her eyebrows, the whiffet of her breath across his face. Then, straightening, she kissed him. The flat of her tongue passed up his chin and over his lips, and, stopping at the ledge of his nose, inverted and traveled back down. Lewis could feel it tensed against him like a spring, and when it swept across the crest of his lips, he lightly kissed its tip. Caroline closed her mouth with a tiny pecking sound. She sniffled, brushed her nose, and settled into him. "'lasses," she said, and her warm brown hair fell against his collarbone. Lewis blinked and touched a finger to his dampened chin. His ears were tingling as if from a breeze. His head was humming like a long flat roadway.

From the front porch came the rattle of house-keys. As the bolt-lock retracted with a ready chink, Caroline dropped to his lap. She turned to watch the television and pillowed her head on his stomach.

"Home!" called Mr. Mitchell, and the door clapped shut behind him.

My brother is three years my senior. When I was first learning to speak, he was the only person to whom my tongue taps and labial stops seemed a language. I would dispense a little train of stochastic syllables—*pa ba mi da*, for instance—and he would translate, for the benefit of my parents: *he wants some more apple-sauce*. My brother understood me, chiefly, from basic sympathy and the will to understand: the world, I am certain, responds to such forces. It was in this fashion that I knew what Caroline told me—though when she said it she was mumbling up from sleep, and though it sounded to the ear as much like *igloo* or *allegory*—when with a quiet and perfect affection she said, "I love you."

With fingers spidery-weak from the cold, Lewis worked the tag of Caroline's zipper into its slide, fastening her jacket with a tidy zzzt. He tightened her laces, straightened her mittens, and wiped her nose with a tissue. He adjusted her socks and trousers, and the buttonless blue puff of her hood. "All right," he said, patting her back. "Off you go." Caroline scampered for the sandbox, her hood flipping from her head to bob along behind her. When she crossed its ledge, she stood for a moment in silence. Then she growled like a bear and gave an angry stamp, felling a hillock of abandoned sand. Lewis watched her from a concrete bench. She found a small pink shovel and arranged a mound of sand into four piles, one at each rail, as if ladling out soup at a dinner table. She buried her left foot and kicked a flurry of grit onto the grass.

Brown leaves shot with threads of red and yellow skittered across the park. They swept past merry-go rounds and picnic tables, past heavy gray stones and rotunda bars. A man and his daughter tottered on a seesaw, a knot of sunlight shuttling along the rod between them like a bubble in a tube of water. Two boys were bouncing tennis balls in the parking lot—hurling them against the asphalt and watching them leap into the sky—and another was descending a decrepit wire fence, its mesh of tendons loose and wobbling. Caroline sat on her knees in the sandbox, burrowing: she unearthed leaves and acorns and pebbles, a shiny screw-top bottlecap and her small pink shovel. A boy with freckles and cowboy boots joined her with a grimace, a ring of white diaper peering from above his pants. His mother handed him a plastic bucket, tousling his plume of tall red hair. "Now you play nice," she told him, and sat next to Lewis on the bench. She withdrew a soda can from her purse, popping its tab and sipping round the edge of its lid. Caroline placed her bottlecap in her shovel, then scolded it—no, no, no—and tipped it to the side. The woman on the bench turned to Lewis—gesturing cheerily, nonchalantly. "Your daughter is *adorable*," she said.

For a moment Lewis didn't know how to respond. He felt a strange coldness shivering up from inside him: it was as if his body were a window, suddenly unlatched, and beyond it was the hard aspen wind of December. Then the sensation dwindled, and his voice took hold of him. "Thanks," he said. "She's not mine, but thank you."

The woman crossed her legs, tapping her soda can with a lacquered red fingernail. "So," she asked, "you're an uncle, then?"

"Sitter."

From the back of her throat came a high little interrogatory *mm*. In the sandbox, her son slid his plastic bucket over his head. *Echo*, he hollered, his face concealed in its trough: *echo, echo, echo*. He was the sort of boy one might expect to find marching loudly into weddings and libraries, chanting the theme songs from television comedies and striking a metal pan with a wooden spoon. "I'm Brooke," said the woman, bending to set her soda can at her feet. "And you are . . . ?"

"Lewis."

She nodded then rummaged in her purse, a sack of brown woven straw as large as a bed-pillow. "Would you like some gum, Lewis? I know it's in here somewhere." Her son lumbered over to Caroline and clapped his bucket over her head. It hit with a loud thumping sound. Lewis, watching, stepped to her side and removed it, then hoisted her to his shoulder as she began to cry.

The woman on the bench glanced up from her purse. "Alex*ander*," she exclaimed. She stomped to the sandbox in counterfeit anger. "*What* did you do?" The boy glowered, his mouth pinching shut like the spiracle of a balloon. He threw the small pink shovel at a litter bin and began punching his left arm. "*That* settles it," said his mother, pointing. "No more fits today from *you*, Mister. To the car."

"Your bucket," said Lewis—it was dangling from his right hand, fingers splayed against Caroline's back.

"Thanks," said the woman, hooking it into her purse. She waved as she left with her son.

Caroline was nuzzling against his neck, her arm folded onto her stomach. Her chest rose and fell against his own and Lewis relaxed his breathing until they were moving in concert. He walked to a wooden picnic table and sat on its roof, brushing a few pine needles to the ground. The wind sighed through the trees, and the creek rippled past beneath a ridge of grass. Silver minnows paused and darted through its shallows, kinks of sunlight agitating atop the water like a sort of camouflage for their movements. Lewis tossed a pine cone into the current and watched it sail—scales flared and glistening—through a tiny cataract. An older couple, arms intertwined, passed by with their adolescent daughter. "I'm not sure I even *believe* in peace of mind," the girl was saying, her hands fluttering at her face as if to fend off a fly. He could hear Caroline slurping on her thumb. "You awake?" he asked, and she mumbled in affirmation. "Do you want to go home or do you want to stay here and play for a while?"

"Play," said Caroline.

Lewis planted her on her feet and, taking her by the hand, walked with her to the playground. A framework of chutes and tiered platforms sat in a bed of sand and gravel, and they climbed a net of ropes into its gallery. A steering-wheel was bolted to a cross-beam at the forward deck, and when Caroline spun it, they beeped like horns and *whoa*ed from side to side. They snapped clots of sand from a hand-rail. They ran across a step-bridge swaying on its chains. A broad gleaming slide descended from a wooden shelf, its ramp speckled with dents and abrasions, and ascending a ladder to its peak, they swooped to the earth. They jumped from a bench onto an old brown stump and climbed a hill of painted rubber tires. They wheeled in slow circles on a merry-go-round, watched the world drift away and return—slide tree parking lot, slide tree parking lot—until their heads felt dizzy and buoyant, like the hollow metal globes that quiver atop radio antennas. Beside a bike rack and a fire hydrant, they discovered the calm blue mirror of a puddle; when Lewis breached it with a stone, they watched themselves pulse across the surface, wavering into pure geometry. A spray of white clouds hovered against the sky, and an airplane drifted through them with a respiratory hush. "Look," said Lewis, and Caroline followed the line of his finger. Behind the airplane were two sharp white condensation trails, cloven with blue sky, that flared and dwindled like the afterlight of a sparkler. Watching, Lewis was seized with a sudden and inexplicable sense of presence, as if weeks and miles of surrounding time and space had contracted around this place, this moment. "My God," he said, and filled his lungs with the rusty autumn air. "Look what we can do."

A man with a stout black camera was taking pictures of the playground equipment. He drew carefully toward the slide and the seesaw, the monkey bars and tire-swings, altering his focus and releasing the shutter. Each print emerged from a vent at the base of the camera, humming into sight on a square of white paper. Lewis approached the man and, nodding to Caroline, asked if he might borrow the device for a moment. "Just one picture?" he asked, his head cocked eagerly. "Well," said the man—and he shrugged, giving a little flutter with his index finger. "Okay. One." Caroline had wandered in pursuit of a whirling leaf to the foot of a small green cypress tree. Its bough was pierced with the afternoon sunlight, and she gazed into the crook of its lowest branches. A flickertail squirrel lay there batting a cone. She raised a mittened hand to her eyes, squinting, and when Lewis snapped her picture, a leaf tumbled onto her forehead.

"Your daughter," said the man, collecting his camera, "is very pretty."

Lewis stared into the empty white photograph "Thank you," he said. He blew across its face until the dim gray ghost of a tree appeared. "She is."

Though it often arises in my memories and dreams, I have not returned to the playground in many days. It is certain to have changed, however minutely, and this is what keeps me away. Were I to visit, I might find the rocking horse rusted on its heavy iron spring, the sidewalk marked with the black prints of leaves, the swings wrapped higher around their crossbars—and though they seem such small things, I'd rather not see them. The sand may have spilled past the lip of the sandbox, and the creek may have eaten away at its banks. The cypress tree might have been taken by saw or risen a few inches closer to the sun. Perhaps a pair of lovers have carved their signet into its bark—a heart and a cross, or a square of initials. My fear, though, is that the park has simply paled with all its contents into an embryonic white—that flattening like a photograph too long exposed, it has curled at its edges and blown away. In my thoughts, though, it grows brighter each day, fresher and finer and more distinct, away from my remembering eyes.

Caroline was nestled in bubbles. Sissing white hills of them gathered and rose, rolling from the faucet to each bank of the tub. They streamed like clouds across the water, rarefying as they accumulated—as those bubbles in the center, collapsing, coalesced into other, slightly larger bubbles, which themselves collapsed into still larger bubbles, and those into still larger (as if a cluster of grapes were to become, suddenly, one large grape), which, bursting, opened tiny chutes and flumes to the exterior—and there sat Caroline, hidden in the thick of them, the tips of her hair afloat on the surface. When she scissored her feet, the great mass of the bubbles swayed atop the water. When she twitched her arm, a little boat of froth released itself from the drift, sailing through the air into a box of tissues. She looked as if she had been planted to her shoulders in snow.

Lewis shut the water off, and the foam that had been rippling away from the head of the tub spread flat, like folds of loose skin drawing suddenly taut. The silence of the faucet left the bathroom loud with hums and whispers—intimate noises were made vibrant and bold: effervescing bubbles, gentle whiffs of breath, metal pipes ticking in the walls. Caroline leaned forward and blew a cove the size of her thumb into a mound of bubbles. The bathwater, swaying with her motion, rocked the mound back upon her, and when she blinked up from inside it, her face was wreathed in white. Lewis pinched the soap from her eyelashes. He cleaned her with a hand towel—brushed the swell of her cheeks and the bead of her nose—and dropped her rubber duck into the bubbles. It struck the water with a *ploop*, then emerged from the glittering suds. "Wack, wack," said Caroline, as it floated into her collarbone. She pulled it to the floor of the tub and watched it hop to the surface.

Lewis squirted a dollop of pink shampoo into his palm and worked it through the flurry of her hair. Its chestnut brown, darkened with water, hung in easy curves along her neck and her cheek and in the dip of skin behind each ear. His fingers, lacing through it, looked as white as slants of moonlight. He flared and collapsed them, rubbing the shampoo into a rich lather, and touched the odd runnel of soap from her forehead. One day, as he was bathing her, a bleb of shampoo had streamed into her eye, and she had kept a hand pressed to it for the rest of the day, quailing away from him whenever he walked past. Ever since then, he had been careful to roll the soap back from her face as it thickened, snapping it into the tub. When it came time to rinse, Caroline tilted her head back and shut her eyes so tightly that they shivered. Lewis braced her in the water, his palm against the smooth of her back.

With a green cotton washcloth and a bar of flecked soap, he washed her chin and her jaw, her round dimpled elbows, the small of her back and the spine of her foot. His sleeves were drawn to his upper arms, his fingertips slowly crimping. His hands passed from station to station with careful diligent presses and strokes. Caroline paddled her duck through the water, then squeezed it and watched the air bubble from under its belly. He washed her arms and her legs and the soft small bowl of her stomach. He washed the hollows of her knees, soaped her neck and soaped her chest, and felt her heart, the size of a robin's egg, pounding beneath him. Her heart, he thought, was driving her blood, and her blood was sustaining her cells, and her cells were investing her body with time. He washed her shoulder blades and the walls of her torso and imagined them expanding as she grew: her muscles would band and bundle, her bones flare open like the frame of an umbrella. He washed the shallow white shoulders that would take on curve and breadth, the waist that would taper, the hips that would round. The vents and breaches, valleys and slopes, that would become as rare and significant to some new husband as they now were to him. The face that, through the measure of its creases, would someday reveal by accident what it now revealed by intent: the feelings that were traveling through her life. He washed her fragile, dissilient, pink-fingered hands. The hands that would unfold and color with age. The hands that would learn how to catch a ball and knot a shoelace, how to hold a pencil and unlock a door—how to drive a car, how to wave farewell, how to shake hello. The hands that would learn how to touch another person, how to carry a child, and on some far day how to die.

The water was lapping against the wall of the tub. Lewis found himself gazing into the twitch of his reflection: his lips and eyes were tense with thought beside a reef of dissipating bubbles. Caroline watched for a moment, then splashed him with a palm of cupped water. When Lewis looked at her through the tiny wet globes that dotted his glasses, she laughed, and he felt some weary thing inside of him ascend and disperse, like fog lifting from a bay. He polished his glasses and his mouth curled into a smile.

When he pulled the bathplug, Caroline started—surprised, as she often was, by the sudden deep gurgle and surge of the water. He welcomed her into the wings of a towel as it serpent-whirled into the drain.

Sums

Number of days we spent together: 144. Number of days we spent apart (supposing that Archbishop James Usher of Meath, who calculated the date of the Creation at 23 October 4004 B.C., was correct): 2,195,195. Number of days since I last saw her: 43. Number of days since I began writing this story: 3. Number of days in her life thus far: 613. Number of days in mine thus far: 12,418; projected: 12,419. Number of times we walked to the park: 102. Number of swings on the swing set there: 3; strap swings: 2; bucket swings: 1. Number of times she rode the bucket swing: 77; the strap swing: 1. Number of times she rode the strap swing and fell: 1. Number of times I pushed her on the bucket swing, average per session: 22; total: 1694. Number of puzzles we constructed: 194. Number of towers we assembled from large cardboard blocks: 112; demolished: 111. Number of stories I told: 58. Number of diapers I changed: 517. Number of lullabies I sang: 64. Number of days I watched, while Caroline napped, Caroline: 74; the television: 23; the sky: 7. Number of times, since we met, that I've laundered my clothing: 93; that I've finished a book: 19; that I've heard songs on the radio with her name in them: 17 (*good times never felt so good: 9; where did your long hair go?*: 2; a song I don't know whose chorus chants *Caroline Caroline Caroline* in a voice like the clittering of dice in a cup: 6). Number of footlong sandwiches I've eaten since we met: 12. Number of Lewises it would take to equal in height the number of footlong sandwiches I've eaten since we met: 2.1; number of Carolines: 4.9. Number of times I've thought today about the color of my walls: 2; about the shape of my chin: 1; about airplanes: 4; about mirrors: 3; about the inset mirror in one of Caroline's flap-books: 1; about Caroline and the turn of her lips: 6; about Caroline and macaroni and cheese: 1; about how difficult it can be to separate one thought from another: 1; about Caroline and moths and childhood fears: 4; about my childhood fear of being drawn through the grate of an escalator: 1; about my childhood fear of being slurped down the drain of a bathtub: 2; about eyes: 9; about hands: 6, about hands, mine: 3. Number of lies I've told you: 2. Number of lies I've told you about my behavior toward Caroline: 0; about fairy tales: 0; about Nabokov: 1. Number of times I've dreamt about her: 14; pleasant: 12. Number of times I've dreamt about her mother: 3; nightmares: 3. Number of nightmares I recall having had in my life: 17. Number of hours I've spent this month: 163; in vain: 163.

Lewis tidied the house while Caroline napped, gathering her toys from the kitchen and the bathroom, the stairway and the den. He collected them in the fold of his arms and quietly assembled them on her toyshelves. Warm air breathed from the ceiling-vents and sunlight ribboned in through the living room windows, striking in its path a thousand little whirling constellations of dust. Lewis pulled a xylophone trolley from under the couch. He stacked rainbow quoits onto a white peg. He carried a pinwheel and a rag doll from the hallway and slipped a set of multiform plastic blocks into the multiform sockets of a block-box. He walked from the oven to the coatrack, from the coatrack to the grandfather clock, fossicking about for the last of a set of three tennis balls, and, finding it behind the laundry hamper, he pressed it into its canister. Then he held the canister to his face, breathing in its flat clean scent before he shelved it in the closet of the master bedroom. Lewis often felt, upon entering this room, as if he had discovered a place that was not an aspect of the house that he knew—someplace dark and still and barren: a cavern or a sepulcher, a tremendous empty seashell. The venetian blinds were always sealed, the curtains drawn shut around them, and both were overshadowed by a fat gray oak tree. The ceiling lamp cast a dim orange light, nebular and sparse, over the bed and the dressers and the carpet. Lewis fell back on the bedspread. The cable of an electric blanket bore into his shoulder, and his head lay in a shallow channel in the center of the mattress—formed, he presumed, by the weight of a sleeping body. He yawned, drumming his hand on his chest, and listened to the sigh of a passing car. He gazed into the tiny red eye of a smoke alarm.

When he left to look in on Caroline, he found her sleeping contentedly, her thumb in her mouth. A stuffed piglet curled from beneath her, its pink snout and the tabs of its ears brushing past her stomach. Her back rose and fell like a parachute tent. He softly shut her door. Returning to the living room, he bent to place a stray red checker in his shirt pocket, then straightened and gave a start: her mother was there, sitting on the sofa and blinking into space. Lisa Mitchell rarely arrived home before the moon was as sharp as a blade in the night sky, never once before evening. Now she sat clutching a small leather purse in her lap, and a stream of sunlight delineated each thread of her hair. It was mid-afternoon.

"Early day?" asked Lewis. He removed a jack-in-the-box from the arm of a chair, sealing the lid on its unsprung clown. Lisa Mitchell neither moved nor spoke; she simply held her purse and stared. "Hello . . . ?" he tested. She sat motionless, queerly mute, like a table lamp or a podium. Then her shoulders gave a single tight spasm, as if an insect had buzzed onto the nape of her neck, and her eyes glassed with tears. Lewis felt, suddenly, understanding and small and human. "Do you need anything?" he asked. "Some water?" Lisa drew a quick high breath and nodded.

Lewis rinsed a glass in the kitchen sink, then filled it from a bay on the door of the refrigerator, watching the crushed ice and a finger of water issue from a narrow spout. When he handed it to Lisa, she sipped until her mouth pooled full, swallowed, and placed it on a sidetable. Her fingertips left transparent annulets across the moist bank of the glass, her lips a wine-red crescent at its rim. Lewis sat next to her on the sofa. "Do you want to talk about it?" he asked. His voice had become as gentle as the aspiration of the ceiling-vents.

"I . . . ," said Lisa, and the corner of her mouth twitched. "He said I. . . ." Her throat gave out a little clicking noise. She trifled with the apron of her purse—snapping it open and shut, open and shut. "I lost my job," she said. And at this she sagged in on herself, shaking, and began to weep. Her head swayed, and her back lurched, and she pressed her hands to her eyes. When Lewis touched a finger to her arm, she fell against him, quaking.

"It's okay," he said. "It will all be okay." Resting against his shoulder, Lisa cried and shivered and slowly grew still. Her purse dropped to the floor as she relaxed into a sequence of calm, heavy breaths. Then, abruptly, she was crying once again. She wavered in this way—between moments of peace and trepidation—for what seemed an hour, as the white midday light slowly windowed across the carpet. After she had fallen quiet, Lewis held her and listened to her breathing. (She sighed placidly, flurrying puffs of air through her nose; she freed a little string of hiccups that seemed both deeply organic and strangely mechanical.) The sleeve of his shirt, steeped with her tears, was clinging to his upper arm, and his hand was pinpricking awake on her back. He could feel the warm pressure of her head against his collar-bone. When she shifted on the cushions, he swallowed, listening to the drumbeat of his heart. He slid his fingers over the rungs of her spine, smoothing the ripples from her blouse, and she seemed to subside into the bedding of the sofa. It was as if she were suddenly just a weight within her clothing, suspended by a hanger from his shoulder, and he thought for a moment that she had fallen asleep—but, when she blinked, he felt the soft flicker of her eyelashes against his neck. Her stockings, sleek and coffee-brown, were beginning to ladder at the knee, and Lewis reached to touch a ravel of loose nylon. He found himself instead curling a hand through her hair.

Lisa lifted her head, looking him in the eye, as his fingers swept across a rise in her scalp. He felt her breath mingling with his own. Her eyes, drawing near, were azure-blue, and walled in black, and staring into his own. They seemed to hover before him like splashes of reflected light, and Lewis wondered what they saw. The tip of her nose met with his, and when she licked her lips, he felt her tongue glance across his chin. His lips were dry and tingling, his stomach as tight as a seed pod. When his hand gave a reflexive flutter on her back, Lisa stiffened.

She tilted away from him, blinking, the stones of her teeth pressing into her lip. The grandfather clock voiced three vibrant chimes, and she stood and planed her blouse into the waist of her skirt.

When she looked down upon him, her eyes were like jigsawed glass. "I think you'd better go now," she said.

Certain places are penetrated with elements of the human spirit. They act as concrete demonstrations of our hungers and capacities. A sudden field in the thick of a forest is a place like reverence, a stand of corn a place like knowledge, a clock tower a place like fury. I have witnessed this and know it to be true. Caroline's house was a place like memory—a place, in fact, like my memory of her: charged with hope and loss and fascination. As I stepped each morning through her front door, I saw the wall-peg hung with a weathered felt hat, the ceiling dotted with stucco, the staircase folding from floor to floor, and it was as if these things were quickened with both her presence and her ultimate departure. The stationary bicycle with its whirring front fan-wheel and the dining room table with its white lace spread, the desk-cup bristling with pencils and pens and the books shelved neatly between ornamental book-ends: they were the hills and trees and markers of a landscape that harbored and kept her. The windows were the windows whose panes she would print with her fingers. The doorstop was the doorstop whose spring she would flitter by its crown. The lamps were the lamps in whose light she would study for school. The sofa was the sofa in whose lap she would grow to adulthood. The mirrors: the mirrors there were backed in silver and framed us in the thick of her house. Yet when we viewed the world inside of them, we did not think *here is this place made silver*, but simply *here is this place*: what does this suggest, we wondered, about the nature of material existence? When I was a small boy, I feared my attic. A ladder depended from a hatch in the hallway, and when my father scaled it into the darkness, I believed, despite the firm white evidence of the ceiling, that he was entering a chamber without a floor. A narrow wooden platform extended into open space, and beneath it lay the deep hidden well of my house: I could see this when I closed my eyes. Though Caroline's house suggested no such fear, it was informed by a similar logic of space: the floors and partitions, the shadows and doorways, were each of them rich with latent dimensions.

It is exactly this sense of latitude and secret depth that my own house is missing. The objects here are only what they are, with nothing to mediate the fact of their existence with the fact of their existence in my life. The walls may be the same hollow blue as a glacier, the carpet as dark as the gravid black sea, and I may be as slight as a boat that skirts the pass—but the walls are only walls, the carpet only carpet, and I am only and ever myself. In the evening, as the sun dwindles to a final red wire at the horizon, I switch on every light and lamp and still my house mushrooms with shadow.

I walk from room to room, and everything that belongs to me drifts by like a mist—the wooden shelves banded with bookspines, the shoes aligned in the closet, the rounded gray stone that I've carried for years . . . they are my life's little accidents, a sediment trickled through from my past: they are nothing to do with me. I look, for instance, at the photograph framed on my desk: it sports a slender green tree, and a piercing blue sky, and a light that is striking the face that I love—and how, I wonder, did I acquire such a thing? It is a gesture of hope simply to open the curtains each morning.

In truth, I don't know why it ended as it did. When Lewis arrives the next morning, the sun has not yet risen. The sidewalks are starred with mica, and the lawns are sheeted with frost, and the streetlamps glow with a clean white light. He steps to the front porch and presses the doorbell. When the door swings open, it is with such sudden violence that he briefly imagines it has been swallowed, pulled down the gullet of the wide front hall. Thomas Mitchell stands before him wearing striped red night clothes, his jaw rough with stubble. He has jostled the coatrack on his way to the door, and behind him it sways into the wall, then shudders upright on its wooden paws. He places his hand on the lock-plate, thick blue veins roping down his forearm.

"We won't be requiring your services any longer," he says, and his eyebrows shelve together toward his nose, as in a child's drawing of an angry man.

"Pardon?" asks Lewis.

"We don't need you here anymore." He announces each syllable of each word, dispassionate and meticulous, as if reciting an oath before a silent courtroom. His body has not moved, only his mouth and eyes.

Lewis would like to ask why, but Thomas Mitchell, taut with bridled anger, stands before him like a dam—exactly that solemn, exactly that impassable—and he decides against it. (*You know why,* the man would say: Lewis can see the words pooled in wait across his features. And yet, though he is coming to understand certain things— that his time here ran to a halt the day before, that his actions then were a form of betrayal—he does not, in fact, know anything.) Instead he asks, "Can I tell her goodbye?" and feels in his stomach a flutter of nervous grief.

"She's not here," says Thomas.

Lisa Mitchell's voice comes questioning from the depths of the house: "What's keeping you?"

Thomas clears his throat. He raises his hand from the lock-plate, and his breath comes huffmg through his nostrils like a plug of steam. "You can go now," he says, tightening his lips. "I don't expect to see you here again." Then, sliding back into the house, he shuts the door. The bolt-lock engages with a heavy thunk.

Lewis does not know where to go or what to do. He feels like a man who, dashing into the post office to mail a letter, discovers his face on a wanted flier. He stands staring at the doorbell—its orange glow like an ember in a settling fire—until he realizes that he is probably being watched. Glancing at the peephole, he feels the keen electric charge of a hidden gaze. Then he walks across the frost-silvered lawn to his car, his staggered footprints a dark rift in the grass. Lewis drives to the end of the block and parks. He looks into the crux of his steering wheel, his hands tented over his temples, and wonders whether Caroline has been told that he won't be returning.

On the sidewalk he passes a paper-boy who is tossing his folded white missiles from a bicycle; they sail in neat arcs through the air, striking porches and driveways with a leathery slap. He walks around the house to the window of Caroline's bedroom, his heart librating in his chest like a seesaw. The sun will soon rise from behind the curved belly of the fields. The frost will dissipate in the slow heat of morning, and his footprints will dwindle into the green of the lawn.

Caroline is awake in her bed, a sharp light streaming across her face from the open bedroom door. Her pacifier falls from her mouth as she yawns. She wiggles in a pair of fuzzy blue pajamas. Lewis presses himself to the brick of the house and watches her for a few moments. Her body casts a wide shadow over her rumpled yellow bedspread, and it looks as if there is an additional head—his—on the pillow next to hers. He touches his fingers to the window. When he curves and sways them, they look like the spindled legs of an insect. He wants to rap against the glass, to pry it from its frame, to reach across Caroline's blankets and pull her into his arms, but he doesn't.

Instead, he lowers his hand to his side, where it hangs like a plummet on a string, and as a hazy form moves into the glare of the doorway, he turns and retreats to his car. Driving away, he spots a filament of dawn sunlight in the basin of the side-view mirror. He will realize as he slows into his driveway that he has just performed one of the most truly contemptible acts of his life. If he were a good man, he would have found a way, no matter the resistance, to tell her goodbye; to hand her like an offering some statement of his love; to leave her with at least this much. He could certainly have tried.

He did not, though. He simply left.

Memories and dreams are the two most potent methods by which the mind investigates itself. Both of them are held by what is not now happening in the world, both of them alert to their own internal motion. I have begun to imagine that they are the same transaction tilted along two separate paths—one into prior possibility, the other into projected. In one of my earliest memories, I am walking through a wooded park with a teacher and my classmates. I carry in my hands a swollen rubber balloon, cherry red and inflated with helium; I don't know where it was purchased, whether it was mine or how long I'd held it, but it was almost as large as the trunk of my body—I remember that. Something jostles me, or my arm grows tired, and I lose my grip. I do not think to reach for the balloon until it has risen into the trees. It floats through a network of leaf-green branches and shrinks in the light of the midday sun. Soon it is only a grain of distant red, and then it vanishes altogether, leaving the blue sky blue and undisturbed.

Remembering this moment, I often dream of Caroline. I dream her resting in my lap and dream her swaying on the swing set. I dream that she is beside me, or I dream that she is approaching. One day, perhaps, we will flee together in my car. We will pass from this town into the rest of our lives, driving through the focus of the narrow black road. On bird-loud summer mornings, as a warm breeze rolls through our windows, we'll watch yellow-green grasshoppers pinging along the verge of the highway. In autumn, the leaves will fall red from the trees as our windshield-blades fan away pepperings of rain. The heat will billow from our dashboard vents in winter, and the houses will chimney into the low gray sky. And on the easy, tonic nights of spring, we'll pull to the side of a quiet street and spread ourselves across our ticking hood: we'll watch the far white stars and the soaring red airplanes, ask *which is the more beautiful?*, *which is the more true?*, and in finding our answers, we will find what we believe in.

✨ A FAMILY SUPPER ✨

Kazuo Ishiguro

Fugu is a fish caught off the Pacific shores of Japan. The fish has held a special significance for me ever since my mother died through eating one. The poison resides in the sexual glands of the fish, inside two fragile bags. When preparing the fish, these bags must be removed with caution, for any clumsiness will result in the poison leaking into the veins. Regrettably, it is not easy to tell whether or not this operation has been carried out successfully. The proof is, as it were, in the eating.

Fugu poisoning is hideously painful and almost always fatal. If the fish has been eaten during the evening, the victim is usually overtaken by pain during his sleep. He rolls about in agony for a few hours and is dead by morning. The fish became extremely popular in Japan after the war. Until stricter regulations were imposed, it was all the rage to perform the hazardous gutting operation in one's own kitchen, then to invite neighbors and friends round for the feast.

At the time of my mother's death, I was living in California. My relationship with my parents had become somewhat strained around that period, and consequently I did not learn of the circumstances surrounding her death until I returned to Tokyo two years later. Apparently, my mother had always refused to eat fugu, but on this particular occasion she had made an exception, having been invited by an old schoolfriend whom she was anxious not to offend. It was my father who supplied me with the details as we drove from the airport to his home in the Kamakura district. When we finally arrived, it was nearing the end of a sunny autumn day.

"Did you eat on the plane?" my father asked. We were sitting on the tatami floor of his tea-room.

"They gave me a light snack."

"You must be hungry. We'll eat as soon as Kikuko arrives."

My father was a formidable-looking man with a large stony jaw and furious black eyebrows. I think now in retrospect that he much resembled Chou En-lai, although he would not have cherished such a comparison, being particularly proud of the pure samurai blood that ran in the family. His general presence was not one which encouraged relaxed conversation; neither were things helped much by his odd way of stating each remark as if it were the concluding one. In fact, as I sat opposite him that afternoon, a boyhood memory came back to me of the time he had struck me several times around the head for "chattering like an old woman." Inevitably, our conversation since my arrival at the airport had been punctuated by long pauses.

"I'm sorry to hear about the firm," I said when neither of us had spoken for some time. He nodded gravely.

"In fact the story didn't end there," he said. "After the firm's collapse, Watanabe killed himself. He didn't wish to live with the disgrace."

"I see."

"We were partners for seventeen years. A man of principle and honor. I respected him very much."

"Will you go into business again?" I said.

"I am—in retirement. I'm too old to involve myself in new ventures now. Business these days has become so different. Dealing with foreigners. Doing things their way. I don't understand how we've come to this. Neither did Watanabe." He sighed. "A fine man. A man of principle."

The tea-room looked out over the garden. From where I sat I could make out the ancient well which as a child I had believed haunted. It was just visible now through the thick foliage. The sun had sunk low and much of the garden had fallen into shadow.

"I'm glad in any case that you've decided to come back," my father said. "More than a short visit, I hope."

"I'm not sure what my plans will be."

"I for one am prepared to forget the past. Your mother too was always ready to welcome you back—upset as she was by your behavior."

"I appreciate your sympathy. As I say, I'm not sure what my plans are."

"I've come to believe now that there were no evil intentions in your mind," my father continued. "You were swayed by certain—influences. Like so many others."

"Perhaps we should forget it, as you suggest."

"As you will. More tea?"

Just then, a girl's voice came echoing through the house.

"At last." My father rose to his feet. "Kikuko has arrived."

Despite our difference in years, my sister and I had always been close. Seeing me again seemed to make her excessively excited and for a while she did nothing but giggle nervously. But she calmed down somewhat when my father started to question her about Osaka and the university. She answered him with short formal replies. She in turn asked me a few questions, but she seemed inhibited by the fear that her questions might lead to awkward topics. After a while, the conversation had become even sparser than prior to Kikuko's arrival. Then my father stood up, saying: "I must attend to supper. Please excuse me for being burdened down by such matters. Kikuko will look after you."

My sister relaxed quite visibly once he had left the room. Within a few minutes, she was chatting freely about her friends in Osaka and about her classes at university. Then quite suddenly she decided we should walk in the garden and went striding out onto the veranda. We put on some straw sandals that had been left along the veranda rail and stepped out into the garden. The daylight had almost gone.

"I've been dying for a smoke for the last half-hour," she said, lighting a cigarette.

"Then why didn't you smoke?"

She made a furtive gesture back toward the house, then grinned mischievously.

"Oh I see," I said.

"Guess what? I've got a boyfriend now."

"Oh yes?"

"Except I'm wondering what to do. I haven't made up my mind yet."

"Quite understandable."

"You see, he's making plans to go to America. He wants me to go with him as soon as I finish studying."

"I see. And you want to go to America?"

"If we go, we're going to hitch-hike." Kikuko waved a thumb in front of my face. "People say it's dangerous, but I've done it in Osaka and it's fine."

"I see. So what is it you're unsure about?"

We were following a narrow path that wound through the shrubs and finished by the old well. As we walked, Kikuko persisted in taking unnecessarily theatrical puffs on her cigarette.

"Well. I've got lots of friends now in Osaka. I like it there. I'm not sure I want to leave them all behind just yet. And Suichi—I like him, but I'm not sure I want to spend so much time with him. Do you understand?"

"Oh perfectly."

She grinned again, then skipped on ahead of me until she reached the well. "Do you remember," she said, as I came walking up to her, "how you used to say this well was haunted?"

"Yes, I remember."

We both peered over the side.

"Mother always told me it was the old woman from the vegetable store you'd seen that night," she said. "But I never believed her and never came out here alone."

"Mother used to tell me that too. She even told me once the old woman had confessed to being the ghost. Apparently she'd been taking a short cut through our garden. I imagine she had some trouble clambering over these walls."

Kikuko gave a giggle. She then turned her back to the well, casting her gaze about the garden.

"Mother never really blamed you, you know," she said, in a new voice. I remained silent. "She always used to say to me how it was their fault, hers and Father's, for not bringing you up correctly. She used to tell me how much more careful they'd been with me, and that's why I was so good." She looked up and the mischievous grin had returned to her face. "Poor Mother," she said.

"Yes. Poor Mother."

"Are you going back to California?"

"I don't know. I'll have to see."

"What happened to—to her? To Vicki?"

"That's all finished with," I said. "There's nothing much left for me now in California."

"Do you think I ought to go there?"

"Why not? I don't know. You'll probably like it." I glanced toward the house. "Perhaps we'd better go in soon. Father might need a hand with the supper."

But my sister was once more peering down into the well. "I can't see any ghosts," she said. Her voice echoed a little.

"Is Father very upset about his firm collapsing?"

"Don't know. You can never tell with Father." Then suddenly she straightened up and turned to me. "Did he tell you about old Watanabe? What he did?"

"I heard he committed suicide."

"Well, that wasn't all. He took his whole family with him. His wife and his two little girls."

"Oh, yes?"

"Those two beautiful little girls. He turned on the gas while they were all asleep. Then he cut his stomach with a meat knife."

"Yes, Father was just telling me how Watanabe was a man of principle."

"Sick." My sister turned back to the well.

"Careful. You'll fall right in."

"I can't see any ghost," she said. "You were lying to me all that time."

"But I never said it lived down the well."

"Where is it, then?"

We both looked around at the trees and shrubs. The light in the garden had grown very dim. Eventually I pointed to a small clearing some ten yards away.

"Just there I saw it. Just there."

We stared at the spot.

"What did it look like?"

"I couldn't see very well. It was dark."

"But you must have seen something."

"It was an old woman. She was just standing there, watching me."

We kept staring at the spot as if mesmerized.

"She was wearing a white kimono," I said. "Some of her hair had come undone. It was blowing around a little."

Kikuko pushed her elbow against my arm. "Oh be quiet. You're trying to frighten me all over again." She trod on the remains of her cigarette, then for a brief moment stood regarding it with a perplexed expression. She kicked some pine needles over it, then once more displayed her grin. "Let's see if supper's ready," she said.

We found my father in the kitchen. He gave us a quick glance, then carried on with what he was doing.

"Father's become quite a chef since he's had to manage on his own," Kikuko said with a laugh. He turned and looked at my sister coldly.

"Hardly a skill I'm proud of," he said. "Kikuko, come here and help."

For some moments my sister did not move. Then she stepped forward and took an apron hanging from a drawer.

"Just these vegetables need cooking now," he said to her. "The rest just needs watching." Then he looked up and regarded me strangely for some seconds. "I expect you want to look around the house," he said eventually. He put down the chopsticks he had been holding. "It's a long time since you've seen it."

As we left the kitchen I glanced back toward Kikuko, but her back was turned.

"She's a good girl," my father said quietly.

I followed my father from room to room. I had forgotten how large the house was. A panel would slide open and another room would appear. But the rooms were all startlingly empty. In one of the rooms the lights did not come on, and we stared at the stark walls and tatami in the pale light that came from the windows.

"This house is too large for a man to live in alone," my father said. "I don't have much use for most of these rooms now."

But eventually my father opened the door to a room packed full of books and papers. There were flowers in vases and pictures on the walls. Then I noticed something
on a low table in the corner of the room. I came nearer and saw it was a plastic model
of a battleship, the kind constructed by children. It had been placed on some newspaper; scattered around it were assorted pieces of grey plastic.

My father gave a laugh. He came up to the table and picked up the model.

"Since the firm folded," he said, "I have a little more time on my hands." He
laughed again, rather strangely. For a moment his face looked almost gentle. "A little
more time."

"That seems odd," I said. "You were always so busy."

"Too busy perhaps." He looked at me with a small smile. "Perhaps I should have
been a more attentive father."

I laughed. He went on contemplating his battleship. Then he looked up. "I hadn't
meant to tell you this, but perhaps it's best that I do. It's my belief that your mother's
death was no accident. She had many worries. And some disappointments."

We both gazed at the plastic battleship.

"Surely," I said eventually, "my mother didn't expect me to live here for ever."

"Obviously you don't see. You don't see how it is for some parents. Not only must
they lose their children, they must lose them to things they don't understand." He
spun the battleship in his fingers. "These little gunboats here could have been better
glued, don't you think?"

"Perhaps. I think it looks fine."

"During the war I spent some time on a ship rather like this. But my ambition was
always the air force. I figured it like this. If your ship was struck by the enemy, all you
could do was struggle in the water hoping for a lifeline. But in an aeroplane—well—
there was always the final weapon." He put the model back onto the table. "I don't
suppose you believe in war."

"Not particularly."

He cast an eye around the room. "Supper should be ready by now," he said. "You
must be hungry."

Supper was waiting in a dimly lit room next to the kitchen. The only source of
light was a big lantern that hung over the table, casting the rest of the room into
shadow. We bowed to each other before starting the meal.

There was little conversation. When I made some polite comment about the food,
Kikuko giggled a little. Her earlier nervousness seemed to have returned to her. My
father did not speak for several minutes. Finally he said:

"It must feel strange for you, being back in Japan."

"Yes, it is a little strange."

"Already, perhaps, you regret leaving America."

"A little. Not so much. I didn't leave behind much. Just some empty rooms."

"I see."

I glanced across the table. My father's face looked stony and forbidding in the half-
light. We ate on in silence.

Then my eye caught something at the back of the room. At first I continued
eating, then my hands became still. The others noticed and looked at me. I went on
gazing into the darkness past my father's shoulder.

"Who is that? In that photograph there?"

"Which photograph?" My father turned slightly, trying to follow my gaze.

"The lowest one. The old woman in the white kimono."

My father put down his chopsticks. He looked first at the photograph, then at me.

"Your mother." His voice had become very hard. "Can't you recognize your own mother?"

"My mother. You see, it's dark. I can't see it very well."

No one spoke for a few seconds, then Kikuko rose to her feet. She took the photograph down from the wall, came back to the table and gave it to me.

"She looks a lot older," I said.

"It was taken shortly before her death," said my father.

"It was the dark. I couldn't see very well."

I looked up and noticed my father holding out a hand. I gave him the photograph. He looked at it intently, then held it toward Kikuko. Obediently, my sister rose to her feet once more and returned the picture to the wall.

There was a large pot left unopened at the center of the table. When Kikuko had seated herself again, my father reached forward and lifted the lid. A cloud of steam rose up and curled toward the lantern. He pushed the pot a little toward me.

"You must be hungry," he said. One side of his face had fallen into shadow.

"Thank you." I reached forward with my chopsticks. The steam was almost scalding. "What is it?"

"Fish."

"It smells very good."

In amidst soup were strips of fish that had curled almost into balls. I picked one out and brought it to my bowl.

"Help yourself. There's plenty."

"Thank you." I took a little more, then pushed the pot toward my father. I watched him take several pieces to his bowl. Then we both watched as Kikuko served herself.

My father bowed slightly. "You must be hungry," he said again. He took some fish to his mouth and started to eat. Then I too chose a piece and put it in my mouth. It felt soft, quite fleshy against my tongue.

"Very good," I said. "What is it?"

"Just fish."

"It's very good."

The three of us ate on in silence. Several minutes went by.

"Some more?"

"Is there enough?"

"There's plenty for all of us." My father lifted the lid and once more steam rose up. We all reached forward and helped ourselves.

"Here," I said to my father, "you have the last piece."

"Thank you."

When we had finished the meal, my father stretched out his arms and yawned with an air of satisfaction. "Kikuko," he said. "Prepare a pot of tea, please."

My sister looked at him, then left the room without comment. My father stood up.

"Let's retire to the other room. It's rather warm in here."

I got to my feet and followed him into the tea-room. The large sliding windows had been left open, bringing in a breeze from the garden. For a while we sat in silence.

"Father," I said, finally.

"Yes?"

"Kikuko tells me Watanabe-San took his whole family with him."

My father lowered his eyes and nodded. For some moments he seemed deep in thought. "Watanabe was very devoted to his work." He said at last. "The collapse of the firm was a great blow to him. I fear it must have weakened his judgment."

"You think what he did—it was a mistake?"

"Why, of course. Do you see it otherwise?"

"No, no. Of course not."

"There are other things besides work."

"Yes."

We fell silent again. The sound of locusts came in from the garden. I looked out into the darkness. The well was no longer visible.

"What do you think you will do now?" my father asked. "Will you stay in Japan for a while?"

"To be honest, I hadn't thought that far ahead."

"If you wish to stay here, I mean here in this house, you would be very welcome. That is, if you don't mind living with an old man."

"Thank you. I'll have to think about it."

I gazed out once more into the darkness.

"But of course," said my father, "this house is so dreary now. You'll no doubt return to America before long."

"Perhaps. I don't know yet."

"No doubt you will."

For some time my father seemed to be studying the back of his hands. Then he looked up and sighed.

"Kikuko is due to complete her studies next spring," he said. "Perhaps she will want to come home then. She's a good girl."

"Perhaps she will."

"Things will improve then."

"Yes, I'm sure they will."

We fell silent once more, waiting for Kikuko to bring the tea.

Mericans

Sandra Cisneros

We're waiting for the awful grandmother who is inside dropping pesos into *la ofrenda* box before the altar to La Divina Providencia. Lighting votive candles and genuflecting. Blessing herself and kissing her thumb. Running a crystal rosary between her fingers. Mumbling, mumbling, mumbling.

There are so many prayers and promises and thanks-be-to-God to be given in the name of the husband and the sons and the only daughter who never attend mass. It doesn't matter. Like La Virgen de Guadalupe, the awful grandmother intercedes on their behalf. For the grandfather who hasn't believed in anything since the first PRI elections. For my father, El Periquín, so skinny he needs his sleep. For Auntie Lightskin, who only a few hours before was breakfasting on brain and goat tacos after dancing all night in the pink zone. For Uncle Fat-Face, the blackest of the black sheep—*Always remember your Uncle Fat-Face in your prayers.* And Uncle Baby—*You go for me, Mamá—God listens to you.*

The awful grandmother has been gone a long time. She disappeared behind the heavy leather outer curtain and the dusty velvet inner. We must stay near the church entrance. We must not wander over to the balloon and punch-ball vendors. We cannot spend our allowance on fried cookies or Familia Burrón comic books or those clear cone-shaped suckers that make everything look like a rainbow when you look through them. We cannot run off and have our picture taken on the wooden ponies. We must not climb the steps up the hill behind the church and chase each other through the cemetery. We have promised to stay right where the awful grandmother left us until she returns.

There are those walking to church on their knees. Some with fat rags tied around their legs and others with pillows, one to kneel on and one to flop ahead. There are women with black shawls crossing and uncrossing themselves. There are armies of penitents carrying banners and flowered arches while musicians play tinny trumpets and tinny drums.

La Virgen de Guadalupe is waiting inside behind a plate of thick glass. There's also a gold crucifix bent crooked as a mesquite tree when someone once threw a bomb. La Virgen de Guadalupe on the main altar because she's a big miracle, the crooked crucifix on a side altar because that's a little miracle.

But we're outside in the sun. My big brother Junior hunkered against the wall with his eyes shut. My little brother Keeks running around in circles.

Maybe and most probably my little brother is imagining he's a flying feather dancer, like the ones we saw swinging high up from a pole on the Virgin's birthday. I want to be a flying feather dancer too, but when he circles past me he shouts, "I'm a B-Fifty-two bomber, you're a German," and shoots me with an invisible machine gun. I'd rather play flying feather dancers, but if I tell my brother this, he might not play with me at all.

"*Girl*. We can't play with a *girl*." *Girl*. It's my brothers' favorite insult now instead of "sissy." "You *girl*," they yell at each other. "You throw that ball like a *girl*."

I've already made up my mind to be a German when Keeks swoops past again, this time yelling, "I'm Flash Gordon. You're Ming the Merciless and the Mud People." I don't mind being Ming the Merciless but I don't like being the Mud People. Something wants to come out of the corners of my eyes, but I don't let it. Crying is what *girls* do.

I leave Keeks running around in circles—"I'm the Lone Ranger, you're Tonto." I leave Junior squatting on his ankles and go look for the awful grandmother.

Why do churches smell like the inside of an ear? Like incense and the dark and candles in blue glass? And why does holy water smell of tears? The awful grandmother makes me kneel and fold my hands. The ceiling high and everyone's prayers bumping up there like balloons.

If I stare at the eyes of the saints long enough, they move and wink at me, which makes me a sort of saint too. When I get tired of winking saints, I count the awful grandmother's mustache hairs while she prays for Uncle Old, sick from the worm, and Auntie Cuca, suffering from a life of troubles that left half her face crooked and the other half sad.

There must be a long, long list of relatives who haven't gone to church. The awful grandmother knits the names of the dead and the living into one long prayer fringed with the grandchildren born in that barbaric country with its barbarian ways.

I put my weight on one knee, then the other, and when they both grow fat as a mattress of pins, I slap them each awake. *Micaela, you may wait outside with Alfredito and Enrique.* The awful grandmother says it all in Spanish, which I understand when I'm paying attention. "What?" I say, though it's neither proper nor polite. "What?" which the awful grandmother hears as "*¿Güat?*" But she only gives me a look and shoves me toward the door.

After all that dust and dark, the light from the plaza makes me squinch my eyes like if I just came out of the movies. My brother Keeks is drawing squiggly lines on the concrete with a wedge of glass and the heel of his shoe. My brother Junior squatting against the entrance, talking to a lady and man.

They're not from here. Ladies don't come to church dressed in pants. And everybody knows men aren't supposed to wear shorts.

"*¿Quieres chicle?*" the lady asks in a Spanish too big for her mouth.

"*Gracias*." The lady gives him a whole handful of gum for free, little cellophane cubes of Chiclets, cinnamon and aqua and the white ones that don't taste like anything but are good for pretend buck teeth.

"*Por favor*," says the lady. "*¿Un foto?*" pointing to her camera.

"*Sí*."

She's so busy taking Junior's picture, she doesn't notice me and Keeks.

"Hey, Michele, Keeks. You guys want gum?"

"But you speak English!"

"Yeah," my brother says, "we're Mericans."

We're Mericans, we're Mericans, and inside the awful grandmother prays.

THE RED CONVERTIBLE

Louise Erdrich

I was the first one to drive a convertible on my reservation. And of course it was red, a red Olds. I owned that car along with my brother Henry Junior. We owned it together until his boots filled with water on a windy night and he bought out my share. Now Henry owns the whole car, and his younger brother Lyman (that's myself), Lyman walks everywhere he goes.

How did I earn enough money to buy my share in the first place? My one talent was I could always make money. I had a touch for it, unusual in a Chippewa. From the first I was different that way, and everyone recognized it. I was the only kid they let in the American Legion Hall to shine shoes, for example, and one Christmas I sold spiritual bouquets for the mission door to door. The nuns let me keep a percentage. Once I started, it seemed the more money I made the easier the money came. Everyone encouraged it. When I was fifteen I got a job washing dishes at the Joliet Café, and that was where my first big break happened.

It wasn't long before I was promoted to bussing tables, and then the short-order cook quit and I was hired to take her place. No sooner than you know it I was managing the Joliet. The rest is history. I went on managing. I soon become part owner, and of course there was no stopping me then. It wasn't long before the whole thing was mine.

After I'd owned the Joliet for one year, it blew over in the worst tornado ever seen around here. The whole operation was smashed to bits. A total loss. The fryalator was up in a tree, the grill torn in half like it was paper. I was only sixteen. I had it all in my mother's name, and I lost it quick, but before I lost it I had every one of my relatives, and their relatives, to dinner, and I also bought that red Olds I mentioned, along with Henry.

The first time we saw it! I'll tell you when we first saw it. We had gotten a ride up to Winnipeg, and both of us had money. Don't ask me why, because we never mentioned a car or anything, we just had all our money. Mine was cash, a big bankroll from the Joliet's insurance. Henry had two checks—a week's extra pay for being laid off, and his regular check from the Jewel Bearing Plant.

We were walking down Portage anyway, seeing the sights, when we saw it. There it was, parked, large as life. Really as *if* it was alive. I thought of the word *repose*, because the car wasn't simply stopped, parked, or whatever. That car reposed, calm and gleaming, a FOR SALE sign in its left front window. Then, before we had thought it over at all, the car belonged to us and our pockets were empty. We had just enough money for gas back home.

We went places in that car, me and Henry. We took off driving all one whole summer. We started off toward the Little Knife River and Mandaree in Fort Berthold and then we found ourselves down in Wakpala somehow, and then suddenly we were over in Montana on the Rocky Boys, and yet the summer was not even half over. Some people hang on to details when they travel, but we didn't let them bother us and just lived our everyday lives here to there.

I do remember this one place with willows. I remember I lay under those trees and it was comfortable. So comfortable. The branches bent down all around me like a tent or a stable. And quiet, it was quiet, even though there was a powwow close enough so I could see it going on. The air was not too still, not too windy either. When the dust rises up and hangs in the air around the dancers like that, I feel good. Henry was asleep with his arms thrown wide. Later on, he woke up and we started driving again. We were somewhere in Montana, or maybe on the Blood Reserve—it could have been anywhere. Anyway it was where we met the girl.

All her hair was in buns around her ears, that's the first thing I noticed about her. She was posed alongside the road with her arm out, so we stopped. That girl was short, so short her lumber shirt looked comical on her, like a nightgown. She had jeans on and fancy moccasins and she carried a little suitcase.

"Hop on in," says Henry. So she climbs in between us.

"We'll take you home," I says. "Where do you live?"

"Chicken," she says.

"Where the hell's that?" I ask her.

"Alaska."

"Okay," says Henry, and we drive.

We got up there and never wanted to leave. The sun doesn't truly set there in summer, and the night is more a soft dusk. You might doze off, sometimes, but before you know it you're up again, like an animal in nature. You never feel like you have to sleep hard or put away the world. And things would grow up there. One day just dirt or moss, the next day flowers and long grass. The girl's name was Susy. Her family really took to us. They fed us and put us up. We had our own tent to live in by their house, and the kids would be in and out of there all day and night. They couldn't get over me and Henry being brothers, we looked so different. We told them we knew we had the same mother, anyway.

One night Susy came in to visit us. We sat around in the tent talking of this and that. The season was changing. It was getting darker by that time, and the cold was even getting just a little mean. I told her it was time for us to go. She stood up on a chair.

"You never seen my hair," Susy said.

That was true. She was standing on a chair, but still, when she unclipped her buns the hair reached all the way to the ground. Our eyes opened. You couldn't tell how much hair she had when it was rolled up so neatly. Then my brother Henry did something funny. He went up to the chair and said, "Jump on my shoulders." So she did that, and her hair reached down past his waist, and he started twirling, this way and that, so her hair was flung out from side to side.

"I always wondered what it was like to have long pretty hair," Henry says. Well we laughed. It was a funny sight, the way he did it. The next morning we got up and took leave of those people.

. . .

On to greener pastures, as they say. It was down through Spokane and across Idaho then Montana and very soon we were racing the weather right along under the Canadian border through Columbus, Des Lacs, and then we were in Bottineau County and soon home. We'd made most of the trip, that summer, without putting up the car hood at all. We got home just in time, it turned out, for the army to remember Henry had signed up to join it.

I don't wonder that the army was so glad to get my brother that they turned him into a Marine. He was built like a brick outhouse anyway. We liked to tease him that they really wanted him for his Indian nose. He had a nose big and sharp as a hatchet, like the nose on Red Tomahawk, the Indian who killed Sitting Bull, whose profile is on signs all along the North Dakota highways. Henry went off to training camp, came home once during Christmas, then the next thing you know we got an overseas letter from him. It was 1970, and he said he was stationed up in the northern hill country. Whereabouts I did not know. He wasn't such a hot letter writer, and only got off two before the enemy caught him. I could never keep it straight, which direction those good Vietnam soldiers were from.

I wrote him back several times, even though I didn't know if those letters would get through. I kept him informed all about the car. Most of the time I had it up on blocks in the yard or half taken apart, because that long trip did a hard job on it under the hood.

I always had good luck with numbers, and never worried about the draft myself. I never even had to think about what my number was. But Henry was never lucky in the same way as me. It was at least three years before Henry came home. By then I guess the whole war was solved in the government's mind, but for him it would keep on going. In those years I'd put his car into almost perfect shape. I always thought of it as his car while he was gone, even though when he left he said, "Now it's yours," and threw me his key.

"Thanks for the extra key," I'd said. "I'll put it up in your drawer just in case I need it." He laughed.

When he came home, though, Henry was very different, and I'll say this: the change was no good. You could hardly expect him to change for the better, I know. But he was quiet, so quiet, and never comfortable sitting still anywhere but always up and moving around. I thought back to times we'd sat still for whole afternoons, never moving a muscle, just shifting our weight along the ground, talking to whoever sat with us, watching things. He'd always had a joke, then, too, and now you couldn't get him to laugh, or when he did it was more the sound of a man choking, a sound that stopped up the throats of other people around him. They got to leaving him alone most of the time, and I didn't blame them. It was a fact: Henry was jumpy and mean.

I'd bought a color TV set for my mom and the rest of us while Henry was away. Money still came very easy. I was sorry I'd ever bought it though, because of Henry. I was also sorry I'd bought color, because with black-and-white the pictures seem older and farther away. But what are you going to do? He sat in front of it, watching it, and that was the only time he was completely still. But it was the kind of stillness that you see in a rabbit when it freezes and before it will bolt. He was not easy. He sat in his chair gripping the armrests with all his might, as if the chair itself was moving at a high speed and if he let go at all he would rocket forward and maybe crash right through the set.

Once I was in the room watching TV with Henry and I heard his teeth click at something. I looked over, and he'd bitten through his lip. Blood was going down his chin. I tell you right then I wanted to smash that tube to pieces. I went over to it but Henry must have known what I was up to. He rushed from his chair and shoved me out of the way, against the wall. I told myself he didn't know what he was doing.

My mom came in, turned the set off real quiet, and told us she had made something for supper. So we went and sat down. There was still blood going down Henry's chin, but he didn't notice it and no one said anything even though every time he took a bite of his bread his blood fell onto it until he was eating his own blood mixed in with the food.

While Henry was not around we talked about what was going to happen to him. There were no Indian doctors on the reservation, and my mom was afraid of trusting Old Man Pillager because he courted her long ago and was jealous of her husbands. He might take revenge through her son. We were afraid that if we brought Henry to a regular hospital they would keep him.

"They don't fix them in those places," Mom said; "they just give them drugs."

"We wouldn't get him there in the first place," I agreed, "so let's just forget about it."

Then I thought about the car.

Henry had not even looked at the car since he'd gotten home, though like I said, it was in tip-top condition and ready to drive. I thought the car might bring the old Henry back somehow. So I bided my time and waited for my chance to interest him in the vehicle.

One night Henry was off somewhere. I took myself a hammer. I went out to that car and I did a number on its underside. Whacked it up. Bent the tail pipe double. Ripped the muffler loose. By the time I was done with the car it looked worse than any typical Indian car that has been driven all its life on reservation roads, which they always say are like government promises—full of holes. It just about hurt me, I'll tell you that! I threw dirt in the carburetor and I ripped all the electric tape off the seats. I made it look just as beat up as I could. Then I sat back and waited for Henry to find it.

Still, it took him over a month. That was all right, because it was just getting warm enough, not melting, but warm enough to work outside.

"Lyman," he says, walking in one day, "that red car looks like shit."

"Well it's old," I says. "You got to expect that."

"No way!" says Henry. "That car's a classic! But you went and ran the piss right out of it, Lyman, and you know it don't deserve that. I kept that car in A-one shape. You don't remember. You're too young. But when I left, that car was running like a watch. Now I don't even know if I can get it to start again, let alone get it anywhere near its old condition."

"Well you try," I said, like I was getting mad, "but I say it's a piece of junk."

Then I walked out before he could realize I knew he'd strung together more than six words at once.

. . .

After that I thought he'd freeze himself to death working on that car. He was out there all day, and at night he rigged up a little lamp, ran a cord out the window, and had himself some light to see by while he worked. He was better than he had been before, but that's still not saying much. It was easier for him to do the things the rest of us did. He ate more slowly and didn't jump up and down during the meal to get this or that or look out the window. I put my hand in the back of the TV set, I admit, and fiddled around with it good, so that it was almost impossible now to get a clear picture. He didn't look at it very often anyway. He was always out with that car or going off to get parts for it. By the time it was really melting outside, he had it fixed.

I had been feeling down in the dumps about Henry around this time. We had always been together before. Henry and Lyman. But he was such a loner now that I didn't know how to take it. So I jumped at the chance one day when Henry seemed friendly. It's not that he smiled or anything. He just said, "Let's take that old shitbox for a spin." Just the way he said it made me think he could be coming around.

We went out to the car. It was spring. The sun was shining very bright. My only sister, Bonita, who was just eleven years old, came out and made us stand together for a picture. Henry leaned his elbow on the red car's windshield, and he took his other arm and put it over my shoulder, very carefully, as though it was heavy for him to lift and he didn't want to bring the weight down all at once.

"Smile," Bonita said, and he did.

That picture. I never look at it anymore. A few months ago, I don't know why, I got his picture out and tacked it on the wall. I felt good about Henry at the time, close to him. I felt good having his picture on the wall, until one night when I was looking at television. I was a little drunk and stoned. I looked up at the wall and Henry was staring at me. I don't know what it was, but his smile had changed, or maybe it was gone. All I know is I couldn't stay in the same room with that picture. I was shaking. I got up, closed the door, and went into the kitchen. A little later my friend Ray came over and we both went back into that room. We put the picture in a brown bag, folded the bag over and over tightly, then put it way back in a closet.

I still see that picture now, as if it tugs at me, whenever I pass that closet door. The picture is very clear in my mind. It was so sunny that day Henry had to squint against the glare. Or maybe the camera Bonita held flashed like a mirror, blinding him, before she snapped the picture. My face is right out in the sun, big and round. But he might have drawn back, because the shadows on his face are deep as holes. There are two shadows curved like little hooks around the ends of his smile, as if to frame it and try to keep it there—that one, first smile that looked like it might have hurt his face. He has his field jacket on and the worn-in clothes he'd come back in and kept wearing ever since. After Bonita took the picture, she went into the house and we got into the car. There was a full cooler in the trunk. We started off east, toward Pembina and the Red River because Henry said he wanted to see the high water.

The trip over there was beautiful. When everything starts changing, drying up, clearing off, you feel like your whole life is starting. Henry felt it, too. The top was down and the car hummed like a top. He'd really put it back in shape, even the tape on the seats was very carefully put down and glued back in layers. It's not that he smiled again or even joked, but his face looked to me as if it was clear, more peaceful. It looked as though he wasn't thinking of anything in particular except the bare fields and windbreaks and houses we were passing.

The river was high and full of winter trash when we got there. The sun was still out, but it was colder by the river. There were still little clumps of dirty snow here and there on the banks. The water hadn't gone over the banks yet, but it would, you could tell. It was just at its limit, hard swollen, glossy like an old gray scar. We made ourselves a fire, and we sat down and watched the current go. As I watched it I felt something squeezing inside me and tightening and trying to let go all at the same time. I knew I was not just feeling it myself; I knew I was feeling what Henry was going through at that moment. Except that I couldn't stand it, the closing and opening. I jumped to my feet. I took Henry by the shoulders and I started shaking him. "Wake up," I says, "wake up, wake up, wake up!" I didn't know what had come over me. I sat down beside him again.

His face was totally white and hard. Then it broke, like stones break all of a sudden when water boils up inside them.

"I know it," he says. "I know it. I can't help it. It's no use."

We start talking. He said he knew what I'd done with the car. It was obvious it had been whacked out of shape and not just neglected. He said he wanted to give the car to me for good now, it was no use. He said he'd fixed it just to give it back and I should take it.

"No way," I says, "I don't want it."

"That's okay," he says, "you take it."

"I don't want it, though," I says back to him, and then to emphasize, just to emphasize, you understand, I touch his shoulder. He slaps my hand off.

"Take that car," he says.

"No," I say, "make me," I say, and then he grabs my jacket and rips the arm loose. That jacket is a class act, suede with tags and zippers: I push Henry backwards, off the log. He jumps up and bowls me over. We go down in a clinch and come up swinging hard, for all we're worth, with our fists. He socks my jaw so hard I feel like it swings loose. Then I'm at his ribcage and land a good one under his chin so his head snaps back. He's dazzled. He looks at me and I look at him and then his eyes are full of tears and blood and at first I think he's crying. But no, he's laughing. "Ha! Ha!" he says. "Ha! Ha! Take good care of it."

"Okay," I says. "Okay, no problem. Ha! Ha!"

I can't help it, and I start laughing, too. My face feels fat and strange, and after a while I get a beer from the cooler in the trunk, and when I hand it to Henry he takes his shirt and wipes my germs off. "Hoof-and-mouth disease," he says. For some reason this cracks me up, and so we're really laughing for a while, and then we drink all the rest of the beers one by one and throw them in the river and see how far, how fast, the current takes them before they fill up and sink.

"You want to go on back?" I ask after a while. "Maybe we could snag a couple nice Kashpaw girls."

He says nothing. But I can tell his mood is turning again.

"They're all crazy, the girls up here, every damn one of them."

"You're crazy too," I say, to jolly him up. "Crazy Lamartine boys!"

He looks as though he will take this wrong at first. His face twists, then clears, and he jumps up on his feet. "That's right!" he says. "Crazier 'n hell. Crazy Indians!"

I think it's the old Henry again. He throws off his jacket and starts swinging his legs up from the knees like a fancy dancer. He's down doing something between a grouse dance and a bunny hop, no kind of dance I ever saw before, but neither has anyone else on all this green growing earth. He's wild. He wants to pitch whoopee! He's up and at me and all over. All this time I'm laughing so hard, so hard my belly is getting tied up in a knot.

"Got to cool me off!" he shouts all of a sudden. Then he runs over to the river and jumps in.

There's boards and other things in the current. It's so high. No sound comes from the river after the splash he makes, so I run right over. I look around. It's getting dark. I see he's halfway across the water already, and I know he didn't swim there but the current took him. It's far. I hear his voice, though, very clearly across it.

"My boots are filling," he says.

He says this in a normal voice, like he just noticed and he doesn't know what to think of it. Then he's gone. A branch comes by. Another branch. And I go in.

By the time I get out of the river, off the snag I pulled myself onto, the sun is down. I walk back to the car, turn on the high beams, and drive it up the bank. I put it in first gear and then I take my foot off the clutch. I get out, close the door, and watch it plow softly into the water. The headlights reach in as they go down, searching, still lighted even after the water swirls over the back end. I wait. The wires short out. It is all finally dark. And then there is only the water, the sound of it going and running and going and running and running.

❧ WHY I LIKE COUNTRY MUSIC ❧

James Alan McPherson

No one will believe that I like country music. Even my wife scoffs when told such a possibility exists. "Go on!" Gloria tells me. "I can see blues, bebop, maybe even a little buckdancing. But not bluegrass." Gloria says, "Hillbilly stuff is not just music. It's like the New York Stock Exchange. The minute you see a sharp rise in it, you better watch out."

I tend to argue the point, but quietly, and mostly to myself. Gloria was born and raised in New York; she has come to believe in the stock exchange as the only index of economic health. My perceptions were shaped in South Carolina; and long ago I learned there, as a waiter in private clubs, to gauge economic flux by the tips people gave. We tend to disagree on other matters too, but the thing that gives me most frustration is trying to make her understand why I like country music. Perhaps it is because she hates the South and has capitulated emotionally to the horror stories told by refugees from down home. Perhaps it is because Gloria is third generation Northernborn. I do not know. What I do know is that, while the two of us are black, the distance between us is sometimes as great as that between Ibo and Yoruba. And I do know that, despite her protestations, I like country music.

"You are crazy," Gloria tells me.

I tend to argue the point, but quietly, and mostly to myself.

Of course I do not like all country stuff; just pieces that make the right connections. I like banjo because sometimes I hear ancestors in the strumming. I like the fiddle-like refrain in "Dixie" for the very same reason. But most of all I like square dancing—the interplay between fiddle and caller, the stomping, the swishing of dresses, the strutting, the proud turnings, the laughter. Most of all I like the laughter. In recent months I have wondered why I like this music and this dance. I have drawn no general conclusions, but from time to time I suspect it is because the square dance is the only dance form I ever mastered.

"I wouldn't say that in public," Gloria warns me.

I agree with her, but still affirm the truth of it, although quietly, and mostly to myself.

Dear Gloria: This is the truth of how it was:

In my youth in that distant country, while others learned to strut, I grew stiff as a winter cornstalk. When my playmates harmonized their rhythms, I stood on the sidelines in atonic detachment. While they shimmied, I merely jerked in lackluster imitation. I relate these facts here, not in remorse or self-castigation, but as a true confession of my circumstances. In those days, down in our small corner of South Carolina, proficiency in dance was a form of storytelling. A boy could say, "I traveled here and there, saw this and fought that, conquered him and made love to her, lied to them, told a few others the truth, just so I could come back here and let you know what things out there are really like." He could communicate all this with smooth,

300

graceful jiggles of his round bottom, synchronized with intricately coordinated sweeps of his arms and small, unexcited movements of his legs. Little girls could communicate much more.

But sadly, I could do none of it. Development of these skills depended on the ministrations of family and neighbors. My family did not dance; our closest neighbor was a true-believing Seventh Day Adventist. Moreover, most new dances came from up North, brought to town usually by people returning to riff on the good life said to exist in those far Northern places. They prowled our dirt streets in rented Cadillacs; paraded our brick sidewalks exhibiting styles abstracted from the fullness of life in Harlem, South Philadelphia, Roxbury, Baltimore and the South Side of Chicago. They confronted our provincial clothes merchants with the arrogant reminder, "But people ain't wearin' this in New Yokkk!" Each of their movements, as well as their world-weary smoothness, told us locals meaningful tales of what was missing in our lives. Unfortunately, those of us under strict parental supervision, or those of us without Northern connections, could only stand at a distance and worship these envoys of culture. We stood on the sidelines—styleless, gestureless, danceless, doing nothing more than an improvised one-butt shuffle—hoping for one of them to touch our lives. It was my good fortune, during my tenth year on the sidelines, to have one of these Northerners introduce me to the square dance.

My dear, dear Gloria, her name was Gweneth Lawson:

She was a pretty, chocolate-brown little girl with dark brown eyes and two long black braids. After all these years, the image of these two braids evokes in me all there is to remember about Gweneth Lawson. They were plaited across the top of her head and hung to a point just above the back of her Peter Pan collar. Sometimes she wore two bows, one red and one blue, and these tended to sway lazily near the place on her neck where the smooth brown of her skin and the white of her collar met the ink-bottle black of her hair. Even when I cannot remember her face, I remember the rainbow of deep, rich colors in which she lived. This is so because I watched them, every weekday, from my desk directly behind hers in our fourth-grade class. And she wore the most magical perfume, or lotion, smelling just slightly of fresh-cut lemons, that wafted back to me whenever she made the slightest movement at her desk. Now I must tell you this much more, dear Gloria: whenever I smell fresh lemons, whether in the market or at home, I look around me—not for Gweneth Lawson, but for some quiet corner where I can revive in private certain memories of her. And in pursuing these memories across such lemony bridges, I rediscover that I loved her.

Gweneth was from the South Carolina section of Brooklyn. Her parents had sent her south to live with her uncle, Mr. Richard Lawson, the brick mason, for an unspecified period of time. Just why they did this I do not know, unless it was their plan to have her absorb more of South Carolina folkways than conditions in Brooklyn would allow. She was a gentle, soft-spoken girl; I recall no condescension in her manner. This was all the more admirable because our unrestrained awe of a Northern-born black person usually induced in him some grand sense of his own importance. You must know that in those days older folks would point to someone and say, "He's from the North," and the statement would be sufficient in itself. Mothers made their children behave by advising that, if they led exemplary lives and attended church regularly, when they died they would go to New York. Only someone who understands what London meant to Dick Whittington, or how California and the suburbs function in the national mind, could appreciate the mythical dimensions of this Northlore.

But Gweneth Lawson was above regional idealization. Though I might have loved her partly because she was a Northerner, I loved her more because of the world of colors that seemed to be suspended above her head. I loved her glowing forehead and I loved her bright, dark brown eyes; I loved the black braids, the red and blue and sometimes yellow and pink ribbons; I loved the way the deep, rich brown of her neck melted into the pink or white cloth of her Peter Pan collar; I loved the lemony vapor on which she floated and from which, on occasion, she seemed to be inviting me to be buoyed up, up, up into her happy world; I loved the way she caused my heart to tumble whenever, during a restless moment, she seemed about to turn her head in my direction; I loved her more, though torturously, on the many occasions when she did not turn. Because I was a shy boy, I loved the way I could love her silently, at least six hours a day, without ever having to disclose my love.

My platonic state of mind might have stretched onward into a blissful infinity had not Mrs. Esther Clay Boswell, our teacher, made it her business to pry into the affair. Although she prided herself on being a strict disciplinarian, Mrs. Boswell was not without a sense of humor. A round, full-breasted woman in her early forties, she liked to amuse herself, and sometimes the class as well, by calling the attention of all eyes to whomever of us violated the structure she imposed on classroom activities. She was particularly hard on people like me who could not contain an impulse to daydream, or those who allowed their eyes to wander too far away from lessons printed on the blackboard. A black and white sign posted under the electric clock next to the door summed up her attitude toward this kind of truancy: NOTICE TO ALL CLOCK-WATCHERS, it read, TIME PASSES, WILL YOU? Nor did she abide timidity in her students. Her voice booming, "Speak up, boy!" was more than enough to cause the more emotional among us, including me, to break into convenient flows of warm tears. But by doing this we violated yet another rule, one on which depended our very survival in Mrs. Esther Clay Boswell's class. She would spell out this rule for us as she paced before her desk, slapping a thick, homemade ruler against the flat of her brown palm. "There ain't no *babies* in here," she would recite. *Thaap!* "Anybody thinks he's still a *baby* . . ." *Thaap!* ". . . should crawl back home to his mama's *titty*." *Thaap!* "You little bunnies shed your *last water* . . ." *Thaap!* ". . . the minute you left home to come in here." *Thaap!* "From now on, you g'on do all your *cryin'* . . ." *Thaap!* ". . . in *church!*" *Thaap!* Whenever one of us compelled her to make this speech it would seem to me that her eyes paused overlong on my face. She would seem to be daring me, as if suspicious that, in addition to my secret passion for Gweneth Lawson, which she might excuse, I was also in the habit of throwing fits of temper.

She had read me right. I was the product of too much attention from my father. He favored me, paraded me around on his shoulder, inflated my ego constantly with what, among us at least, was a high compliment: "You my nigger if you don't get no bigger." This statement, along with my father's generous attentions, made me selfish and used to having my own way. I *expected* to have my own way in most things, and when I could not, I tended to throw tantrums calculated to break through any barrier raised against me.

Mrs. Boswell was also perceptive in assessing the extent of my infatuation with Gweneth Lawson. Despite my stealth in telegraphing emissions of affection into the back part of Gweneth's brain, I could not help but observe, occasionally, Mrs. Boswell's cool glance pausing on the two of us. But she never said a word. Instead, she would settle her eyes momentarily on Gweneth's face and then pass quickly to mine. But in that instant she seemed to be saying, "Don't look back now, girl, but I *know* that bald-headed boy behind you has you on his mind." She seemed to watch me daily, with a combination of amusement and absolute detachment in her brown eyes. And when she stared, it was not at me but at the normal focus of my attention: the end of Gweneth Lawson's black braids. Whenever I sensed Mrs. Boswell watching I would look away quickly, either down at my brown desktop or across the room to the blackboard. But her eyes could not be eluded this easily. Without looking at anyone in particular, she could make a specific point to one person in a manner so general that only long afterward did the real object of her attention realize it had been intended for him.

"Now you little brown bunnies," she might say, "and you black buck rabbits and you few cottontails mixed in, some of you starting to smell yourselves under the arms without knowing what it's all about." And here, it sometimes seemed to me, she allowed her eyes to pause casually on me before resuming their sweep of the entire room. "Now I know your mamas already made you think life is a bed of roses, but in *my* classroom you got to know the footpaths through the *sticky* parts of the rosebed." It was her custom during this ritual to prod and goad those of us who were developing reputations for meekness and indecision; yet her method was Socratic in that she compelled us, indirectly, to supply our own answers by exploiting one person as the walking symbol of the error she intended to correct. Clarence Buford, for example, an oversized but good-natured boy from a very poor family, served often as the helpmeet in this exercise.

"Buford," she might begin, slapping the ruler against her palm, "how does a tongue-tied country boy like you expect to get a wife?"

"I don't want no wife," Buford might grumble softly.

Of course the class would laugh.

"Oh yes you do," Mrs. Boswell would respond. "All you buck rabbits want wives." *Thaap!* "So how do you let a girl know you're not just a bump on a log?"

"I know! I know!" a high voice might call from a seat across from mine. This, of course, would be Leon Pugh. A peanut-brown boy with curly hair, he seemed to know everything. Moreover, he seemed to take pride in being the only one who knew answers to life questions and would wave his arms excitedly whenever our attentions were focused on such matters. It seemed to me his voice would be extra loud and his arms waved more strenuously whenever he was certain that Gweneth Lawson, seated across from him, was interested in an answer to Mrs. Esther Clay Boswell's question. His eager arms, it seemed to me, would be reaching out to grasp Gweneth instead of the question asked.

"Buford, you twisted-tongue, bunion-toed country boy," Mrs. Boswell might say, ignoring Leon Pugh's hysterical arm waving, "you gonna let a cottontail like Leon get a girlfriend before you?"

"I don't want no girlfriend," Clarence Buford would almost sob. "I don't like no girls."

The class would laugh again while Leon Pugh manipulated his arms like a flight navigator under battle conditions. "I know! I know! I swear to *God* I know!"

When at last Mrs. Boswell would turn in his direction, I might sense that she was tempted momentarily to ask me for an answer. But as in most such exercises, it was the worldly-wise Leon Pugh who supplied this. "What do *you* think, Leon?" she would ask inevitably, but with a rather lifeless slap of the ruler against her palm.

"My daddy told me . . ." Leon would shout, turning slyly to beam at Gweneth, ". . . my daddy and my big brother from the Bronx New York told me that to git *anythin'* in this world you gotta learn how to blow your own horn."

"Why, Leon?" Mrs. Boswell might ask in a bored voice.

"Because," the little boy would recite, puffing out his chest, "because if you don't blow your own horn ain't nobody else g'on blow it for you. That's what my daddy said."

"What do you think about that, Buford?" Mrs. Boswell would ask.

"I don't want no girlfriend anyhow," the puzzled Clarence Buford might say.

And then the cryptic lesson would suddenly be dropped.

This was Mrs. Esther Clay Boswell's method of teaching. More than anything written on the blackboard, her questions were calculated to make us turn around in our chairs and inquire in guarded whispers of each other, and especially of the wise and confident Leon Pugh, "What does she mean?" But none of us, besides Pugh, seemed able to comprehend what it was we ought to know but did not know. And Mrs. Boswell, plump brown fox that she was, never volunteered any more in the way of confirmation than was necessary to keep us interested. Instead, she paraded around us, methodically slapping the homemade ruler against her palm, suggesting by her silence more depth to her question, indeed, more implications in Leon's answer, than we were then able to perceive. And during such moments, whether inspired by self-ishness or by the peculiar way Mrs. Boswell looked at me, I felt that finding answers to such questions was a task she had set for me, of all the members of the class.

Of course Leon Pugh, among other lesser lights, was my chief rival for the affections of Gweneth Lawson. All during the school year, from September through the winter rains, he bested me in my attempts to look directly into her eyes and say a simple, heartfelt "hey." This was my ambition, but I never seemed able to get close enough to get her attention. At Thanksgiving I helped draw a bounteous yellow cornucopia on the blackboard, with fruits and flowers matching the colors that floated around Gweneth's head; Leon Pugh made one by himself, a masterwork of silver paper and multicolored crepe, which he hung on the door. Its silver tail curled upward to a point just below the face of Mrs. Boswell's clock. At Christmas, when we drew names out of a hat for the exchange of gifts, I drew the name of Queen Rose Phipps, a fairly unattractive squash-yellow girl of absolutely no interest to me. Pugh, whether through collusion with the boy who handled the lottery or through pure luck, pulled forth from the hat the magic name of Gweneth Lawson. He gave her a set of deep purple bows for her braids and a basket of pecans from his father's tree. Uninterested now in the spirit of the occasion, I delivered to Queen Rose Phipps a pair of white socks. Each time Gweneth wore the purple bows she would glance over at Leon and smile. Each time Queen Rose wore my white socks I would turn away in embarrassment, lest I should see them pulling down into her shoes and exposing her skinny ankles.

After class, on wet winter days, I would trail along behind Gweneth to the bus stop, pause near the steps while she entered, and follow her down the aisle until she chose a seat. Usually, however, in clear violation of the code of conduct to which all gentlemen were expected to adhere, Leon Pugh would already be on the bus and shouting to passersby, "Move off! Get away! This here seat by me is reserved for the girl from Brooklyn New York." Discouraged but not defeated, I would swing into the seat next nearest her and cast calf-eyed glances of wounded affection at the back of her head or at the brown, rainbow profile of her face. And at her stop, some eight or nine blocks from mine, I would disembark behind her along with a crowd of other love-struck boys. There would then follow a well-rehearsed scene in which all of us, save Leon Pugh, pretended to have gotten off the bus either too late or too soon to wend our proper paths homeward. And at slight cost to ourselves we enjoyed the advantage of being able to walk close by her as she glided toward her uncle's green-frame house. There, after pausing on the wooden steps and smiling radiantly around the crowd like a spring sun in that cold winter rain, she would sing, "Bye, y'all," and disappear into the structure with the mystery of a goddess. Afterward I would walk away, but slowly, much slower than the other boys, warmed by the music and light in her voice against the sharp, wet winds of the February afternoon.

I loved her, dear Gloria, and I danced with her and smelled the lemony youth of her and told her that I loved her, all this in a way you would never believe:

You would not know or remember, as I do, that in those days, in our area of the country, we enjoyed a pleasingly ironic mixture of Yankee and Confederate folkways. Our meals and manners, our speech, our attitudes toward certain ambiguous areas of history, even our acceptance of tragedy as the normal course of life—these things and more defined us as Southern. Yet the stern morality of our parents, their toughness and penny-pinching and attitudes toward work, their covert allegiance toward certain ideals, even the directions toward which they turned our faces, made us more Yankee than Cavalier. Moreover, some of our schools were named for Confederate men of distinction, but others were named for the stern-faced believers who had swept down from the North to save a people back, back long ago, in those long-forgotten days of once upon a time. Still, our schoolbooks, our required classroom songs, our flags, our very relation to the statues and monuments in public parks, negated the story that these dreamers from the North had ever come. We sang the state song, memorized the verses of homegrown poets, honored in our books the names and dates of historical events both before and after that Historical Event which, in our region, supplanted even the division of the millennia introduced by the followers of Jesus Christ. Given the silent circumstances of our cultural environment, it was ironic, and perhaps just, that we maintained a synthesis of two traditions no longer supportive of each other. Thus it became traditional at our school to celebrate the arrival of spring on May first by both the ritual plaiting of the Maypole and square dancing.

On that day, as on a few others, the Superintendent of Schools and several officials were likely to visit our schoolyard and stand next to the rusty metal swings, watching the fourth, fifth, and sixth graders bob up and down and behind and before each other, around the gaily painted Maypoles. These happy children would pull and twist long runs of billowy crepe paper into wondrous, multicolored plaits. Afterward, on the edges of thunderous applause from teachers, parents and visiting dignitaries, a wave of elaborately costumed children would rush out onto the grounds in groups of eight and proceed with the square dance. "Doggone!" the Superintendent of Schools was heard to exclaim on one occasion. "Y'all do it so good it just makes your *bones* set up and take notice."

Such was the schedule two weeks prior to May first, when Mrs. Boswell announced to our class that as fourth graders we were now eligible to participate in the festivities. The class was divided into two general sections of sixteen each, one group preparing to plait the pole and a second group, containing an equal number of boys and girls, practicing turns for our part in the square dance. I was chosen to square dance; so was Leon Pugh. Gweneth Lawson was placed with the pole plaiters. I was depressed until I remembered, happily, that I could not dance a lick. I reported this fact to Mrs. Boswell just after drawing, during recess, saying that my lack of skill would only result in our class making a poor showing. I asked to be reassigned to the group of Maypole plaiters. Mrs. B. looked me over with considerable amusement tugging at the corners of her mouth. "Oh, you don't have to *dance* to do the square dance," she said. "That's a dance that was made up to mock folks that couldn't dance." She paused a second before adding thoughtfully: "The worse you are at dancing, the better you can square dance. It's just about the best dance in the world for a stiff little bunny like you."

"I want to plait the Maypole," I said.

"You'll square dance or I'll grease your little butt," Mrs. Esther Clay Boswell said.

"I ain't gonna do *nothin'*!" I muttered. But I said this quietly, and mostly to myself, while walking away from her desk. For the rest of the day she watched me closely, as if she knew what I was thinking.

The next morning I brought a note from my father. "Dear Mrs. Boswell:" I had watched him write earlier that morning, "My boy does not square dance. Please excuse him as I am afraid he will break down and cry and mess up the show. Yours truly . . ."

Mrs. Boswell said nothing after she had read the note. She merely waved me to my seat. But in the early afternoon, when she read aloud the lists of those assigned to dancing and Maypole plaiting, she paused as my name rolled off her tongue. "You don't have to stay on the square dance team," she called to me. "You go on out in the yard with the Maypole team."

I was ecstatic. I hurried to my place in line some three warm bodies behind Gweneth Lawson. We prepared to march out.

"Wait a minute," Mrs. Boswell called. "Now it looks like we got seventeen bunnies on the Maypole team and fifteen on the square dance. We have to even things up." She made a thorough examination of both lists, scratching her head. Then she looked carefully up and down the line of stomping Maypoleites. "Miss Gweneth Lawson, you cute little cottontail you, it looks like you gonna have to go over to the square dance team. That'll give us eight sets of partners for the square dance . . . but now we have another problem." She made a great display of counting the members of the two squads of square dancers. "Now there's sixteen square dancers all right, but when we pair them off we got a problem of higher mathematics. With nine girls and only seven *boys*, looks like we gotta switch a girl from square dancing to Maypole and a boy from Maypole to square dancing"

I waited hopefully for Gweneth Lawson to volunteer. But just at that moment the clever Leon Pugh grabbed her hand and began jitterbugging as though he could hardly wait for the record player to be turned on and the dancing to begin.

"What a cute couple," Mrs. Boswell observed absently. "Now which one of you other girls wants to join up with the Maypole team?"

Following Pugh's example, the seven remaining boys grabbed the girls they wanted as partners. Only skinny Queen Rose Phipps and shy Beverly Hankins remained unclaimed. Queen Rose giggled nervously.

"Queen Rose," Mrs. B. called, "I know you don't mind plaiting the Maypole." She waved her ruler in a gesture of a casual dismissal. Queen Rose raced across the room and squeezed into line.

"*Now*," Mrs. Boswell said, "I need a boy to come across to the square dancers."

I was not unmindful of the free interchange of partners involved in square dancing, even though Leon Pugh had beat me in claiming the partner of my choice. All I really wanted was one moment swinging Gweneth Lawson in my arms. I raised my hand slowly.

"Oh, not *you*, little bunny," Mrs. Boswell said. "You and your daddy claim you don't like to square dance." She slapped her ruler against her palm. *Thaap! Thaap!* Then she said, "Clarence Buford, I *know* a big-footed country boy like you can square dance better than anybody. Come on over here and kiss cute little Miss Beverly Hankins."

"I don't like no girls *noway*," Buford mumbled. But he went over and stood next to the giggling Beverly Hankins.

"Now!" said Mrs. B. "March on out in that yard and give that pole a good plaiting!"

We started to march out. Over my shoulder, as I reached the door, I glimpsed the overjoyed Leon Pugh whirling lightly on his toes. He sang in a confident tone:

> I saw the Lord give Moses a pocketful of roses.
> I skid Ezekiel's wheel on a ripe banana peel.
> I rowed the Nile, flew over a stile,
> Saw Jack Johnson pick his teeth
> With toenails from Jim Jeffries' feets . . ."

"Grab your partners!" Mrs. Esther Clay Boswell was saying as the oak door slammed behind us.

I had been undone. For almost two weeks I was obliged to stand on the sidelines and watch Leon Pugh allemande left and do-si-do my beloved Gweneth. Worse, she seemed to be enjoying it. But I must give Leon proper credit: he was a dancing fool. In a matter of days he had mastered, and then improved on, the various turns and bows and gestures of the square dance. He leaped while the others plodded, whirled each girl through his arms with lightness and finesse, chattered playfully at the other boys when they tumbled over their own feet. Mrs. Boswell stood by the record player calling, "Put some *strut* in it, Buford, you big potato sack. Watch Leon and see how *he* does it." I leaned against the classroom wall and watched the dancers, my own group having already exhausted the limited variations possible in matters of Maypole plaiting.

At home each night I begged my father to send another note to Mrs. Boswell, this time stating that I had no interest in the Maypole. But he resisted my entreaties and even threatened me with a whipping if I did not participate and make him proud of me. The real cause of his irritation was the considerable investment he had already made in purchasing an outfit for me. Mrs. Boswell had required all her students, square dancers and Maypole plaiters alike, to report on May first in outfits suitable for square dancing. My father had bought a new pair of dungarees, a blue shirt, a red and white polka-dot bandanna and a cowboy hat. He was in no mood to bend under the emotional weight of my new demands. As a matter of fact, early in the morning of May first he stood beside my bed with the bandanna in his left hand and his leather belt in his right hand, just in case I developed a sudden fever.

I dragged myself heavily through the warm, blue spring morning toward school, dressed like a carnival cowboy. When I entered the classroom I sulked against the wall, being content to watch the other children. And what happy buzzings and jumping and excitement they made as they compared costumes. Clarence Buford wore a Tom Mix hat and a brown vest over a green shirt with red six-shooter patterns embossed on its collar. Another boy, Paul Carter, was dressed entirely in black, with a fluffy white handkerchief puffing from his neck. But Leon Pugh caught the attention of all our eyes. He wore a red and white checkered shirt, a loose green bandanna clasped at his throat by a shining silver buffalo head, brown chaps sewed onto his dungarees, and shiny brown cowboy boots with silver spurs that clanked each time he moved. In his hand he carried a carefully creased brown cowboy hat. He announced his fear that it would lose its shape and planned to put it on only when the dancing started. He would allow no one to touch it. Instead, he stood around clanking his feet and smoothing the crease in his fabulous hat and saying loudly, "My daddy says it pays to look good no matter what you put on."

The girls seemed prettier and much older than their ages. Even Queen Rose Phipps wore rouge on her cheeks that complemented her pale color. Shy Beverly Hankins had come dressed in a blue and white checkered bonnet and a crisp blue apron; she looked like a frontier mother. But Gweneth Lawson, my Gweneth Lawson, dominated the group of girls. She wore a long red dress with sheaves and sheaves of sparkling white crinoline belling it outward so it seemed she was floating. On her honey-brown wrists golden bracelets sparkled. A deep blue bandanna enclosed her head with the wonder of a summer sky. Black patent leather shoes glistened like half-hidden stars beneath the red and white of her hemline. She stood smiling before us and we marveled. At that moment I would have given the world to have been able to lead her about on my arm.

Mrs. Boswell watched us approvingly from behind her desk. Finally, at noon, she called, "Let's go on out!" Thirty-two living rainbows cascaded toward the door. Pole plaiters formed one line. Square dancers formed another. Mrs. Boswell strolled officiously past us in review. It seemed to me she almost paused while passing the spot where I stood in line. But she brushed past me, straightening an apron here, applying spittle and a rub to a rouged cheek there, waving a wary finger at an over-anxious boy. Then she whacked her ruler against her palm and led us out into the yard. The fifth and sixth graders had already assembled. On one end of the playground were a dozen or so tall painted poles with long, thin wisps of green and blue and yellow and rust-brown crepe floating lazily on the sweet spring breezes.

"Maypole teams *up!*" called Mr. Henry Lucas, our principal, from his platform by the swings. Beside him stood the white Superintendent of Schools (who said later of the square dance, it was reported to all the classes, "Lord y'all square dance so *good* it makes me plumb *ashamed* us white folks ain't takin' better care of our art stuff."). "Maypole teams up!" Mr. Henry Lucas shouted again. Some fifty of us, screaming shrilly, rushed to grasp our favorite color crepe. Then, to the music of "Sing Praise for All the Brightness and the Joy of Spring," we pulled and plaited in teams of six or seven until every pole was twisted as tight and as colorfully as the braids on Gweneth Lawson's head. Then, to the applause of proud teachers and parents and the whistles of the Superintendent of Schools, we scattered happily back under the wings of our respective teachers. I stood next to Mrs. Boswell, winded and trembling but confident I had done my best. She glanced down at me and said in a quiet voice, "I do believe you are learning the rhythm of the thing."

I did not respond.

"Let's *go!*" Leon Pugh shouted to the other kids, grabbing Gweneth Lawson's arm and taking a few clanking steps forward.

"Wait a minute, Leon," Mrs. Boswell hissed. "Mr. Lucas has to change the record."

Leon sighed. "But if we don't git out there first, all them other teams will take the best spots."

"Wait!" Mrs. Boswell ordered.

Leon sulked. He inched closer to Gweneth. I watched him swing her hand impatiently. He stamped his feet and his silver spurs jangled.

Mrs. Boswell looked down at his feet. "Why, Leon," she said, "you can't go out there with razors on your shoes."

"These ain't razors," Leon muttered. "These here are spurs my brother in Bronx New York sent me just for this here dance."

"You have to take them off," Mrs. Boswell said.

Leon growled. But he reached down quickly and attempted to jerk the silver spurs from the heels of his boots. They did not come off. "No time!" he called, standing suddenly. "Mr. Lucas done put the record on."

"Leon, you might *cut* somebody with those things," Mrs. Boswell said. "Miss Gweneth Lawson's pretty red dress could get caught in those things and then she'll fall as surely as I'm standin' here."

"I'll just go out with my boots off," Leon replied.

But Mrs. Boswell shook her head firmly. "You just run on to the lunchroom and ask Cook for some butter or mayo. That'll help 'em slip off." She paused, looking out over the black dirt playground. "And if you miss the first dance, why, there'll be a second and maybe even a third. We'll get a Maypole plaiter to sub for you."

My heart leaped. Leon sensed it and stared at me. His hand tightened on Gweneth's as she stood radiant and smiling in the loving spring sunlight. Leon let her hand drop and bent quickly, pulling at the spurs with the fury of a Samson.

"Square dancers *up!*" Mr. Henry Lucas called.

"Sonofa*bitch!*" Leon grunted.

"Square dancers *up!*" called Mr. Lucas.

The fifth and sixth graders were screaming and rushing toward the center of the yard. Already the record was scratching out the high, slick voice of the caller. "*Sonofabitch!*" Leon moaned.

Mrs. Boswell looked directly at Gweneth, standing alone and abandoned next to Leon. "Miss Gweneth Lawson," Mrs. Boswell said in a cool voice, "it's a cryin' shame there ain't no prince to take you to that ball out there."

I do not remember moving, but I know I stood with Gweneth at the center of the yard. What I did there I do not know, but I remember watching the movements of others and doing what they did just after they had done it. Still, I cannot remember just when I looked into my partner's face or what I saw there. The scratchy voice of the caller bellowed directions and I obeyed:

> "*Allemande left with your left hand*
> *Right to your partner with a right and left grand . . .*"

Although I was told later that I made an allemande right instead of left, I have no memory of the mistake.

> "*When you get to your partner pass her by*
> *And pick up the next girl on the sly . . .*"

Nor can I remember picking up any other girl. I only remember that during many turns and do-si-dos I found myself looking into the warm brown eyes of Gweneth Lawson. I recall that she smiled at me. I recall that she laughed on another turn. I recall that I laughed with her an eternity later.

> "*. . . promenade that dear old thing*
> *Throw your head right back and sing be-cause, just be-cause . . .*"

I do remember quite well that during the final promenade before the record ended, Gweneth stood beside me and I said to her in a voice much louder than that of the caller, "When I get up to Brooklyn I hope I see you." But I do not remember what she said in response. I want to remember that she smiled.

I know I smiled, dear Gloria. I smiled with the lemonness of her and the loving of her pressed deep into those saving places of my private self. It was my plan to savor these, and I did savor them. But when I reached New York, many years later, I did not think of Brooklyn. I followed the old, beaten, steady paths into uptown Manhattan. By then I had learned to dance to many other kinds of music. And I had forgotten the savory smell of lemon. But I think sometimes of Gweneth now when I hear country music. And although it is difficult to explain to you, I still maintain that I am no mere arithmetician in the art of the square dance. I am into the calculus of it.

"Go on!" you will tell me, backing into your Northern mythology. "I can see the hustle, the hump, maybe even the Ibo highlife. But no hillbilly."

These days I am firm about arguing the point, but, as always, quietly, and mostly to myself.

❧ I Stand Here Ironing ❧

Tillie Olsen

I stand here ironing, and what you asked me moves tormented back and forth with the iron.

"I wish you would manage the time to come in and talk with me about your daughter. I'm sure you can help me understand her. She's a youngster who needs help and whom I'm deeply interested in helping."

"Who needs help." . . . Even if I came, what good would it do? You think because I am her mother I have a key, or that in some way you could use me as a key? She has lived for nineteen years. There is all that life that has happened outside of me, beyond me.

And when is there time to remember, to sift, to weigh, to estimate, to total? I will start and there will be an interruption and I will have to gather it all together again. Or I will become engulfed with all I did or did not do, with what should have been and what cannot be helped.

She was a beautiful baby. The first and only one of our five that was beautiful at birth. You do not guess how new and uneasy her tenancy in her now-loveliness. You did not know her all those years she was thought homely, or see her poring over her baby pictures, making me tell her over and over how beautiful she had been—and would be, I would tell her—and was now, to the seeing eye. But the seeing eyes were few or non-existent. Including mine.

I nursed her. They feel that's important nowadays. I nursed all the children, but with her, with all the fierce rigidity of first motherhood, I did like the books then said. Though her cries battered me to trembling and my breasts ached with swollenness, I waited till the clock decreed.

Why do I put that first? I do not even know if it matters, or if it explains anything.

She was a beautiful baby. She blew shining bubbles of sound. She loved motion, loved light, loved color and music and textures. She would lie on the floor in her blue overalls patting the surface so hard in ecstasy her hands and feet would blur. She was a miracle to me, but when she was eight months old I had to leave her daytimes with the woman downstairs to whom she was no miracle at all, for I worked or looked for work and for Emily's father, who "could no longer endure" (he wrote in his good-bye note) "sharing want with us."

I was nineteen. It was the pre-relief, pre-WPA world of the Depression. I would start running as soon as I got off the streetcar, running up the stairs, the place smelling sour, and awake or asleep to startle awake, when she saw me she would break into a clogged weeping that could not be comforted, a weeping I can hear yet.

After a while I found a job hashing at night so I could be with her days, and it was better. But it came to where I had to bring her to his family and leave her.

It took a long time to raise the money for her fare back. Then she got chicken pox and I had to wait longer. When she finally came, I hardly knew her, walking quick

312

and nervous like her father, looking like her father, thin, and dressed in a shoddy red that yellowed her skin and glared at the pockmarks. All the baby loveliness gone.

She was two. Old enough for nursery school they said, and I did not know then what I know now—the fatigue of the long day, and the lacerations of group life in the kinds of nurseries that are only parking places for children.

Except that it would have made no difference if I had known. It was the only place there was. It was the only way we could be together, the only way I could hold a job.

And even without knowing, I knew. I knew the teacher that was evil because all these years it has curdled into my memory, the little boy hunched in the corner, her rasp, "why aren't you outside, because Alvin hits you? that's no reason, go out, scaredy." I knew Emily hated it even if she did not clutch and implore "don't go Mommy" like the other children, mornings.

She always had a reason why we should stay home. Momma, you look sick. Momma, I feel sick. Momma, the teachers aren't there today, they're sick. Momma, we can't go, there was a fire there last night. Momma, it's a holiday today, no school, they told me.

But never a direct protest, never rebellion. I think of our others in their three-, four-year-oldness—the explosions, the tempers, the denunciations, the demands— and I feel suddenly ill. I put the iron down. What in me demanded that goodness in her? And what was the cost, the cost to her of such goodness?

The old man living in the back once said in his gentle way: "You should smile at Emily more when you look at her." What *was* in my face when I looked at her? I loved her. There were all the acts of love.

It was only with the others I remembered what he said, and it was the face of joy, and not of care or tightness or worry I turned to them—too late for Emily. She does not smile easily, let alone almost always as her brothers and sisters do. Her face is closed and sombre, but when she wants, how fluid. You must have seen it in her pantomimes, you spoke of her rare gift for comedy on the stage that rouses a laughter out of the audience so dear they applaud and applaud and do not want to let her go.

Where does it come from, that comedy? There was none of it in her when she came back to me that second time, after I had had to send her away again. She had a new daddy now to learn to love, and I think perhaps it was a better time.

Except when we left her alone nights, telling ourselves she was old enough.

"Can't you go some other time, Mommy, like tomorrow?" she would ask. "Will it be just a little while you'll be gone? Do you promise?"

The time we came back, the front door open, the clock on the floor in the hall. She rigid awake. "It wasn't just a little while. I didn't cry. Three times I called you, just three times, and then I ran downstairs to open the door so you could come faster. The clock talked loud. I threw it away, it scared me what it talked."

She said the clock talked loud again that night I went to the hospital to have Susan. She was delirious with the fever that comes before red measles, but she was fully conscious all the week I was gone and the week after we were home when she could not come near the new baby or me.

She did not get well. She stayed skeleton thin, not wanting to eat, and night after night she had nightmares. She would call for me, and I would rouse from exhaustion to sleepily call back: "You're all right, darling, go to sleep, it's just a dream," and if she still called, in a sterner voice, "now go to sleep, Emily, there's nothing to hurt you." Twice, only twice, when I had to get up for Susan anyhow, I went in to sit with her.

Now when it is too late (as if she would let me hold and comfort her like I do the others) I get up and go to her at once at her moan or restless stirring. "Are you awake, Emily? Can I get you something?" And the answer is always the same: "No, I'm all right, go back to sleep, Mother."

They persuaded me at the clinic to send her away to a convalescent home in the country where "she can have the kind of food and care you can't manage for her, and you'll be free to concentrate on the new baby." They still send children to that place. I see pictures on the society page of sleek young women planning affairs to raise money for it, or dancing at the affairs, or decorating Easter eggs or filling Christmas stockings for the children.

They never have a picture of the children so I do not know if the girls still wear those gigantic red bows and the ravaged looks on the every other Sunday when parents can come to visit "unless otherwise notified"—as we were notified the first six weeks.

Oh it is a handsome place, green lawns and tall trees and fluted flower beds. High up on the balconies of each cottage the children stand, the girls in their red bows and white dresses, the boys in white suits and giant red ties. The parents stand below shrieking up to be heard and the children shriek down to be heard, and between them the invisible wall "Not To Be Contaminated by Parental Germs or Physical Affection."

There was a tiny girl who always stood hand in hand with Emily. Her parents never came. One visit she was gone. "They moved her to Rose Cottage" Emily shouted in explanation. "They don't like you to love anybody here."

She wrote once a week, the labored writing of a seven-year-old. "I am fine. How is the baby. If I write my leter nicly I will have a star. Love." There never was a star. We wrote every other day, letters she could never hold or keep but only hear read—once. "We simply do not have room for children to keep any personal possessions," they patiently explained when we pieced one Sunday's shrieking together to plead how much it would mean to Emily, who loved so to keep things, to be allowed to keep her letters and cards.

Each visit she looked frailer. "She isn't eating," they told us.

(They had runny eggs for breakfast or mush with lumps, Emily said later, I'd hold it in my mouth and not swallow. Nothing ever tasted good, just when they had chicken.)

It took us eight months to get her released home, and only the fact that she gained back so little of her seven lost pounds convinced the social worker.

I used to try to hold and love her after she came back, but her body would stay stiff, and after a while she'd push away. She ate little. Food sickened her, and I think much of life too. Oh she had physical lightness and brightness, twinkling by on skates, bouncing like a ball up and down up and down over the jump rope, skimming over the hill; but these were momentary.

She fretted about her appearance, thin and dark and foreign-looking at a time when every little girl was supposed to look or thought she should look a chubby blonde replica of Shirley Temple. The doorbell sometimes rang for her, but no one seemed to come and play in the house or be a best friend. Maybe because we moved so much.

There was a boy she loved painfully through two school semesters. Months later she told me how she had taken pennies from my purse to buy him candy. "Licorice was his favorite and I brought him some every day, but he still liked Jennifer better'n me. Why, Mommy?" The kind of question for which there is no answer.

School was a worry to her. She was not glib or quick in a world where glibness and quickness were easily confused with ability to learn. To her overworked and exasperated teachers she was an overconscientious "slow learner" who kept trying to catch up and was absent entirely too often.

I let her be absent, though sometimes the illness was imaginary. How different from my now-strictness about attendance with the others. I wasn't working. We had a new baby, I was home anyhow. Sometimes, after Susan grew old enough, I would keep her home from school, too, to have them all together.

Mostly Emily had asthma, and her breathing, harsh and labored, would fill the house with a curiously tranquil sound. I would bring the two old dresser mirrors and her boxes of collections to her bed. She would select beads and single earrings, bottle tops and shells, dried flowers and pebbles, old postcards and scraps, all sorts of oddments; then she and Susan would play Kingdom, setting up landscapes and furniture, peopling them with action.

Those were the only times of peaceful companionship between her and Susan. I have edged away from it, that poisonous feeling between them, that terrible balancing of hurts and needs I had to do between the two, and did so badly, those earlier years.

Oh there are conflicts between the others too, each one human, needing, demanding, hurting, taking—but only between Emily and Susan, no, Emily toward Susan that corroding resentment. It seems so obvious on the surface, yet it is not obvious. Susan, the second child, Susan, golden- and curly-haired and chubby, quick and articulate and assured, everything in appearance and manner Emily was not; Susan, not able to resist Emily's precious things, losing or sometimes clumsily breaking them; Susan telling jokes and riddles to company for applause while Emily sat silent (to say to me later: that was *my* riddle, Mother, I told it to Susan); Susan, who for all the five years' difference in age was just a year behind Emily in developing physically.

I am glad for that slow physical development that widened the difference between her and her contemporaries, though she suffered over it. She was too vulnerable for that terrible world of youthful competition, of preening and parading, of constant measuring of yourself against every other, of envy, "If I had that copper hair," "If I had that skin. . . ." She tormented herself enough about not looking like the others, there was enough of the unsureness, the having to be conscious of words before you speak, the constant caring—what are they thinking of me? without having it all magnified by the merciless physical drives.

Ronnie is calling. He is wet and I change him. It is rare there is such a cry now. That time of motherhood is almost behind me when the ear is not one's own but must always be racked and listening for the child cry, the child call. We sit for a while and I hold him, looking out over the city spread in charcoal with its soft aisles of light. "*Shoogily*," he breathes and curls closer. I carry him back to bed, asleep. *Shoogily*. A funny word, a family word, inherited from Emily, invented by her to say: *comfort*.

In this and other ways she leaves her seal, I say aloud. And startle at my saying it. What do I mean? What did I start to gather together, to try and make coherent? I was at the terrible, growing years. War years. I do not remember them well. I was working, there were four smaller ones now, there was not time for her. She had to help be a mother, and housekeeper, and shopper. She had to set her seal. Mornings of crisis and near hysteria trying to get lunches packed, hair combed, coats and shoes found, everyone to school or Child Care on time, the baby ready for transportation. And always the paper scribbled on by a smaller one, the book looked at by Susan then mislaid, the homework not done. Running out to that huge school where she was one, she was lost, she was a drop; suffering over her unpreparedness, stammering and unsure in her classes.

There was so little time left at night after the kids were bedded down. She would struggle over books, always eating (it was in those years she developed her enormous appetite that is legendary in our family) and I would be ironing, or preparing food for the next day, or writing V-mail to Bill, or tending the baby. Sometimes, to make me laugh, or out of her despair, she would imitate happenings or types at school.

I think I said once: "Why don't you do something like this in the school amateur show?" One morning she phoned me at work, hardly understandable through the weeping: "Mother, I did it. I won, I won; they gave me first prize; they clapped and clapped and wouldn't let me go."

Now suddenly she was Somebody, and as imprisoned in her difference as she had been in her anonymity.

She began to be asked to perform at other high schools, even in colleges, then at city and statewide affairs. The first one we went to, I only recognized her that first moment when thin, shy, she almost drowned herself into the curtains. Then: Was this Emily? The control, the command, the convulsing and deadly clowning, the spell, then the roaring, stamping audience, unwilling to let this rare and precious laughter out of their lives.

Afterwards: You ought to do something about her with a gift like that—but without money or knowing how, what does one do? We have left it all to her, and the gift has as often eddied inside, clogged and clotted, as been used and growing.

She is coming. She runs up the stairs two at a time with her light graceful step, and I know she is happy tonight. Whatever it was that occasioned your call did not happen today.

"Aren't you ever going to finish the ironing, Mother? Whistler painted his mother in a rocker. I'd have to paint mine standing over an ironing board." This is one of her communicative nights and she tells me everything and nothing as she fixes herself a plate of food out of the icebox.

She is so lovely. Why did you want me to come in at all? Why were you concerned? She will find her way.

She starts up the stairs to bed. "Don't get *me* up with the rest in the morning." "But I thought you were having midterms." "Oh, those," she comes back in, kisses me, and says quite lightly, "in a couple of years when we'll all be atom-dead they won't matter a bit."

She has said it before. She *believes* it. But because I have been dredging the past, and all that compounds a human being is so heavy and meaningful in me, I cannot endure it tonight.

I will never total it all. I will never come in to say: She was a child seldom smiled at. Her father left me before she was a year old. I had to work away from her her first six years when there was work, or I sent her home and to his relatives. There were years she had care she hated. She was dark and thin and foreign-looking in a world where the prestige went to blondeness and curly hair and dimples, she was slow where glibness was prized. She was a child of anxious, not proud, love. We were poor and could not afford for her the soil of easy growth. I was a young mother, I was a distracted mother. There were the other children pushing up, demanding. Her younger sister seemed all that she was not. There were years she did not let me touch her. She kept too much in herself, her life was such she had to keep too much in herself. My wisdom came too late. She has much to her and probably little will come of it. She is a child of her age, of depression, of war, of fear.

Let her be. So all that is in her will not bloom—but in how many does it? There is still enough left to live by. Only help her to know—help make it so there is cause for her to know—that she is more than this dress on the ironing board, helpless before the iron.

CREDITS

Jeremy Blodgett. "Not Even Angels Are Immortal" by Jeremy Blodgett, copyright © 2003 by Jeremy Blodgett. Used by permission of the author.

Jorge Luis Borges. "The Aleph" translated by Anthony Kerrigan, from *A Personal Anthology* by Jorge Luis Borges, copyright © 1967 by Grove Press, Inc. Used by permission of Grove/Atlantic, Inc.

Kevin Brockmeier. "These Hands" from *Things That Fall from the Sky* by Kevin Brockmeier, copyright © 2002 by Kevin Brockmeier. Used by permission of Pantheon Books, a division of Random House, Inc.

Sandra Cisneros. "Mericans" from *Woman Hollering Creek* by Sandra Cisneros, copyright © 1991 by Sandra Cisneros. Published by Vintage Books, a division of Random House, Inc., New York and originally in hardcover by Random House, Inc. Reprinted by permission of Susan Bergholz Literary Services, New York. All rights reserved.

Sarah Cornwell. "Pretty Little Things" by Sarah Cornwell, first appeared in *The Grinnell Review*, Volume XXII, Spring 2003, copyright © 2003 by Sarah Cornwell. Used by permission of the author.

Louise Erdrich. "The Red Convertible" from *Love Medicine*, new and expanded version by Louise Erdrich, copyright © 1984, 1993 by Louise Erdrich. Reprinted by permission of Henry Holt and Company, LLC.

Ernest Hemingway. Excerpt from "A Way You'll Never Be" from *The Short Stories of Ernest Hemingway* by Ernest Hemingway, copyright © 1933 by Charles Scribner's Sons. Copyright renewed © 1961 by Mary Hemingway. Reprinted by permission of Scribner, a Division of Simon & Schuster.

Kazuo Ishiguro. "A Family Supper" by Kazuo Ishiguro, copyright © 1982 by Kazuo Ishiguro. Reproduced by permission of the author c/o Rogers, Coleridge & White Ltd., 20 Powis Mews, London W11 1JN.

James Alan McPherson. "Why I Like Country Music" by James Alan McPherson, first appeared in *Elbow Room*, which was published by Fawcett Books/Random House in 1972. Copyright shall remain in the name of James Alan McPherson.

Judith Claire Mitchell. "A Man of Few Words" by Judith Claire Mitchell, copyright © 1998 by Judith Claire Mitchell. First published in *Scribner's Best of the Fiction Workshops 1998*. Reprinted by permission of the author.

Flannery O'Connor. "Revelation," from *The Short Stories* by Flannery O'Connor, copyright © 1971 by the estate of Mary Flannery O'Connor. Reprinted by permission of Farrar, Straus and Giroux, LLC.

Tillie Olsen. "I Stand Here Ironing," from *Tell Me A Riddle* by Tillie Olsen, introduction by John Leonard, copyright © 1956, 1957, 1960, 1961 by Tillie Olsen. Introduction 1994, by Dell Publishing. Used by permission of Dell Publishing, a division of Random House, Inc.

Wallace Stegner. "The Traveler" from *Collected Stories of Wallace Stegner* by Wallace Stegner, copyright © 1990 by Wallace Stegner. Used by permission of Random House, Inc.

Tobias Wolff. "Bullet in the Brain" from *On the Night in Question: Stories* by Tobias Wolff, copyright © 1996 by Tobias Wolff. Used by permission of Alfred A. Knopf, a division of Random House, Inc.

INDEX